AUSTIN MAXI 1969-71 AUTOBOOK

Workshop Manual for
Austin Maxi 1500 1969-71
Austin Maxi 1750 1970-71

by

Kenneth Ball G I Mech E

and the

Autopress team of Technical Writers

AUTOPRESS LTD   GOLDEN LANE   BRIGHTON   BN1 2QJ   ENGLAND

The AUTOBOOK series of Workshop Manuals covers the majority of British and Continental motor cars.

For a full list see the back of this manual.

CONTENTS

Introduction

Acknowledgement

Appendix

ISBN 0 85147 226 5

First Edition   December 1969
Second Edition, fully revised   June 1971

© Autopress Ltd 1971

Printed in Brighton England for Autopress Ltd by G Beard & Son Ltd

ACKNOWLEDGEMENT

My thanks are due to British Leyland Motor Corporation for their unstinted co-operation and also for supplying data and illustrations.

I am also grateful to a considerable number of owners who have discussed their cars at length, and many of whose suggestions have been included in this manual.

Kenneth Ball G I Mech E
Associate Member Guild of Motoring Writers
Ditchling Sussex England

INTRODUCTION

This do-it-yourself Workshop Manual has been specially written for the owner who wishes to maintain his car in first class condition and to carry out his own servicing and repairs. Considerable savings on garage charges can be made, and one can drive in safety and confidence knowing the work has been done properly.

Comprehensive step-by-step instructions and illustrations are given on all dismantling, overhauling and assembling operations. Certain assemblies require the use of expensive special tools, the purchase of which would be unjustified. In these cases information is included but the reader is recommended to hand the unit to the agent for attention.

Throughout the Manual hints and tips are included which will be found invaluable, and there is an easy to follow fault diagnosis at the end of each chapter.

Whilst every care has been taken to ensure correctness of information it is obviously not possible to guarantee complete freedom from errors or to accept liability arising from such errors or omissions.

Instructions may refer to the righthand or lefthand sides of the vehicle or the components. These are the same as the righthand or lefthand of an observer standing behind the car and looking forward.

CHAPTER 1

THE ENGINE

1:1 Description

The Maxi power unit continues the well-proven and accepted concept of a transverse engine and front-wheel drive which has been so successful in BLMC productions like the Mini, the 1100, 1300 and 1800. There is, however, a big change in engine design, the traditional pushrod operation of the valves being replaced by overhead camshaft operation, the drive being by chain. **FIG 1:1** shows this feature and many more can be identified from the following description.

The new engine is mounted transversely in unit with the clutch, a fivespeed gearbox and the final drive, the assembly being carried in a subframe which is bolted to the body of the car.

Two engine sizes are available and are known as the 1500 and 1750. The former is of 1485cc with a bore and stroke of 76.2 x 81.28mm, the latter is 1748cc having dimensions of 76.2 x 95.75mm. Their respective outputs are 74 bph at 5500 rev/min and 84 bhp at 5000 rev/min.

The cast iron cylinder block encloses part of the camshaft chain drive at the front, and the bottom flange, which is on the centre line of the crankshaft, bolts to the transmission casing. The exceptionally stiff crankshaft is machined from SG iron and is carried in five main bearings. At the lefthand end of the crankshaft is a combined crankshaft pulley and torsional vibration damper. Behind this is an oil seal, the camshaft driving sprocket and a skew gear which drives an almost-vertical shaft. The shaft drives a distributor at its top end and a rotor-type oil pump at the bottom. The lower end also incorporates a cam which operates the fuel pump through the agency of a pushrod. The righthand end of the crankshaft carries the flywheel and a diaphragm spring clutch, the driven plate of which is connected to a single-helical gear free to rotate independently of the crankshaft and taking the drive down to the transmission gears below. The main bearings have split steel-backed liners with a running surface of reticular tin.

The short, stiff connecting rods are split horizontally and have similar bearings to those for the crankshaft. The big-ends will pass upwards through the bores. The gudgeon pin is a tight press fit in the small-end and fully-floating in the piston bosses. The aluminium pistons have solid skirts and a flat crown and carry three compression rings and an oil-control ring apiece .

A cast iron cylinder head is provided with valves set at a small angle from the vertical. The inlet ports are round and

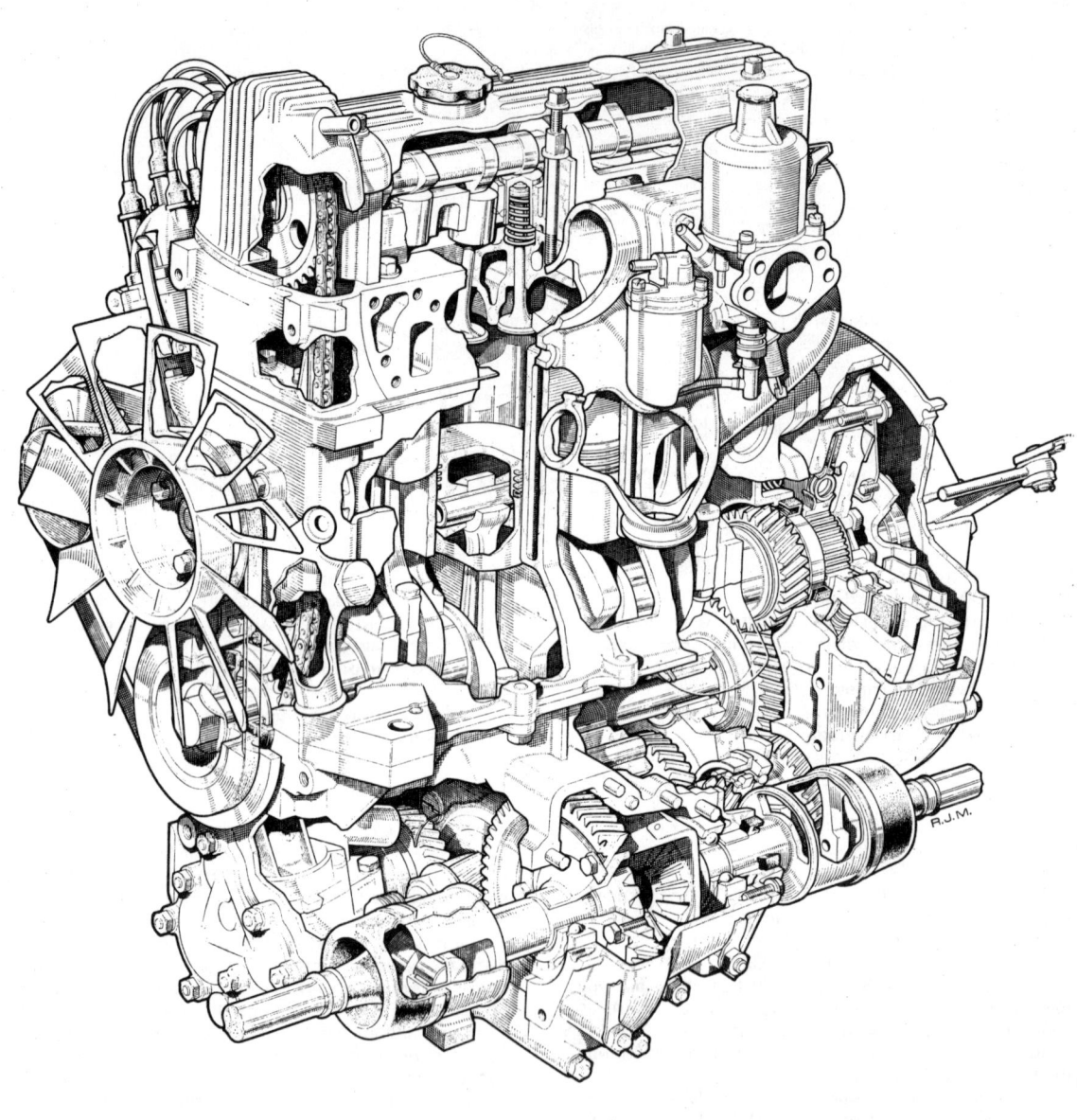

FIG 1:1   A cutaway view of the power unit showing the chain-driven overhead camshaft. Note the inverted tappets which bear directly on the valve stems

the exhaust rectangular, the manifold being a one-piece casting. Bolted to the top face of the cylinder head is an aluminium casting which carries the camshaft in three bearings machined directly in the aluminium. Below each cam is a large bore in which a bucket-type tappet is fitted. The hollow part of the tappet accepts the valve stem and spring, clearance between the tappet and the valve stem being adjusted by shims. At the front end of the camshaft is a large sprocket. There are three devices to guide and tension the chain, two of them being vertical plates inside the tight and loose sides of the chain. The third is a self-adjusting tensioner with a slipper head bearing on the chain low down on the front run of the chain.

The oil pump takes oil from the transmission casing and passes it to a fullflow filter with a renewable element. A non-adjustable oil relief valve is fitted in the transmission casing under the filter head. From the filter, oil under pressure passes to drillings feeding the various bearings in the usual way. A crankcase ventilator is fitted to the flywheel housing and this incorporates a renewable filter element.

From the crankshaft pulley a V-belt drives the water pump and a multi-bladed cooling fan on a common shaft and then makes a three-point drive round the generator pulley. Cooling water is circulated through the block and head by the pump impeller, passing a thermostat on its way to the radiator header tank. When the water is cold the thermostat remains closed and water is recirculated through the engine to give a fast warm-up.

1:2 Overhauling methods

Before proceeding with instructions on engine overhaul we feel that many readers will find the following comments useful.

The owner who is competent to do most of his own car repairs may not necessarily be a trained engineer. This is no disadvantage if he is prepared to be clean, careful, systematic and observant. We appreciate that working on a car which has been well-used may pose many problems associated with dirt, corrosion and wear. Very often a little science will solve such problems without the need for excessive force. For this reason, and to ensure that operations are tackled in the right way, we suggest that a few minutes spent in reading 'Hints on Maintenance and Overhaul' at the end of this manual will be time well spent.

Although the 'Introduction' to this manual has already made the point, it will probably be useful to repeat the information that the righthand and lefthand sides of a car are those seen from the driver's seat looking forward. It is essential to remember this because there will be frequent references to locations in this way. As we are dealing with a transverse engine the traditional front and rear ends of the engine do not apply but components in these locations will be described as viewed.

Other useful information is that No. 1 cylinder is at the lefthand end and the firing order is 1, 3, 4, 2. Additional technical information will be found in the 'Appendix' at the back of this manual, together with a 'Glossary of Terms' which explains the meaning of possibly unfamiliar expressions.

Operations with the engine in the car:

All work on the head can be tackled with the engine in the car. The crankshaft pulley can be removed and so can

the flywheel and clutch. Behind the flywheel is the primary gear. End float of this gear can be adjusted and the primary gear oil seal can be renewed.

Components which can be removed are the belt, water pump and generator, the starter motor, the fuel pump, the distributor, carburetter and the exhaust system.

Operations entailing removal of the power unit:

Because the transmission is bolted to the underside of the engine it is necessary to remove the complete power unit to attend to the crankshaft, the connecting rods and pistons and the timing chain. It is also necessary when servicing the primary gear and the drive shaft to the oil pump, fuel pump and distributor.

1:3 Removing and refitting the power unit

Cable gearchange (without subframe, see Fig 1:2):

Drain the engine and transmission oil. Drain the cooling system.

Remove the bonnet, battery and tray.

Remove the air cleaner and carburetter as described in **Chapter 2, Section 2:5**. Remove the clamp and detach the exhaust pipe from the manifold. Disconnect the servo pipe from the manifold.

Remove two bolts to detach the engine steady bracket 10 from the subframe. Release the clutch slave cylinder from the flywheel housing and disconnect the earthing cable.

Disconnect the spill pipe from the radiator and remove the expansion tank. Disconnect the heater hoses. Disconnect the fuel pipe. Disconnect all electrical leads from the thermal transmitter, oil pressure switch, distributor and coil, starter and generator.

Jack up the front of the car, and support it under the lower suspension arms. Support the engine on lifting tackle.

Remove the bolts from the front lefthand engine mounting 21 and from the rear mounting to the displacer housing. Detach the exhaust clamp from the differential housing bracket.

Mark the gearchange cables ready for reassembly and disconnect them as instructed in **Chapter 6**.

Using tool 18G1146, item 26, release the drive shafts from their locating rings in the differential. Remove the centre nut from the rear engine mounting and lower the rear of the engine sufficiently to disengage the mounting. Then push the engine as far forward as possible, and lift it sufficiently for the rear mounting to clear the subframe.

Disconnect the speedometer cable and move the engine as far as possible over to the left and disengage the righthand drive shaft. Move the engine over to the right and disengage the lefthand drive shaft. Tie the shafts out of the way and lift the engine assembly out of the car, then disconnect and remove the radiator assembly.

Rod gearchange (see Fig 1:3):

The procedure for removing this type will be the same as for cable change up to the point when the engine is supported on lifting tackle, then:

Detach the damper bracket from the transmission 21 and remove the pin retaining the extension rod to the

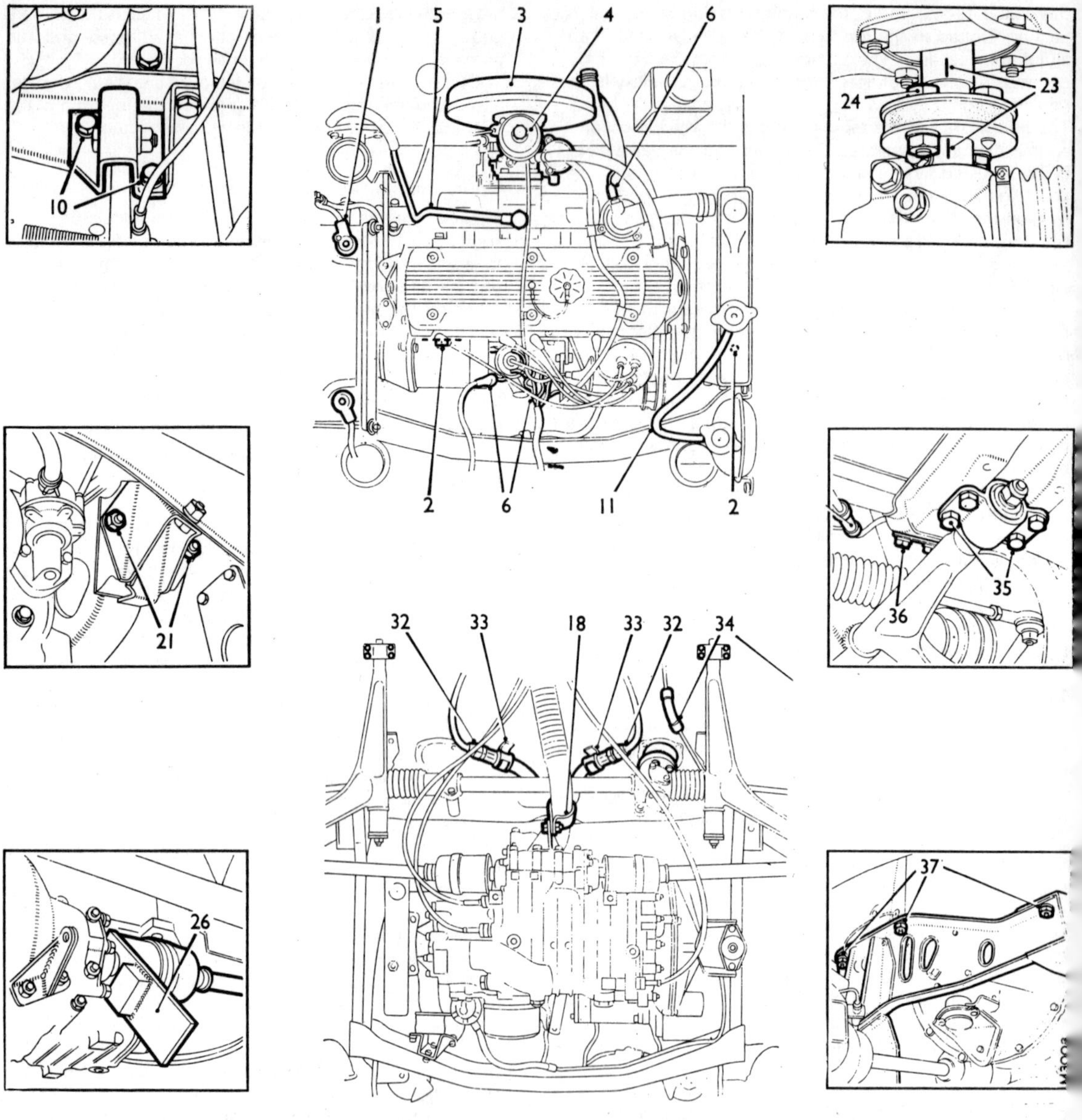

FIG 1:2 Removing power unit (cable gearchange)

Key to Fig 1:2   1 Battery connectors   2 Water drain plugs   3 Air cleaner   4 Carburetter   5 Servo pipe   6 Electric cables   10 Steady bracket   11 Radiator spill pipe   18 Exhaust pipe clip   21 Lefthand engine mounting   23 Steering column alignment marks   24 Coupling bolts   26 Releasing drive shafts   32 Connectors for suspension pipes   33 Clip   34 Fuel pipe connector   35 Suspension arm bolts   36 Bolts (subframe to toeboard)   37 Bolts (subframe to wing valance)

selector shaft 22. Detach the steady rod 23 from the differential housing and also the two nuts 24 securing the exhaust bracket.

Slacken the exhaust bracket U-bolt nuts 25 and slide the bracket down the pipe, then remove the bolts securing the front 26 and rear 27 lefthand engine mountings. Release the drive shafts from their location rings using Tool 18G.1146, item 28, and slacken the bolts 29 securing the rear engine mounting to the subframe bracket. Remove

the nuts 30 securing the rear mounting to the clutch cover and push the engine as far forward as possible raising it enough for the rear mounting to clear the bracket on the clutch cover.

Disconnect the speedometer cable and then move the engine over to left and then right to permit the removal of the right and left drive shafts.

Temporarily secure the drive shafts and lift out the engine. Disconnect and remove the radiator assembly.

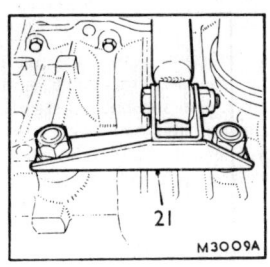

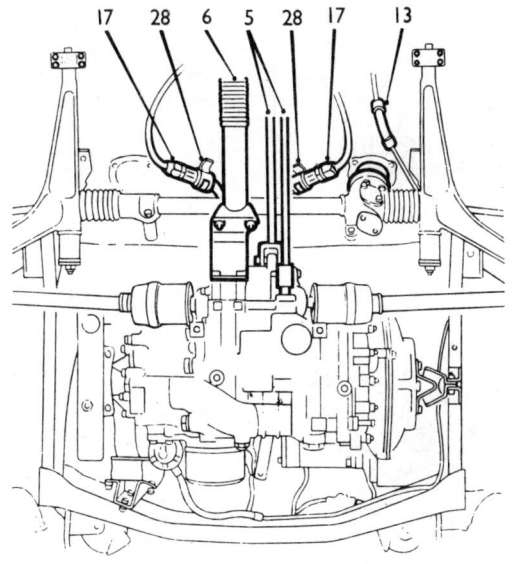

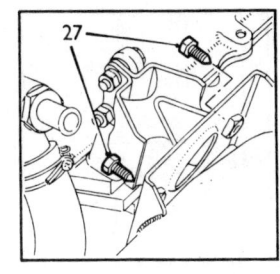

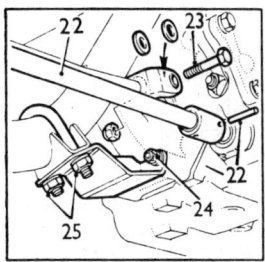

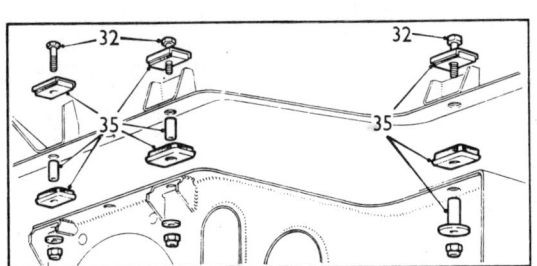

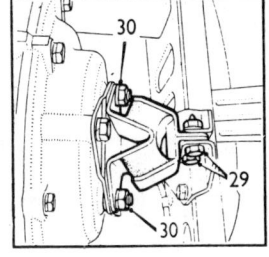

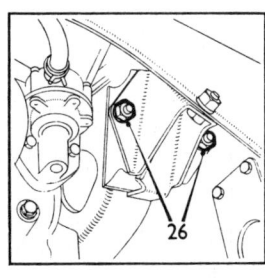

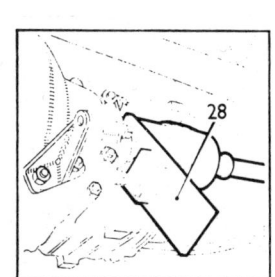

FIG 1:3   Removing power unit (rod gearchange)

Key to Fig 1:3   5 Remote control rods   6 Exhaust pipe   13 Fuel pipe   17 Suspension pipe connectors   21 Damper bracket   22 Extension rod and pin   23 Steady rod   24 Exhaust bracket nuts   25 Exhaust U-bolt nuts   26 Lefthand front mounting   27 Lefthand rear mounting   28 Releasing drive shafts   29 Bolt (rear mounting to subframe bracket)   30 Bolt (rear mounting to clutch cover)   32 Bolts (subframe to wing valance)   35 Rubber mountings and sleeves

Refitting (cable gearchange):

Temporarily secure the exhaust pipe to the displacer housing and lower the engine enough to permit the drive shafts to be engaged, fitting the lefthand shaft first. Connect the speedometer cable.

Lower the engine slowly, making sure the drive shafts are not strained and are engaging the differential correctly. The exhaust pipe must lie to the right of its differential bracket. The engine steady rod must not foul the displacer housing.

Lower the engine until the rear mounting engages its centre bolt. Raise the engine and fit the rear mounting nut.

Fit and tighten the front mounting bolts. Connect the exhaust pipe.

Connect the gear selector cables. Pull the rod out when connecting the inner cable, using Service Tool No. 18G.1158 to retain the balls and springs in the selector jaws (see **Chapter 6**). Adjust the cables if necessary, using the instructions in the same chapter.

Check that the drive shafts are fully engaged in the differential gears. Complete the operation by reversing the dismantling procedure then lower the car, refill the cooling system and fill the engine and transmission with the correct grade of oil.

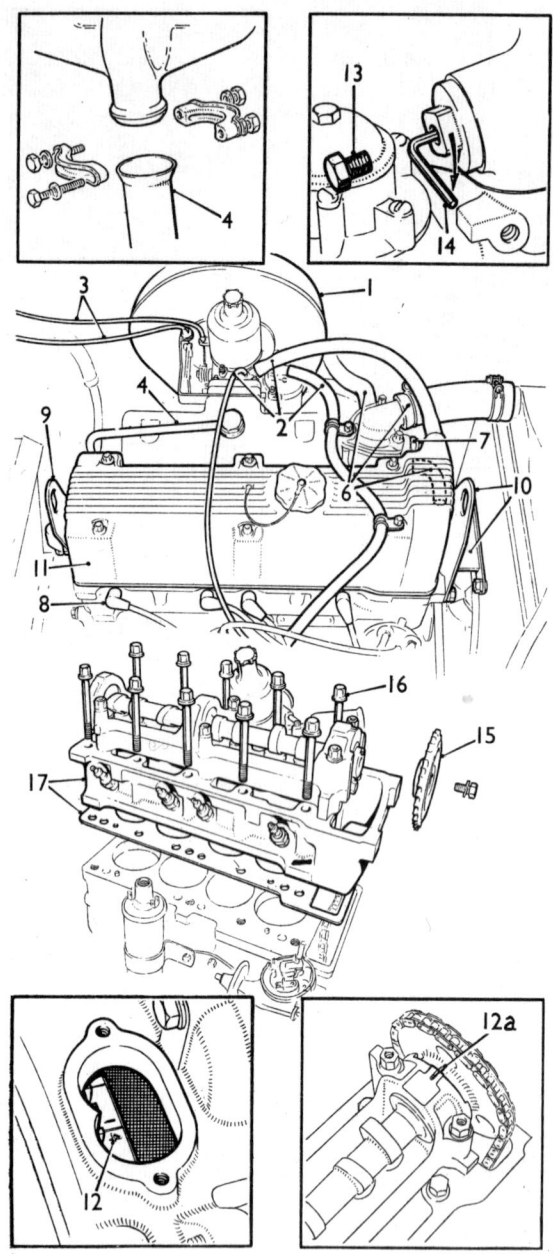

FIG 1 : 4 Operations for removing the cylinder head

Key to Fig 1 : 4   1 Air cleaner   2 Fuel, breather and distributor vacuum pipes   3 Choke and throttle cables   4 Brake servo and exhaust pipes   7 Thermal transmitter   8 Plug leads   9 Rear lifting bracket   10 Front lifting bracket   11 Cylinder head cover   12 Flywheel timing marks   12a Camshaft alignment marks   13 Chain tensioner adapter bolt   14 Allen key   15 Camshaft sprocket   16 Cylinder head bolts   17 Cylinder head and gasket

Refitting (rod gearchange):

This procedure is slightly different from that given earlier. After connecting the speedometer cable and engaging the drive shafts, check that the engine steady rod does not foul the displacer housing then secure the rear engine mounting to the bracket on the clutch housing. Tighten the bolts securing the rear mounting to the bracket on the subframe.

Fit and tighten both front mountings. Secure the exhaust bracket to the differential housing and replace the steady rod. Fit a new pin to retain the extension rod to the selector shaft. Reattach the damper bracket to the transmission.

Check that the drive shafts are fully engaged in the differential gears then remove the engine lifting tackle.

Refit the remaining items in the reverse order to removal. Check the adjustment of the remote control steady rod as described in **Chapter 6**.

Lower the car and refill with oil and coolant.

Cable gearchange (with subframe):

Before commencing this operation the suspension system must be depressurized at the local service station. It is quite in order to drive the car for short distances in this condition at speeds of less than 30 mile/hr.

Drain the cooling system and disconnect the battery. Remove the air cleaner and carburetter as instructed in **Chapter 2, Section 2 : 5**. Disconnect the servo pipe.

Disconnect all wiring and the heater hose. Detach the heater control valve. Release the clutch return spring, unbolt the slave cylinder and earth cable. Disconnect the expansion hose from the radiator.

Disconnect the speedometer cable and the exhaust pipe. Remove the bolt securing the brake servo unit. Remove the knob on the gearchange lever. Disconnect the reverse light switch.

Release the exhaust pipe clip from the differential bracket. Unbolt the silencer and remove the exhaust pipe.

Unbolt the heat shield and lower the gearchange control from the body.

Mark the steering column and the pinion shaft 23 for later reassembly and remove the two bolts 24 by which they are secured. Now lift up the front of the car under the sub-frame and remove the road wheels. Disconnect the brake pipes from the flexible hoses. Support the front of the body.

Disconnect the suspension pipes at the front connectors, release the flexible pipes from the body clips. Disconnect the fuel supply pipe.

Remove the bolts securing the lower suspension arm bearings 35 and those securing the subframe to the toe-board 36 and the wing valances 37. Lower the subframe and raise the body to clear.

Rod gearchange (with subframe):

This procedure will be similar to that described for cable change models, but before removing the carburetter, remove the remote control assembly as described in **Chapter 6** and also the exhaust system. Slacken the screws securing the front door kicking plates and remove the carpet.

Remove the carburetter. Disconnect the brake servo pipe and all electrical wiring. Disconnect the heater hoses and the control valve and continue the operation as for the cable change models.

Refitting:

This is a reversal of the removal procedure in each case with a few points to be noted.

Cable change:

Check that the subframe dowels are aligned with the holes in the wing valances.

Ensure that the rear suspension displacer unit struts are correctly positioned before repressurizing the suspension.

Check that the metal bushes are fitted in the exhaust mountings before refitting.

Rod change:

Ensure that the flanged sleeve locates the front subframe mounting rubber to the wing valance, and plain sleeves 35 locate the remaining rubbers.

The subframe mounting rubbers are located by small sleeves to the body.

Ensure that the rear suspension displacer unit struts are correctly positioned before repressurizing.

1:4 Removing and refitting the cylinder head

This can be done with the engine in the car. Proceed as follows, using **FIG 1:4** for reference:

Removing:

1 Remove the air cleaner 1 and disconnect the vacuum, breather and fuel pipes 2. Disconnect the carburetter

2 Disconnect the brake servo and exhaust pipes 4. Drain the cooling system and disconnect the radiator, water pump and heater hoses 6 from the thermostat housing. **Never at any time attempt to release the cylinder head without draining the cooling system or water will enter the bores and the transmission casing.**

3 Disconnect the leads from the thermal transmitter 7 and the spark plugs 8. Detach the engine steady arm and lifting bracket 9. Detach the radiator bracket and front lifting bracket 10. Remove the cylinder head cover 11 (6 bolts).

4 Remove the flywheel housing timing cover and turn the crankshaft until the 1/4 mark on the flywheel is at TDC with No. 1 cylinder firing, as at 12. Line-up the marks on the camshaft and bearing housing 12a. From low down near the fuel pump, remove bolt 13 from the chain tensioner adapter. With an $\frac{1}{8}$inch Allen key, locate the socket in the tensioner and turn it clockwise.

5 Remove the camshaft sprocket 15. Using a diagonal sequence, slacken the cylinder head bolts 16 part of a turn at a time until they can be removed. Lift off the cylinder head and gasket 17.

Refitting:

Use a new cylinder head gasket and fit the head. Tighten the bolts gradually in a diagonal sequence, finishing with a torque wrench setting of 60 lb ft. Fit the camshaft sprocket using a torque of 35 lb ft on the bolt. Check all timing marks. Release the chain tensioner by turning the Allen key anticlockwise. Follow the dismantling operations in reverse, using a torque of 6 lb ft on the head cover

bolts. The torque for the front and rear lifting bracket bolts is 30 lb ft.

1:5 Servicing head, camshaft and valves

Removing camshaft and tappets (refer to FIG 1:5):

Before dismantling the valve gear it is a good plan to check the tappet clearance as described in **Section 1:6** so that adjustments can be made if necessary. Having done this, proceed as follows:

1 Remove the timing cover 2 so that the timing marks on the flywheel can be seen. Make up a simple peg spanner to engage the three holes in the camshaft sprocket as shown by 3. Turning the sprocket will enable the crankshaft to be set so that the timing marks 3a are in the 1/4 position at TDC with No. 1 cylinder firing. The official Service Tool shown in the illustration is 18G.1153.

2 Align the camshaft and bearing housing marks as shown at 4. Remove the battery 5 and detach the radiator stay and front lifting bracket 6. Remove the engine steady and rear lifting bracket 7.

3 From below the distributor, unscrew the chain tensioner adapter screw. 8. Insert a $\frac{1}{8}$inch Allen key 9 and turn it clockwise to retract the tensioner. Remove the camshaft sprocket 10.

4 Slacken bolts 11 a little at a time in a diagonal sequence until all pressure from the valve springs is released. When the camshaft housing 12 is lifted still more the tappets 14 will fall clear to enable the camshaft 13 to be withdrawn to the rear. Now remove the tappets and store them in the correct order for replacement. Some numbered nails in a strip of wood could be used, or simply an indication to show which nail and tappet is located at the front or lefthand end of the engine.

Camshaft details:

End float and location of the camshaft is controlled by plate 11 in **FIG 1:6**. This will be found bolted to the camshaft housing behind the sprocket. If end float of the camshaft exceeds .002 to .007 inch it must be cured by fitting a new plate.

Examine the camshaft and housing bearing surfaces for signs of scoring and excessive wear. The journal diameters are given in Technical Data at the end of this manual. See that the cam surfaces are not worn or pitted and that the sprocket driving dowel is a perfect fit. Check the fit of the tappets in the housing and renew worn parts.

Reassembling:

The first operation is to determine the correct shimming for any tappets which showed a deviation from the required clearance. This is described in **Section 1:6**. The correct shims can be smeared with petroleum jelly and stuck inside the tappets. Then do the following:

1 Refit the camshaft housing and turn bolts 11 to engage two or three threads only. Fit the tappets in the correct order. Refit the camshaft.

2 Without fitting the chain, lightly attach the sprocket and turn until the marks 4 are in line. Remove the sprocket. Tighten the housing bolts gradually in a diagonal sequence to a torque of 20 lb ft. Check the crankshaft timing marks to ensure that they have not moved from the original setting and fit the camshaft sprocket

FIG 1:5 Removing the camshaft and tappets. Note tappet adjusting shims **17**

Key to Fig 1:5   2 Flywheel housing cover   3 Service Tool 18G.1153   4 Camshaft alignment marks   5 Battery
6 Front lifting bracket   7 Rear lifting bracket   8 Chain tensioner adapter bolt   9 Allen key   10 Camshaft sprocket
11 Camshaft housing bolts   12 Camshaft housing   13 Camshaft   14 Tappets   17 Tappet adjusting shims

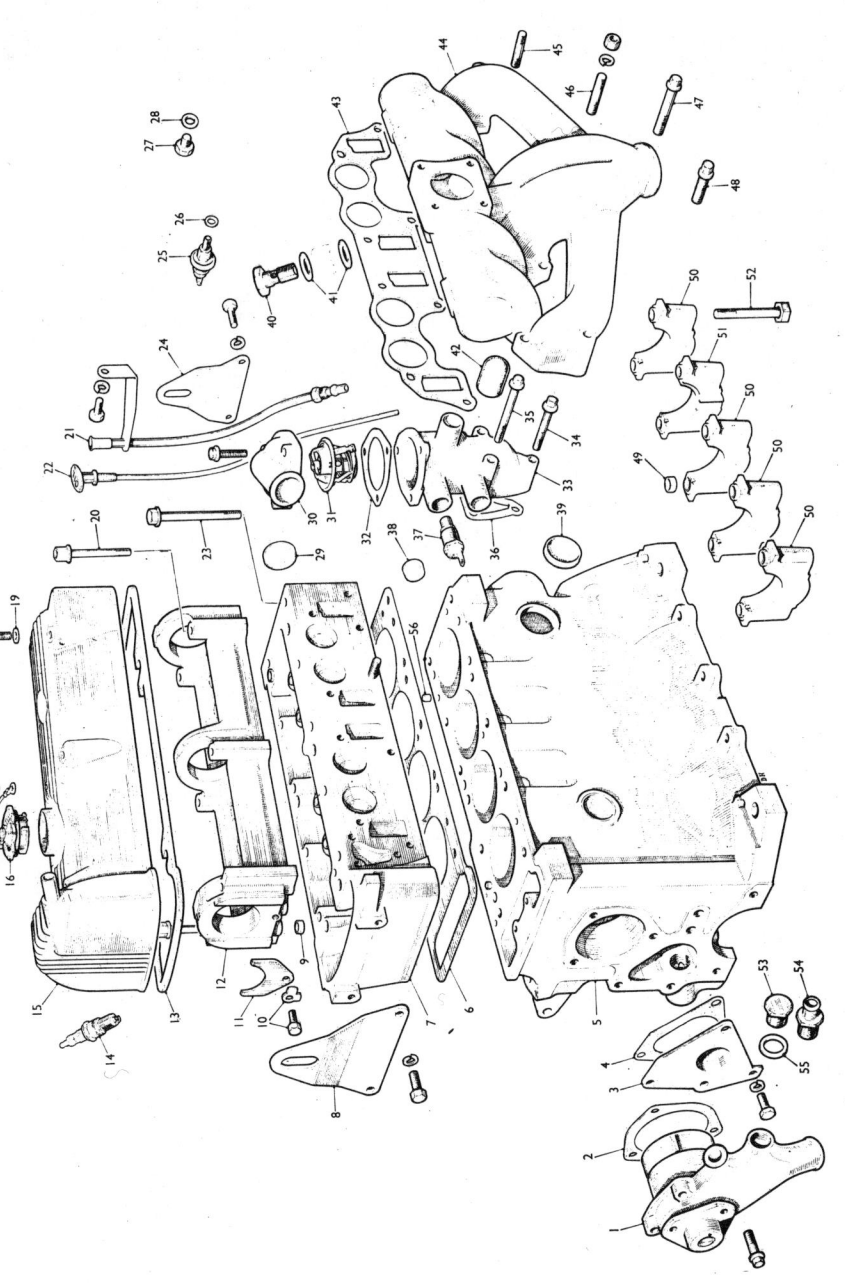

FIG 1:6 External components of the engine. There are grooves in the fourth main bearing cap **51** to accommodate thrust washers

Key to Fig 1:6 1 Water pump 2 Gasket for water pump 3 Engine front cover 4 Gasket for front cover 5 Cylinder block 6 Gasket for cylinder head
7 Cylinder head 8 Engine front lifting bracket 9 Ring dowel 10 Bolt and lockwasher 11 Locating plate for camshaft 12 Housing for camshaft and tappets
13 Gasket 14 Sparking plug 15 Cylinder head cover 16 Oil filler cap 17 Rivet 18 Bolt 19 O-ring 20 Bolt for camshaft and tappet housing
21 Oil dipstick tube 22 Oil dipstick 23 Bolt for cylinder head 24 Engine rear lifting bracket 25 Oil pressure switch 26 Washer for oil pressure switch
27 Cylinder block drain plug 28 Washer for drain plug 29 Core plug for cylinder head 30 Water outlet elbow 31 Thermostat 32 Gasket for water outlet elbow
33 Thermostat housing 34 Short bolt for thermostat housing 35 Long bolt for thermostat housing 36 Gasket for thermostat housing 37 Thermal transmitter
38 Plug for main oil gallery 39 Core plug for cylinder block 40 Screw for servo banjo union 41 Washers for banjo union 42 Heater connection blanking plug
43 Gasket for inlet and exhaust manifold 44 Inlet and exhaust manifold 45 Short stud 46 Long stud 47 Long bolt 48 Short bolt 49 Dowel for main bearing cap
50 Main bearing cap 51 No. 4 (thrust) main bearing cap 52 Bolt for main bearing cap 53 Plug 54 Adapter for heater connection 55 Sealing washer
56 Dowel for cylinder head

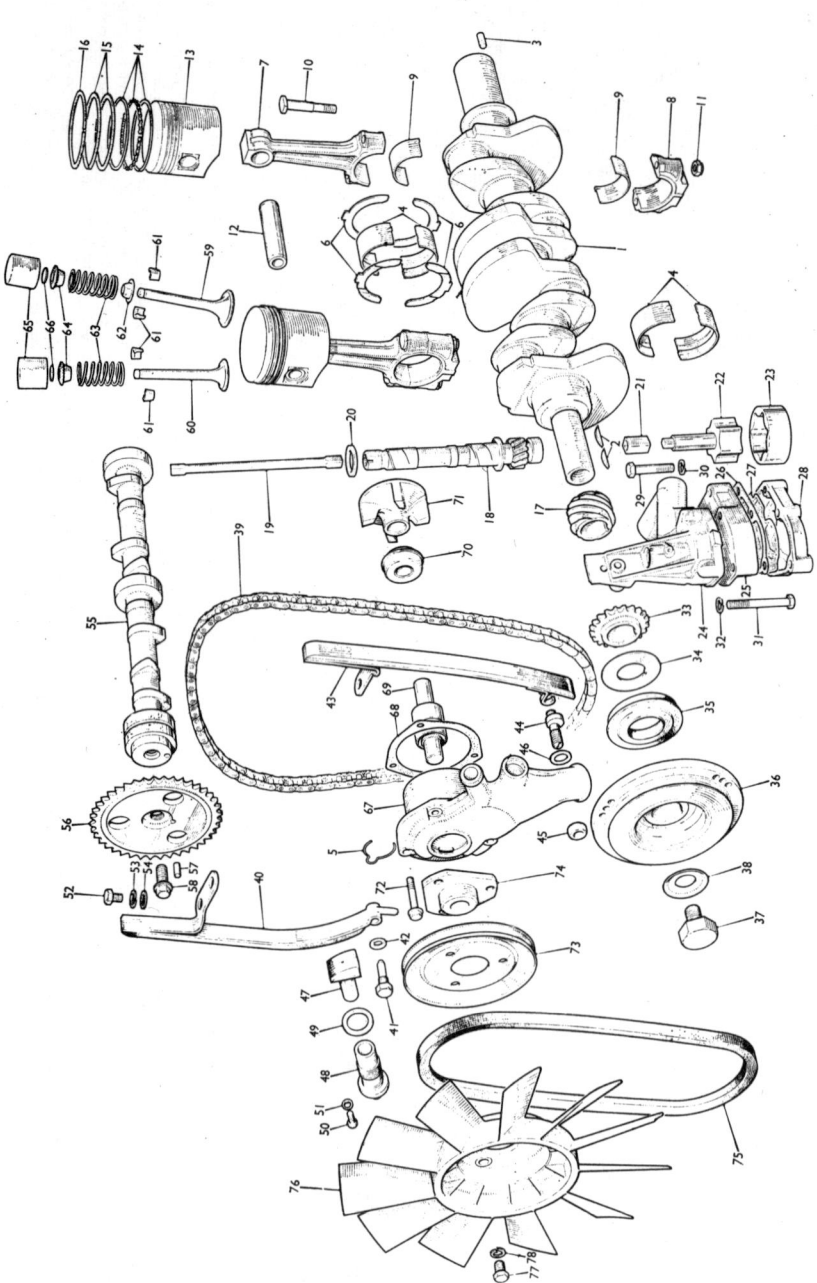

FIG 1:7 Internal components of the engine. The oil pump is driven by squared shaft **19** which passes down through distributor drive shaft **18**

Key to Fig 1:7 1 Crankshaft   2 Keys for timing gear and sprocket   3 Dowel for flywheel   4 Main bearing shells   5 Retainer for water pump bearing
6 Crankshaft thrust washers   7 Connecting rod   8 Big-end bearing cap   9 Big-end bearing shell   10 Main bearing shells   11 Nut for bolt   12 Gudgeon pin
13 Piston   14 Oil control ring   15 Tapered compression rings   16 Top compression ring   17 Distributor, oil pump and fuel pump drive gear
18 Distributor and fuel pump drive shaft   19 Oil pump drive shaft   20 Thrust washer for shaft   21 Oil pump drive coupling   22 Oil pump rotor
23 Oil pump outer ring   24 Oil pump body   25 Oil strainer body   26 Gasket   27 Oil strainer   28 Oil strainer cover   29 Bolt for oil pump—short
30 Spring washer   31 Bolt for oil pump—long   32 Spring washer   33 Crankshaft sprocket   34 Oil thrower   35 Crankshaft front oil seal
36 Crankshaft pulley and vibration damper   37 Bolt for pulley   38 Lockwasher for bolt   39 Chain for camshaft   40 Chain guide—tensioner side
41 Dowel bolt for guide   42 Washer for bolt   43 Chain guide—tight side   44 Lockwasher for bolt   45 Locknut for adjuster   46 Washer for nut
47 Chain tensioner assembly   48 Adapter for chain tensioner   49 Washer for adapter   50 Bolt for adapter   51 Washer for bolt   52 Bolt for chain guides
53 Spring washer   54 Plain washer   55 Camshaft   56 Camshaft sprocket   57 Dowel for sprocket   58 Bolt for sprocket   59 Inlet valve
60 Oil seal   61 Valve cotters   62 Oil seal   63 Valve springs   64 Valve spring cup   65 Tappets   66 Shim for tappets   67 Water pump body
68 Gasket for water pump   69 Bearing and shaft assembly   70 Seal for water pump   71 Vane for water pump   72 Bolt for water pump
75 Hub for fan and pulley   76 Fan   77 Bolt for fan   78 Spring washer for bolt

without disturbing either the crankshaft or the cam-shaft. The timing will then be correct. Tighten the sprocket bolt to a torque of 35 lb ft.

3 Follow the rest of the dismantling operations in the reverse order, tightening the lifting bracket bolts to a torque of 30 lb ft.

Dismantling the head:

Having removed the camshaft housing as just described, it will be possible to work on the valves. Using a suitable spring compressor, compress the valve springs 63 in **FIG 1 : 7** and remove the cotters 61, the spring cups 64 and the springs 63. Remove the oil seals and spring seats from the inlet valves. Remove the valves and store them in the correct order so that they can be replaced in their respective guides during reassembly.

If the valves and seats have seen considerable service it will be necessary to have them reconditioned by an agent with the proper tools. Valve seats can be reground to the correct angle of $45\frac{1}{4}$ deg., but if the seatings in the head need reconditioning, the following operations are required:

1 The glazing of the seats must be removed.

2 The seats must be recut to an angle of 45 deg., removing the minimum of metal.

3 The seats must be narrowed to the correct width.

The valves can then be lapped in with fine grinding paste. Note that seats in the head which have gone too far can be restored by having inserts fitted. This is done by accurate machining with special equipment. After fitting, the insert seats are cut to the correct dimensions.

To grind in the valves, put a light spring under the head and smear the valve seat with a little fine grinding paste. Use a reciprocating movement of a suction tool stuck to the head of the valve. Let the valve rise occasionally under the influence of the spring so that the paste becomes evenly distributed and concentric scoring of the seats is avoided. Grind no more than is necessary to produce an even matt grey finish.

Refitting the valves:

This is a simple reversal of the dismantling procedure, but fit new oil seals to the inlet valve stems. Adjust the tappets as instructed in the following Section.

Noisy valve gear on early engines may be due to valve stem scuffing or picking-up. This will be evident from the roughness of the stems and the only cure is renewal. A BMC agent will give advice on whether the guide bores are fit for further service. At engine No. 14H.283.EH. 13473 the finish of the guides and the methods of assembly were modified to eliminate scuffing.

1 : 6 Tappet adjustment

Because the cams bear directly on tappets which con-tact the valve stems, the possibility of wear is much reduced. This means that what seems a complicated procedure will be rarely tackled. When it is, it will be necessary to provide a small micrometer to check the thickness of the adjusting shims. The method of adjust-ment is then as follows:

1 Refer to **FIG 1 : 8** and disconnect the breather hose 1. Disconnect fuel pipe 2 and withdraw it from the ther-mostat clip. Plug this pipe at 3 so that fuel is not lost

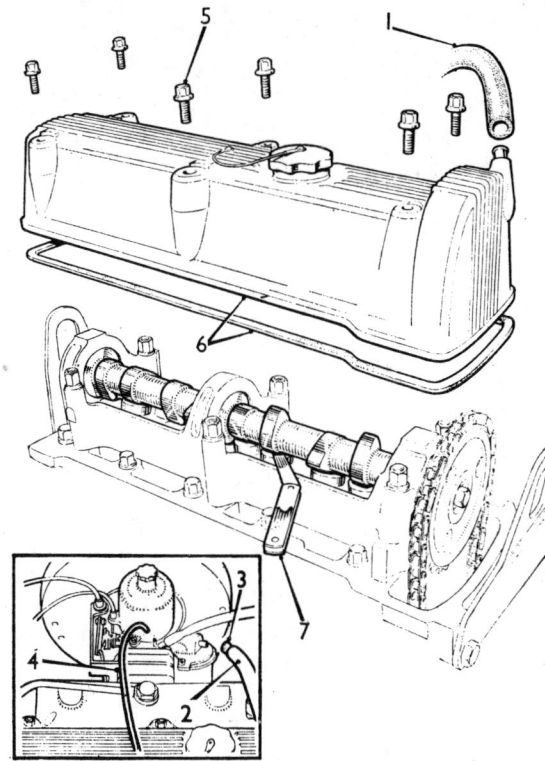

FIG 1 : 8 Sequence of operations when adjusting tappet clearances

Key to Fig 1 : 8   1 Breather hose   2 Carburetter fuel pipe   3 Plug   4 Distributor vacuum pipe
5 Cylinder head cover bolts   6 Cover and gasket
7 Feeler gauges

when the crankshaft is turned by means of the cam-shaft. Disconnect the ignition vacuum pipe 4 from the carburetter.

2 Remove the six cover bolts 5. Remove the cover and gasket 6.

3 With a feeler gauge 7 check the clearance between the back of each cam and the tappet as shown. To turn the camshaft make a replica of Service Tool 18G.1153 which has three pegs engaging the holes in the sprocket. The camshaft must be turned against the normal direc-tion of rotation. Use the following sequence when checking:

Check No. 1 tappet with No. 8 valve fully open
Check No. 3 tappet with No. 6 valve fully open
Check No. 5 tappet with No. 4 valve fully open
Check No. 2 tappet with No. 7 valve fully open
Check No. 8 tappet with No. 1 valve fully open
Check No. 6 tappet with No. 3 valve fully open
Check No. 4 tappet with No. 5 valve fully open
Check No. 7 tappet with No. 2 valve fully open

Write down the clearances in the correct order. Notice that each line of numbers adds up to nine. This enables checking to proceed without constant reference to the table.

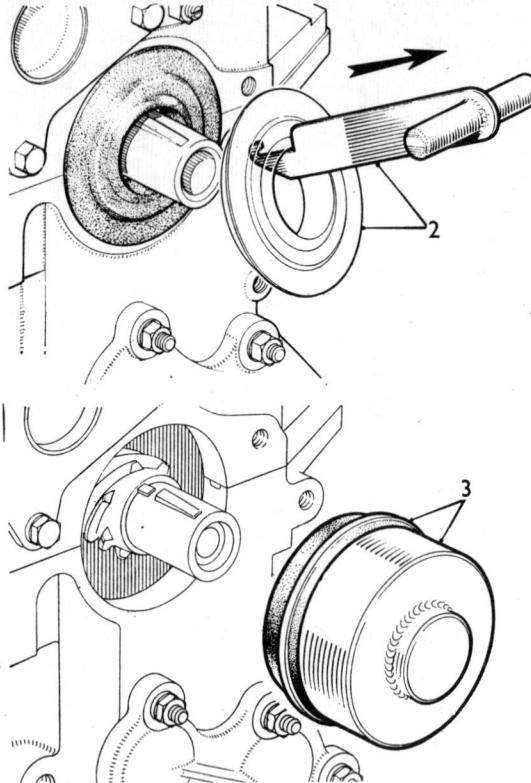

Check the shimming of all the other tappets with incorrect clearances.

6 Stick the shims inside the tappets with a little petroleum jelly and refit all the dismantled parts in the reverse order of dismantling. Check the tappet clearance again when the camshaft is in place. When fitting the camshaft sprocket make certain that the crankshaft and camshaft marks are still correctly aligned as specified early in **Section 1:5**.

1:7 Crankshaft pulley and front oil seal

Removing pulley:

1 Remove the radiator complete with cowl as described in **Chapter 4**. Slacken the generator mounting bolts as instructed in the same Chapter when dealing with fan belt adjustment. Remove the belt and the fan (3 bolts).

2 Remove the lower bracket which supports the radiator. Refer to **FIG 1:7** and unscrew the pulley retaining bolt 37. The combined pulley and vibration damper 36 is provided with two tapped holes to take an extractor. Using two long bolts and a tapped plate, a central screw can be made to bear on a pad placed on the end of the crankshaft 1 so that the pulley can be drawn off.

Refitting pulley:

Reverse the dismantling instructions, tightening the pulley retaining bolt to a torque of 60 to 70 lb ft. After the radiator is refitted and the hoses coupled, refill the cooling system.

Renewing the front oil seal:

After the crankshaft pulley is removed as just described, make up a simple hooked tool to slide along the crankshaft pulley keyway so that the hook can be engaged behind the seal. This can then be pulled out. The BLMC Service Tool is 18G.1087 as shown in **FIG 1:9**. The new seal must be fitted without tilting and the BLMC Service Tool is a large cup 3 which slides on the crankshaft and presses on the outer flange of the seal. This tool ensures that the seal is fitted squarely into its recess, and its number is 18G.1162.

FIG 1:9 Service Tool 18G.1087 removing the front oil seal (top). The lower view shows a new seal being fitted with Service Tool 18G.1162

4 The standard setting of the tappet clearance is .016 to .018 inch for inlet valves and .020 to .022 inch for exhaust valves. Adjustment is only necessary if the clearance for either valve is reduced to less than .012 inch, if new parts have been fitted or if valve grinding has been carried out. However, if the valve gear has been noisy, it is now suggested that valve clearances are reduced to .016 inch for inlets and .020 inch for exhausts. Again, the clearance in each case must be not less than .012 inch.

5 Refer to **Section 1:5** and repeat the first Operations 1 to 4 to reach the point where the tappets can be removed. Notice that there is a shim inside each tappet as shown by 17 in **FIG 1:5**. From the list of recorded clearances take the first tappet to need clearance adjustment and measure the thickness of the shim removed from it. Let 'A' be the clearance as measured, 'B' the thickness of the shim removed and 'C' the correct clearance specified in Operation 4. The thickness of shim required can then be calculated from the formula $A + B - C$. Shims are available in the following thicknesses:

.097 inch	.105 inch	.113 inch
.099 inch	.107 inch	.115 inch
.101 inch	.109 inch	.117 inch
.103 inch	.111 inch	.119 inch

1:8 The flywheel and housing

Removing flywheel with engine in car:

As the task of removing the clutch also involves removal of the flywheel, refer to **Chapter 5** where full instructions are given for this operation.

Removing flywheel with engine out of car:

Refer to **FIG 1:10** and proceed as follows:

1 Remove the power unit as described in **Section 1:3**. Remove the starter 3. Remove the clutch housing cover 4.

2 Remove the clutch thrust plate 5. The flywheel is retained by four bolts 6. Remove these and drift the flywheel squarely off the crankshaft. Remove the clutch as in **Chapter 5**.

Refitting flywheel with engine in car:

This is simply a matter of using the instructions for refitting the clutch as given in **Chapter 5**. Refer to the following notes on dowels and retaining bolt torque.

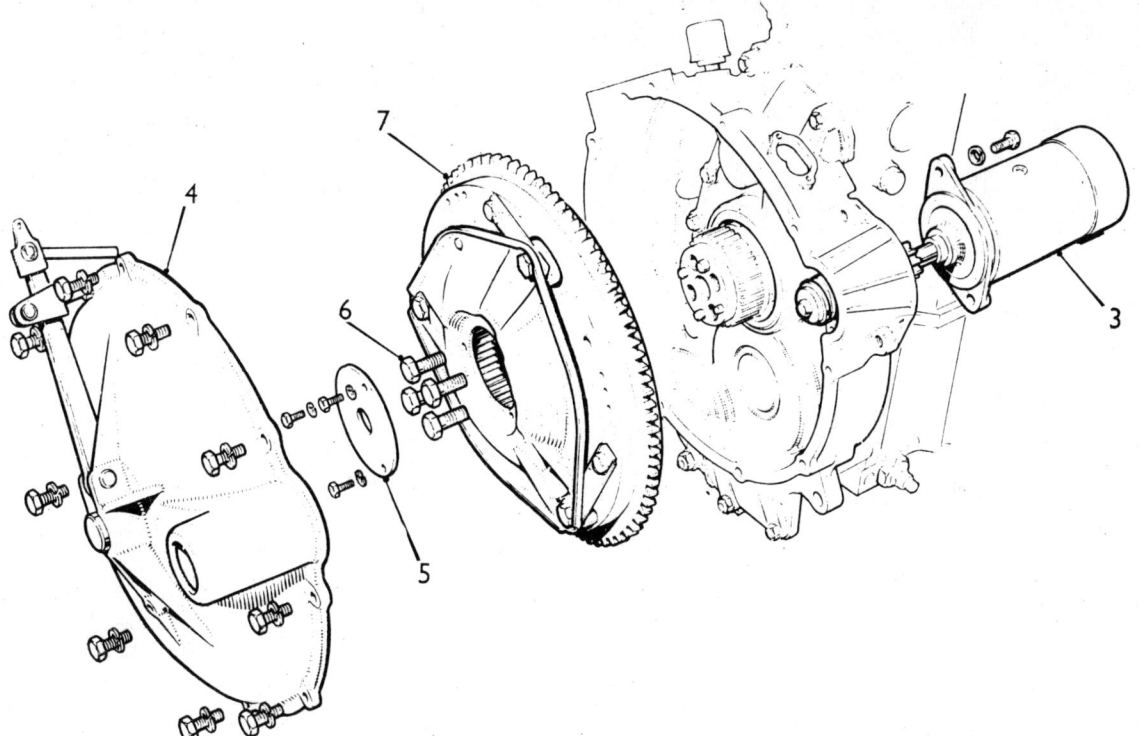

FIG 1 :10   Parts to be dismantled when removing the flywheel

Key to Fig 1 :10   3 Starter   4 Clutch housing cover   5 Clutch thrust plate   6 Flywheel bolts   7 Flywheel

Refitting the flywheel with engine out of car:

There are three small dowel holes in the flywheel centre. If a new or reconditioned flywheel is being fitted, these holes must be line-reamed with those in the crankshaft. Oversize dowels are available to fit the increased hole diameter.

Check the crankshaft primary gear end float as described in **Section 1 :9** and adjust it if necessary. Reverse the dismantling procedure to reassemble the parts. Tighten the flywheel retaining bolts to a torque of 60 lb ft, and those for the clutch housing cover to 15 to 18 lb ft.

Removing the flywheel housing:

Remove the power unit as instructed in **Section 1 :3**. Remove the flywheel as described in this Section. Looking on the face of the housing, remove the two top bolts. From inside the housing remove the two sets of three bolts each and below these the two sets of two nuts. From the flange under the housing remove five nuts. The next step needs some care as the primary gear oil seal might sustain damage from the gear splines. There is a Service Tool 18G.1152 which is essentially a length of thin-walled tubing, the outward-facing end being tapered as a lead-in. This fits over the splines to present a smooth surface to the oil seal. A strip of masking tape might make a good substitute.

With the splines suitably covered, withdraw the flywheel housing. Note the large ring dowel which locates the recess in the housing and surrounds the first motion shaft.

Refitting the flywheel housing:

Before fitting a new or reconditioned housing it will be necessary to check the ring dowel just mentioned. This operation is covered in **Chapter 6**. The rest of the refitting is the reverse of the dismantling sequence.

1 :9 The crankshaft primary gear and oil seal
Checking end float (engine in car):

1 Remove the flywheel as in **Section 1 :8**. Refer to **FIG 1 :11** and measure the depth in the flywheel of the recess 2. Fit the existing thrust washer and gear to the crankshaft and measure the amount the crankshaft protrudes, as indicated at 4.

2 As the end float must lie between .003 and .005 inch it is necessary for dimension 4 to exceed dimension 2 by that amount. Select a suitable thrust washer to achieve this result. Washers are available in thicknesses of .153 to .155 inch, .156 to .158 inch, .159 to .161 inch and .162 to .164 inch.

Checking end float (engine out of car):

1 Remove the flywheel and housing as described in **Section 1 :8**. Refit the flywheel with the existing thrust washer and primary gear in place. Tighten the flywheel bolts to a torque of 60 lb ft.

2 Using a feeler gauge, check the clearance between the rear face of the thrust washer and the flange on the crankshaft as indicated at 10. Select a thrust washer

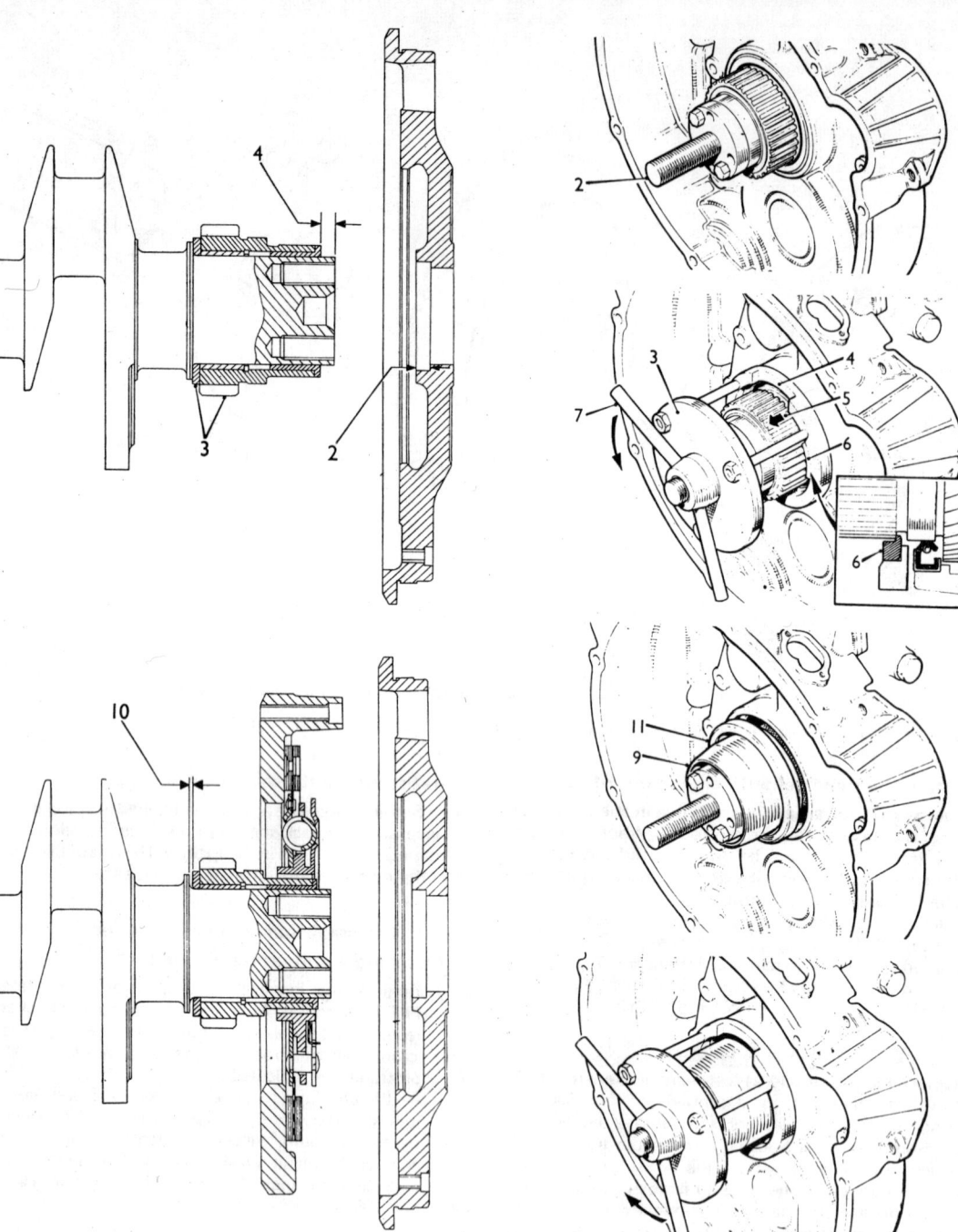

FIG 1:11 Checking the end float of the crankshaft primary gear. In the car (top view). Out of the car (bottom view)

Key to Fig 1:11   2 Depth of crankshaft recess in flywheel
3 Primary gear and thrust washer   4 Amount crankshaft protrudes   10 Clearance between crankshaft flange and thrust washer

FIG 1:12 Removing and fitting a primary gear oil seal using Service Tool 18G.1152

Key to Fig 1:12   2 Stud bolted to crankshaft
3 Cage of tool   4 Slot in cage   5 Primary gear
6 Collets hooked behind primary gear   7 Turn nut to remove gear   9 Protective sleeve   11 Oil seal

which will give the correct end float of .003 to .005 inch. The selection of washers which are available is given in the preceding Operation.

Renewing the primary gear oil seal (engine in car):

This is best accomplished by using the Service Tool 18G.1152 which is shown in **FIG 1:12**. This consists of a stud 2 which is bolted to the end of the crankshaft and a cage 3 which can be drawn outwards along the stud by a captive nut 7. The inner flange 4 of the cage is provided with two loose collets 6 which drop behind the splines on the primary gear. The abutment thus made allows the cage to draw the primary gear off the crankshaft, bringing the seal with it. The clutch must be removed before the tool can be used.

To fit a new seal it is necessary to cover the primary gear splines to protect the seal from damage. The Service Tool is a length of thinwalled tubing 9 with a tapered lead at the front end. A strip of masking tape over the splines might be an effective substitute. The seal 11 is pressed into its recess after a liberal coating of oil, using the Service Tool in reverse. The final operation is to check and adjust the primary gear end float as described in a preceding Operation. The clutch can then be refitted.

1:10 Camshaft drive gear

Removing the sprockets:

1 Remove the power unit from the car as instructed in **Section 1:3**. Remove the transmission assembly as described in **Chapter 6**.
2 Remove the crankshaft pulley (see **Section 1:7**). Remove the camshaft sprocket (see **Section 1:4**). Remove the front oil seal (see **Section 1:7**). Behind the seal is an oil thrower, part 34 in **FIG 1:7**.
   Remove this to allow the sprocket 33 to be pulled off the crankshaft.

Renewing the timing chain:

Having removed the camshaft and crankshaft sprockets, the timing chain can be removed, but only by parting the bright link. Working on the link is possible by using Service Tool 18G.1151, which is like a small but powerful vice 12 equipped with special pins on an adapter 9 and a loose bridge piece 10, as shown in **FIG 1:13**. The first pins to be used are pointed and both of them coincide with the riveted ends of the bright link pins. Find the bright link of the chain and fit the bridge piece into it. Position the adapter so that the points will press on the ends of the linkpins which have horizontal depressions and tighten the press to force the pins out of the side plate 11. Remove the press and part the chain, which can then be withdrawn from the cylinder block.

Fit a new chain and join the ends with a new link, the pins facing the moving jaw of the press. Locate the loose link plate 18 in the moving jaw 19 with the chamfered side away from the chain. Fit the locating bridge 10 in the bright link so that its legs centralize the link in the fixed jaw or anvil. Tighten the press to force the side plate onto the pins. Fit the riveting adapter 13 to the moving jaw 19 and tighten with hand pressure only. The chisel points will rivet the ends of the pins to secure the side plate. Check that the link is free to move without tight spots.

Refitting the sprockets:

1 Refit the crankshaft sprocket with its tapered face outwards. Check that the crankshaft is set at TDC with No. 1 cylinder firing and the 1/4 timing marks on the flywheel aligned. Check that the camshaft marks are also in line.
2 Fit the camshaft sprocket into the chain and assemble the sprocket to the camshaft without turning the crankshaft. Tighten the fixing bolt to a torque of 35 lb ft.
3 Reverse the dismantling procedure to complete the operation.

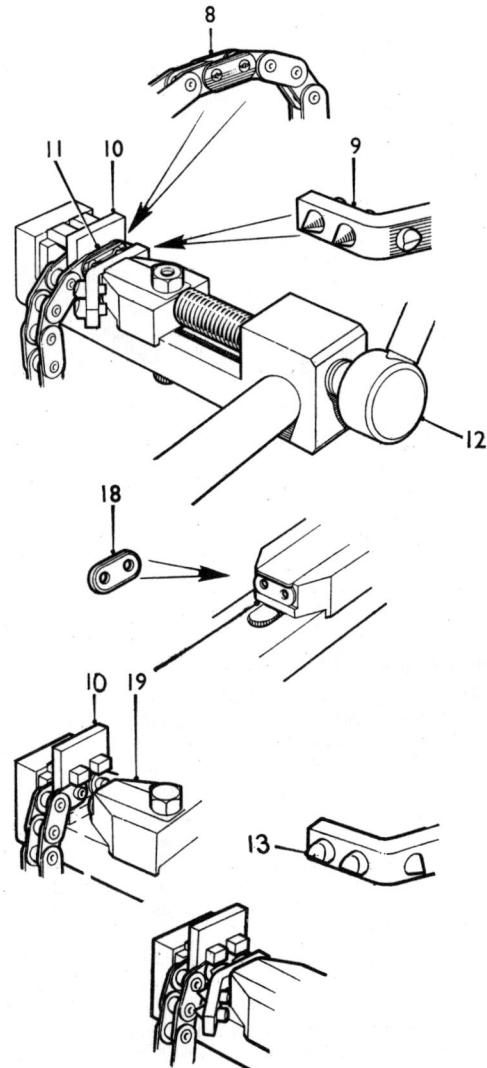

FIG 1:13 Parting and joining the timing chain using Service Tool 18G.1151

Key to Fig 1:13
9 Pointed extractor pins
11 Side plate being removed
13 Riveting pins
19 Moving jaw of tool
8 Bright link of chain
10 Loose bridge piece
12 Service Tool
18 Side plate fitted to moving jaw

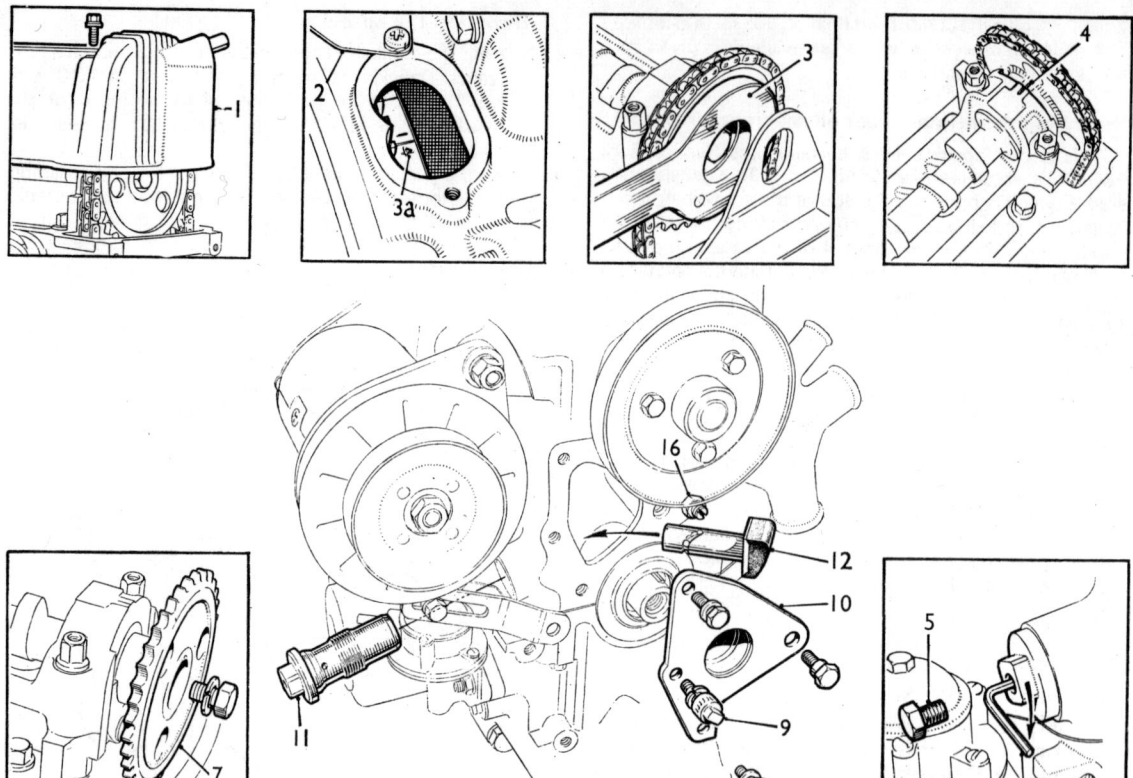

FIG 1 :14   Removing and refitting the timing chain tensioner

Key to Fig 1 :14   1 Camshaft cover   2 Timing cover on flywheel housing   3 Service Tool 18G.1153 for turning crankshaft
3a Flywheel timing marks   4 Camshaft alignment marks   5 Bolt for tensioner adapter   6 Allen key   7 Camshaft sprocket
9 Pivot bolt for generator link   10 Engine front cover   11 Chain tensioner adapter   12 Tensioner
16 Adjuster for righthand chain guide

Removing the chain tensioner:

The location of the tensioner adapter will be seen to be
immediately under the generator as shown by part 11 in
FIG 1 :14. To remove the tensioner do the following:

1 Remove the camshaft cover 1 (six bolts). Remove the
flywheel housing timing cover 2 and set the crankshaft
at TDC with No. 1 cylinder firing. The 1/4 marks 3a on
the flywheel will then be aligned with the pointer. The
spanner with three pegs shown as part 3 is used on the
camshaft sprocket to turn both camshaft and crankshaft. A replica of the BLMC Service Tool 18G.1153
could be made up.

2 The alignment marks 4 must also be checked. These
will be found on the camshaft sprocket and the bearing
housing.

3 Remove the chain tensioner adapter bolt 5. Introduce a
⅛ inch Allen key into the hole and turn it clockwise to
retract the tensioner.

4 Remove the camshaft sprocket 7 and the crankshaft
pulley as described in **Section 1 :7**. Remove the pivot
bolt 9 for the generator adjusting link.

5 Remove the cover plate 10 to gain access for the
removal of the tensioner 12. This can be done after the
adapter 11 is unscrewed.

Check the head of the tensioner for wear and also the
fit of the shank in the bore of the adapter. Renew worn
parts.

Refitting the chain tensioner:

1 Refit the tensioner and the adapter. Fit the camshaft
sprocket and make sure the timing marks on the flywheel
and the camshaft are still correctly aligned. Tighten the
sprocket bolt to 35 lb ft.

2 Locate locknut 16 and slacken it. This locks the adjusting screw for the righthand chain guide which is part 13
in **FIG 1 :15**. Turn the adjuster until the chain is tight
but not taut and tighten the locknut.

3 Turn the Allen key anticlockwise to release the tensioner. Refit all the dismantled parts in the reverse order
to dismantling.

Removing the chain guides:

Refer to **FIG 1 :15** which shows the guides in the lower
view. Note that every reference to the righthand and lefthand guides is as seen in the external view on the left. Do
the following:

1 Remove the radiator complete with cowl (see
Chapter 4). Remove the crankshaft pulley (see

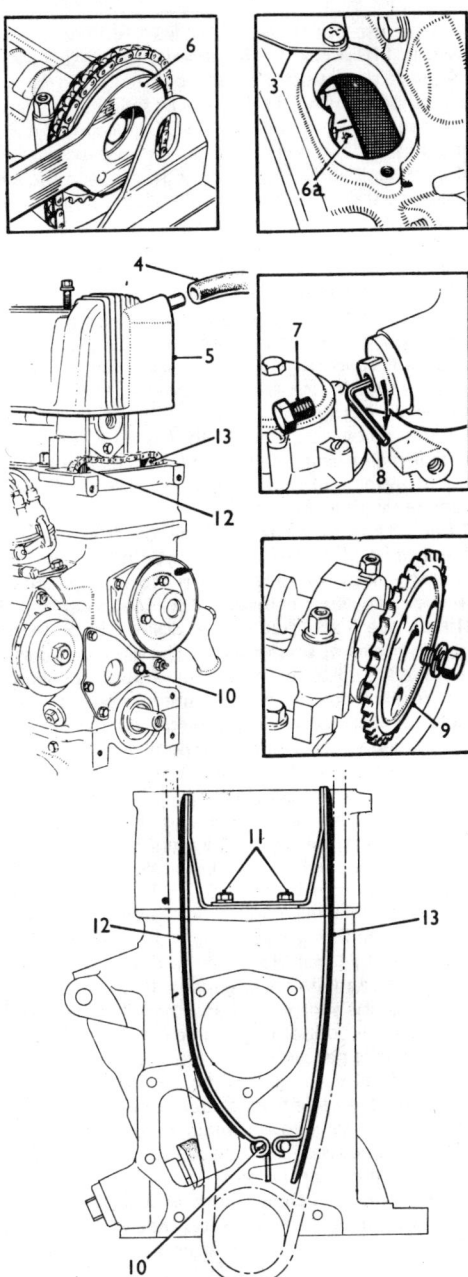

FIG 1:15 Removing and refitting timing chain guides

Key to Fig 1:15
3 Flywheel housing timing cover
4 Breather hose   5 Camshaft cover   6 Service Tool
18G.1153 for turning crankshaft   6a Crankshaft timing
marks   7 Bolt for tensioner adapter   8 Allen key
9 Camshaft sprocket   10 Dowel bolt for lefthand guide
11 Guide retaining bolts   12 Lefthand guide
13 Righthand guide

Section 1 : 7) and the flywheel housing timing cover 3.
Disconnect the breather hose 4. Remove the cover 5.

2 Use peg spanner 6 on the camshaft sprocket to turn the
crankshaft until the 1/4 mark 6a on the flywheel is in
line with the pointer when No. 1 cylinder is firing.

3 Remove the tensioner adapter bolt 7, insert a $\frac{1}{8}$ inch
Allen key in the hole and turn clockwise to retract the
tensioner. Remove the camshaft sprocket 9.

4 Remove the dowel bolt 10 from the lower end of the
lefthand guide 12. Remove bolts 11 from the upper
guide and lift away the lefthand guide. Disengage the
lower end of the righthand guide 13 from its eccentric
adjuster, turn it through 90 deg. and withdraw it.

Refitting the chain guides:

Having renewed worn guides and checked the adjuster
44 in **FIG 1 : 7**, reassembly can be started. If the adjuster
was removed, make sure that it is correctly refitted so that
the guide is in vertical alignment.

1 Fit the righthand guide with its lower end engaged in
the adjuster.

2 Fit the lefthand guide and the dowel bolt 41 in **FIG
1 : 7**. Tighten the bolt to a torque of 18 to 20 lb ft.
Make sure that the dowel bolt correctly engages the
guide. Use the same torque for bolts 11.

3 Check that the camshaft and crankshaft marks are still
correctly aligned and continue reassembling in the
reverse order to dismantling. Turn the Allen key anticlockwise to release the chain tensioner.

Noisy chain drive:

If a noisy drive is caused by the chain fouling the side
of the tunnel in the block, check that there is not less
than .125 inch clearance between the chain and the
block at the nearest point. Insufficient clearance can be
rectified by judicious filing of the tunnel, but the greatest
care must be taken to prevent filings from dropping into
the crankcase.

1:11 Servicing pistons and connecting rods

Removing:

This can only be done with the power unit out of the
car (see **Section 1 : 3**). It is also necessary to remove the
transmission assembly as instructed in **Chapter 6**. Then
proceed as follows:

1 Remove the cylinder head (see **Section 1 : 4**). Refer to
FIG 1 : 16 and check the markings on rod and cap 4.
These should coincide with the cylinder bore numbers
starting with No. 1 at the front or lefthand end of the
engine.

2 When the big-end nuts 5 are removed they must be
scrapped, so be prepared to fit new nuts on reassembly.
When the nuts are off, tap the connecting rod bolts
upwards until a downward pull on the caps 6 will
release them. Remove the bearing shells 9 in **FIG 1 : 7**,
keeping them in the order of removal.

3 If the engine is due for decarbonizing there will be a
ring of carbon round the top of each cylinder bore.
Remove this with a scraper and then push the connecting rod and piston upwards and out. If the bearing
shells and caps are restored to their respective rods
there will be no confusion when it comes to reassembly.

A design feature of the piston and connecting rod
assembly is that the gudgeon pin is a tight press fit in the
small-end of the rod. Removing and refitting the pin

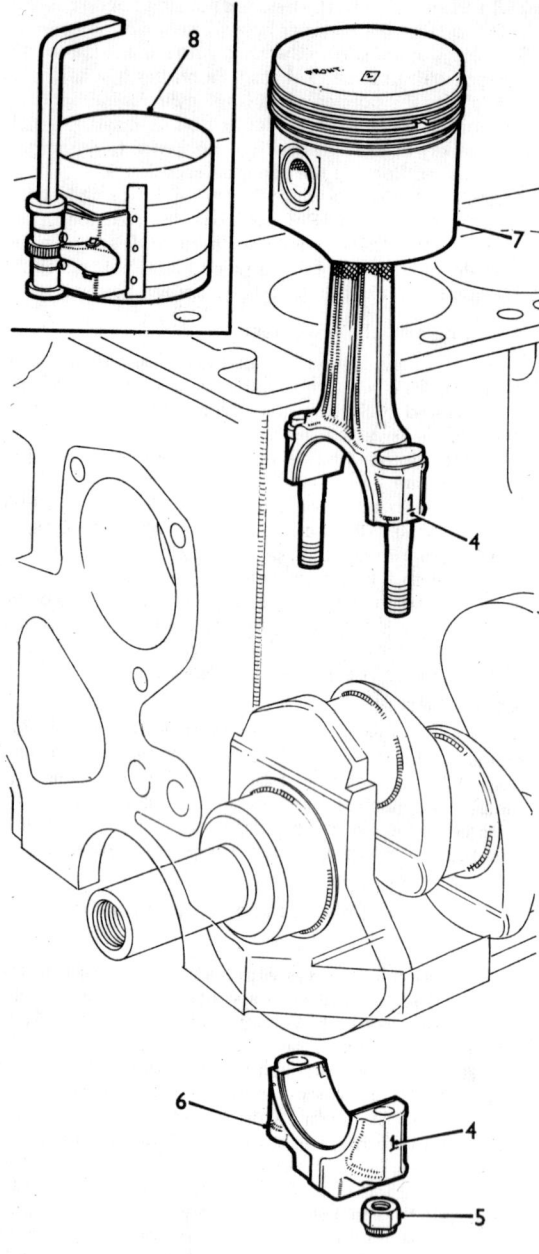

entails the use of Service Tools 18G.1150 and 1150B as shown in **FIG 1:17**. In the absence of these Tools the work must be entrusted to an agent suitably equipped. The method of using the Tools is as follows:

1 Hold the hexagon body 1 in a vice. Unscrew nut 2 until it is flush with the end then push it in direction 3 until it contacts the thrust race. Fit adapter 4 on the centre screw so that its cutaway for the piston rings is uppermost.

2 Slide sleeve 5 onto the centre screw with the groove entering first as shown by the arrow. The piston crown is marked 'FRONT'. Fit the piston onto the centre screw so that the marking is adjacent to the adapter 4. **This position is important because the gudgeon pin is offset towards the front of the engine and the piston would not fit the recess in the adapter if wrongly assembled.**

3 Fit the remover/replacer bush 7 on the centre screw with its flange last. Screw on the stopnut 8 until there is about $\frac{1}{32}$ inch of end play at 'A'. Lock the stopnut securely with lockscrew 9.

4 **Check that the curved face of the adapter is clean and slide the piston into place so that it fits the adapter face. The piston rings must lie in the cutaway of the adapter. Make certain that the sleeve 5 and bush 7 are correctly positioned in the bores at each side of the piston.** Screw the large nut 2 up to the face of the thrust race as at 14. Use plenty of oil on the large nut and centre screw.

5 Hold the lockscrew while turning the large nut so that the gudgeon pin is withdrawn. Remove the piston rings one at a time over the top of the piston, working a thin strip of steel from the gap and under each ring while pressing it upwards onto the land above.

Check all parts for wear, renewing the assembly if the gudgeon pin is slack in the piston bosses. The correct diameter of the pin is .8123 to .8125 inch. Renew the piston rings if they have seen much service and check the ring gap before fitting them (see 17 in **FIG 1:18**). Press each ring about 1 inch down the bore with a piston and measure the gap with feeler gauges. It should be .012 to .022 inch for the top, second and third rings and .015 to .045 for the oil control ring. Judicious filing of the ring ends will enable gaps which are too small to be increased. Check the fit of the rings in the piston grooves, but first clean the grooves free from carbon without scraping the metal. The ring to groove clearance 18 of the top three rings must lie between .0015 to .0035 inch. Note that the top ring 26 is a plain chrome one and the second and third 25 are tapered. Dimensions for widths of rings and ring grooves are given in Technical Data at the end of this manual.

Reassembling pistons to connecting rods:

Fit the rings to the piston, feeding them over the top or crown. Start with the oil control ring, fitting the bottom rail 19 first and moving it out of the groove to rest just below. Fit the expander 20 into the bottom groove and then restore the bottom rail to the groove. Fit the top rail 22. Check that the ends of the expander are butting as shown at 23. They must not overlap. Set the gaps of the rails and the expander at 90 deg. to each other as shown.

Follow on by fitting the third and second tapered rings. These are marked 'TOP' and the marking must face up-

FIG 1:16 A piston and connecting rod. The inset shows a ring compressor for use when refitting the piston in the bore

Key to Fig 1:16 4 Bore numbers stamped on connecting rod and cap 5 Big-end nut 6 Big-end cap 7 Piston 8 Ring compressor

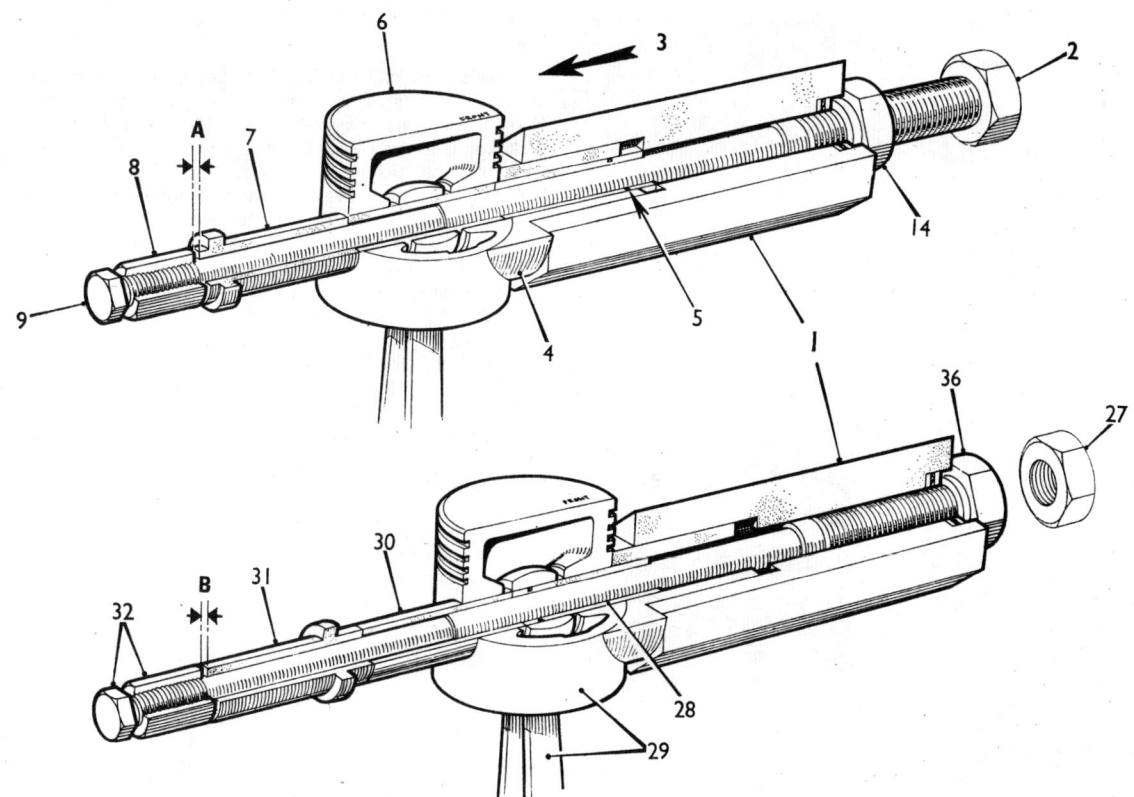

FIG 1:17   Gudgeon pin removal (above) and replacement (below), using Service Tools 18G.1150 and 18G.1150B

Key to Fig 1:17   1 Hexagon body   2 Nut for centre screw   3 Screw pushed in direction of arrow   4 Adapter 18G.1150B
5 Groove in parallel sleeve   6 Piston   7 Remover/replacer bush   8 Stop nut   9 Lockscrew   A End play of $\frac{1}{32}$ inch
14 Large nut contacting thrust race   27 Large nut removed   28 Parallel sleeve   29 Piston and connecting rod
30 Gudgeon pin   31 Remover/replacer bush   32 Stop nut and lockscrew   B End play of $\frac{1}{32}$ inch
36 Large nut screwed up to thrust race

wards. On 1750 engines the tapered compression ring is fitted in the second groove only. Fit the top ring. Fit the piston to the connecting rod in the following sequence:

1 Refer to the lower view in **FIG 1:17** and remove the large nut 27. Pull the centre screw out of the body a few inches.
2 Fit the parallel sleeve 28 with the grooved end trailing. Fit the piston and connecting rod, the small-end being entered on the sleeve up to the groove.
3 Use thin oil on the gudgeon pin 30 and fit it so that it enters the piston boss right up to the connecting rod small-end. Fit the remover/replacer bush 31 with its flange nearest the pin.
4 Screw on the stop nut 32 until there is $\frac{1}{32}$ inch end play at 'B'. Lock the nut securely with the lockscrew.
5 The curved face of the adapter must be clean. The piston rings must lie over the cutaway in the adapter. Screw the large nut 27 up to thrust race as at 36. Set a torque wrench to break at 12 lb ft. This is the minimum

load for an acceptable fit of the pin in the small-end. **If the wrench does not break during the operation the gudgeon pin is not tight enough in the small-end and new parts must be fitted. It is also important to keep the large nut and the centre screw well lubricated, as excessive friction may give a false torque wrench reaction.**
6 Hold the lockscrew and turn the large nut so that the gudgeon pin is drawn in until the flange of bush 31 is $\frac{1}{16}$ inch from the piston skirt. **Never allow the flange to contact the piston.**
7 Being satisfied that the pin is a correct fit, check it for freedom in the piston bosses. The piston must be free to slide sideways. If it is tight, wash the assembly in petrol or paraffin and lubricate the pin with Achesons Colloids 'Oildag'. If it is still tight after this, dismantle the assembly and check for damage or ingrained dirt.
8 After checking the piston and connecting rod for alignment, use 'Oildag' on the gudgeon pin and prepare to fit the piston into its bore by oiling liberally.

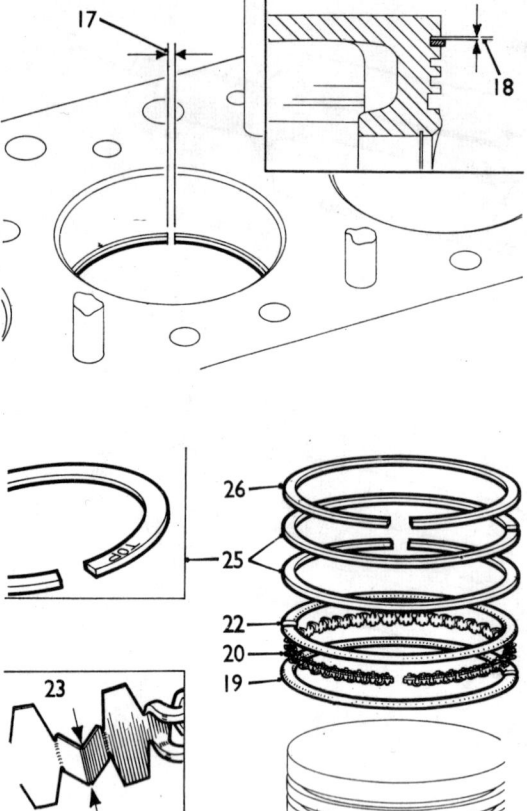

FIG 1:18 Top view shows piston ring gap and side clearance in piston groove. Lower view shows the rings, the marking 'TOP' and the butted ends of the oil control ring expander

Key to Fig 1:18 17 Ring gap measured in bore 18 Side clearance of ring   19 Bottom rail of oil control ring   20 Expander of oil control ring   22 Top rail of oil control ring   23 Butted ends of expander 25 Second and third tapered rings are marked 'TOP' 26 Chromium-plated top ring

Refitting pistons and connecting rods:

Reverse the dismantling sequence but be careful to ensure that each assembly is fitted into its correct bore. The piston crown is marked 'FRONT' and the connecting rod oil hole must be on the distributor side. Use a piston ring compressor to introduce the piston into the oiled bore and then pull the assembly down until the upper bearing shell can be fitted to the rod. Be careful to fit the tag on the shell into the notch in the rod and oil the big-end journal. Fit the cap and lower shell with the marks aligned and screw **new** nuts on the bolts. Tighten to a torque of 30 lb ft.

When the engine and transmission have been bolted together and restored to the car, fill with the correct grade and quantity of lubricating oil and also fill the cooling system.

1:12 Crankshaft servicing

Removing:

Work on the crankshaft cannot begin until the power unit is removed from the car and the transmission unbolted. These operations are described in **Section 1:3** and **Chapter 6** respectively. Refer to **FIG 1:19** and do the following operations:

1 Remove the front oil seal 3, the oil thrower and crankshaft sprocket 4 and the distributor drive gear 5. These operations are described in **Sections 1:7, 1:10** and **1:13** respectively. Remove the crankshaft primary gear and thrust washer 6 as in **Section 1:9**.

2 Use a dial gauge on one end of the crankshaft and lever the shaft backwards and forwards to check the end float. Check the big-end markings 4 in **FIG 1:16** and the main bearing marks 7 in **FIG 1:19**. In each case No. 1 should start at the front or lefthand end of the engine. Remove big-end caps 8 and main bearing caps 9.

3 Lift away the crankshaft 10. On each side of No. 4 main bearing there are thrust washers to control end float. They are shown as items 6 in **FIG 1:7**. Keep the bearing shells with their caps so that they can be fitted in their original positions if they are not to be renewed.

Refitting the crankshaft:

Check the main and big-end bearings for wear. Diametrical clearance and end float figures will be found in Technical Data at the end of this manual. If necessary, the main and big-end journals can be reground to undersizes of .010, .020, .030 and .040 inch and undersize bearings fitted. Excessive end float is cured by selecting suitable thrust washers 10. Renew all bearing shells which are scored or show signs of breaking up.

Adjustment of main and big-end clearances by filing the caps and shells is not permissible. It immediately renders the parts unacceptable on an exchange basis. The shells are ready to fit and the running clearances will be correct without any need for adjustment. If a bearing has 'run', flush out all oil passages under high pressure and inject fresh engine oil.

If the crankshaft is a new or reconditioned one it will be necessary to line-ream the three small dowel holes at the flywheel end with those in the flywheel. Oversize dowels can then be fitted. Proceed to refit the crankshaft as follows:

1 Oil the journals and lower the crankshaft into place after positioning the timing chain correctly. Make sure the thrust washer halves are correctly fitted and have their oilways facing outwards.

2 Check that the bearing shell tags are seated in their notches and fit the main bearing caps. Tighten the bolts to a torque of 70 lb ft.

3 Fit the big-end caps, tightening the nuts to a torque of 30 lb ft. Fit the distributor drive gear as described in **Section 1:13**. Follow the rest of the dismantling sequence in reverse. Fill the engine and transmission assembly with the correct grade and quantity of oil and refill the cooling system when the radiator assembly is complete. Refer to **Section 1:15** for hints on the problem of bearings which become too tight when the nuts are tightened.

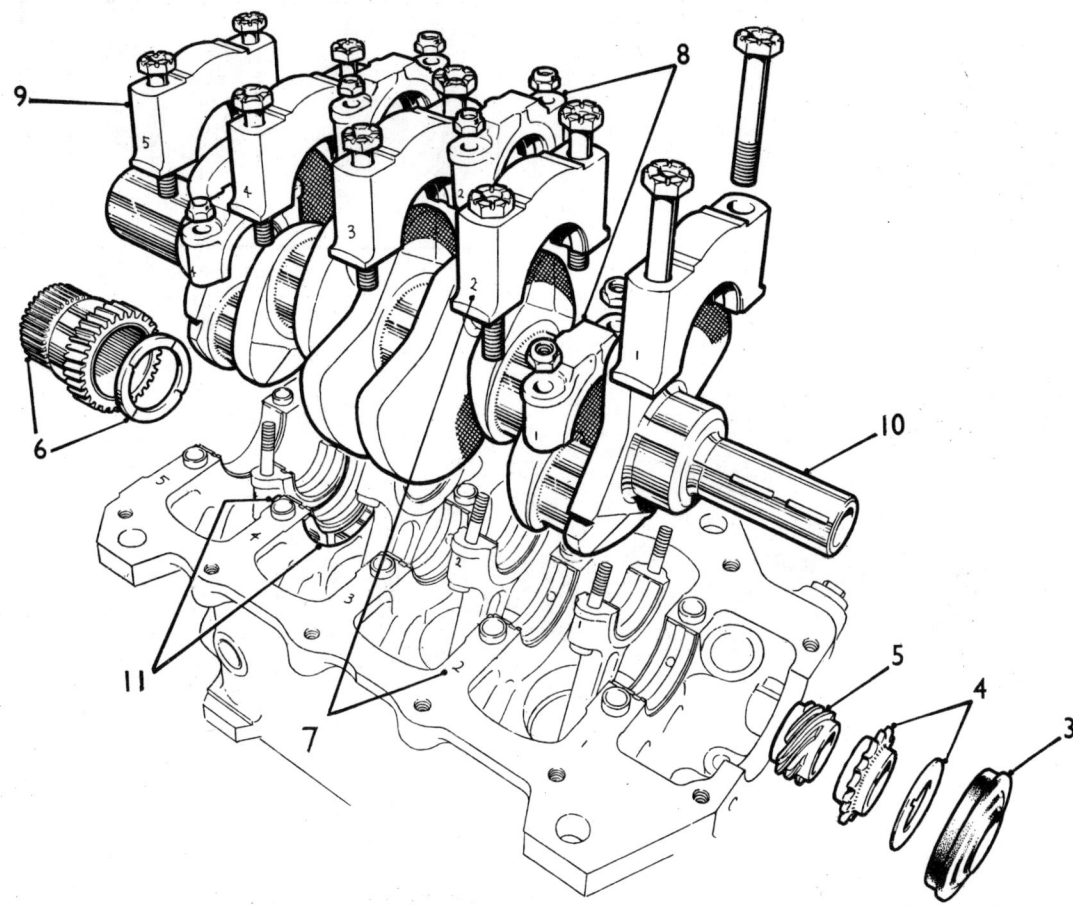

FIG 1:19 The crankshaft and main bearing caps lifted from the cylinder block

Key to Fig 1:19   3 Front oil seal   4 Oil thrower and crankshaft sprocket   5 Distributor drive gear
7 Primary gear and thrust washer   7 Mating marks on cap and block   8 Big-end caps   9 Main bearing cap
10 Crankshaft   11 Thrust washers

1:13 The distributor drive shaft

Use **FIG 1:20** for reference purposes. Note the drive shaft and thrust washer 15. An internal shaft not shown drives the oil pump through the agency of squared ends. It is important to observe that the distributor drive at the top end consists of an offset slot as shown by the top insets 12 and 13. This ensures that the drive can only be meshed in one position. Above the gear on the shaft is a face cam which drives a short pushrod to operate the fuel pump. Remove the drive shaft as follows:

1 Remove the power unit (see **Section 1:3**) and the transmission (see **Chapter 6**). Remove the crankshaft pulley (see **Section 1:7**) and the camshaft cover 4.
2 Remove the flywheel timing cover and turn the crankshaft until the 1/4 mark is at TDC with No. 1 cylinder firing as shown at 5.
3 Remove bolt 6 from the chain tensioner adapter near the fuel pump. Insert a $\frac{1}{8}$ inch Allen key and turn it clockwise to retract the tensioner. Remove the camshaft sprocket 8.
4 Remove the front oil seal 9 (see **Section 1:7**). Withdraw oil thrower 10 and sprocket 11. Make sure the crankshaft is still as set and note the position of the distributor driving slot. It should be as shown in inset 12 where the slot is at 2 o'clock and the large lobe is uppermost.
5 Pull the distributor drive gear 14 off the crankshaft and watch the distributor drive shaft at the same time. It will be seen to turn through approximately 90 deg. Remove the drive shaft and thrust washer 15. Note the squared driving shaft for the oil pump.

Check the shaft for wear of the bearing surfaces, the drive slot at the top and the drive shaft for the oil pump. Excessive wear of the gear teeth or the fuel pump cam will necessitate the renewal of the complete shaft. If the gear is worn it is always desirable to renew the crankshaft gear at the same time.

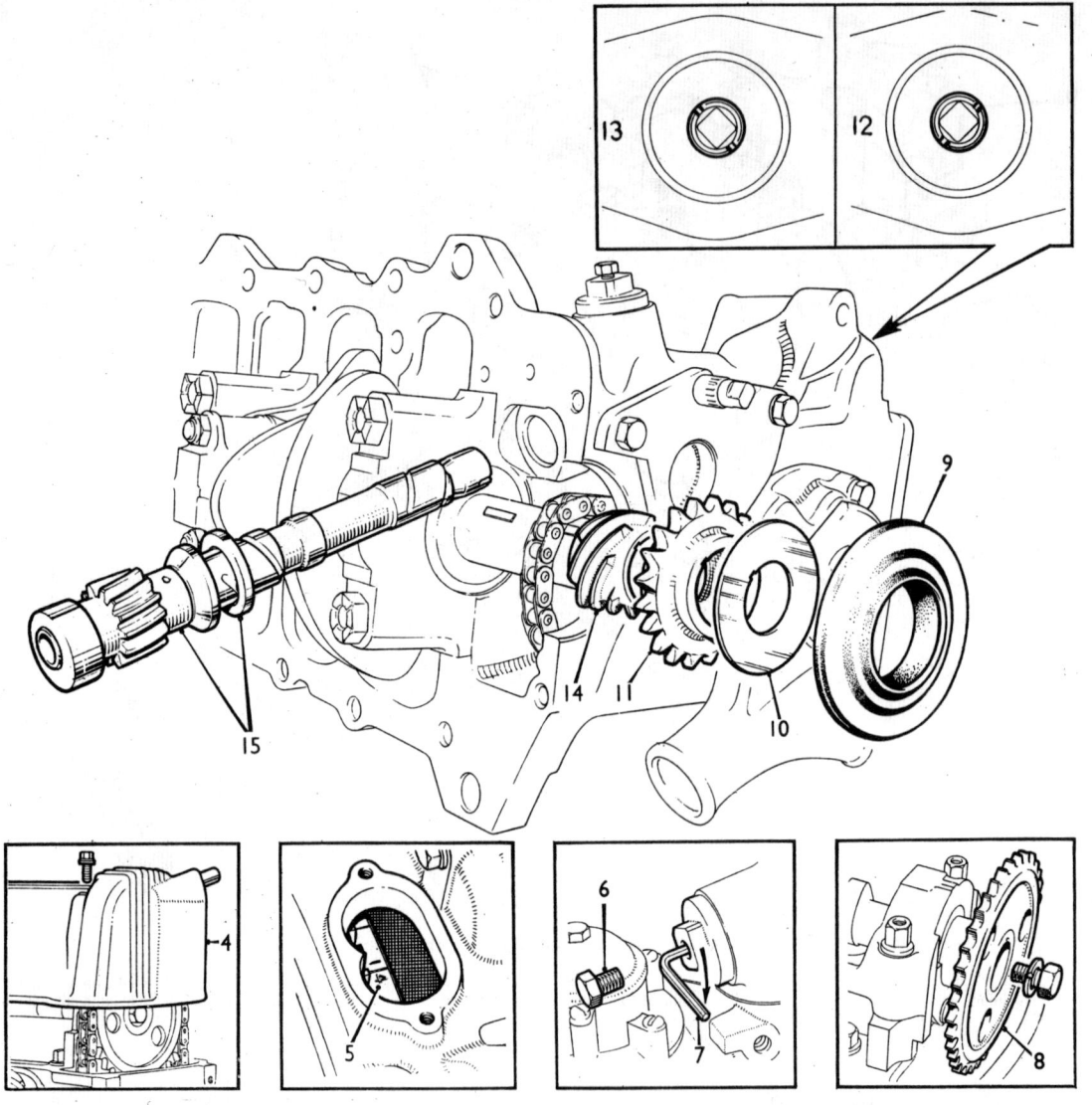

FIG 1:20 Removing and refitting the distributor and fuel pump drive shaft. Insets **12** and **13** show the offset slot in the top end

Key to Fig 1:20   4 Camshaft cover   5 Crankshaft timing mark   6 Bolt for tensioner adapter   7 Allen key
8 Camshaft sprocket   9 Front oil seal   10 Oil thrower   11 Sprocket   12 Position of offset slot after meshing gears
13 Position of offset slot before meshing gears   14 Distributor drive gear   15 Distributor and fuel pump drive shaft with thrust washer

Refitting the drive shaft:

    Some care is needed in this operation because the shaft turns as the gear teeth are meshed. **It is essential, for the accuracy of ignition timing, to ensure that the drive slot at the top end finishes up in the right position.** Proceed as follows:

1 Fit thrust washer 15. Check that the crankshaft has not moved from the original setting.

2 Refer to inset 13 in the illustration. Fit the drive shaft so that the slot is in the 10 o'clock position with the large lobe uppermost. Now mesh the gears and note how the shaft turns anticlockwise until the slot has moved through approximately 90 deg. to bring it to 2 o'clock as shown at inset 12. The large lobe will still be uppermost. This is the correct position for No. 1 cylinder to be firing.

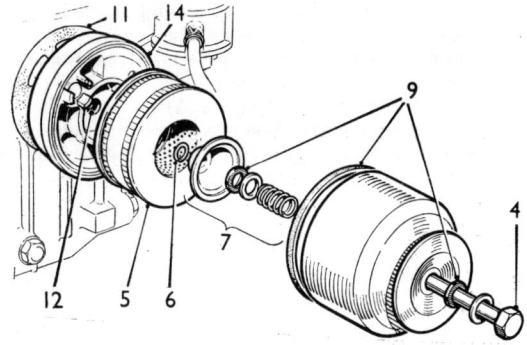

FIG 1:21 Components of the fullflow oil filter

Key to Fig 1:21   4 Centre bolt   5 Renewable element
6 Centre bolt circlip   7 Pressure plate, rubber and steel
washers and spring for centre bolt   9 Rubber washers and
sealing ring   11 Gasket for filter head   12 Centre bolt
sealing ring   14 Filter head

3 Temporarily fit the distributor, turning the distributor shaft by the rotor arm until the slot and driving key mesh. There is only one place where this can be done because of the offset. Check that the rotor arm is now so placed that it faces the distributor cap segment and lead to No. 1 sparking plug with the contact breaker points about to open. Check the ignition timing with a stroboscope (see **Chapter 3**).

4 Continue the dismantling operations in reverse.

1:14 The lubrication system

The oil filter:

The fullflow oil filter has a renewable element which should be changed every 6000 miles. The filter will be found low down under the generator. Change the element as follows, referring to **FIG 1:21**:

1 Unscrew bolt 4. With a container handy to catch draining oil, pull off the casing and element 5, leaving the head 14 in position. Discard the old element. **Never attempt to clean it.**

2 From inside the casing, remove circlip 6 from the centre bolt. Remove parts 7. Wash all the components in petrol and examine the condition of the rubber washers and particularly the large head washer 9. Renew all defective parts and then reassemble items 7 on the centre bolt in the order shown. Do not forget the washers under the head of the bolt.

3 Reassemble using a new element, checking that the centre bolt sealing ring 12 is correctly positioned in the head. If the head was removed, clean the joint faces and fit a new gasket 11.

4 Tighten the bolt to a torque of 20 lb ft, run the engine and check for leaks. This is most important as serious loss of lubricating oil might otherwise occur. Check the oil level with the dipstick.

Draining and refilling:

Always drain the lubricating oil when it is warm and thin. The drain plug is at the bottom of the transmission casing under the fan. Remove it and drain out the old oil

every 6000 miles. The peg sticking out of the plug is a magnet. Clean it of adhering particles of steel and fit a new copper washer if necessary. Refit the plug and refill with the correct grade of oil. Use $8\frac{1}{2}$ pints but add an extra pint if the oil filter element has been changed. Run the engine for a few minutes, let it stand for a short time and check the level.

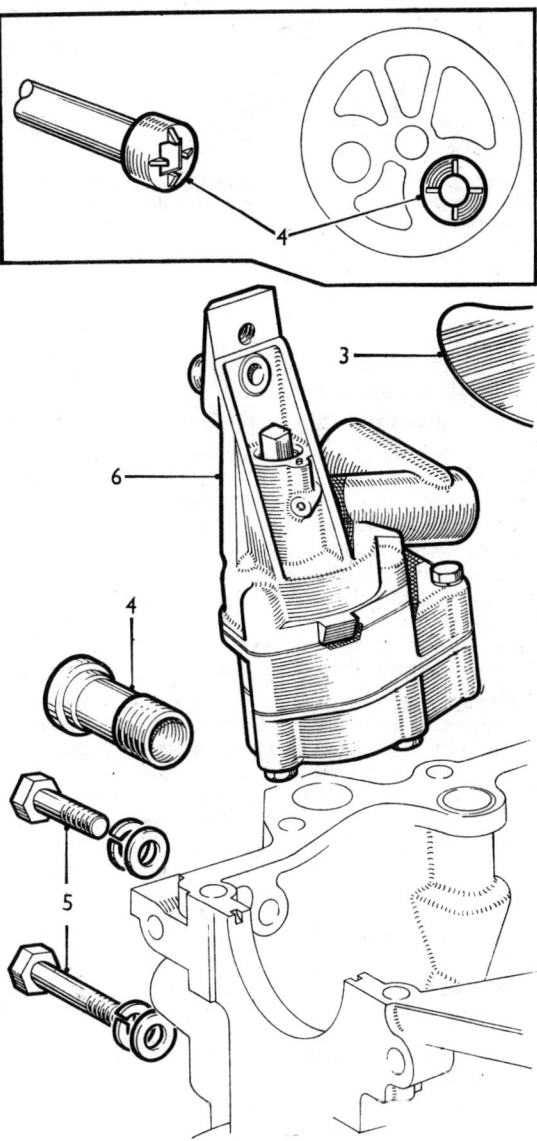

FIG 1:22 Removing the oil pump. On the left in the inset is Service Tool 18G.1149 for removing the outlet connection

Key to Fig 1:22   3 Transmission baffle   4 Pump
outlet connection   5 Pump securing bolts   6 Pump
assembly

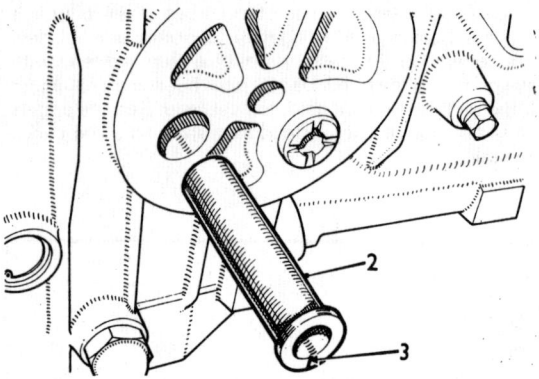

FIG 1:23 The oil pressure relief valve 2. Marking 3 indicates the position of the release hole. It must face downwards

Oil pump and drive shaft:

Removing and refitting shaft:

When the distributor is removed as instructed in **Chapter 3** a squared shaft will be seen. This is part 19 in **FIG 1:7**. Prepare a short piece of tubing with a cross slot so that it will grip the shaft when pressed down on it. Withdraw the shaft.

When refitting the shaft make sure that it fully engages with the oil pump drive. Tighten the distributor bolts to 8 to 10 lb ft.

Removing and refitting oil pump:

1 Remove the power unit as in **Section 1:3** and the transmission as in **Chapter 6**. Remove the transmission baffle 31 in the exploded view of the transmission casing in the same chapter.
2 Refer to the inset in **FIG 1:22** and unscrew the pump outlet connection 4 using Service Tool 18G.1149 as illustrated or a large screwdriver specially ground.
3 Remove the pump fixing bolts 5 and lift out the pump 6. Dismantle the pump into the component parts shown in **FIG 1:7**. Check the fit of the inner rotor and shaft 22 in the pump housing. Do the same for the outer rotor 23. The efficiency of the pump depends on the minimum variation from the original clearances. Renew all defective parts.
4 Clean the filter gauze 27 with a brush and clean fuel. Do not use fluffy rag. If it is necessary to remove the oil pump pickup, fifth-speed gear must be removed from the transmission as instructed in **Chapter 6**.
5 Refit all the parts in the reverse order of dismantling, lubricating well and making sure that gasket 26 is in good condition.

Removing and refitting oil pressure relief valve:

Refer to **FIG 1:23** for details of the valve. It is not adjustable and must be renewed as an assembly. If any variation from normal oil pressure is known not to be due to wear in the oil pump or the engine bearings, particularly those of the crankshaft and big-ends, then renewal of the relief valve might effect a cure. The valve is accessible after the filter and its head are removed as instructed earlier in this Section. It is readily withdrawn. When refitting the valve make sure the release hole is pointing downwards. The mark 3 is in line with the hole for easy verification. When refitting the filter, check that the head joint washer and the casing gasket are in good condition. Check the oil level with the dipstick.

Ventilation filter:

Although not primarily a part of the lubrication system, this item is included because the filter ensures that dirt cannot enter the engine through the ventilator. The domed cover is located on the flywheel housing adjacent to the clutch slave cylinder. Every 12,000 miles undo the centre screw and remove the old element. Clean the inside of the cover, fit a new element and replace the cover.

1:15 Reassembling the engine

All the operations concerned with ʻdismantling and refitting the various components of the engine have been covered in **Sections 1:3 to 1:14**. The task of reassembling the transmission to the engine is covered early in **Chapter 6**. It is essential to be clean and methodical when performing the operations and to lubricate all bearing surfaces liberally with clean engine oil. Always renew all joint gaskets as these are available in complete sets.

Start off by fitting the crankshaft. As each bearing cap is tightened check the freedom of the shaft. If it suddenly becomes tight, dismantle the last cap to be tightened and check the bearing shells for dirt and burrs. This method must also be adopted when refitting the big-ends. Make quite sure that the shaft has been correctly assembled with all gears and the timing chain in position. Continue to refit the components in the reverse order to dismantling, being careful to use the torque wrench figures given in the text and also in Technical Data at the end of this manual. Always check that the crankshaft and camshaft are correctly positioned so that the ignition and valve timings are not wrongly set.

Fit a new gasket before attaching the inlet and exhaust manifold. There are four short bolts in the top row, two long bolts in the outer holes in the bottom row and two nuts and spring washers for studs in the third and fourth bottom holes.

Before fitting the exhaust pipe, check the condition of the flare on the pipe where it contacts the manifold. It is also important to ensure that the two clamps are neither strained nor broken. Renew faulty parts and fit new bolts if the old ones are bent or it will be difficult to make a leak-tight joint.

The servicing of associated components such as the carburetter fuel pump, generator and water pump are covered in the various Chapters devoted to those subjects. When reassembling is completed and the power units restored to the car, check that the oil level is correct and refill the cooling system. Run the engine and immediately check that there are no leaks from the oil filter nor from the hose connections. Check the ignition timing with a strobo-scope (see **Chapter 3**). After the engine has been running in service and has had a chance to settle down, check the tappet adjustment and the tightness of the bolts and nuts.

1 :16 Fault diagnosis

(a) Engine will not start

1 Defective coil
2 Faulty distributor capacitor (condenser)
3 Dirty, pitted or incorrectly set contact breaker points
4 Ignition wiring loose or insulation faulty
5 Water on plug leads, damp distributor
6 Battery discharged, terminals corroded
7 Faulty or jammed starter. Switch defective
8 Plug leads wrongly connected
9 Vapour lock in fuel pipes due to heat
10 Defective fuel pump or float mechanism
11 Overchoking or underchoking, sticking carburetter piston
12 Blocked petrol filter or carburetter jet
13 Leaking valves, broken springs
14 Sticking valves
15 Valve timing incorrect
16 Ignition timing incorrect

(b) Engine stalls

1 Check 1, 2, 3, 4, 5, 10, 11, 12, 13 and 14 in (a)
2 Sparking plugs defective or gaps incorrect
3 Retarded ignition
4 Mixture too weak
5 Water in fuel system
6 Petrol tank vent blocked
7 Incorrect valve clearances

(c) Engine idles badly

1 Check 2, 4 and 7 in (b)
2 Air leak at manifold joints
3 Carburetter jet wrongly positioned
4 Air leak in carburetter
5 Over-rich mixture
6 Worn piston rings
7 Worn valve stems or guides
8 Weak exhaust valve springs

(d) Engine misfires

1 Check 1, 2, 3, 4, 5, 8, 10, 12, 13, 14, 15 and 16 in (a); 2, 3, 4 and 7 in (b)
2 Weak or broken valve springs

(e) Engine overheats (see Chapter 4)

(f) Compression low

1 Check 13 and 14 in (a), 6 and 7 in (c) and 2 in (d)
2 Worn piston ring grooves
3 Scored or worn cylinder bores
4 Breakdown of head gasket

(g) Engine lacks power

1 Check 3, 10, 11, 12, 13, 14, 15 and 16 in (a); 2, 3, 4 and 7 in (b); 6 and 7 in (c) and 2 in (d)
2 Leaking joint washers
3 Fouled sparking plugs
4 Automatic ignition advance not operating

(h) Burnt valves or head seats

1 Check 13 and 14 in (a); 7 in (b); 2 in (d) and also check (e)
2 Excessive carbon build-up round valve seats and head

(j) Sticking valves

1 Check 2 in (d)
2 Bent valve stem
3 Scored valve stem or guide
4 Incorrect valve clearance

(k) Excessive cylinder wear

1 Check 11 in (a) and see Chapter 4
2 Lack of oil
3 Dirty oil
4 Piston rings gummed up or broken
5 Badly fitting piston rings, gaps too small
6 Bent connecting rod

(l) Excessive oil consumption

1 Check 6 and 7 in (c) and check (k)
2 Ring gaps too wide
3 Oil control rings defective
4 Scored cylinders
5 Oil level too high
6 Leaking oil seals, filter, joints
7 Ineffective inlet valve stem oil seals

(m) Crankshaft or connecting rod bearing failure

1 Check 2 in (k)
2 Restricted oilways
3 Worn journals or crankpins
4 Loose bearing caps
5 Very low oil pressure
6 Bent connecting rod

(n) Internal water leakage (see Chapter 4)

(o) Poor water circulation (see Chapter 4)

(p) Corrosion (see Chapter 4)

(q) High fuel consumption (see Chapter 2)

(r) Engine vibration

1 Loose generator bolts
2 Mounting rubbers loose or ineffective
3 Exhaust pipe mountings defective
4 Engine steady loose or faulty
5 Misfiring due to mixture, ignition or mechanical faults

CHAPTER 2

THE FUEL SYSTEM

2:1 Description

Fuel pump:

The SU fuel pump is mechanically operated by a short pushrod and by a cam which is part of the distributor drive shaft. The pushrod can be seen in **FIG 2:3**. The principle of operation will be readily understood from the following description and an examination of **FIGS 2:1** and **2:5**. The part numbers in brackets are those to be found in the second illustration. It must be understood that the rocker lever 3 (7) is not the correct shape and does not bear directly on the cam as shown in view 'A'.

Movement of the rocker lever by the cam and pushrod pulls down diaphragm 12 (8), the partial vacuum created sucking in fuel through inlet 11 and filter 10 (2a) past valve 7 (4). When the rocker lever returns, spring 13 (8) pushes the diaphragm upwards to force fuel past the outlet slot in the top of valve 7 (4), through outlet 9 to the carburetter. If the carburetter needle valve is closed, the diaphragm cannot rise and the rocker lever will reciprocate idly in the slotted diaphragm pullrod until there is a further demand for fuel.

The carburetter:

The type HS6 carburetter is of SU make and is mounted horizontally. The following description will refer to the components to be seen in **FIG 2:7**.

The air intake bore through body 1 is fitted with a butterfly valve 36 in throttle spindle 35 to control the volume of mixture passing to the engine. Piston 9 rises and falls inside chamber 7 and when at rest virtually blocks the air intake. Its movement is due to the depression in the air intake system associated with engine load and throttle opening. This depression affects the space above the piston, causing the piston to rise and fall, thus producing a variable choke aperture in the body. This constantly changing volume of air which is drawn into the engine demands a variable quantity of fuel to produce the correct mixture. Tapered needle 11 is attached to the underside of the piston so that it also rises and falls inside a jet 44. The smallest diameter of the needle is in the jet when the piston is fully raised, so that there is maximum air and fuel when required. Rapid fluctuations of the piston and needle are damped out by hydraulic damper 13.

Rich mixture for starting from cold is obtained by pulling the jet down to a smaller diameter of the tapered needle. Fuel is supplied to the jet by the usual system of a float-controlled needle valve in chamber 22. The cam on lever 57 comes into play when the choke control is pulled out. It provides for a small throttle opening at the same time as the rich mixture needed for easy starting from cold.

2:2 Fuel pump testing

A dual gauge is shown in **FIG 2:2** and this is Service Tool 18G.1116, but there is no reason why two separate instruments should not be used.

Before using the gauge, test the pump on the engine as follows:

1 First test the flow from the pump by disconnecting the feed hose from the float chamber and turning the end into a container. Disconnect the positive lead from the ignition coil.

2 Operate the starter and see whether fuel emerges from the hose end in spurts. If the flow is normal, look for carburation or starting difficulties elsewhere.

3 If the flow starts off well but rapidly falls off, suspect a blockage in the fuel tank venting system. Test with the filler cap removed. Other causes might be choked filters in the tank or pump.

4 If air bubbles emerge from the immersed end of the hose, there is an air leak on the suction side of the pump.

In cases where failure is evident, take off the pump and subject it to a dry test with the gauges. **Never pass compressed air through the pump.**

Dry test of pump:

This is carried out before dismantling a suspected pump, and is also made as a check for a reassembled pump.

Suction:

Connect the gauge to the inlet nozzle 1 as shown in the top view and operate the rocker lever 2 through three full strokes. The minimum reading on the vacuum side of the gauge must not drop more than 2 inches of mercury (Hg) in 15 seconds.

Delivery:

Connect the gauge to the outlet nozzle 3 as shown in the lower view. Operate the rocker lever 4 through two full strokes. The minimum pressure reading must not drop more than .5 lb/sq in in 15 seconds.

Testing without a gauge:

Although not strictly accurate, this test will indicate whether pump is working at all. Check the suction by holding a finger over the inlet nozzle and working the rocker lever through three full strokes. When the finger is released there should be a distinct sucking sound.

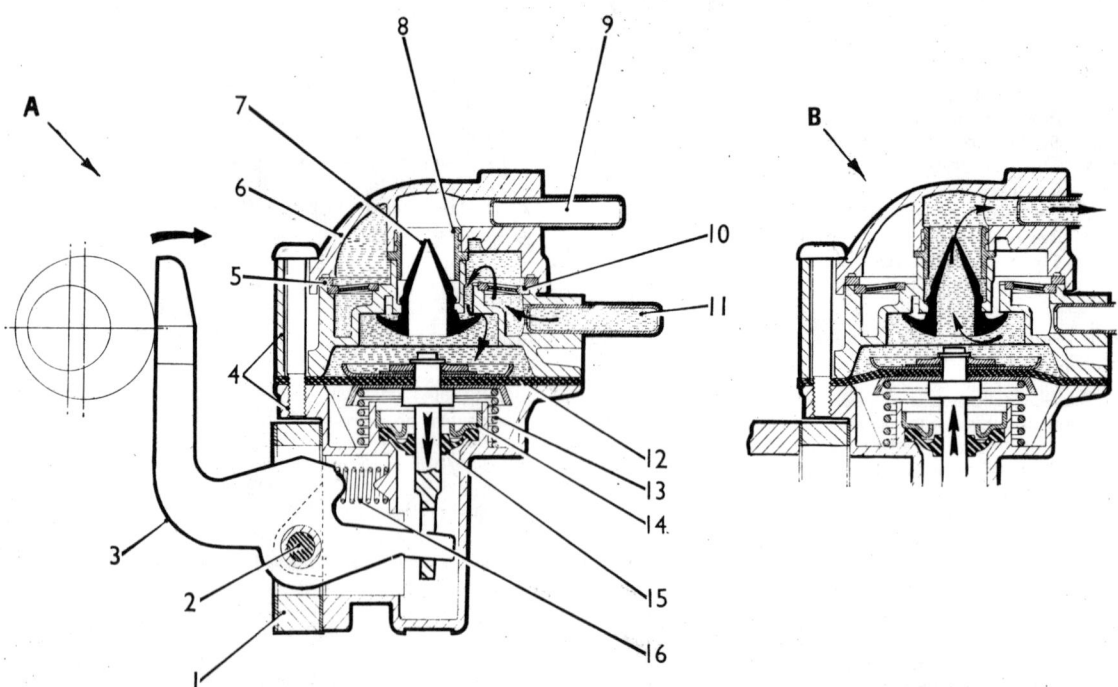

FIG 2:1 The mechanical fuel pump in section. Note that the rocker lever **3** is operated by a cam and pushrod and not directly by a cam as shown on the left. View **A** shows the fuel intake stroke and view **B** the delivery stroke

Key to Fig 2:1   1 Insulating and joint washer assembly   2 Pivot pin   3 Rocker lever   4 Upper and lower bodies
5 Sealing washer   6 Outlet cover   7 Inlet and outlet valve   8 Insert—outlet cover   9 Outlet nozzle   10 Filter
11 Inlet nozzle .   12 Diaphragm assembly   13 Diaphragm spring   14 Retaining cup   15 Crankcase seal
16 Rocker lever tension spring

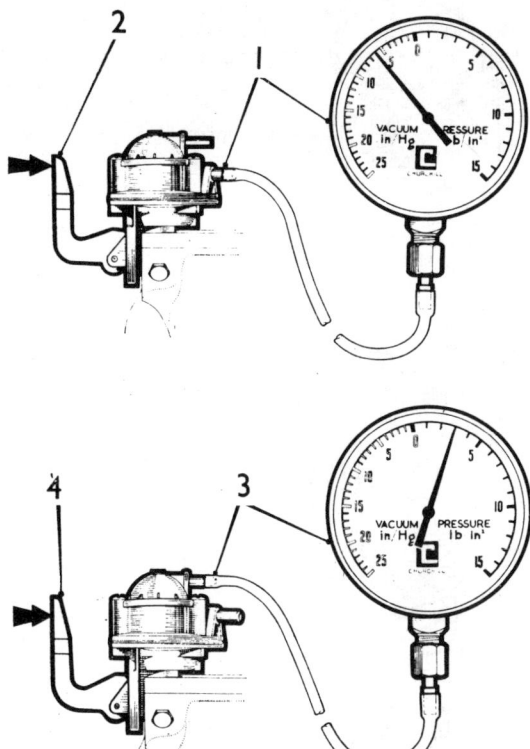

bodies as indicated at 1. This will facilitate correct reassembly.

2 Remove three screws to release the cover and take off sealing washer and filter 2a. Remove screws 3 to part the body halves.

3 The combined inlet and outlet valve 4 is a press fit in the upper body. When removing it be careful not to damage the inlet seating, which is the fine edge on the largest diameter. Withdraw insert 5 from the outlet cover.

4 Press the diaphragm down against spring pressure 8 and remove the pin 6 from the rocker lever 7. Remove the lever and spring.

5 Put some lubricant on the pullrod of the diaphragm and pull it through seal 9 to release the diaphragm and spring. The lubricant will prevent damage to the seal.

6 The seal need not be disturbed unless there has been leakage past it. To remove and replace the seal use Service Tool 18G.1119 as illustrated in **FIG 2:6**. Screw the centre of the tool into the retaining cup and draw it from the lower body.

Inspecting:

Examine the diaphragm for deterioration. Check the fine edges and lips of the inlet/outlet valve and the cover insert. Renew the cover gasket and the flange gasket if necessary. Check the lever and pin for wear and renew both parts and the lower body if excessive. Clean the top chamber and the filter, using a brush and fuel. Make sure no brush hairs are left behind. Do not use a fluffy rag for cleaning.

Reassembling:

Reverse the dismantling procedure, noting the following:

1 The retaining cup for the crankcase seal 9 is pressed in using Service Tool 18G.1119.

2 Before fitting the diaphragm, remove all sharp edges from the stirrup at the lower end of the pullrod, then lightly oil the rod to prevent damage to the seal. Line-up the slot for engagement with the rocker lever.

3 Press the inlet/outlet valve carefully into place until the groove registers with the flange at the entrance to the

FIG 2:2 Testing the fuel pump suction and delivery using a combined gauge, Service Tool 18G.1116

Key to Fig 2:2
2 Pump rocker lever
4 Pump rocker lever
1 Gauge connected to inlet nozzle
3 Gauge connected to outlet nozzle

To test the delivery, hold the finger over the outlet nozzle and depress the rocker arm fully. The pressure should hold up for about 15 seconds.

Data:

The suction of a pump in good condition should be a minimum of 6 inches of mercury (Hg) and the minimum pressure should be 3 lb/sq in.

1:3 Removing and servicing the fuel pump

Removing:

Referring to **FIG 2:3**, disconnect the fuel pipes 1, remove nuts 2 and lift away the pump. Withdraw the operating pushrod 3.

Refitting:

Reverse the procedure, using a new gasket.

Dismantling:

Refer to **FIG 2:5** and do the following:

1 Clean the outside of the pump so that dirt cannot enter. Mark the flanges of cover 2 and the upper and lower

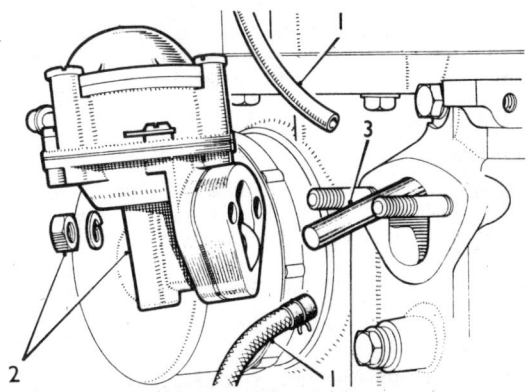

FIG 2:3 Removing the fuel pump

Key to Fig 2:3   1 The fuel pipes   2 Pump and retaining nuts   3 Pushrod

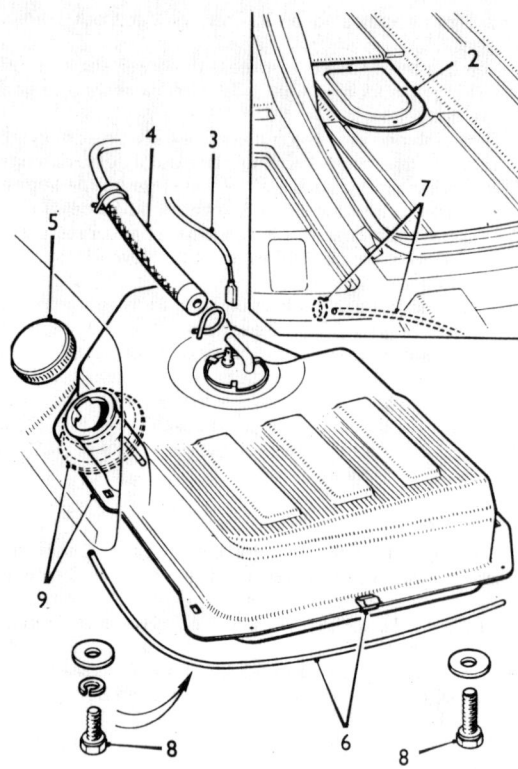

FIG 2 : 4   Removing the fuel tank

Key to Fig 2 : 4   2 Access panel in boot   3 Fuel
gauge cable   4 Fuel pipe   5 Filler cap   6 Breather
pipe and clip   7 Pipe and grommet   8 Tank bolts
9 Tank and grommet

outlet passage. Check that the edge on the large diameter is making an effective seal on the face in the
upper half of the body.
4 Line-up the holes in the diaphragm with those in the
  lower body. Press on the rocker lever until the diaphragm is flat, fit the top half and fit the short screws,
  leaving them slack. Fit the filter, sealing washer and
  outlet cover and tighten all screws evenly.
5 Test the pump as instructed in **Section 2 : 2.**

2 : 4 The fuel tank

Removing:

1 Disconnect the battery. Remove the access panel 2
  from the floor of the boot as shown in **FIG 2 : 4.**
2 Disconnect fuel gauge cable 3 and fuel pipe 4. Remove
  the filler cap 5.
3 Detach breather pipe 6 from the clip on the tank flange.
  Push the pipe back through the body grommet as
  shown at 7.
4 Remove the tank securing bolts 8. Remove the tank,
  disengaging the filler neck from body grommet 9.

Refitting:

Reverse the dismantling procedure, feeding the breather
pipe through the body grommet as the tank is raised.

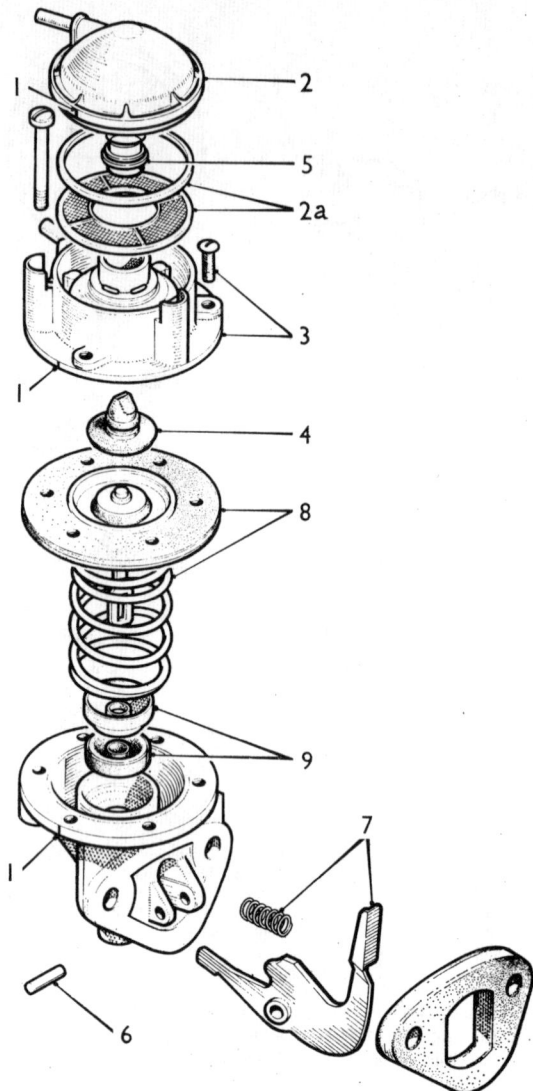

**FIG 2 : 5   The fuel pump exploded. Part 4 is the combined
inlet and outlet valve**

Key to Fig 2 : 5   1 Alignment marks for correct assembling
2 Outlet cover   2a Cover seal and filter   3 Upper
body and flange screws   4 Inlet/outlet valve   5 Outlet
cover insert   6 Rocker lever pivot pin   7 Rocker lever
and spring   8 Diaphragm and spring   9 Crankcase
seal and retaining cup

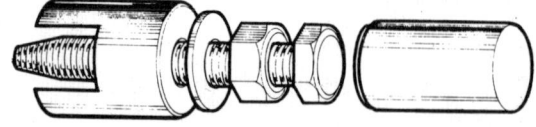

**FIG 2 : 6   Service Tool 18G.1119 for removing and
replacing the fuel pump oil seal retainer**

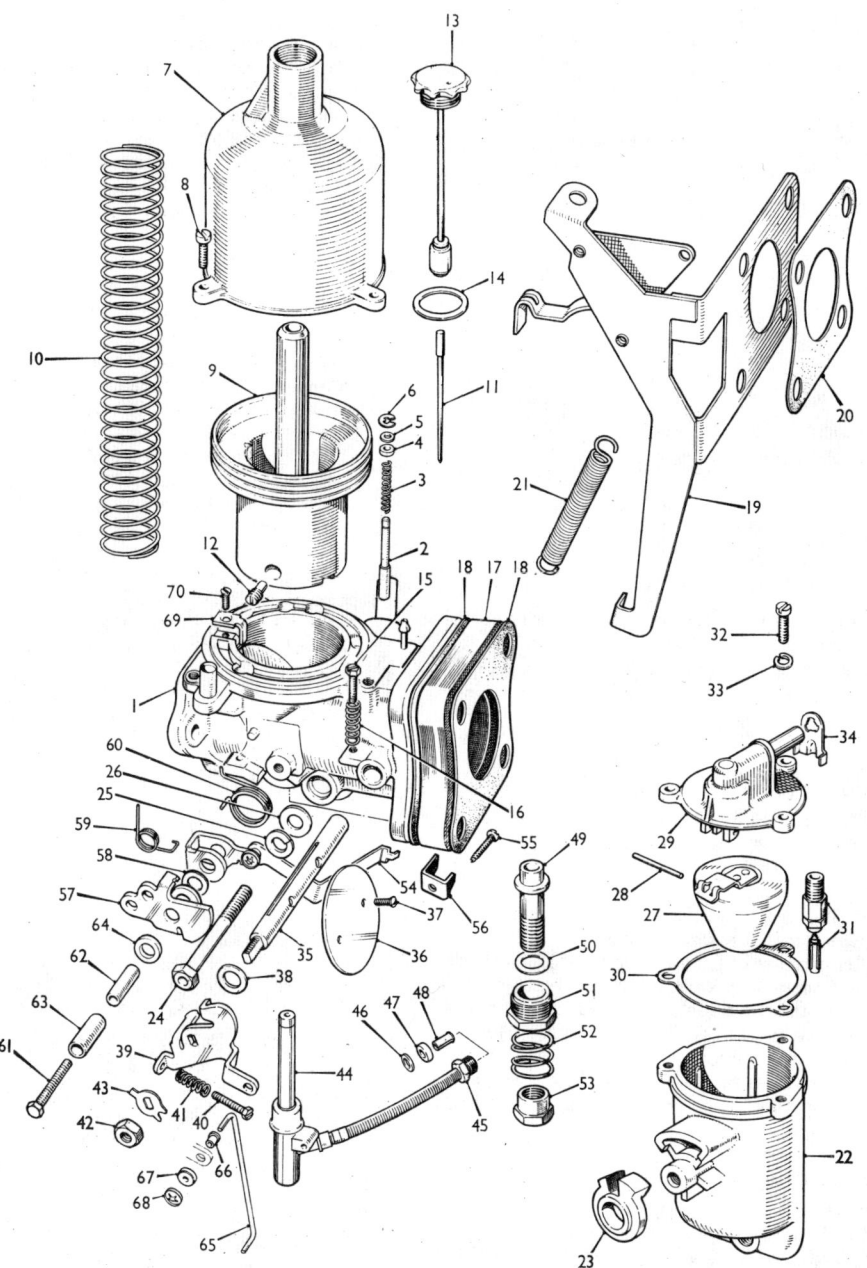

FIG 2:7 The SU carburetter exploded

Key to Fig 2:7   1 Body   2 Piston lifting pin   3 Spring for pin   4 Sealing washer   5 Plain washer
6 Circlip   7 Piston chamber   8 Screw for chamber   9 Piston   10 Spring   11 Needle   12 Needle locking screw
13 Piston damper   14 Sealing washer   15 Throttle adjusting screw   16 Spring for screw   17 Spacer   18 Gasket
19 Progressive throttle linkage   20 Gasket   21 Spring   22 Float chamber   23 Adapter   24 Bolt for float chamber
25 Spring washer   26 Plain washer   27 Float   28 Hinge pin for float   29 Lid for float chamber   30 Gasket
31 Needle and seat   32 Screw for lid   33 Spring washer   34 Baffle plate   35 Throttle spindle   36 Throttle disc
37 Screw for disc   38 Washer for spindle   39 Throttle return lever   40 Cam stop screw   41 Spring for screw
42 Nut for spindle   43 Tab washer for nut   44 Jet assembly   45 Nut   46 Washer   47 Gland   48 Ferrule
49 Jet bearing   50 Washer   51 Jet locking nut   52 Spring   53 Jet adjusting nut   54 Pickup lever and link
55 Screw for link   56 Bracket for link   57 Cam lever   58 Washer   59 Spring for cam lever   60 Spring for pickup lever
61 Pivot bolt   62 Pivot tube—inner   63 Pivot tube—outer   64 Distance washer   65 Throttle lever rod
66 Bush   67 Washer   68 Lockwasher   69 Piston guide   70 Screw for guide

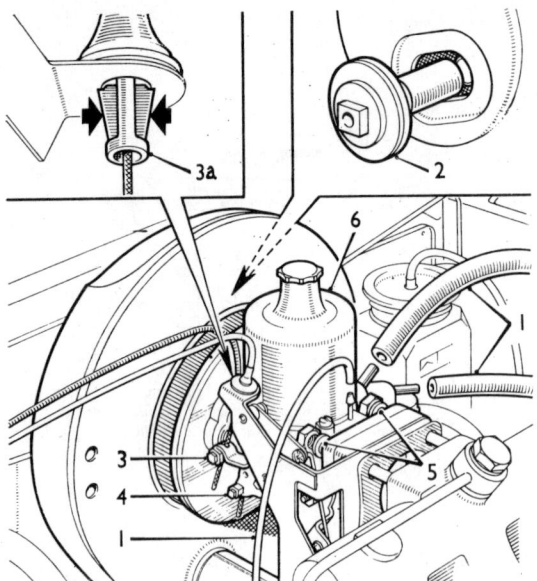

FIG 2:8 Sequence of operations for removing carburetter

Key to Fig 2:8   1 Distributor vacuum, breather and fuel pipes   2 Air cleaner fixing   3 Throttle cable fixing   3a Throttle outer cable fixing   4 Mixture or choke cable fixing   5 Carburetter securing nuts and washers   6 Carburetter

2:5 Carburetter removal and refitting

Refer to **FIG 2:8** and follow these instructions:
1 Disconnect the distributor vacuum pipe, engine breather pipe and fuel supply pipe 1. Remove the air cleaner 2.
2 Disconnect the throttle cable 3 and detach the outer cable 3a. Disconnect the choke cable 4.
3 Remove the carburetter flange nuts 5 and pull off the carburetter 6 complete with abutment bracket and linkage. Check the condition of the spacer and the two gaskets. Air leakage at the flange will cause tuning problems and weak mixture.

To refit the carburetter follow the instructions in reverse. Adjust the throttle and choke cables as described in **Section 2:10**.

2:6 Carburetter tuning

If the carburetter is correctly adjusted, the only operation needed to keep it working properly is to top up the damper periodically with 20W engine oil. Refer to **FIG 2:9** which shows the location of the damper and the fluid 1. Fill until the level is $\frac{1}{2}$ inch above the top of the hollow piston rod.

If it is felt that the carburetter needs tuning, remember that it cannot be satisfactory unless the engine is at normal running temperature. It is also wise to ensure that the throttle opens smoothly and that the choke cable is correctly adjusted.

Idling adjustment:

Having checked that the damper fluid is at the correct height, the next step is to check the idling speed. Remember that the normal idling speed is slower than the fast idle which is obtained when the choke is pulled out for starting from cold. With the engine hot and the choke inoperative, the idling speed should be 500 rev/min. If the speed is not correct, refer to **FIG 2:9** and do the following:
1 Turn screw 3 in the required direction until the correct speed is obtained. If the engine does not run smoothly at this speed, check the mixture.

Mixture adjustment:

1 Locate the piston lifting pin marked 4 in the inset to **FIG 2:9**. With the engine stopped, lift the piston by pressing the pin upwards to its fullest extent and then release the pin smartly. The piston should fall freely and stop with a distinct metallic click. If it does not do so, remove the damper and try again. Failure of the piston to fall freely can be caused by dirt in the top chamber or to the piston needle being out-of-centre to the jet. If the piston is found to be quite free in the top chamber, centralize the jet by referring to **Section 2:7**.
2 Being satisfied that the needle and jet are centralized, continue with the tuning operation for correct mixture strength. Turn jet adjusting nut 5 upwards to its highest position, noting the number of turns. Repeat the raising of the piston by lifting pin 4. If the piston now fails to fall freely, recheck the jet centralizing.

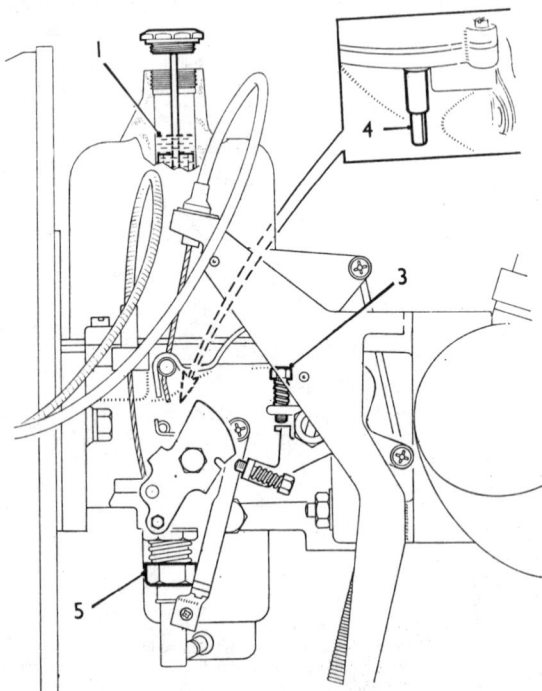

FIG 2:9 Tuning the carburetter for correct idling and mixture strength

Key to Fig 2:9   1 Piston damper oil well   3 Slow-running screw   4 Piston lifting pin   5 Jet adjusting nut

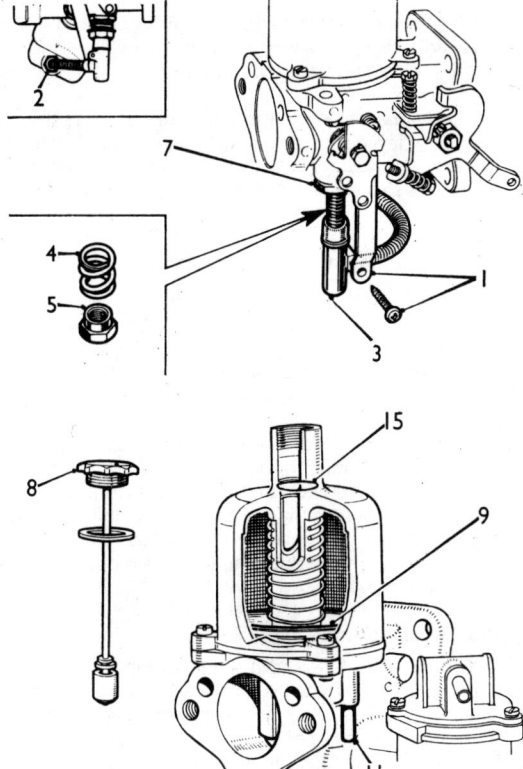

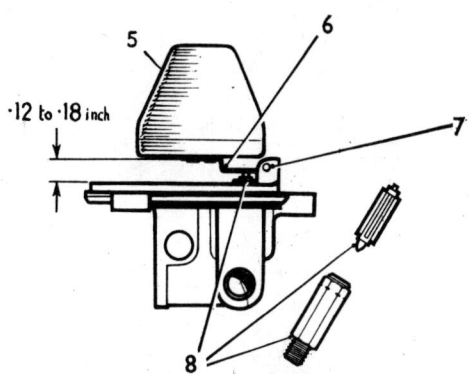

FIG 2:11   Adjusting the float chamber fuel level

Key to Fig 2:11   5 Float   6 Bending point for adjustment   7 Float lever pivot   8 Needle valve and seat

1 Remove screw 1 to disconnect the link from jet 3. Disconnect fuel feed pipe 2 from the float chamber. Pull out the jet.
2 Remove the jet adjusting nut 5 and spring 4. Refit the nut without the spring and screw it on as far as possible. Refit the jet.
3 Slacken the jet locking nut 7. This is part 51 in **FIG 2:7**. When the locking nut is loose it allows jet bearing 49 in the same illustration to move about freely in its enlarged bore.
4 Remove the piston damper 8. Press down on piston 9 by introducing a pencil or piece of rod into the bore vacated by the damper. While the piston is firmly pressed down, tighten locknut 7.
5 Lift the piston with pin 11 and check that it falls freely. Lower the adjusting nut and check again. If there is any difference in the sound of piston impact, repeat the jet centring operation.
6 Remove the jet. Remove the adjusting nut, refit the spring and restore the nut. Connect up the fuel pipe and the jet link. Finally top up the damper oil well with 20W

FIG 2:10   Centring the carburetter needle and jet

Key to Fig 2:10   1 Jet link and fixing   2 Fixing for fuel pipe to float chamber   3 Jet   4 Spring   5 Jet adjusting nut   7 Jet bearing locknut   8 Damper   9 Piston   15 Damper oil well

3 When all is well, restore the jet adjusting nut 5 to its original position. Start the engine, making sure that it is still at normal running temperature and turn the nut upwards or downwards to obtain the smoothest running and fastest speed. Turning the nut upwards will weaken the mixture and turning downwards will enrich it. Smooth running may also result in a much faster idling speed, so reset screw 3 until correct idling is obtained.
4 Check the mixture setting by using the lifting pin to raise the piston about $\frac{1}{32}$ inch, listening carefully for any change in engine speed. If speed drops immediately, the mixture is too weak. If it rises and continues to do so, even when the piston is raised still further, the mixture is too rich. If there is only a momentary increase in engine speed then the mixture is correct.

2:7 Jet centring

This operation is necessary if it is suspected that the piston sticks and that this sticking is not due to grit in the top chamber. Refer to **FIG 2:10** and carry out the following procedure:

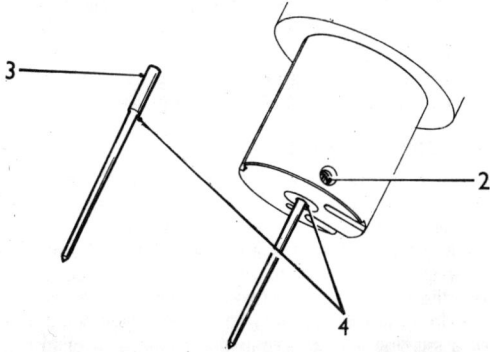

FIG 2:12   Changing a jet needle. **2** is the securing screw, **3** the needle identification and **4** the needle shoulder flush with the piston

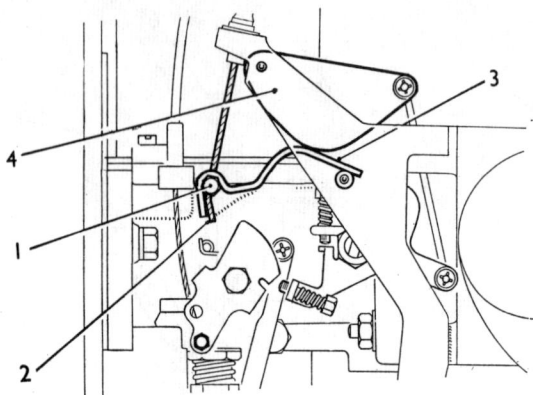

FIG 2:13 Adjusting the throttle cable

Key to Fig 2:13   1 Cable fixing   2 Inner cable
3 Operating lever   4 Operating cam

engine oil until it is $\frac{1}{2}$ inch above the hollow piston rod and refit the damper. Check the idling speed and mixture strength as described in **Section 2:6**.

2:8 Float chamber fuel level

If there has been trouble with fuel starvation or flooding and it is known that there is nothing wrong with the float or needle valve, check the fuel level as shown in **FIG 2:11**. Proceed as follows:

1 Before removing the three securing screws from the float chamber lid, mark across the flanges so that the lid can be refitted correctly. Disconnect the fuel pipe and remove the lid.
2 Hold the lid upside down as shown. The gap between the float 5 and the lid should be between .12 and .18 inch. Adjust the gap by bending the float lever at the point marked 6. **Do not bend anywhere else.**
3 Withdraw pivot pin 7 to remove the float and the needle valve assembly 8. If a punctured float is suspected, immerse it in hot water and look for the bubbles which will emerge from any hole which is present.
4 Unscrew the needle valve and check the seat of the needle. If it is not a smooth taper but is shouldered, it is wise to renew both needle and seating. It is the only cure if flooding has been a nuisance. Clean the parts with air pressure and reassemble. Clean out the float chamber by washing in fuel before refitting the lid.

2:9 Changing the jet needle

Refer to **FIG 2:7** and remove screws 8. Before lifting off the piston chamber 7 it is a good plan to mark the flanges so that it can be restored to its original position on reassembly. Piston 9 can be withdrawn. It may be of interest to know that the rim of the piston does not contact the bore of the chamber. Dirt or damage may be the reason for actual contact and this is sometimes the cause of a sticking piston. When the piston and chamber are removed, treat them with respect. They are precision-machined parts which must not be dropped or otherwise damaged. The purpose of spring 10 is to assist gravity in returning a falling piston.

With the piston detached, refer to **FIG 2:12** and slacken the needle clamping screw 2. Pull out the needle and note the identification stamped on the shank at 3. The standard needle is KP.

Check that the needle is not bent before refitting it. Whether it is a new needle or the original one, fit it so that the shoulder 4 is flush with the base of the piston and tighten the securing screw. Restore the parts and check the jet centring as described in **Section 2:7**.

2:10 Throttle and mixture controls

Throttle cable:

To adjust the cable, refer to **FIG 2:13** and do the following:

1 Slacken the cable trunnion bolt 1. Pull down on inner cable 2 until all free play of the accelerator pedal is eliminated.
2 With the cable held taut, raise lever 3 until it just contacts cam 4. With the parts held in this position, slide the trunnion up the cable and tighten the bolt.
3 The final check is to press down on the accelerator pedal to see whether there is about $\frac{1}{16}$ inch of free movement in the cable before the cam operating lever starts to move.

Removing throttle cable:

Refer to **FIG 2:8** and disconnect the inner cable by undoing bolt 3. Detach the outer cable from the bracket by squeezing, as indicated by the arrows at 3a. The top end of the accelerator pedal rod is slotted, as shown in **FIG 2:16**. Disconnect the inner cable by pulling on the nipple until the cable can be lifted out of the slot. Release the cable from the brake servo pipe clip. Withdraw the cable assembly from the servo mounting plate in a forward direction.

To refit the cable, reverse the operations and finally adjust the inner cable as described at the beginning of this Section.

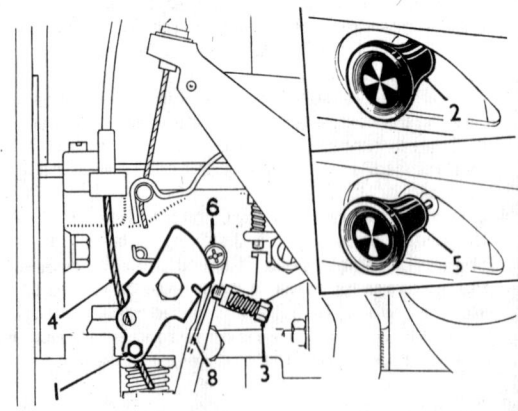

FIG 2:14 Adjusting the mixture or choke control

Key to Fig 2:14   1 Inner cable fixing   2 Control knob   3 Fast-idle screw   4 Inner cable   5 Knob pulled out $\frac{1}{4}$ inch   8 Small gap between cam and screw

Mixture or choke control:

To adjust the cable, refer to **FIG 2:14**.

1 Slacken cable trunnion bolt 1. Push control knob 2 right in.

2 Turn the fast-idle screw 3 so that there is a small amount of clearance between the screw and the cam as indicated at 8.

3 Adjust the position of the trunnion on inner cable 4 so that there is about $\frac{1}{16}$ inch of free movement before the cam lever begins to move.

4 Pull out the control knob about $\frac{1}{4}$ inch, in which position 5 the link 6 should be about to move the jet. Start the engine.

5 Adjust screw 3 until the fast-idle is at 1000 to 1100 rev/min. Then push the control knob right in again and check that there is a small gap at 8.

Removing mixture or choke control:

Refer to **FIG 2:15** and follow these instructions:

1 Disconnect the battery. Disconnect choke cable 2 from the carburetter.

2 Remove screws 3 which secure the instrument panel. Disconnect speedometer cable 4 from the back of the instrument.

3 Pull out the wiring plug 5 from the panel. Remove the panel 6.

4 Remove nut and shake proof washer 7 which secure the outer cable to the facia. Withdraw the knob and cable assembly 8 through the body grommet.

Reverse the dismantling sequence to reassemble. Note that the inner cable is connected to the lower of the two holes in the carburetter choke lever, as shown in **FIG 2:14**. When the operation is completed, adjust the cable as instructed.

2:11 Removing accelerator pedal

Disconnect the throttle cable from the top end of the accelerator pedal arm by holding the nipple and pressing the arm away from it so that the cable can be slipped out of the slot. From the pedal arm pivot, remove the splitpin and washer. Lever the pivot far enough from the mounting bracket to allow the pedal to be withdrawn. Refit in the reverse order.

2:12 Dismantling the carburetter

Having removed the carburetter according to the instructions in **Section 2:5**, refer to **FIG 2:7** and dismantle as follows:

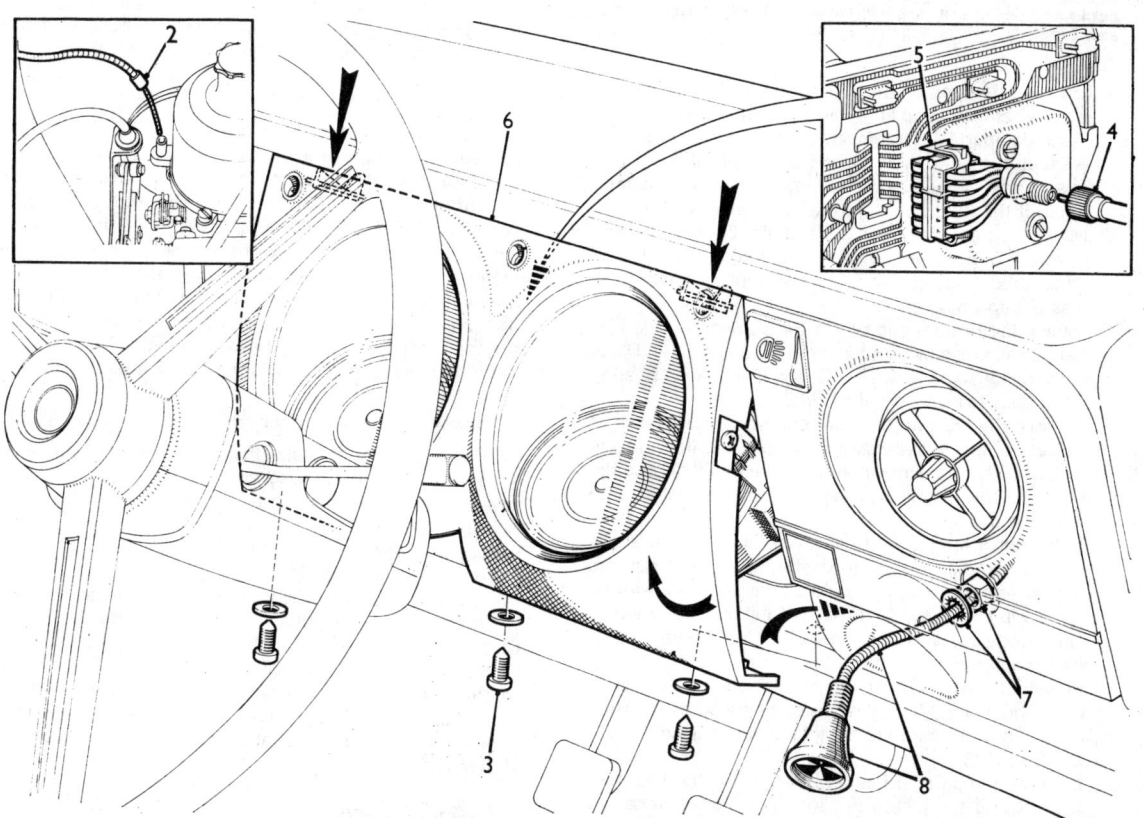

FIG 2:15 Removing the mixture or choke control

Key to Fig 2:15

	2 Choke cable	3 Panel securing screws	4 Speedometer cable	5 Wiring plug
6 Instrument panel	7 Control knob fixing	8 Knob and cable assembly		

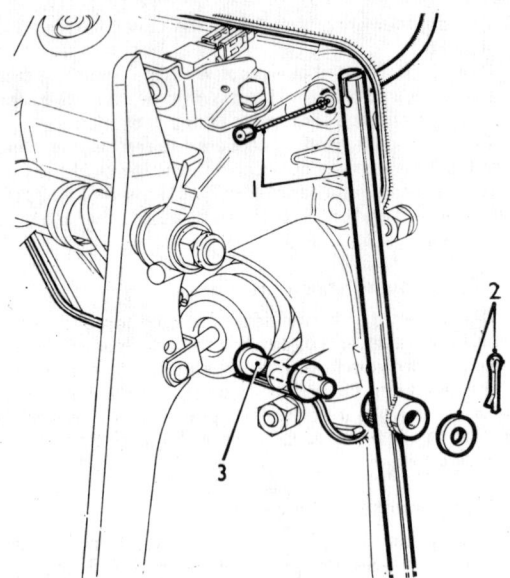

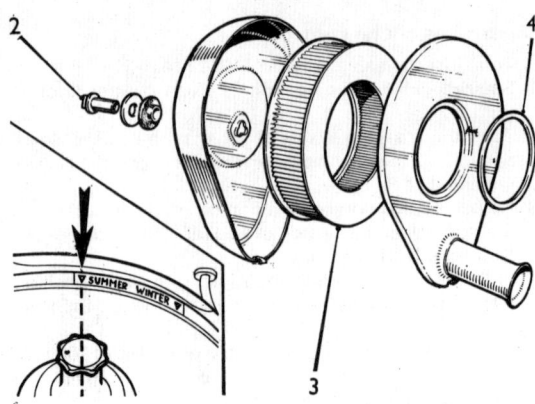

FIG 2:17 The air cleaner dismantled showing the securing nut **2**, the element **3** and the seal **4**. The inset shows the air intake setting for summer

FIG 2:16 Removing the accelerator pedal. The throttle cable and pedal arm are indicated at **1**, pivot fixing at **2** and pivot **3**

1 Mark the flanges of the top chamber 7 and body 1, remove screws 8 and lift away the chamber and piston. If the damper 13 is removed or the piston pulled out without due care, there will be a loss of damper fluid. The correct sequence is to remove the damper and pour off the fluid before further dismantling.

2 Mark the float chamber 22 and lid 29 and slacken screws 32. Remove bolt 24, pipe union nut 45 and detach the float chamber, taking care to collect the washers and adapter.

3 Detach the bottom end of link 54 from jet 44 and pull out the jet. Unscrew nut 53, remove spring 52 and then unscrew the locking nut 51. This will enable jet bearing 49 to be removed from the body.

4 Remove the lid from the float chamber, taking care of gasket 30. If it is necessary to remove the float needle and seat 31, first remove pin 28, which will release the float 27. The needle will fall out and the seat can be unscrewed.

5 Only after a long period of service is it likely that the throttle spindle 35 will need attention. To remove it, unlock screws 37 which secure disc 36 in the slotted spindle in side body 1. If the spindle and the bearings in the body are worn there will be air leaks. These make for a weak mixture and difficult tuning.

6 Removing pivot bolt 61 will release the mixture controls. The piston lifting pin can be removed by pressing off circlip 6. Attention to the jet needle 11 is covered in **Section 2:9**.

7 Clean all the parts in fuel and check that the needle is straight and the piston not touching the chamber by spinning it with the piston rod inserted. Take the utmost care not to damage either piston or chamber by dropping. **Do not stretch spring 10 in an attempt to influence performance.** Clean the float chamber and

adjust the float level, if required, by following the instructions in **Section 2:8**. Renew faulty gaskets, particularly those on each side of spacer 17. Note that although other needles may be available, it is normally unwise to depart from the one which is fitted as standard, namely needle KP. The jet is fixed in size and will not need renewal unless a bent or badly centred needle has worn it oval.

2:13 Reassembling carburetter

This is a straightforward reversal of the dismantling procedure. Fitting a new needle in the piston is covered in **Section 2:9. When assembling the piston and top chamber, do not oil any other parts except the piston rod.** When the carburetter is complete, refit it to the engine as in **Section 2:5** and check the cable adjustments according to **Section 2:10**. Centralize the jet by following the instructions in **Section 2:7** and fill up the damper oil well with 20W engine oil until it is $\frac{1}{2}$ inch above the top of the piston rod. The last operation will be to set the idling and mixture as described in **Section 2:6**.

2:14 Air cleaner maintenance

The frequency with which the element must be changed depends entirely upon road conditions. If the car is running on very dusty roads it is essential to service the air cleaner more frequently, as a choked element will have a serious restricting effect on the air intake to the engine.

To change an element, refer to **FIG 2:17** and release the speedometer cable clip from the air cleaner intake tube. Unscrew the centre nut 2 and withdraw the assembly. Clean the container thoroughly and fit a new element 3. Check the condition of sealing washer 4. Fit the cleaner to the carburetter and position the air intake tube as required. The arrow heads for summer or winter positions should line up with the central axis of the carburetter as shown by the inset.

2:15 Fault diagnosis

(a) Restricted flow or no fuel from pump

1 Air vent in tank restricted
2 Fuel pipes blocked

3 Air leaks at pipe connections
4 Pump filter blocked
5 Pump diaphragm defective
6 Pump spring broken
7 Faulty valve assembly in pump
8 Worn rocker pivot, pushrod or cam
9 Fuel vapourizing in pipelines due to heat

(b) Float chamber lacks fuel

1 Check (a)
2 Sticking float needle valve
3 Float level set too low

(c) Float chamber floods

1 Defective float needle valve
2 Float level set too high
3 Punctured float

(d) Excessive fuel consumption

1 Carburetter needs adjusting
2 Fuel leakage
3 Sticking mixture control
4 Dirty air cleaner
5 Wrong carburetter needle

6 Engine running too hot
7 Brakes binding
8 Tyres too soft
9 Idling speed too high
10 Car overloaded

(e) Idling speed too high

1 Rich fuel mixture
2 Throttle or mixture controls sticking
3 Idling screws wrongly adjusted
4 Worn throttle butterfly valve or spindle

(f) Poor idling

1 Check (c)
2 Vacuum pipe to distributor faulty
3 Vacuum pipe to brake servo faulty
4 Sticking piston

(g) Difficult starting

1 Check most of preceding Sections
2 Faulty ignition
3 Mechanical defects in engine
4 Air leaks at manifold joints
5 Jet and needle need recentring

CHAPTER 3

THE IGNITION SYSTEM

3:1 Description

The distributor is of Lucas make, type 25.D4. It incorporates two automatic timing controls, the first being a centrifugal mechanism and the second a vacuum unit. These can be seen in **FIG 3:6**.

Fine adjustments to the ignition timing can be made by turning the milled nut 1 in **FIG 3:1**. These small alterations can be made to compensate for changes in engine condition or grades of fuel.

Turning to the automatic timing controls we will deal first with the centrifugal device. In this, weights fly outwards against the tension of small springs as engine speed rises. This movement advances the contact breaker cams relative to the distributor driving shaft, so that the points open earlier to give advanced ignition timing.

The vacuum unit is connected to the carburetter by a small-bore pipe. Depression in the carburetter intake system operates the vacuum unit, the suction varying according to engine load. At small throttle openings, with no load on the engine, there is a high degree of vacuum which causes the unit to advance the ignition timing. Large throttle openings with low speeds and a heavily-loaded engine—conditions which are met when hill-climbing, result in a much-reduced degree of vacuum. The unit will then retard the ignition. The components of the centrifugal and vacuum units can be seen in **FIG 3:6**.

Note that the distributor shaft is driven in an anticlockwise direction, as indicated by the lower arrow in **FIG 3:1**.

3:2 Routine maintenance

The following operations should be carried out every 6,000 miles:

Distributor lubrication:

1 Refer to **FIG 3:2** which shows the lubrication points to be found after the distributor cap has been removed. Use an oilcan filled with 20W engine oil. Remove the rotor arm 2 in **FIG 3:1**.

2 Apply a thin smear of grease to the cam 13.

3 Apply one drop of oil to the contact breaker pivot 14.

4 Inject two or three drops of oil into the space indicated at 15. This will lubricate the centrifugal mechanism below the plate.

5 Apply two or three drops of oil into the recess marked **16. Do not remove the central screw.** There is clearance provide for oil to pass.

When lubricating, make quite sure that no oil reaches the contact breaker points 5 in **FIG 3:3**. Wipe off all surplus oil and grease.

Distributor checking:

Refer to **FIG 3:1** which shows the distributor with the cap removed. Turn the rotor arm 2 in the direction of the lower arrow and then release it. It should return freely to its original position.

The contact breaker plate 3 should be free to move. Push on the plate at the point indicated by the upper arrow.

Adjusting and cleaning the contact breaker:

To adjust the contact points refer to **FIG 3:3** and do the following:

1 Turn the crankshaft until the points 5 are fully open. This can be done by removing the sparking plugs, engaging top gear and moving the car gently in the required direction.

2 Check the gap between the points with feeler gauges. It should be .014 to .016 inch. If adjustment is necessary, slacken screw 6 and insert a screwdriver in the notches indicated at 7. Turning the screwdriver clockwise will decrease the gap and turning it anticlockwise will increase it. Retighten the securing screw when satisfied.

To clean the contact breaker points unscrew nut 9. Lift off the washers, insulator and terminals. The spring and moving contact can then be lifted off. Remove screw 6 to release the fixed contact. The contact points should be a clean matt grey. It is normal, after much service, for one of them to have a central pip and the other a small depression. Using a fine carborundum stone or emery cloth, dress the points to remove any pip or rim. The points must finish up quite flat, so that when they are installed they meet squarely. It is not necessary to remove all the depression just mentioned, only the pip. Clean off all emery dust and refit the points, taking care to fit the insulator, the terminals and the washers in the correct order when reassembling the fixed end of the spring (see **FIG 3:7**). Adjust the contact gap when the assembly is complete.

The rotor arm:

Slight erosion of the outer edge of the brass plate is normal and is not detrimental to performance. When refitting the arm, ensure that it is clean and free from oil and that the key correctly engages the slot in the shaft.

The distributor cap:

Clean the cap inside and out and look for signs of 'tracking' round the brass segments. This shows as a black line on the inner surface of the cap and is evidence of arcing. The only cure is to fit a new cap. Slight signs of erosion of the segments is not harmful.

Check the carbon brush 4 in the central boss inside the cap (see **FIG 3:4**). It must be free to move when pressed in, and should spring out when released.

Sparking plugs:

The plugs must be removed and cleaned, preferably on a sand-blasting machine. After cleaning, the gaps must be reset to the correct gap, which is .024 to .026 inch. **Do not try to bend the central electrode** but set the gap by bending the one on the side. The electrodes should be bright and clean. Heavy erosion of the side electrode is a sign that the plug is due for renewal.

Clean the outsides of the plug insulators and refit each plug with a new gasket washer. Tighten to a torque of 30 lb ft. It is not necessary to over-tighten to make a gastight joint.

3:3 Testing ignition system

If the ignition system is suspected as the cause of engine failure, the first step is to test the spark in the following way:

1 Refer to **FIG 3:5** and remove the centre lead 7 from the distributor cap. It is a simple push fit. Switch on the ignition and turn the engine by means of the starter. At the same time get an assistant to hold the detached cable **by the insulation** with the metal end about $\frac{3}{16}$ inch away from a good earth such as the cylinder block. As the engine rotates there should be regular sparking across the gap.

2 If there is no spark, remove distributor cap 2. Examine the plug leads 2 in **FIG 3:4** and renew them if the insulation is cracked or perished. Make sure the conductor makes good contact at the ends. The carbon brush 4 is housed in the central moulding inside the cap. It should protrude, and when pressed in, should spring out again quite freely. The end will be polished where it contacts the rotor arm (see 2 in **FIG 3:1**). The rotor arm should have a bright spot where the brush has been rubbing. If all is well, test the rotor arm by substitution to ensure that it is not at fault.

3 If none of these tests and possible rectification leads to successful sparking, carry out more intensive testing with a voltmeter as follows:

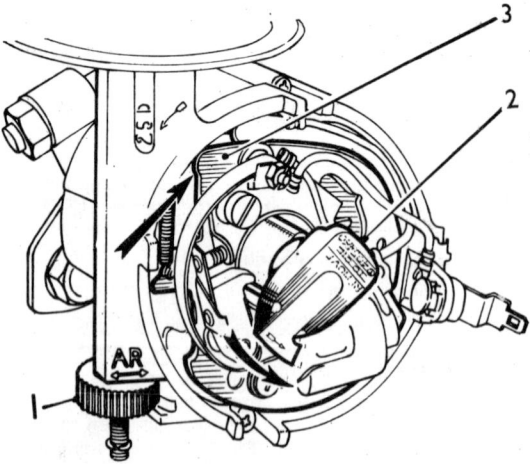

FIG 3:1 Checking the centrifugal and vacuum advance mechanisms. The micrometer timing adjustment is milled nut **1**. Check centrifugal action by turning rotor arm **2** in direction of lower arrow. Check that vacuum advance moving plate **3** is free to move

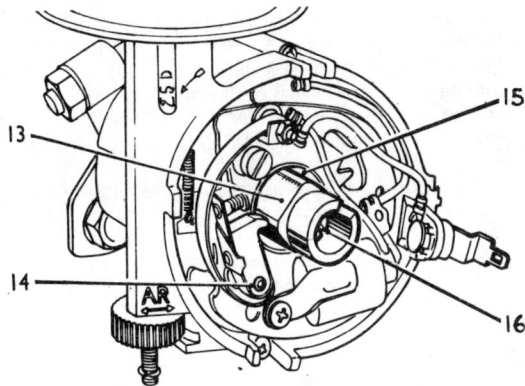

FIG 3:2   Distributor lubrication points

Key to Fig 3:2   13 Contact breaker cam   14 Contact breaker pivot   15 Aperture leading to centrifugal device   16 Cam spindle and centre screw

Testing the low-tension circuit in the event of ignition failure:

1 Remove the distributor cap and rotor arm. Locate the LT terminal on the coil. There will be a white cable with a black tracer in it attached to the terminal. Do not disturb the wiring but connect a 0–20-volt moving coil meter between the terminal and a good earth.

2 Look at the contact breaker points 5 in **FIG 3:3** and if they are closed, separate them with a piece of clean card.

3 Switch on the ignition and watch the voltmeter. It should read 12-volts. If there is no reading with the contacts separated, transfer the voltmeter lead from the LT terminal to the other terminal on the coil which has a white lead attached to it. If there is now a reading, disconnect the white/black cable from the coil terminal and reconnect the voltmeter to the disconnected terminal. No reading will indicate a faulty coil. A reading of battery voltage indicates faulty contact breaker insulation or a faulty capacitor (condenser). Check the capacitor by substitution. The correct capacity is .18 to .24 mF.

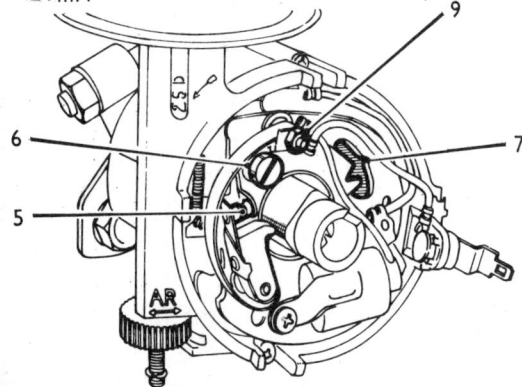

FIG 3:3   Servicing the contact breaker

Key to Fig 3:3   5 Contact points   6 Screw for contact plate   7 Screwdriver notches for adjusting gap   9 Nut securing spring and terminals

4 If the voltmeter reads 12-volts with the contact points separated, remove the card. The reading should drop to zero as the points meet. If it does, the LT ignition circuit is in order. If there is still no spark it will probably be due to a break in the secondary winding of the coil. The easiest way to check this is to substitute the suspected coil with one of known performance. If the battery voltage reading persists with the points in contact, or the reading does not drop right back to zero, transfer the voltmeter lead to the LT terminal on the distributor (see 4 in **FIG 3:5**).

5 If the reading now drops back to zero then the cable between the coil and the distributor is at fault. If the reading is still at battery voltage it means that the contact points are not making electrical contact. If a low reading on the voltmeter persists it indicates a high resistance across the points. Clean or renew the contact points.

Testing the high-tension circuit:

Having tested the low-tension circuit as just described, and having rectified any faults, proceed to recheck for sparking as outlined at the beginning of this Section.

3:4 Servicing the distributor

Removing:

1 Refer to **FIG 3:5** and remove the flywheel housing cover 1. Check which sparking plug lead comes from No. 1 cylinder (the first cylinder adjacent to the fan). Remove the distributor cover 2.

2 Turn the crankshaft to the 1/4 TDC mark with No. 1 cylinder firing. The rotor arm in the distributor will then be pointing to the segment inside the distributor cap which leads to the plug lead for No. 1 cylinder (if the cap was in place). The rotor arm is item 2 in **FIG 3:1**.

3 Disconnect the low-tension lead 4 by pulling it off the terminal tag. Disconnect vacuum pipe 5.

4 Mark the position of the clamping (or securing) plate, remove bolts 6 and withdraw the distributor. **Do not slacken the clamping plate bolt or the plate may shift on the distributor body and the timing will then be lost. It is necessary to use a stroboscope to retime the ignition.**

Dismantling:

Refer to **FIG 3:6** which shows the distributor components but not the cap. **Before dismantling, make a careful note of the relative positions of the driving dog at the bottom end of the shaft, and the slot for the rotor arm above the contact breaker cams. This** is important because the tongue on the face of the dog is offset and this must be refitted in the correct position or the timing will be 180 deg. out. Dismantle as follows:

1 Having sprung back the clips, lift off the cap. Pull off the rotor arm.

2 Lift the vacuum control unit link off the peg attached to the contact breaker moving plate. Take out the two screws securing the contact breaker baseplate and lift out the complete contact breaker assembly together with the external LT terminal.

3 Remove the circlip from the shaft at the micrometer adjustment end of the vacuum control unit. Unscrew the milled nut to release the unit. There is a spring under

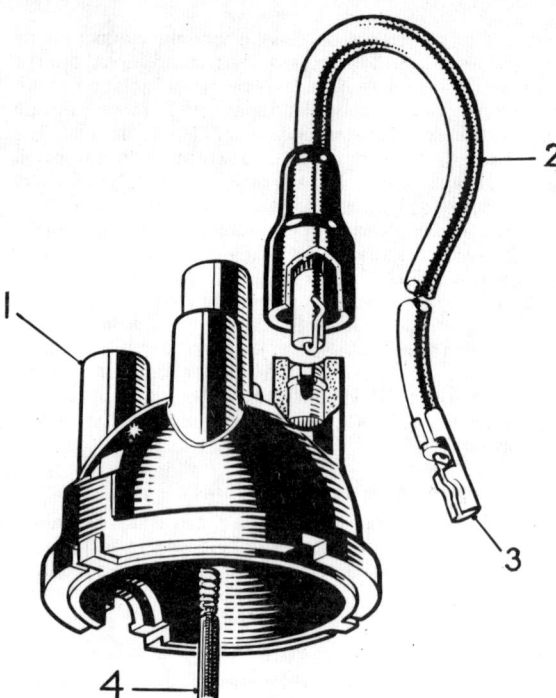

FIG 3:4   Features of the distributor cap

Key to Fig 3:4   1 Cap   2 Sparking plug lead (HT)
3 Plug connector   4 Carbon brush and spring

the nut and a ratchet device clipped to the body.

4 Drive out the cross-pin to release the driving dog from the shaft. Pull out the shaft and centrifugal timing mechanism. There is a distance collar under the action plate.

4 To dismantle the shaft, first remove the springs from the centrifugal device. Remove the screw from inside the rotor arm socket above the cams. Lift off the cam shaft and weights.

Reconditioning:

Check the fit of the shaft in the bearing bush in the distributor body. If the bush is worn it is possible to renew it with a stepped mandrel having the smaller end highly polished and of the same diameter as the distributor shaft. This will ensure that the bush, which will close in slightly as it is fitted, will nevertheless be the correct bore for the shaft without reaming. **Being a self-lubricating bush of sintered metal it is not possible to ream the bore without ruining the self-lubricating properties.**

To fit a new bush, first prepare it by immersing it in SAE 30 engine oil for 24 hours. Press out the old bush from inside the body.

Insert the new bush from the drive end with the smaller diameter part entering first. This will ensure that the bush is fitted accurately and without tilt. Fit the polished mandrel and use steady pressure from a press or large vice to push the bush right home. The bush must be a tight fit and flush with the body face at the driving end. It should then protrude slightly inside the body.

Lubricate the shaft with clean engine oil after checking that there are no burrs on the end, or round the cross-pin hole. Push in the shaft and check for excessive tightness. Binding may be rectified by tapping out the shaft and refitting it several times. Finally, run the shaft for 15 minutes by driving it in a lathe, or by any other suitable means.

Check the centrifugal assembly, renewing the parts if weights, pins or springs are worn or otherwise defective. Check the fit of the camshaft on the driving shaft. Slackness here may cause erratic contact breaker operation.

Renovate the contact breaker according to the instructions in **Section 3:2**.

Reassembling:

Apply engine oil or Ragosine Molybdenized non-creep oil to the shaft and refit it in the body. Do not forget the distance collar. Fit the driving dog and cross-pin with the thrust washer between the dog and the body.

Fit the camshaft with the pins engaging in the centrifugal weights. Make quite sure that the rotor arm slot is in the correct relationship to the driving dog tongue as instructed at the beginning of the 'Dismantling' notes. Lubricate the pins with engine oil.

Reassemble the contact breaker moving plate by referring to **FIG 3:7**. Note that insulating washers are fitted to the terminal pillar and under the contact breaker lever or rocker. Put a tiny spot of oil on the pin and fit the rocker and spring. Slip the insulating bush into the terminal tags and fit over the terminal pillar to locate the spring eye. Continue to reassemble in the reverse order to dismantling.

Refitting:

Assuming that the engine has not been turned over and that the distributor clamp plate has not been moved, refitting is a simple matter of pressing the distributor shank into the housing and turning the shaft by means of the rotor arm until the driving dogs are engaged. This can happen in one place only, because the dogs are offset. The clamping

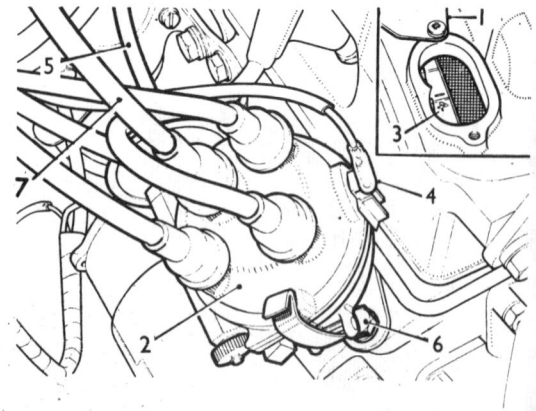

FIG 3:5   Removing the distributor

Key to Fig 3:5   1 Flywheel housing timing cover
2 Distributor cap   3 Timing marks on flywheel
4 Low-tension (LT) lead   5 Vacuum pipe
6 Securing bolt   7 High-tension (HT) lead from coil

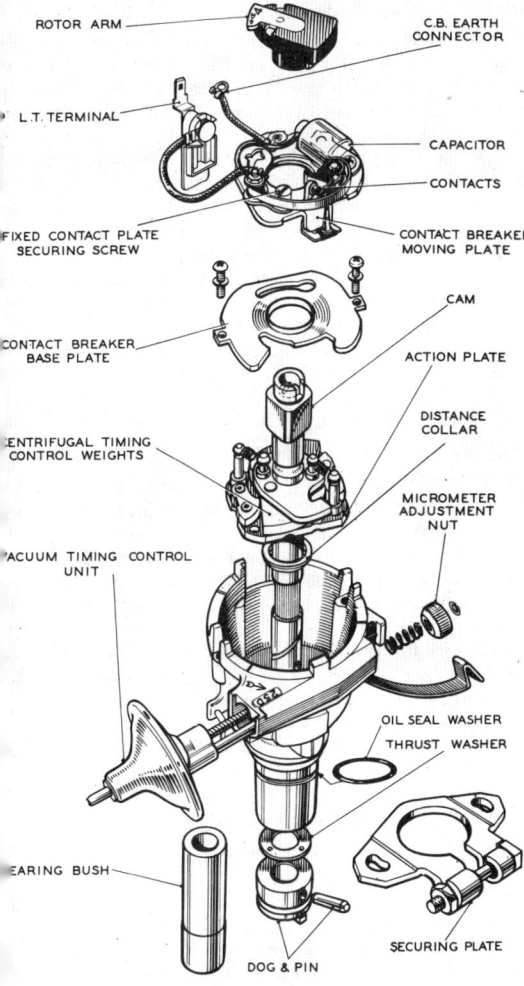

ROTOR ARM

C.B. EARTH
CONNECTOR

L.T. TERMINAL

CAPACITOR

CONTACTS

FIXED CONTACT PLATE
SECURING SCREW

CONTACT BREAKER
MOVING PLATE

CAM

CONTACT BREAKER
BASE PLATE

ACTION PLATE

DISTANCE
COLLAR

CENTRIFUGAL TIMING
CONTROL WEIGHTS

MICROMETER
ADJUSTMENT
NUT

VACUUM TIMING CONTROL
UNIT

OIL SEAL WASHER

THRUST WASHER

BEARING BUSH

SECURING PLATE

DOG & PIN

FIG 3:6 The Lucas 25.D4 distributor exploded

late can then be secured in the position it originally occupied and the timing should be more or less correct. Tighten the bolts to a torque of 8 to 10 lb ft. Only if the micrometer adjustment is in exactly the same position as it was before dismantling, can the timing be exactly as before. Finally, connect the vacuum pipe, and set the contact breaker gap as in **Section 3:2**.

:5 Timing the ignition

If the position for correct ignition timing has been lost, it will be necessary to use a stroboscope to retime it correctly.

The first step is to turn the crankshaft until the 1/4 TDC mark on the flywheel is aligned with the pointer as shown in **FIG 3:5**. Fit the distributor and engage the driving dogs. If the distributor drive shaft is correctly fitted, the distributor rotor arm should now point to the segment in the cap which leads to No. 1 sparking plug (the nearest to the fan).

If this is not so, the distributor drive shaft has been incorrectly fitted or the rotor arm-to-distributor driving dog relationship is wrong. In the first case refer to **Section 1:13**. In the second case the timing will be 180 deg. out and the cure is to refit the camshaft pins in the centrifugal weight holes after turning the shaft through half-a-turn.

Having established that the rotor arm is in the correct position, slacken the bolt across the distributor clamp plate and turn the distributor body until the contact breaker points are just beginning to open.

Now restore the cap and sparking plug leads and disconnect the vacuum pipe so that the vacuum control cannot operate. Start the engine and keep the rev/min below 650 so that the centrifugal advance mechanism is also inoperative. Use the stroboscope so that the ignition timing can be set at 12 deg. BTDC. Fine adjustments can be made with the milled nut 1 in **FIG 3:1**. Note the adjacent arrows for 'Advance' and 'Retard'. This nut can also be used if an exceptional circumstance like the use of low-octane fuel calls for slight retarding of the ignition.

3:6 Sparking plugs and leads

The correct sparking plugs for the 'Maxi' are Champion, type N9Y. It is good practice to renew the complete set every 12,000 miles or every 12 months depending on the condition of the engine. Faulty carburation or excessive oil consumption may cause sparking plug troubles due to overheating or fouling, so that more frequent renewal may be necessary until the troubles are cured.

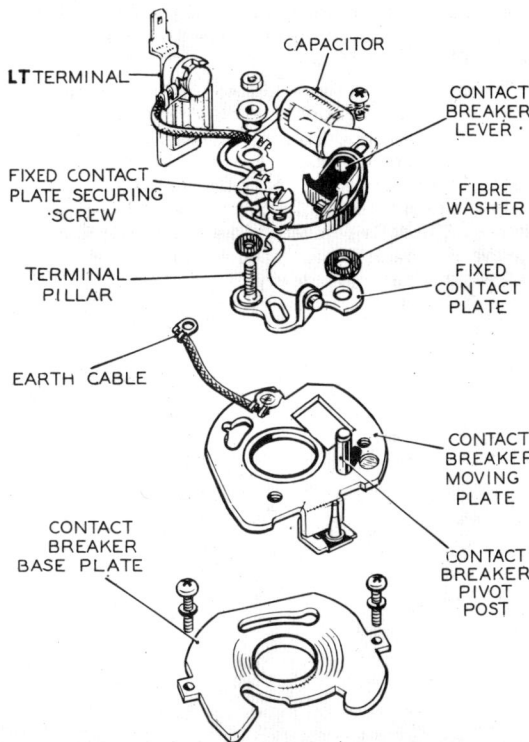

LT TERMINAL

CAPACITOR

CONTACT
BREAKER
LEVER

FIXED CONTACT
PLATE SECURING
SCREW

FIBRE
WASHER

FIXED
CONTACT
PLATE

TERMINAL
PILLAR

EARTH CABLE

CONTACT
BREAKER
MOVING
PLATE

CONTACT
BREAKER
BASE PLATE

CONTACT
BREAKER
PIVOT
POST

FIG 3:7 The components of the contact breaker assembly. The vacuum control is hooked onto the tapered pin on the foreground of the moving plate

The sparking plugs should be cleaned and adjusted every 6,000 miles. Remove them with a box spanner, taking great care to keep the spanner square. If it is allowed to tilt it may contact the plug insulator and crack it. Examine the deposits round the electrodes for the evidence which gives a clue to firing conditions.

A normal deposit should be brown to greyish tan in colour, this being the result of correct carburation and a mixture of high-speed and low-speed driving. If the deposits are white or yellowish they indicate greater heat due to long periods of constant-speed driving, probably rather fast. Black, wet deposits are caused by oil entering the combustion chamber past worn pistons and bores or down valve stems. If the black deposits are dry and fluffy they usually indicate running with a rich mixture, but they may also be due to incomplete combustion through defective ignition or excessive idling.

Overheated sparking plugs have a white, blistered look about the centre electrode and the side electrode may be badly eroded. The cause may be poor cooling, wrong ignition timing or sustained high speeds with heavy loads.

Although some cleaning can be done by hand it is difficult to reach the inner surfaces and the best plan is to have the plugs cleaned on a shot-blasting machine. They can be tested under pressure at the same time. A sparking plug which shows a good spark in the open air may not spark at all under pressure. The garage will also set the gaps correctly. If the owner does this setting himself, it is most important to make sure the electrodes are bright and clean and the gap adjusted by bending the side electrode. **Never try to bend the central electrode.** The correct gap is .024 to .026 inch.

The plugs should screw in easily by hand. Any difficulty will be due to deposits on the threads. Clean those on the plugs with a wire brush. The holes in the head can be cleaned out with a tap or by using an old plug with crossed saw cuts down the threads. Always fit new gaskets and do not overtighten. The correct torque wrench figure is 30 lb ft. Wipe over the insulators after fitting to remove any smears from oily fingers. Oil on the insulators makes dirt adhere more readily.

Sparking plug leads and cap:

Renew the plug leads if there is any suspicion that they have deteriorated in any way. Make sure the end connections make good metallic contact with the core of the cable. **FIG 3:4** shows the leads 2 and also the carbon brush 4. The brush should protrude from the centre housing inside cap 1 about $\frac{3}{16}$ inch and be quite free to spring out again after being pressed in. Renew the brush and spring if the brush is obviously worn too short. If the hole in the cap is worn so that the brush moves too freely from side to side, renew the cap. Also renew the cap if the brass segments inside are badly eroded. Some marking is inevitable because the spark jumps across from the rotor arm and slight erosion is not detrimental.

Check the cap for 'tracking' as explained in **Section 3:2.**

3:7 Fault diagnosis

(a) Engine will not fire

1 Battery discharged
2 Distributor contact points dirty, pitted or badly adjusted
3 Distributor cap dirty, cracked or 'tracking'
4 Carbon brush inside cap not touching rotor
5 Faulty cable, switch, or loose connections in low-tension circuit
6 Distributor rotor arm cracked
7 Faulty coil
8 Broken contact breaker spring
9 Contact points stuck open
10 High-tension lead from coil to distributor detached or broken

(b) Engine misfires

1 Check 2, 3, 5 and 7 in (a)
2 Weak contact breaker spring
3 High-tension plug or coil leads cracked or damaged
4 Loose sparking plug(s)
5 Sparking plug insulation cracked
6 Sparking plug gap incorrectly set
7 Ignition timing too far advanced

CHAPTER 4

THE COOLING SYSTEM

4:1 Description

The system is pressurized to raise the boiling point of the coolant. The rise in pressure is, however, restricted to 15 lb/sq in by a spring-loaded valve in the expansion tank filler cap.

The natural thermo-syphon action of heated water tending to rise to the top tank of the radiator, and falling down through the core to be cooled, is augmented by a centrifugal impeller pump which is mounted on the lefthand end of the cylinder block. The outer end of the pump spindle carries a pulley and a plastic fan, the drive being by V-belt from a pulley on the crankshaft.

To secure a rapid warm-up from cold, there is a thermostat valve in a housing attached to the head. This is closed when the coolant is cold, thus preventing circulation through the top hose to the radiator. When the coolant heats up, the thermostat valve opens and coolant is then free to pass through the radiator.

In the bottom righthand corner of **FIG 4:1** can be seen an expansion tank which is mounted low down beside the radiator. It is connected by a hose to the top tank of the radiator, and as the coolant expands with heat it escapes down the pipe into the expansion tank. When the engine stops and the coolant temperature drops, the partial vacuum created in the radiator top tank causes coolant to be drawn back up the hose.

4:2 Routine maintenance

Every 3,000 miles check the level of coolant in the radiator and the expansion tank. **Allow the system to cool before removing the two filler caps. Never release the radiator filler cap while the system is hot.** If there is any reason for removing the expansion tank cap while the system is still hot, do so with extreme caution as there is a serious risk of scalding by escaping steam at high pressure. Turn the cap slowly and protect the hand with several layers of cloth. Refer to **FIG 4:1** where cap 2 is the plain one which must be fitted to the radiator.

If there is a persistent demand for extra coolant, check that there are no leaks in the system. Overheating is also a contributory cause. If antifreeze is in use, remember that the addition of plain water will dilute the concentration, so add more antifreeze too.

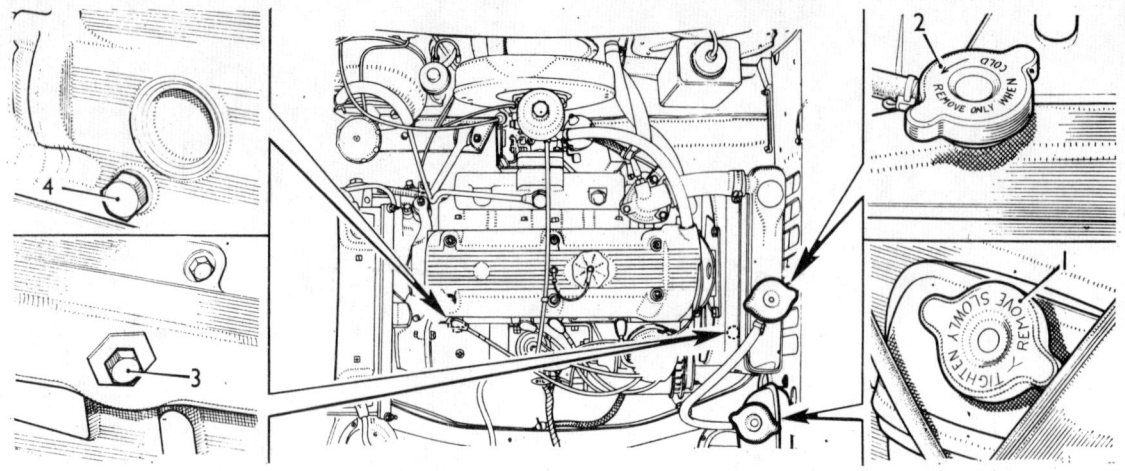

FIG 4:1   Sequence of operations to drain and refill the cooling system

Key to Fig 4:1   1 Expansion tank filler cap (with valve)   2 Radiator filler cap (plain)   3 Radiator drain plug
4 Cylinder block drain plug

With the cap 1 removed, check the level of coolant in the expansion tank. The depth should be at least 2.5 inch. Top up if required. Check the level in the radiator top tank and top up if required.

Fan belt adjustment:

Every 6,000 miles, check the fan belt and its adjustment. If there are cracks or frayed edges, renew the belt by slackening off the tension. Lift the belt off the pulleys and manoeuvre it over the fan blades and out through the enlarged part of the radiator cowling aperture.

To adjust the tension of the belt, refer to **FIG 4:2**. First check the tension by applying moderate finger pressure to the longest run of the belt. The amount of deflection should not exceed $\frac{1}{2}$ inch. Do not run the engine with a tight belt as it causes rapid belt deterioration and possible damage to generator and pump bearings. A slack belt might result in overheating and lack of charging current from the generator.

The correct tension can be obtained by slackening the two generator fixing bolts 1 in the illustration. Also slacken the adjusting link bolt 2. Lift the generator by hand pressure, tighten the bolts and check the tension. **If it is necessary to lift the generator with a lever, apply it at the driven end bracket only.** Tighten the bolts to a torque of 18 to 20 lb ft.

Pump bearing lubrication:

The bearing assembly is sealed for life and there is no provision for introducing extra lubricant.

4:3 Draining and refilling radiator

Draining:

Refer to **FIG 4:1** and remove the caps from the radiator and expansion tanks, 2 and 1 respectively. Remove the radiator drain plug 3 and the cylinder block drain plug 4. Save the coolant for re-use if it contains antifreeze and is not two years old.

It is important to note that neither the heater nor the expansion tank can be drained. For this reason the cooling system must be filled with an antifreeze solution during freezing conditions, and the expansion tank must have $\frac{1}{4}$ pint of antifreeze added to it.

Refilling:

1 Refit both drain plugs and open the heater valve. Fill the system through the radiator filler opening and refit the cap.
2 If necessary, top up the coolant in the expansion tank until it is half full and fit the cap.
3 Run the engine at a fast idle for 30 seconds and then stop it. Top up the system through the radiator filler neck. Run the engine until it reaches normal operating temperature. Stop the engine and let the system cool down. Check that the expansion tank is about half full.

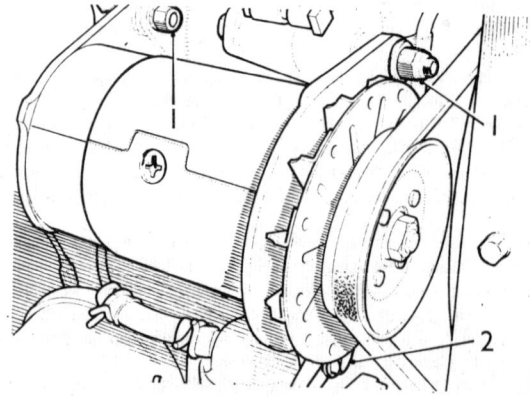

FIG 4:2   To adjust the tension of the fan belt, slacken fixing bolts **1** and link bolt **2**

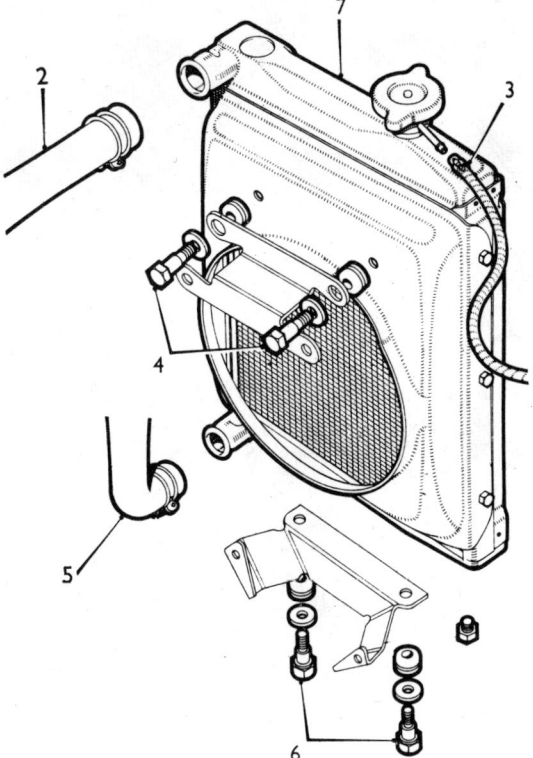

FIG 4:3 Removing the radiator and cowling complete

Key to Fig 4:3   2 Top hose   3 Spill hose
4 Top fixing bolts   5 Bottom hose   6 Bottom fixing
bolts   7 Radiator and cowling

Flushing:

Before adding antifreeze, or when changing the coolant, flush through the system with water from a hose. First open both drain points, remove the thermostat as shown in **FIG 4:4** and insert the hose in the radiator filler neck.

4:4 Removing and refitting radiator

Removing:

Refer to **FIG 4:3** and do the following:
1 Drain the cooling system and disconnect the top hose 2. Disconnect the spill pipe 3.
2 Remove the top fixing bolts 4, disconnect the bottom hose 5 and remove the bottom bolts 6.
3 Lift out the radiator complete with cowl 7.

If there has been trouble with overheating and a blocked radiator is suspected, back-flush it by passing water through it from the bottom hose connection. Continue flushing until the water runs clear. Any trouble with leaks is best cured by radiator experts.

Refitting:

This is a matter of reversing the order of removal, the final operation being to refill the system according to the instructions in **Section 4:3**.

4:5 The thermostat and housing

Removing thermostat:

Refer to **FIG 4:4**. Drain the cooling system and disconnect the top hose from the thermostat cover 3. Remove the three bolts and lift off the cover and gasket. Lift out the thermostat 4.

Checking thermostat:

There are two possible causes of trouble with a thermostat. If it sticks open it leads to overcooling and a slow warming-up period. If it remains persistently closed it will cause overheating. In the case of overheating it is possible to run without the thermostat until it can be renewed.

To check the action of the thermostat, suspend it in a container of water so that it is fully immersed but not touching the bottom or sides. Using a thermometer, heat the water and watch the valve. It should start to open at the temperature stamped on the base. The correct thermostat settings are:

Standard	82°C or 180°F
Hot countries	74°C or 165°F
Cold countries	88°C or 190°F

If the thermostat is found to be faulty do not try to repair it or to modify its performance.

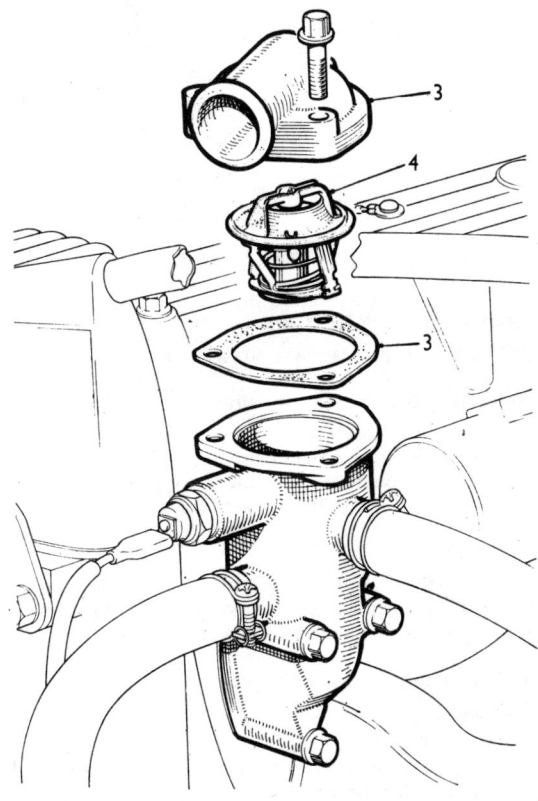

FIG 4:4 Removing the thermostat. Parts **3** are the cover and gasket, **4** is the thermostat

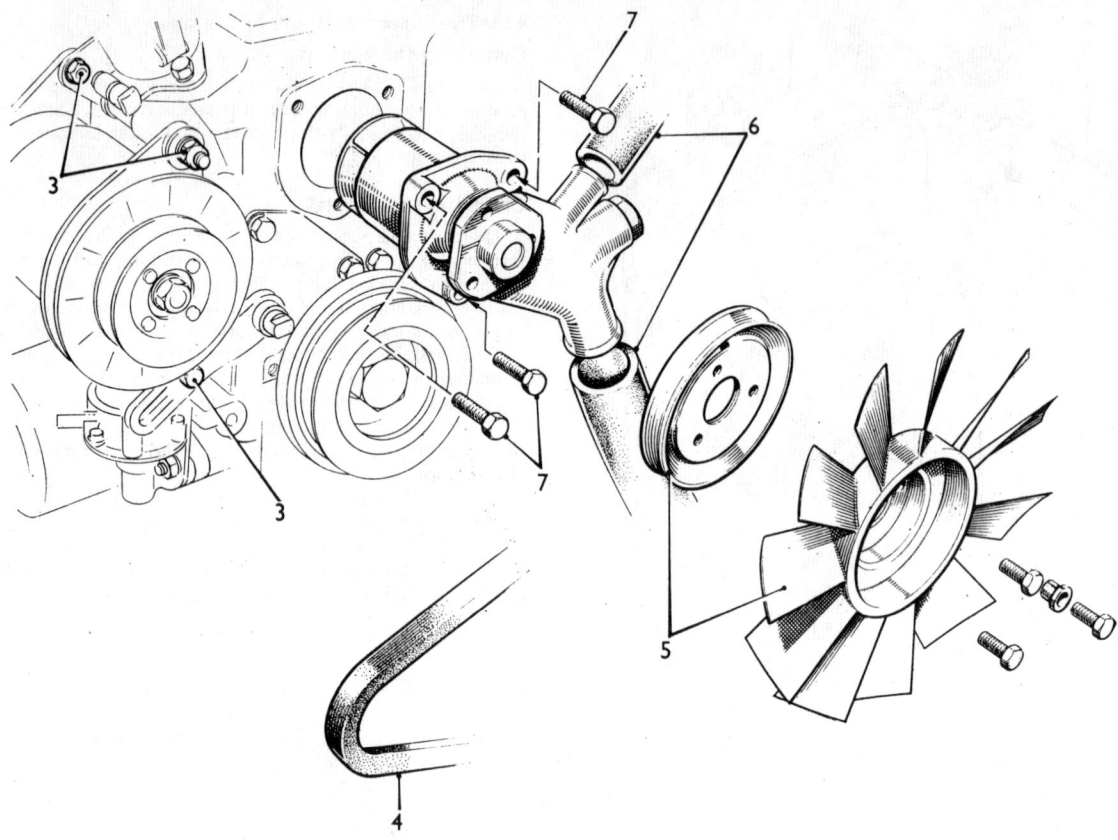

FIG 4:5   Removing the water pump

Key to Fig 4:5   3 The generator fixings   4 Fan belt   5 Fan and pulley   6 Hoses   7 Pump fixing bolts

Refitting:

This is a reversal of the removal sequence.

Removing thermostat housing:

Disconnect the cable from the thermal transmitter, and all three hoses, after draining the cooling system. Remove the three long bolts securing the housing to the cylinder block and lift it away. Take care of the gasket.

Refitting:

Reverse the dismantling sequence, but use a new gasket between the housing and the block. Refill the cooling system as described in **Section 4:3.**

4:6 Servicing the water pump

Removal:

Refer to **FIG 4:5** and follow these instructions:
1 Drain the cooling system. Remove the radiator and cowl as in **Section 4:4.**
2 Slacken the three generator fixings 3 and remove the fan belt 4.
3 Remove three bolts to detach the fan pulley 5. Disconnect the hoses 6 from the pump.

4 Remove bolts 7 and withdraw the pump from the block. Note that there is a gasket under the mounting flange, which is not shown.

Dismantling:

The pulley hub and impeller are press fits on the shaft. Be prepared to renew the parts if this fit is impaired during dismantling.
1 Refer to **FIG 4:6** and remove the hub 1 from the shaft, using a puller.
2 Pull out the bearing locating wire 2 from the body. Press the spindle and bearing assembly 3 rearwards out of the body.
3 Pull the impeller 4 off the shaft with an extractor. The seal 5 can now be withdrawn.

Check the condition of the spindle and bearing assembly and renew if worn, corroded or losing lubricant through the seals. Check seal 5. The carbon ring must be undamaged and polished by contact with the impeller boss. Renew the seal if leakage of coolant has been evident.

Reassembling:

Press the bearing assembly into the body until the groove in the bearing housing lines up with the holes for

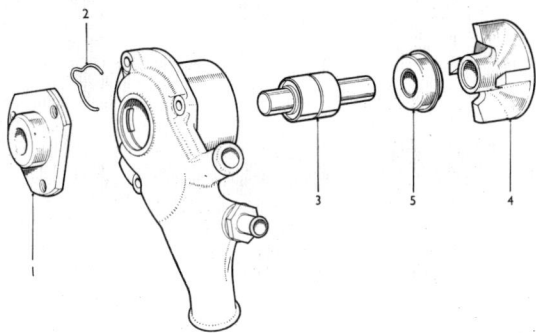

FIG 4:6   Components of the water pump

Key to Fig 4:6   1 Fan and pulley hub   2 Bearing
locating wire   3 Bearing and shaft assembly   4 Pump
impeller   5 Seal

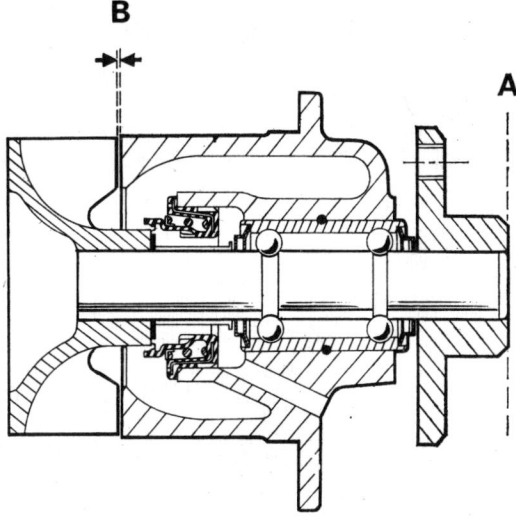

FIG 4:7   A sectioned water pump showing assembly
details. Hub and shaft must be flush at **A**, clearance
between impeller and body must be .010 to .020 inch at
B

the locating wire. Press the pulley hub onto the spindle
until its face is flush with the end of the spindle as shown
in **FIG 4:7** at 'A'. If the hub is not a tight press fit, renew it.
    Press the impeller onto the shaft after fitting the seal.
This too must be a tight press fit. Continue pressing until
the impeller blades clear the body face by .010 to .020 inch
as shown at 'B'. Fit the bearing locating wire.

Refitting:

    Reverse the removal instructions, using a new gasket
between the pump and the cylinder block. Tighten the

securing bolts to a torque of 18 to 20 lb ft. Use the same
torque wrench setting for the generator bolts. Refill the
cooling system as in **Section 4:3**.

4:7 Antifreeze solutions

    **When a heater is fitted and freezing conditions
prevail, it is essential to use antifreeze in the cooling system.** This is so because draining the system does
not drain the heater.
    Antifreeze must also be added to the water in the
expansion tank because this cannot be drained either.
    Antifreeze solution can remain in the system for two
years, but the Specific Gravity must be maintained.
Topping up the system with water will dilute the concentration, so check with an hydrometer and add neat antifreeze as necessary. After the second winter of use, drain
and flush out the system and refill with fresh water and
the correct amount of antifreeze according to the quantity
specified later.
    Use only antifreeze of the ethylene glycol or glycerine
type such as Bluecol. Other makes will do if they conform
to specifications BS.3151 or BS.3152. **Do not use
radiator antifreeze solution in the windscreen
washer.**
    The correct quantities of antifreeze for various degrees
of frost protection are as follows:

Antifreeze	Amount (pints)	Starts to freeze	Frozen solid
25 per cent	5.5	—13°C or 9°F	—26°C or —15°F
33 ⅓ per cent	7.25	—19°C or —2°F	—36°C or —33°F
50 per cent	10.75	—36°C or —33°F	—48°C or —53°F

4:8 Fault diagnosis

(a) Poor coolant circulation

1 Radiator core blocked
2 Engine water passages restricted
3 Coolant level too low
4 Loose fan belt
5 Defective thermostat
6 Collapsed radiator hoses

(b) Overheating

1 Check (a)
2 Faulty ignition or carburation
3 Tight engine
4 Binding brakes, slipping clutch

(c) Internal water leakage

1 Cracked cylinder wall or head
2 Loose cylinder head bolts
3 Faulty head gasket

(d) Corrosion

1 Impurities in water
2 Infrequent draining and flushing

CHAPTER 5

THE CLUTCH

5:1 Description

FIG 5:1 shows the clutch in section and its components can be seen in FIG 5:2. The following description will refer to the part numbers in the first illustration but the numbers in brackets can be used to identify the same parts in the second.

The flywheel 8 (12) is bolted to the end of the crankshaft. Inside the flywheel is a pressure plate 17 (16) and a driven plate 11 (17). When the clutch is engaged, the pressure plate is pulled hard to the left by bolts 9 (14) and diaphragm spring 7. This pressure nips the driven plate friction linings against the flywheel and pressure plate driving faces. The plate is thus carried round, to transmit power to the primary gear 15, and through an idler gear not shown, to input gear 14 and so to the gearbox.

When the clutch pedal is depressed, hydraulic fluid under pressure is transmitted from the clutch master cylinder to the slave cylinder 1. The movement of the slave cylinder piston to the left moves operating lever 2 in the direction of the arrow 'A' so that the bottom end presses release bearing 3 to the right. This action results in diaphragm 6 (15) moving to the right, deflecting the diaphragm spring and pushing the pressure plate to the right too. This releases the driven plate from pressure and it no

longer transmits power to the gearbox. The primary gear 15 also forms the hub for the driven plate and this hub and gear assembly is free to rotate or stay still with respect to the crankshaft. In this way, the crankshaft can continue turning while the driven plate and gearing is stationary. The object of the driving straps 18 is to provide a positive yet flexible connection between the flywheel and the pressure plate. Thus, these two parts will revolve together but the flexibility of the straps will permit the pressure plate to move axially.

5:2 Routine maintenance

It is important to check the fluid level in the clutch master cylinder reservoir every 3,000 miles. FIG 5:3 shows the location close to the battery. Note that the clutch reservoir is the smaller of the two.

Before unscrewing the cap, wipe all round it to remove any dirt. The fluid level is indicated by the line 1 on the outside. Top up to this level using Castrol Girling Brake Fluid Amber. **Do not use unknown substitutes and never introduce mineral oil into the system or complete failure will ensue.** Before refitting the cap, make sure that the vent hole 2 is clear.

The only other maintenance required is to check the

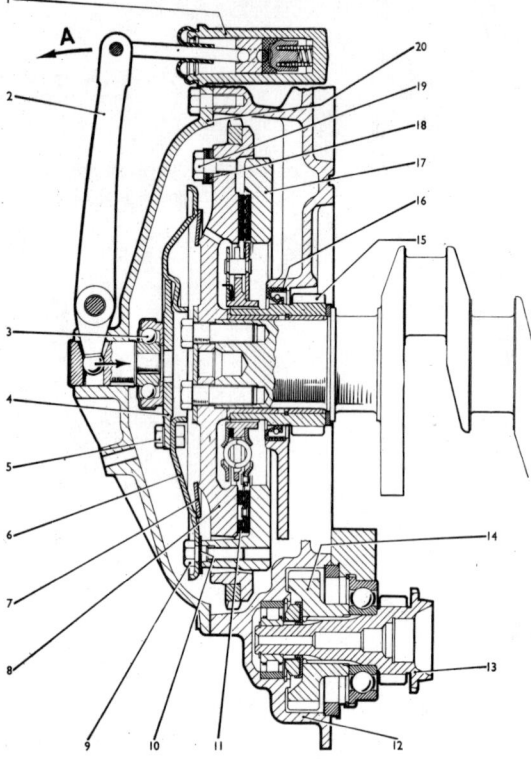

FIG 5:1 A section through the clutch showing the slave cylinder at the top. Arrow A indicates the movement of the operating lever when the clutch pedal is depressed

Key to Fig 5:1   1 Slave cylinder   2 Operating lever
3 Release bearing   4 Thrust plate   5 Bolt for thrust
plate   6 Diaphragm   7 Diaphragm spring
8 Flywheel   9 Bolt for drive strap   10 Drive strap
11 Driven plate   12 Flywheel housing   13 First
motion shaft (gearbox)   14 Input gear   15 Primary
gear (crankshaft)   16 Oil seal   17 Pressure plate
18 Drive strap   19 Bolt for drive strap   20 Clutch cover

clearance between the clutch operating lever and its stop. This is indicated at point 3 in **FIG 5:4**. Use feeler gauges to verify the clearance and if it deviates from the required .020 inch, slacken the locknut 1 and turn the squared shank of the stop 2 anticlockwise to reduce and clockwise to increase the clearance.

5:3 The clutch release bearing

Removing:

Refer to **FIG 5:5** and do the following:

1 Remove the clutch cover as instructed in the first 4 operations for removing the clutch in **Section 5:4**.
2 Remove pivot pin 2 and pull out the operating lever 3. Remove the bearing assembly 4. The shaft can be pressed out of the bearing as shown at 5.

Check the parts for undue wear, which may be the cause of backlash or lost motion. Check the release bearing for roughness and wear.

Refitting:

1 Reverse the removal sequence. It is important to fit the operating lever correctly. The inset on the right shows the lever ready for fitting with the offset ball-end nearest the release bearing.
2 When assembly is completed, set the operating lever clearance correctly as outlined in **Section 5:2**.

5:4 Removing and refitting the clutch

Removing:

1 Refer to **FIG 5:2**. Disconnect and remove the battery. Remove the battery tray.
2 Disconnect and remove the starter 3. Support the power unit under the transmission casing.
3 Remove nut 5 from the engine rear mounting centre-bolt. Remove bolts 6 to release the engine rear mounting 7.
4 Unhook the clutch lever return spring 8. Remove the clutch housing cover 9.
5 Remove the clutch thrust bearing plate 10. Remove flywheel bolts 11 and drive the flywheel squarely off the crankshaft dowels. Mark the clutch and flywheel for correct reassembly and then unscrew bolts 14 evenly to release the diaphragm spring tension. Remove the diaphragm and spring assembly 15.
6 Separate the flywheel and pressure plate 16 to remove the driven plate 17. If the drive straps are removed from the flywheel, mark them first so that they can be restored to their original positions on reassembly.

Clean and examine all the components. The driven plate friction linings should stand well clear of the rivets and be light in colour, with the grain of the material quite visible. A high polish is not detrimental. A dark, glazed appearance may be caused by oil getting on to the linings and there will be other signs that oil has been present. This will be due to leakage past the crankshaft oil seal, which will need renewal.

Check the friction surfaces of the flywheel and pressure plate. These must not be cracked, deeply scored or show signs of overheating due to a slipping clutch.

If the driving straps are faulty it is best to renew them in sets. Renew all other defective parts. It is not advisable to try to rivet new linings on the driven plate as distortion and out-of-balance effects may cause trouble. If the linings are worn, it is likely that the hub splines and shock-absorbing springs in the hub will also be worn and the whole plate is best renewed on an exchange basis.

Refitting:

Before reassembling the clutch and flywheel to the crankshaft, check the crankshaft primary gear end float and adjust it if necessary by referring to **Section 1:9**. Then proceed as follows:

1 Look at the inset in the top righthand corner of **FIG 5:2** and lie the pressure plate 19 on a flat surface with the lugs uppermost.
2 Examine the driven plate 20 for the marking 'FLYWHEEL SIDE'. This is also the side where the shock-absorbing assembly in the hub is offset to stand well proud of the friction linings. Position the plate with the marking uppermost.
3 Lower the flywheel 21 into position. Fit the diaphragm

and spring assembly 22, aligning the marks made when dismantling. Fit bolts 24 but do not tighten them.

4 Fit the assembly to the crankshaft, tightening the bolts to a torque of 60 lb ft. Now tighten the diaphragm bolts to a torque of 15 to 18 lb ft. Fit the clutch release bearing plate.

5 Reverse the rest of the dismantling instructions, using a torque of 15 to 18 lb ft on the clutch housing cover bolts. When reassembly is complete, check the clearance between the withdrawal lever and its stop. Adjust if necessary by referring to **Section 5:2**.

5:5 The hydraulic system

The master cylinder:

An exploded view of the master cylinder parts is shown in **FIG 5:6**, and a section through the assembly is given in **FIG 5:7**. Note how the inner end of bore 12 communicates with the fluid reservoir. This port is closed by valve seal 10 when the clutch pedal is initially depressed. Thus, fluid between the piston 5 and the valve is under pressure and passes out of the cylinder through outlet port 13. From here, a metal and flexible pipe takes the fluid to the

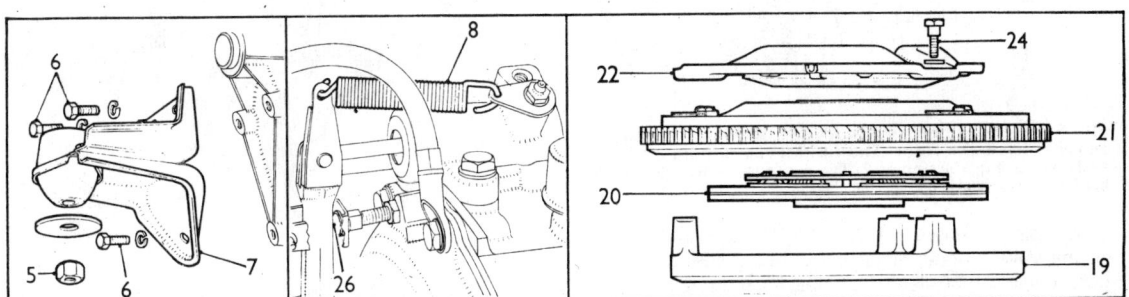

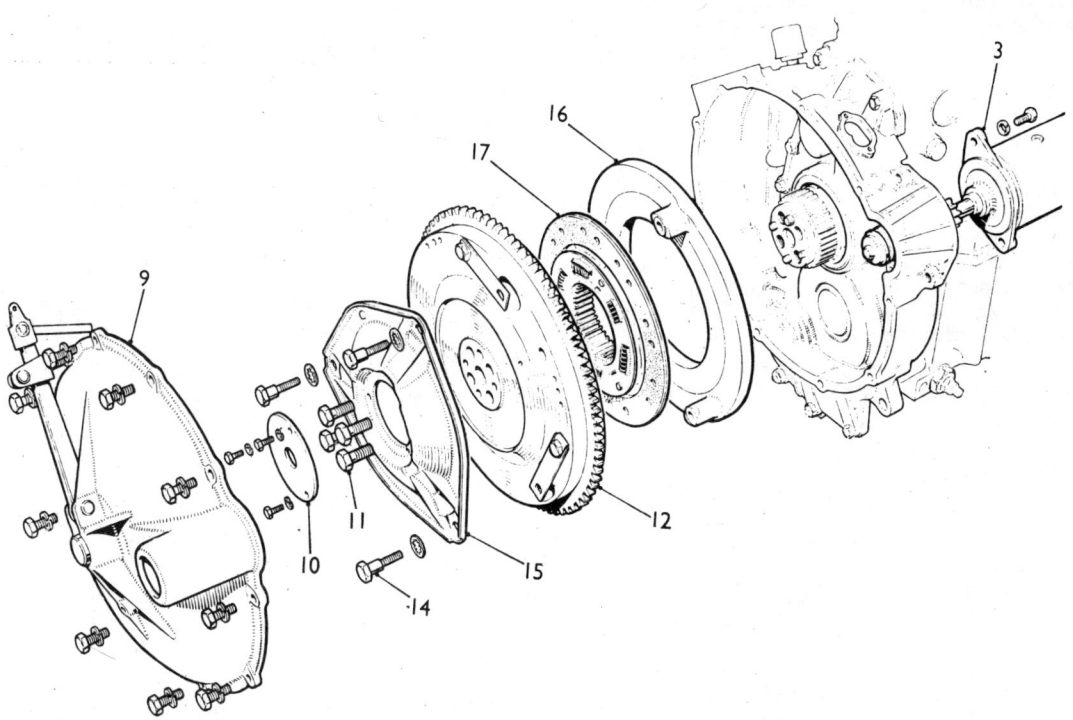

FIG 5:2 Removing and refitting the clutch, showing the sequence of operations

Key to Fig 5:2   3 Starter   5 Nut—engine rear mounting   6 Bolts—engine rear mounting   7 Rear mounting
8 Clutch lever return spring   9 Clutch housing cover   10 Clutch thrust plate   11 Flywheel bolts   12 Flywheel
14 Diaphragm bolts   15 Diaphragm   16 Pressure plate   17 Driven plate   **Inset (top right):**   19 Pressure plate
20 Driven plate   21 Flywheel   22 Diaphragm   24 Diaphragm bolts   **Inset (top centre):**   26 Clearance between clutch operating lever and stop

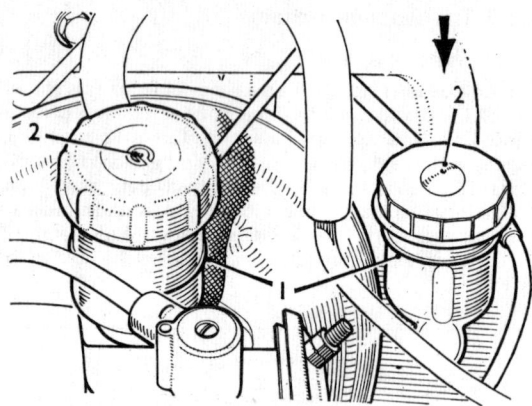

FIG 5:3 The small reservoir for the clutch master cylinder is on the right. The fluid level is indicated at **1** and the vent in the cap at **2**. The large reservoir is for the brake master cylinder

slave cylinder shown in **FIG 5:10**. The pressure of fluid on the slave cylinder piston forces the piston down the bore to operate the clutch operating lever through a pushrod.

When working on the hydraulic system it is essential to be clean, particularly when handling the internal parts. Do not re-use fluid drained from the system and renew all seals which have seen much service.

Removing master cylinder:

1 Refer to **FIG 5:8** and remove clevis pin 1 to detach the pushrod from the clutch pedal. Disconnect the right-hand demister tube from the heater.
2 Remove securing nuts 3. Disconnect pipe 4 from the slave cylinder.
3 Remove the master cylinder complete with pipe. The pipe can then be removed. Drain out the fluid.

Dismantling master cylinder:

1 Peel back the dust cover 1 in **FIG 5:6** and remove the circlip 2 with long-nosed pliers. It may help to push the

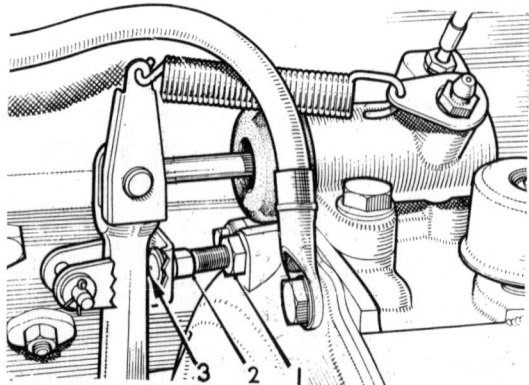

FIG 5:4 Setting the clearance between the clutch operating lever and its stop. The stop locknut is **1**, the squared shank of stop is **2** and the clearance of .020 inch is indicated at **3**

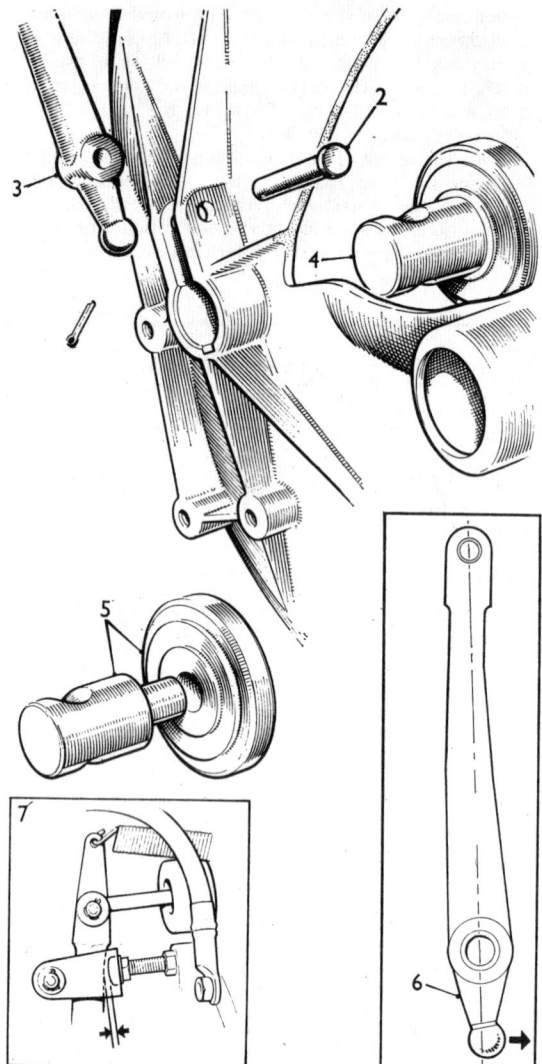

FIG 5:5 Components of the clutch release bearing. Inset **7** shows the clearance between lever and stop and **6** shows the offset ball of the lever positioned nearest to the release bearing

Key to Fig 5:5
3 Operating lever
5 Shaft and bearing separated
2 Operating lever pivot pin
4 Bearing and shaft assembly

piston a short way down the bore to facilitate this operation. Take away the pushrod assembly 3.
2 Remove the piston assembly 4. Gentle air pressure applied to the outlet port will help to blow the parts out of the bore, with the reservoir vent blocked, but be ready to catch the parts in a cloth.
3 Lift thimble leaf 22 and withdraw the piston 5. With the fingers, remove piston seal 6. Compress spring 18 and slip the valve stem 7 out of the elongated hole in the thimble. Pull the thimble out of the spring.

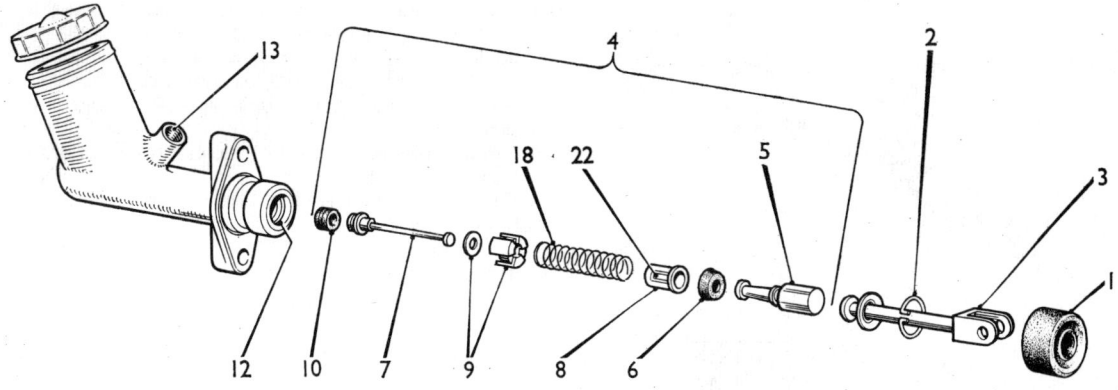

FIG 5:6   Components of the clutch master cylinder

Key to Fig 5:6   1 Dust cover   2 Circlip   3 Pushrod   4 Piston assembly   5 Piston   6 Piston seal
7 Valve stem   8 Thimble   9 Valve spacer and curved washer   10 Valve seal   12 Master cylinder bore
13 Outlet port   22 Leaf on thimble

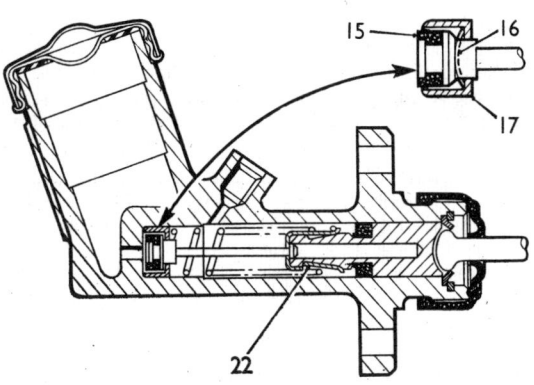

FIG 5:7   Section through master cylinder showing the correct assembly of the valve parts (top right)

Key to Fig 5:7   15 Valve seal   16 Curved washer
17 Valve spacer   22 Leaf on thimble

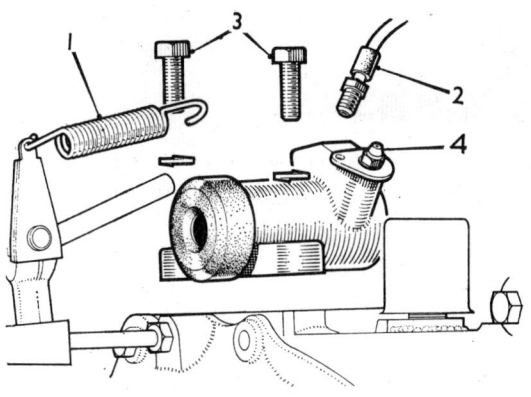

FIG 5:9   Removing the slave cylinder

Key to Fig 5:9   1 Lever return spring   2 Pipe from
master cylinder   3 Securing bolts   4 Bleed screw

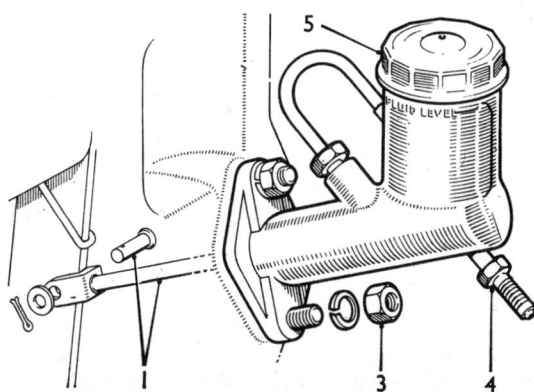

FIG 5:8   Removing the clutch master cylinder

Key to Fig 5:8   1 Pushrod and clevis pin   3 Securing nut
4 Pipe to slave cylinder   5 Master cylinder

4   Remove spacer and washer 9 from the stem. Peel the seal 10 off the valve head.

Wash all the parts in Girling Cleaning Fluid or industrial methylated spirits only. **Do not use solvents such as petrol.** Check the cylinder bore for corrosion, scoring or ridging. It will be useless to fit new seals to a bore which is not perfectly smooth and polished. The seals are available in kit form and it is always wise to renew them.

Make sure the two ports at the inner end of the bore are free from obstruction. Wash the main casting in methylated spirit and allow to dry. Do not dry off with a fluffy rag.

Reassembling the master cylinder:

1   Start by dipping all the internal parts in the correct grade of fluid and assemble them wet. Use Castrol Girling Brake Fluid. Amber.

2   Fit valve seal 15 in **FIG 5:7** to the valve head. Refer to the inset in the same illustration and fit curved washer

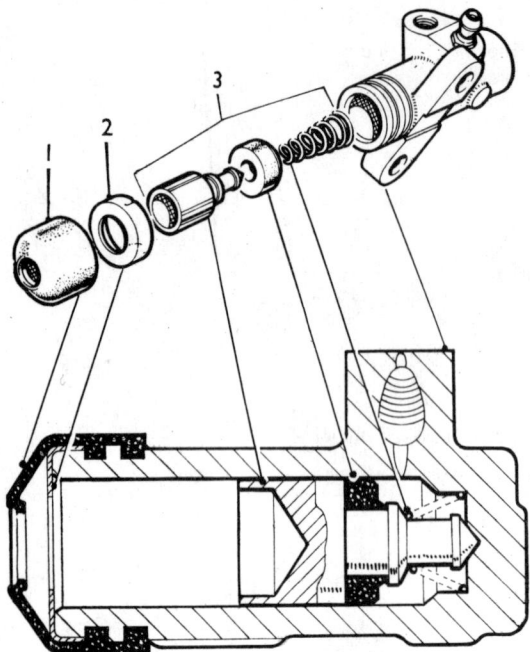

FIG 5:10 Section and components of slave cylinder

Key to Fig 5:10   1 Dust cover   2 End cap
3 Piston assembly

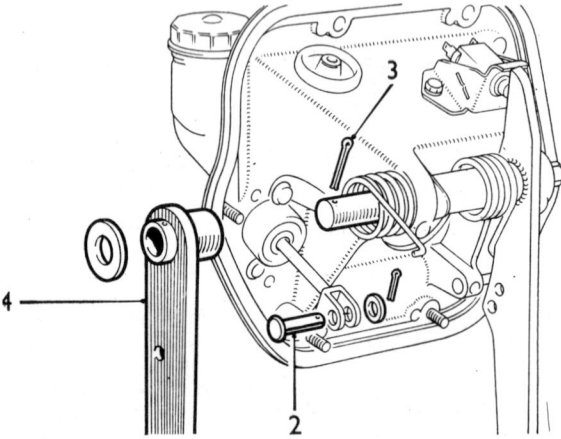

FIG 5:11 Removing the clutch pedal. 2 is the pushrod clevis pin, 3 is the securing splitpin and 4 is the clutch pedal lever

16 so that the domed side is against the shoulder on the stem. Fit spacer 17 so that the legs face the seal.
3 Position the spring centrally on the valve spacer. Insert the thimble in the other end. Push on the thimble to compress the spring and insert the valve stem in the elongated hole in the thimble end. Locate the stem centrally in the thimble.

4 Fit seal 6 with its flat face against the piston. Insert the small end of the piston into the thimble and press it home until the thimble leaf 22 engages behind the shoulder on the piston. Fit the piston assembly into the bore, being careful not to trap or turn back the lip of the seal.
5 Fit the pushrod, followed by the circlip on top of the dished washer. Smear the pushrod and master cylinder side of the dust cover with Girling Rubber Grease and fit the cover.

Refitting the master cylinder:

This is a simple reversal of the removal sequence. When the operation is completed, fill the reservoir with the correct fluid and bleed the system as instructed in **Section 5:6.**

The slave cylinder:
Removal:

Refer to **FIG 5:9** and unhook spring 1. Disconnect fluid pipe 2, unscrew the securing bolts 3 and lift away the cylinder.

Dismantling:

Refer to **FIG 5:10** and remove the dust cover 1. Lift the crimped retainer and remove the end cap 2. Using gentle air pressure, blow out the piston, seal and spring assembly 3.

Clean the parts in Girling Cleaning Fluid or industrial methylated spirits. **Do not use solvents like petrol.**
Examine the cylinder bore. It must be smooth, and polished. If it is scored, ridged or corroded it must be renewed. Do not fit new seals to a worn or damaged piston or cylinder bore. Seals are available in kit form, so renew both seal and dust cover at each overhaul.

Reassembling:

Assemble all internal parts after wetting with Castrol Girling Brake Fluid. Fit the seal with its flat surface against the face of the piston. Press the small end of the spring over the stem of the piston. Insert the piston in the cylinder, taking care not to trap or turn back the lip of the seal. Fit the end cap and dust cover.

Refitting:

Reverse the order of removal. Finish off by bleeding the system as instructed in the following Section.

5:6 Bleeding the system

Fill the clutch master cylinder reservoir with Castrol Girling Brake Fluid Amber. Attach a rubber or plastic tube to the bleed screw nipple 4 in **FIG 5:9**. Immerse the open end of this tube in a small quantity of the same fluid in a clean glass jar.
Obtain the help of an assistant to pump the clutch pedal. Undo the bleed screw about three-quarters of a turn and watch the submerged end of the tube as the assistant depresses the clutch pedal for a full stroke. Air bubbles will be seen to emerge from the tube. At the end of the down stroke, close the bleed screw and return the pedal. Pause a second or two and repeat the operation with the bleed screw opened again. Continue depressing and returning

the pedal until no more air bubbles emerge and then tighten the bleed screw on a slow down stroke of the pedal.

The operation of bleeding the system is always necessary if the pipelines are disconnected or any part of the system is dismantled. It is also necessary if the fluid in the reservoir has dropped so low that air has entered the system.

Discard fluid which has been bled from the system. It may contain dirt and will certainly be aerated. In an emergency, fluid which is known to be clean can be de-aerated by being left to stand for twenty-four hours.

Removing and refitting clutch pedal:

Refer to **FIG 5 :11**. Remove the brake pedal as instructed in **Chapter 10**. Remove clevis pin 2 and splitpin 3 and withdraw the pedal 4. Refit the pedal in the reverse order.

5:8 Fault diagnosis

(a) Drag or spin

1 Oil on driven plate linings
2 Leaking hydraulic system
3 Driven plate distorted
4 Warped or damaged pressure plate
5 Broken driven plate linings
6 Air in the hydraulic system

(b) Fierceness or snatch

1 Check 1, 2, 3 and 4 in (a)
2 Worn linings
3 Worn release mechanism

(c) Slip

1 Check 1 in (a) and 2 in (b)
2 Weak spring
3 Seized slave cylinder piston
4 No clearance between operating lever and stop
5 Release bearing shaft tight in housing

(d) Judder

1 Check 1 and 3 in (a)
2 Warped pressure plate
3 Broken drive straps
4 Contact area of linings not evenly distributed
5 Faulty rubber mountings and steady

(e) Tick or knock

1 Worn driven plate splines
2 Worn release bearing
3 Faulty starter pinion drive
4 Defective drive straps
5 Broken shock-absorber springs in driven plate hub
6 Flywheel loose on crankshaft

CHAPTER 6

THE GEARBOX

6:1 Description

The gearbox has five forward ratios and reverse, with synchromesh engagement on all the forward ratios. The fifth- or top-speed is in effect an overdrive ratio which enables the car to cruise at high speeds with lower engine revolutions than is normal without an overdrive.

The general layout of the gearbox can be seen in **FIG 6:1**, the input of power from the crankshaft and primary gears being to first motion shaft gear 3. The first motion shaft runs in bearings 4 and 5 and carries a needle-roller bearing 6 to support the lefthand end of third motion shaft 34. The inner gear on the first motion shaft meshes with the largest gear of the layshaft cluster 42. In consequence, whenever the first motion shaft is turning, the laygears for the first four forward speeds and reverse are also turning. Splined to the righthand end of the lay-shaft 43 is the synchronizer for the fifth-speed gear 51. This gear is free on the layshaft and it runs on needle roller bearings 52. When the gearchange control moves the outer sleeve of the synchronizer to the left, dogs are

meshed to provide a drive from the layshaft to the fifth-speed gear and so to the final drive pinion 31. This in turn drives the crownwheel and final drive mechanism.

The helical gears for first-, second- and third-speed gears are parts 24, 16 and 15 respectively. These are free to turn on the third motion shaft and are in constant mesh with their counterparts on the layshaft. They are thus always turning when the first motion shaft gear is being driven. To engage any of these gears, and the one at the inner end of the first motion shaft, with the third motion shaft 34, there are two synchromesh assemblies 11 and 20. Movement of the outer synchromesh sleeves and dogs to right or left will engage the required gear. A gear which is not shown can be engaged between the straight-toothed gear on the sleeve of synchronizer 20 and the small straight-toothed gear in the centre of the layshaft to provide reverse. Note that the synchronizer sleeves are splined to hubs which are also splined to the shafts so that when the dogs on the sleeve are engaged with any gear, that gear is then coupled to the shaft. Baulk rings 10,

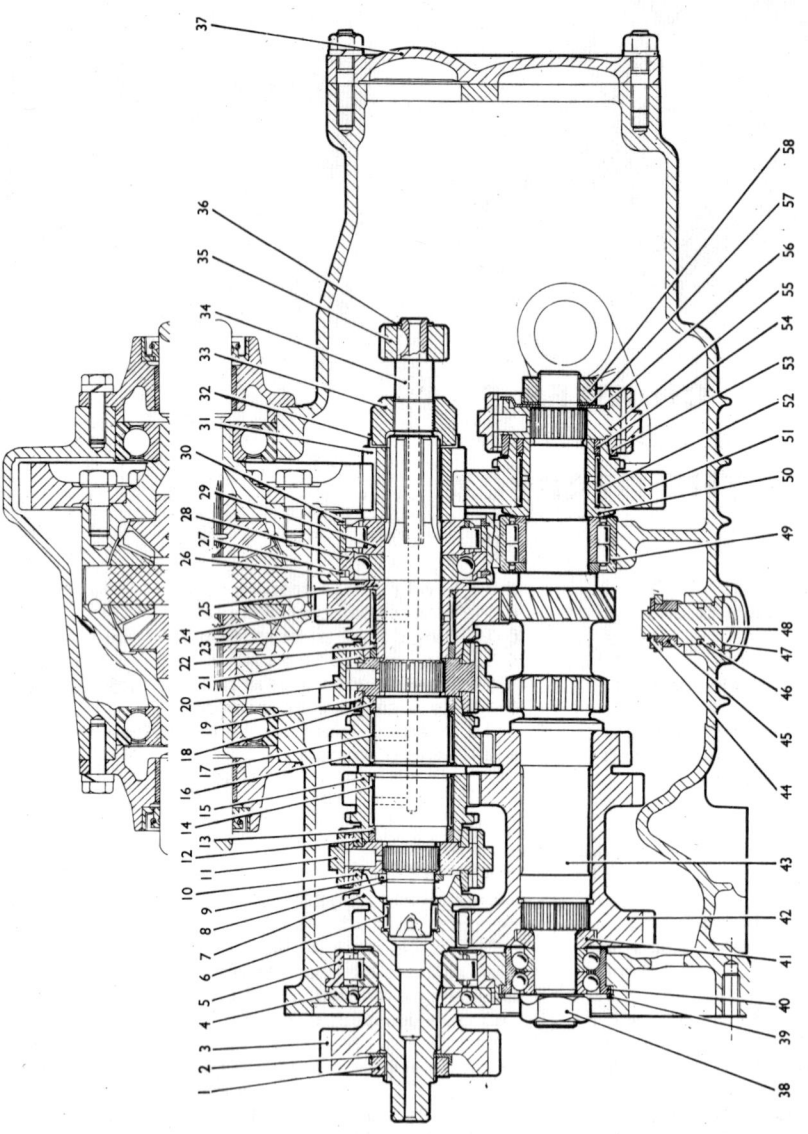

FIG 6:1   A section through the gearbox showing the first motion shaft gear **3**, the third motion shaft **34**, the layshaft **43** and the fifth-speed gear **51**.

Key to Fig 6:1   1 Nut for first-motion shaft gear   2 Lockwasher for nut   3 First-motion shaft gear   4 Ballbearing   5 Roller bearing   6 Needle-roller bearing
7 First-motion shaft   8 Circlip   9 Selective spacer   10 Baulk ring   11 Third- and fourth-speed synchronizer   12 Baulk ring   13 Collar for bearing
14 Needle-roller bearing   15 Third-speed gear   16 Second-speed gear   17 Needle-roller bearing   18 Spacer for bearing   19 Baulk ring
20 First- and second-speed synchronizer   21 Baulk ring   22 Spacer for bearing   23 Needle-roller bearing   24 First-speed gear   2b Hub for gear
26 Casing centre web   27 Circlip   28 Ballbearing   29 Roller bearing   30 Circlip   31 Final drive pinion   32 Lockwasher for nut   33 Nut for pinion
34 Third motion shaft   35 Speedometer pinion   36 Circlip   37 Gearbox front cover   38 Nut for layshaft—rear   39 Circlip   40 Ballbearing   41 Spacer
42 Laygear   43 Layshaft   44 Circlip   45 Reverse selector lever   46 O-ring   47 Circlip   48 Reverse selector pivot pin   49 Roller bearing
50 Hub for gear   51 Fifth-speed   52 Needle-roller bearing   53 Baulk ring   54 Spacer for bearing   55 Fifth-gear synchronizer   56 Retainer for synchronizer
57 Lockwasher for nut   58 Nut for layshaft—front

12, 19, 21 and 53 provide the cone clutches which enable the speeds of the dogs on the gears and the sleeves to be synchronized. Perspective views of the parts mentioned can be seen in **FIG 6:4**.

The connection between the gearlever selectors and those in the gearbox is achieved with flexible inner-and-outer cables as shown in **FIG 6:20** on early cars, or by a system of rods on later models.

6:2 Removing and refitting the transmission assembly

Apart from work on the gearlever control and the selector cables or rods, all other operations on the transmission involve removal of the power unit from the car.

Removing:

1 Remove the power unit as described in **Chapter 1**. Refer to **FIG 6:2** and remove the dipstick and guide tube 2. Remove the distributor 3. Withdraw the oil pump drive shaft 4 from the bore of the distributor drive shaft as explained in **Chapter 1**.
2 Remove the starter 5 and the oil filter 6. Remove the fuel pump and pushrod 7.
3 Remove the clutch housing cover 8, the thrust plate 9 and the flywheel retaining bolts 10. Drift flywheel 11 from the crankshaft. Remove all retaining bolts and nuts

from the flywheel housing as shown by the inset 12 in the top lefthand corner of the illustration. Fit protecting sleeve 18G.1152 over the splines on the crankshaft primary gear to prevent damage to the oil seal and withdraw the flywheel housing 14.
4 Refer to insets 15, remove all the bolts securing the transmission to the engine.

Refitting:

Reverse the removal sequence but note the following:
1 The crankshaft primary gear end float must be checked as described in **Chapter 1**.
2 If a new or reconditioned transmission casing has been fitted, the ring dowel for the first motion shaft bearing must be checked as in **Section 6:12**.
3 Certain bolts securing the transmission to the engine must be fitted first. These are above the oil filter, the fuel pump boss and on the crownwheel side of the differential housing. They cannot be fitted once the engine and transmission are together.
4 Make sure that the O-ring for the oil feed is correctly positioned.
5 Check that the front oil seal and sealing plugs are correctly positioned.
6 Tighten the $\frac{3}{8}$ inch engine-to-transmission securing

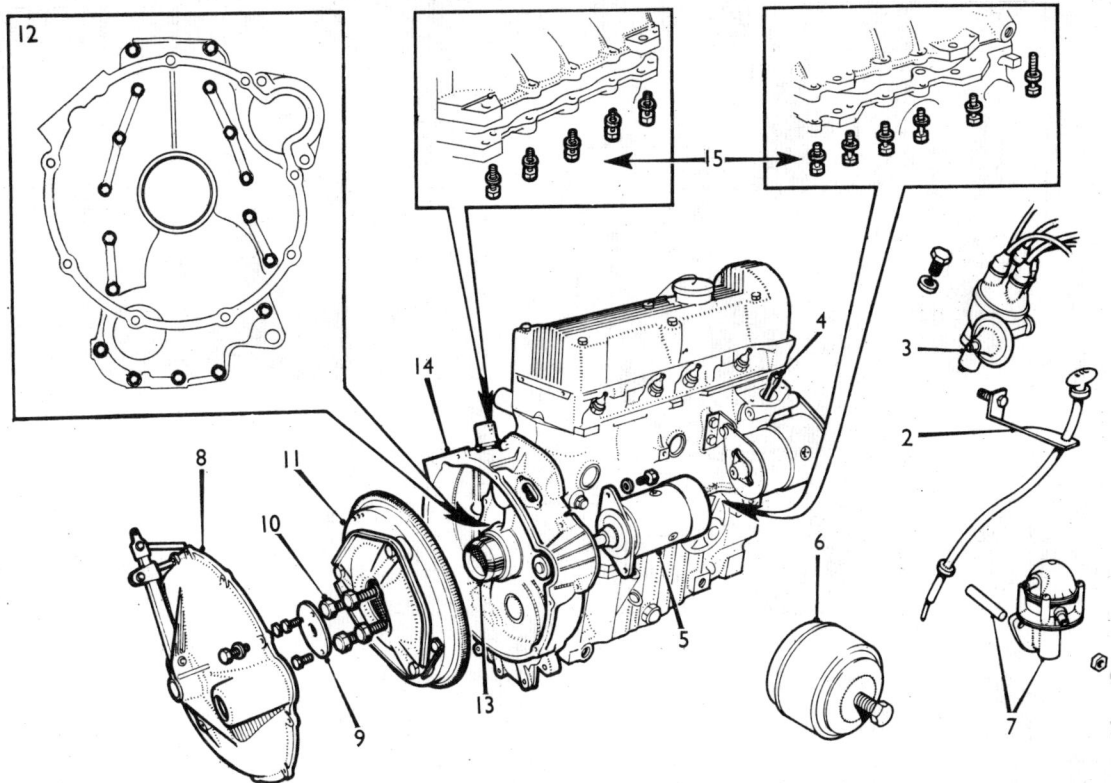

FIG 6:2   Removing the transmission assembly

Key to Fig 6:2   2 Dipstick and guide tube   3 Distributor   4 Oil pump drive shaft   5 Starter   6 Oil filter
7 Fuel pump and pushrod   8 Clutch housing cover   9 Clutch thrust plate   10 Flywheel bolts   11 Flywheel
12 Flywheel housing nuts and bolts   13 Protecting sleeve   14 Flywheel housing   15 Transmission-to-engine bolts

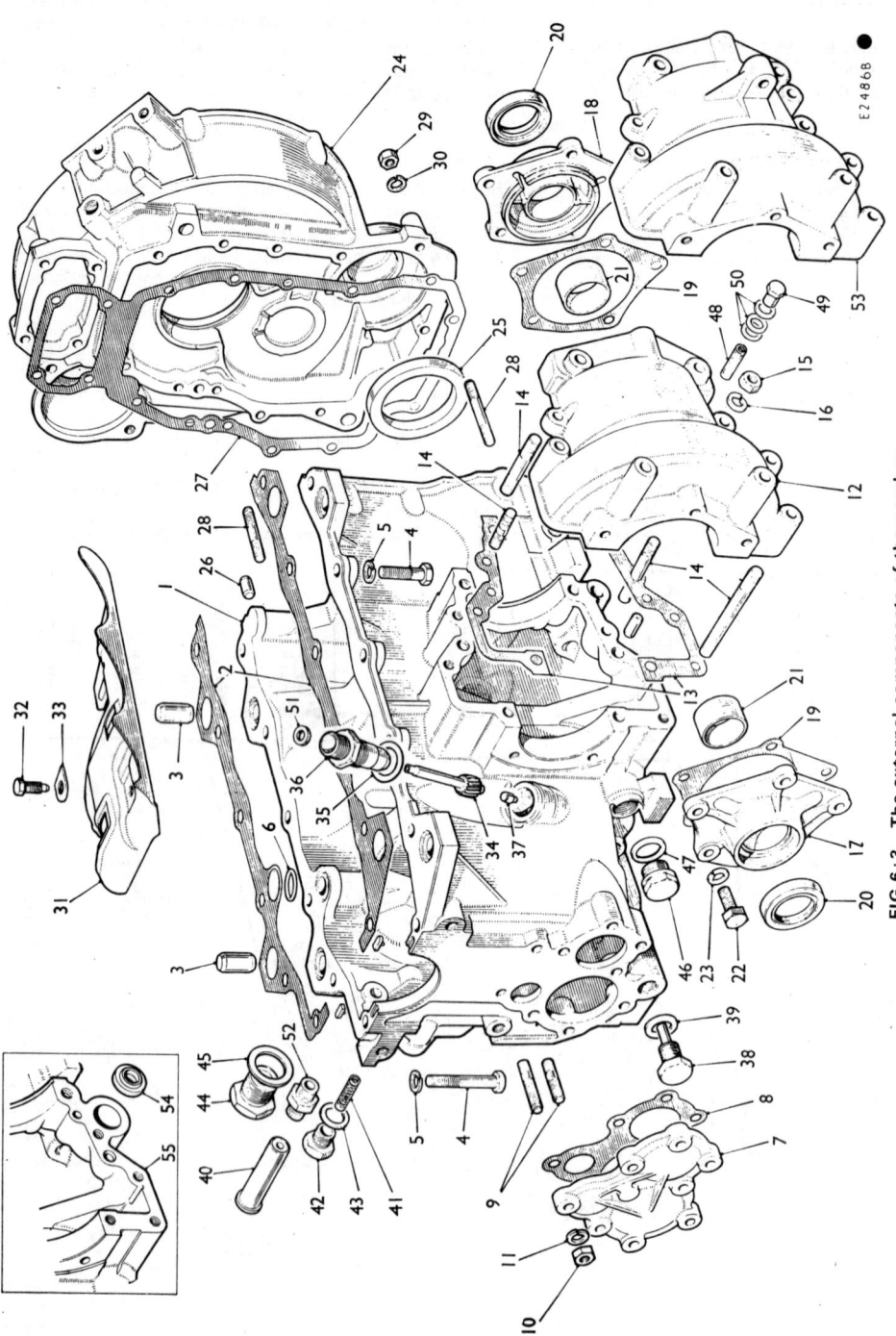

FIG 6:3   The external components of the gearbox

Key to Fig 6:3   1 Gearbox casing (cable gearchange)   2 Gasket for casing   3 Dowel for cylinder block   4 Bolt gearbox to cylinder block   5 Spring washer
6 Oil sealing ring   7 Gearbox front cover   8 Gasket for cover   9 Stud for cover   10 Nut for stud   11 Spring washer for nut   12 Differential housing   13 Gasket for housing
14 Stud for housing   15 Nut for stud   16 Spring washer   17 Lefthand differential side cover   18 Righthand differential side cover   19 Gasket for side cover
20 Oil seal for side cover   21 Bush for side cover   22 Bolt for side cover   23 Spring washer for bolt   24 Flywheel housing   25 Ring dowel for housing
26 Dowel for housing   27 Gasket for housing   28 Stud for housing   29 Nut for stud   30 Spring washer for stud   31 Baffle for gearbox   32 Bolt for reverse shaft and baffle
33 Lockwasher for bolt   34 Speedometer pinion   35 Thrust washer for pinion   36 Adaptor for pinion   37 Thrust pad for drive shaft   38 Magnetic drain plug
39 Washer for drain plug   40 Oil pressure relief valve   41 Reverse and 5th detent spring   42 Reverse and 5th detent plug   43 Washer for plug
44 3rd and 4th fork access plug   45 Washer for plug   46 1st and 2nd selector plug   47 Washer for plug   48 1st and 2nd detent spring   49 1st and 2nd detent plug
50 Washers for plug   51 Seal for drive shaft   52 Detent plug (rod gearchange)   53 Differential housing (rod gearchange)   54 Oil seal for selector shaft (rod
gearchange)   55 Gearbox casing (rod gearchange)

E2486B

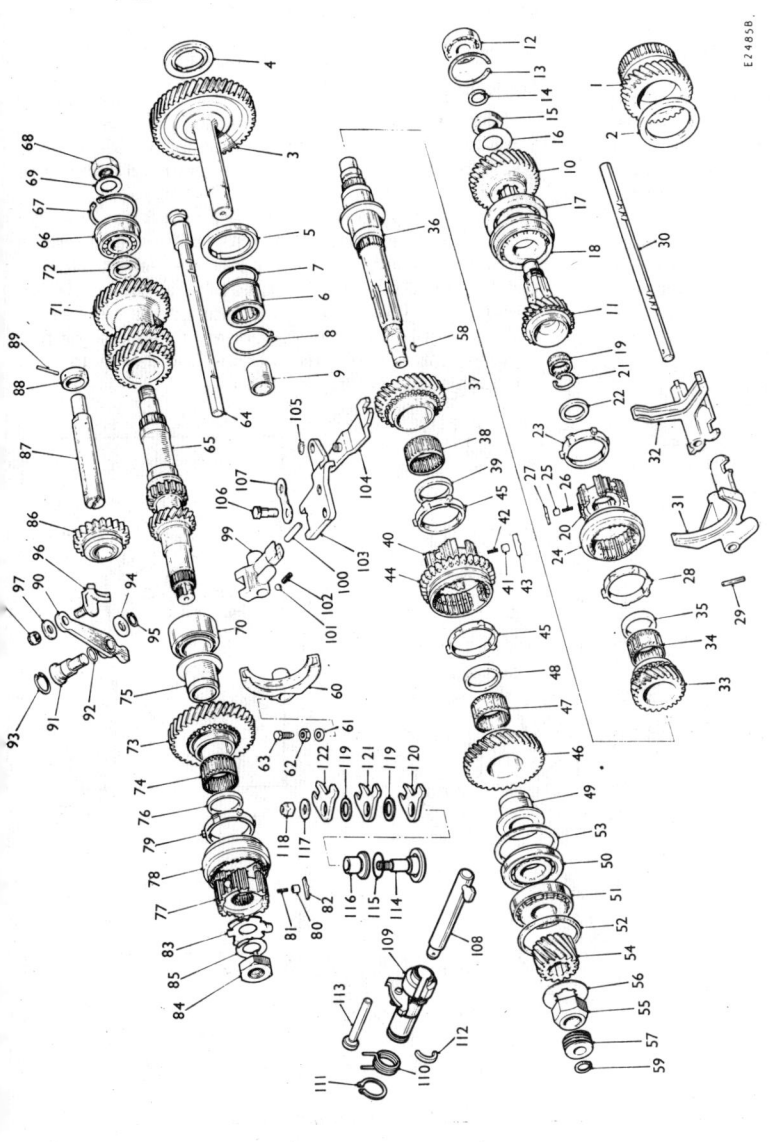

FIG 6:4   The internal components of the gearbox

Key to Fig 6:4   1 Primary gear (crankshaft)   2 Thrust washer for gear   3 Idler gear   4 Outer thrust washer for idler gear   5 Inner thrust washer for idler gear
6 Outer bearing for idler gear   7 Outer circlip for bearing   8 Inner circlip for bearing   9 Inner bearing for idler gear   10 First motion shaft (input)   11 First motion shaft
12 Spigot bearing for shaft   13 Circlip for bearing outer track   14 Circlip for bearing inner track   15 Nut for first motion shaft   16 Lockwasher for nut   17 Ballbearing
for shaft   18 Roller bearing for shaft   19 Needle roller bearing for shaft   20 Synchronizer hub   21 Circlip for synchronizer   22 Spacer for synchronizer (selective)
23 Baulk ring   24 Sycnronizer collar   25 Plunger for synchronizer   26 Spring for plunger   27 Key   28 Baulk ring   29 Slotted spring pin   30 1st to 4th speed selector rod
31 1st and 2nd speed fork   32 3rd and 4th speed selector fork   33 3rd speed gear   34 Bearing for gear   35 Spacer for bearing   36 Third motion shaft   37 2nd speed gear
38 Bearing for gear   39 Spacer for bearing   40 Synchronizer hub   41 Plunger for synchronizer   42 Spring for plunger   43 Key   44 Synchronizer collar/reverse mainshaft gear
45 Baulk ring   46 First speed gear   47 Bearing for gear   48 Spacer for bearing   49 Hub for gear   50 Ballbearing for third motion shaft   51 Roller bearing for third motion shaft
52 Circlip for roller bearing   53 Circlip for ballbearing   54 Final drive pinion   55 Nut for pinion   56 Synchronizer collar/reverse mainshaft gear   57 Speedometer pinion   58 Key for pinion
59 Circlip for pinion   60 5th and reverse speed selector fork   61 Washer for locknut   62 Locknut for bolt   63 Bolt for fork   64 5th and reverse speed selector rod
65 Layshaft   66 Rear bearing for layshaft   67 Circlip for bearing   68 Rear nut for layshaft   69 Lockwasher for nut   70 Front bearing for layshaft   71 Laygear
72 Spacer for laygear   73 5th speed gear   74 Bearing for gear   75 Hub for gear   76 Spacer for bearing   77 Synchronizer hub   78 Synchronizer collar   79 Baulk ring
80 Plunger for synchronizer   81 Spring for plunger   82 Key   83 Retainer for synchronizer   84 Front nut for layshaft   85 Lockwasher for nut   86 Reverse idler gear
87 Shaft for gear   88 Collar for shaft   89 Roll pin for collar   90 Reverse selector lever   91 Pivot pin for lever   92 O-ring for pin   93 O-ring for pin   94 Washer for pin
95 Inner circlip for pin   96 Reverse selector fork   97 Washer   98 Nut   99 Reverse selector interlock   100 Plunger for interlock   101 Ball for interlock   102 Spring for ball
103 Reverse interlock plate   104 Reverse operating lever   105 Circlip for reverse operating lever   106 Bolt for plate   107 Lockwasher for bolt   108 Selector shaft
109 Interlock spool   110 Torsion spring   111 Circlip for interlock spool   112 Retaining collar for interlock spool   113 Pin   114 Pivot post   115 O-ring seal
116 Bush for bellcrank levers   117 Washer   118 Nut   119 Spacer for bellcrank levers   120 Lower bellcrank lever   121 Centre bellcrank lever   122 Upper bellcrank lever

E2485B.

bolts to a torque of 30 lb ft. Tighten the $\frac{5}{16}$ inch bolts to 20 to 25 lb ft.

7 Before fitting the flywheel housing, fit sleeve 18G.1152 over the primary gear to protect the oil seal.

8 Tighten the flywheel housing nuts and bolts evenly and to a torque of 18 lb ft.

6:3 Notes on overhauling

To avoid repetition in the various operations covered in the following Sections, it is assumed that after parts are dismantled they will be thoroughly cleaned and examined for wear. Bearings should be tested in a dry condition. Any wear or roughness when spun calls for renewal. Worn gear teeth will also imply renewal. In most cases it is not advisable to renew a single gear but also to renew those which mate with it. Noisy operation might otherwise be troublesome.

Difficulty in engaging a gear, particularly if accompanied by noise, is likely to be due to worn synchromesh cones or baulk rings. When withdrawing the synchronizing collar or sleeve, be ready to catch the parts 41, 42 and 43 in **FIG 6:4**. Wrap the assembly in a cloth to perform this operation.

Be particularly diligent in looking for wear if the magnetic drain plug is heavily coated with steel particles.

When satisfied that all parts are ready for reassembly, lubricate liberally with clean engine oil. If jointing compound is used, make sure the metal surfaces are free from oil. Note that the use of home-made joints will lead to trouble through a variation in thickness from those supplied as genuine spare parts. This is most important where the thickness regulates the choice of such items as the ring dowel mentioned in **Section 6:12**.

6:4 The primary gears and bearings

Removing the gears:

Refer to **FIG 6:5** and follow these instructions:

1 Remove the power unit as described in **Chapter 1**. Remove the flywheel housing as instructed in the same chapter.

2 Withdraw the crankshaft primary gear 3 and the idler gear 4. Using Service Tool 18G.1158 as illustrated in **FIG 6:6**, select two gears to lock the transmission.

3 Refer to **FIG 6:7** which shows Service Tools 18G.705 and 705H. These are used to remove the first motion shaft spigot bearing as shown at 6. Remove the first motion shaft nut and lockwasher 7. Withdraw the first motion shaft gear 8.

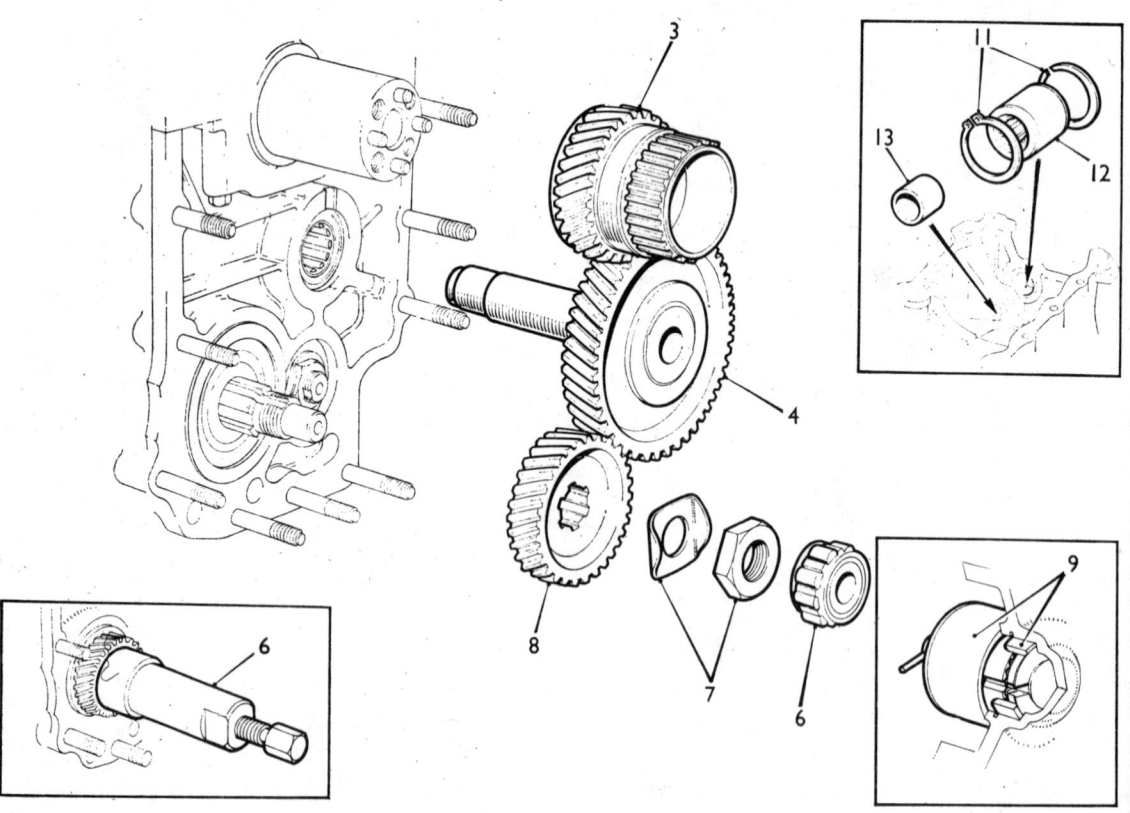

FIG 6:5 The primary gears and bearings

Key to Fig 6:5   3 Crankshaft primary gear   4 Idler gear   6 Removing spigot bearing (first motion shaft)
7 Nut and lockwasher (first motion shaft)   8 Gear (first motion shaft)   9 Removing outer race of spigot bearing
11 Circlips   12 Needle roller (idler gear)   13 Sleeve bearing (idler gear)

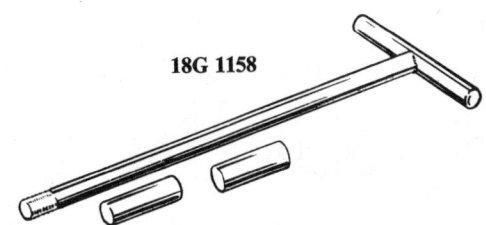

FIG 6:6 Service Tool 18G.1158 for removing, replacing and assembling gear selectors

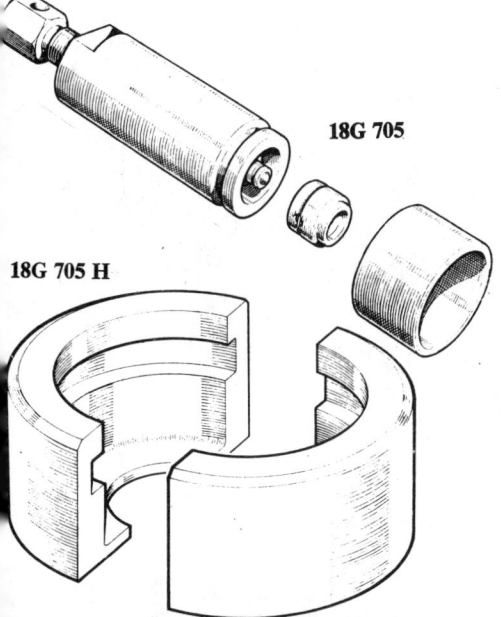

FIG 6:7 Service Tool 18G.705 for removing bearing centre race. Tool 18G.705H is an adapter for removing the spigot bearing of the first motion shaft

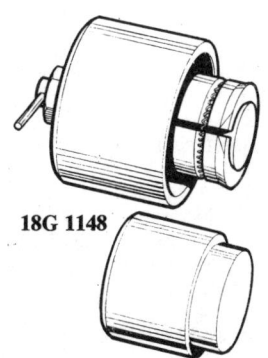

FIG 6:8 Service Tool 18G.1148 is a bearing outer race remover and replacer

4 Use Service Tool 18G.1148 to remove the outer race of the spigot bearing as shown at 9. The tool is illustrated in **FIG 6:8**.

Removing the bearings:

1 Remove the transmission by following operations 1 and 2 in **Section 6:2** but ignore the first sentence. Repeat operation 4.
2 Remove circlips 11 from the idler gear needle roller bearing. Drift the bearing 12 inwards from the casing. Using a spigoted drift, drive the idler gear sleeve bearing 13 from the casing.

Refitting gears and bearings:

1 Drive a new idler gear sleeve bearing into the casing until its face is flush with the inside face of the casing web. The spigoted drift is Service Tool 18G.1160.
2 Fit a circlip into the outer groove of the idler gear needle roller bearing. Fit the bearing into the casing with Service Tool 18G.1159. Fit the inner circlip.
3 Fit the first motion shaft gear, nut and lockwasher. Tighten to a torque of 120 lb ft. Fit the spigot bearing to the first motion shaft.
4 Fit the bearing outer race into the flywheel housing. Check the end float of the crankshaft primary gear as described in **Chapter 1**.
5 Reverse operations 1 and 2 at the beginning of this Section. Fit the transmission to the engine by referring to the instructions in **Section 6:2**.

6:5 Removing and refitting the reverse idler gear

Removing:

Refer to **FIG 6:9** which shows the parts to be removed. Do the following:
1 Remove the power unit as described in **Chapter 1**. Remove the transmission assembly as instructed in **Section 6:2**. Remove the differential assembly as instructed in **Chapter 7**.
2 Remove the oil filter. Remove the oil pressure relief valve as instructed in **Chapter 1**. Remove the baffle plate. Remove the oil pump as described in **Chapter 1**.
3 Remove the idler gear 8 and the transmission cover 9. Remove the fifth-speed/reverse selector rod end plug 10. Remove the detent plug 11 for the same rod.
4 Unlock and slacken the retaining screw 12 for the fifth-speed selector fork. Rotate the fifth/reverse selector rod 180 deg. so that the flat machined face will clear the reverse arm. Withdraw the selector rod enough to disengage it from the fork but take care not to withdraw it from the interlock shown in the bottom lefthand inset. One of the retainers of Service Tool 18G.1158 is shown at 14. The tool is illustrated in **FIG 6:6**. With this introduced into the interlock, press the rod out (15) so that the ball and spring are kept in place as shown.
5 Remove the speedometer drive pinion 16, remove circlip 17 from the end of the third motion shaft. Withdraw the speedometer drive gear and its key 18. Unlock the layshaft nut 22 and the final drive pinion nut 21. Use tool 18G.1158 to select two gears to lock the transmission. Remove nut 21. **Note that it has a lefthand thread.** Remove nut 22.
6 Disengage the gears to unlock the transmission and remove the final drive pinion. From the end of the layshaft remove the fifth-speed assembly 25 together with the needle roller bearing and hub for the gear.

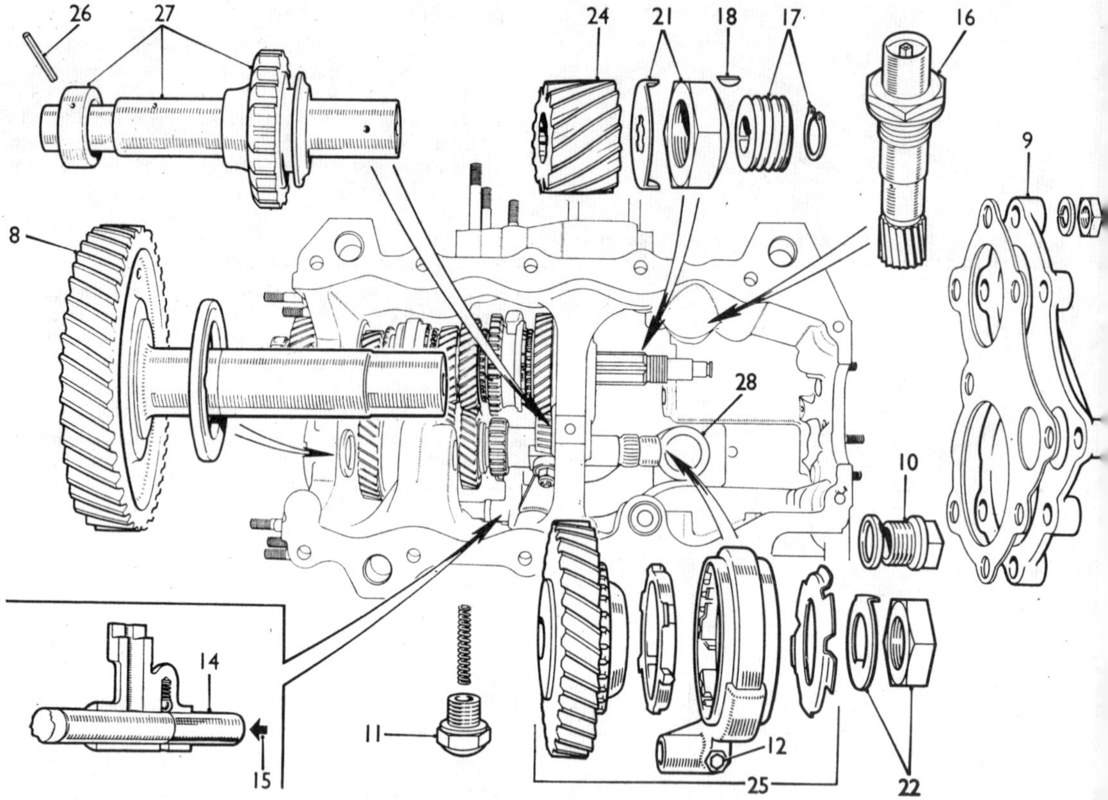

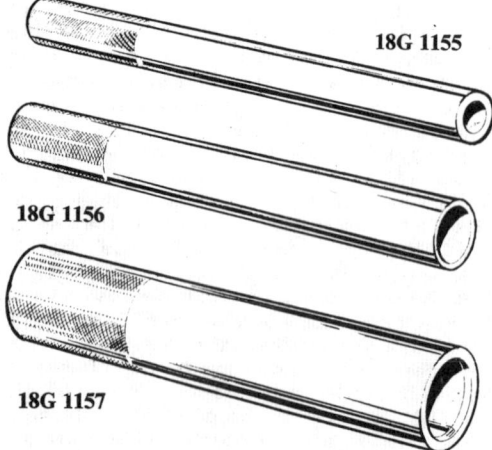

FIG 6:9 Removing and refitting the reverse idler gear

Key to Fig 6:9   8 Idler gear   9 Front cover   10 Plug (fifth/reverse selector rod)   11 Detent plug (fifth/reverse selector)
12 Screw (fifth-speed selector fork)   14 Service Tool (part of 18G.1158)   15 Press to remove selector roo
16 Speedometer pinion assembly   17 Speedometer drive gear and circlip   18 Key   21 Final drive pinion nut and lockwasher
22 Layshaft rear nut and lockwasher   24 Final drive pinion   25 Fifth-speed synchronizer assembly   26 Pin
27 Reverse idler shaft, collar and gear

18G 1155

18G 1156

18G 1157

FIG 6:10 Service Tool 18G.1155 is a third motion shaft remover. Tool 18G.1156 is a third motion shaft replacer and 18G.1157 is a final drive pinion replacer

7 Remove pin 26 from the collar on the reverse idler shaft and separate the parts 27.

Refitting:

Reverse the dismantling operations but note that the oil pump pick-up must be correctly positioned before the fifth-speed gear and synchronizer assembly is fitted. Tighten the layshaft rear nut to a torque of 120 lb ft. When refitting the final drive pinion, support the shaft with Service Tool 18G.1156 and fit the pinion with Tool 18G.1157. The tools are shown in **FIG 6:10**. Tighten the lefthand-threaded nut to a torque of 150 lb ft. When the power unit is restored to the car, refill with the correct quantities of lubricant and coolant.

6:6 Removing and refitting the layshaft

Removing:

1 Remove the power unit (see **Chapter 1**). Remove the transmission assembly as in **Section 6:2**. Remove the reverse idler gear as in **Section 6:5**.

2 Refer to **FIG 6:11** and unlock and remove the layshaft rear nut 4. **This has a lefthand thread.** The layshaft complete with front bearing 5 can now be pulled out

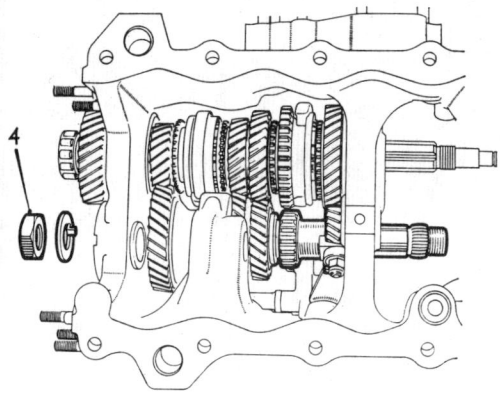

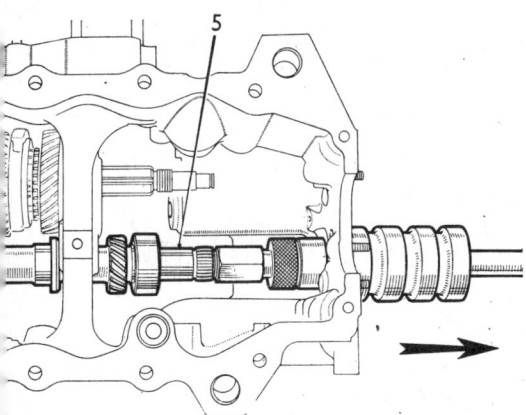

3 Remove ring dowel 8. Move the laygear out of mesh with the fourth-speed gear and clear of the synchronizer teeth as shown at 9. On rod change models push the fifth/reverse selector rod inwards to clear the laygear then move the laygear out of mesh with the fourth-speed gear.

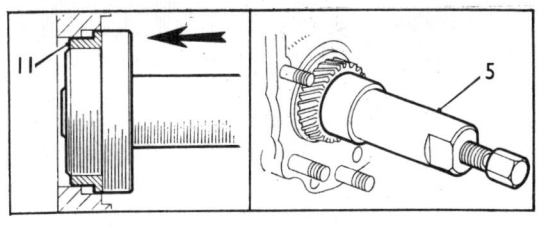

FIG 6:11 Removing the layshaft. The layshaft rear nut 4 has a lefthand thread. In the lower view an impulse extractor is shown removing the layshaft 5

The illustration shows this being done with an impulse extractor 18G.284 and an adapter 18G.284.AE screwed onto the end of the shaft. The extractor is a weight which can be slid rapidly along a shaft until it reaches a stop at the outer end. This impulse provides the extracting force. The tools are shown in FIG 6:13.

Refitting:

Reverse the order of dismantling. Use new lockwashers and gaskets and tighten the layshaft rear nut to a torque of 120 lb ft. Fill the power unit with the correct quantity and grade of lubricant and fill the cooling system.

6:7 Removing and refitting the first motion shaft

Removing:

Refer to FIG 6:12. To recognize the parts it may also be useful to refer to FIG 6:4. Follow these instructions:
Remove the power unit (see Chapter 1). Remove the transmission assembly (see Section 6:2). Remove the reverse idler gear (see Section 6:5). Remove the layshaft (see Section 6:6).
Remove spigot bearing 5, using the tools shown in FIG 6:7. Unlock and remove nut 6. This has a lefthand thread. Remove input gear 7.

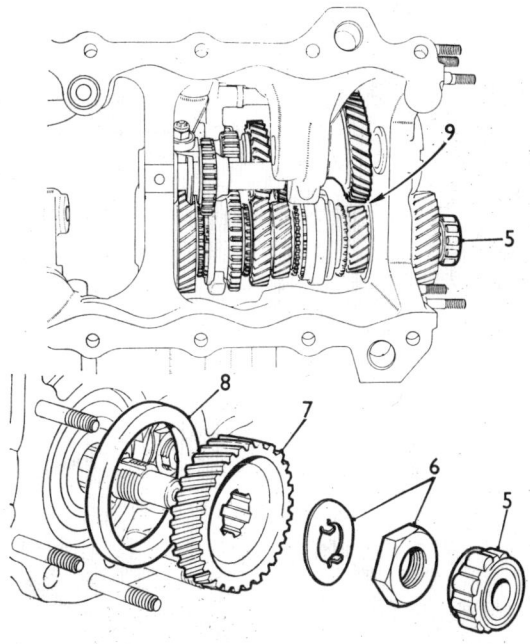

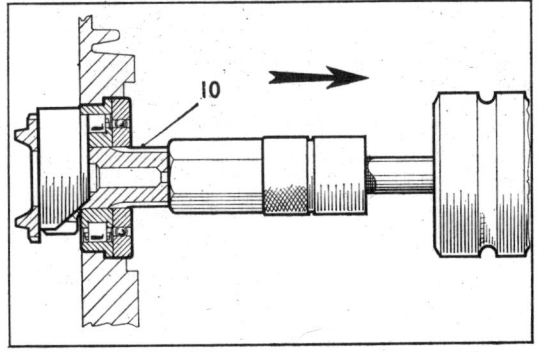

FIG 6:12 Removing and refitting the first motion shaft

Key to Fig 6:12   5 Spigot bearing (top view, Service Tools 18G.705 and 705.H in use)   6 First motion shaft nut and lockwasher (nut has lefthand thread)   7 Input gear   8 Ring dowel   9 Laygear clear of synchronizer   10 Impulse extractor removing shaft and bearing   11 Refitting bearing outer race

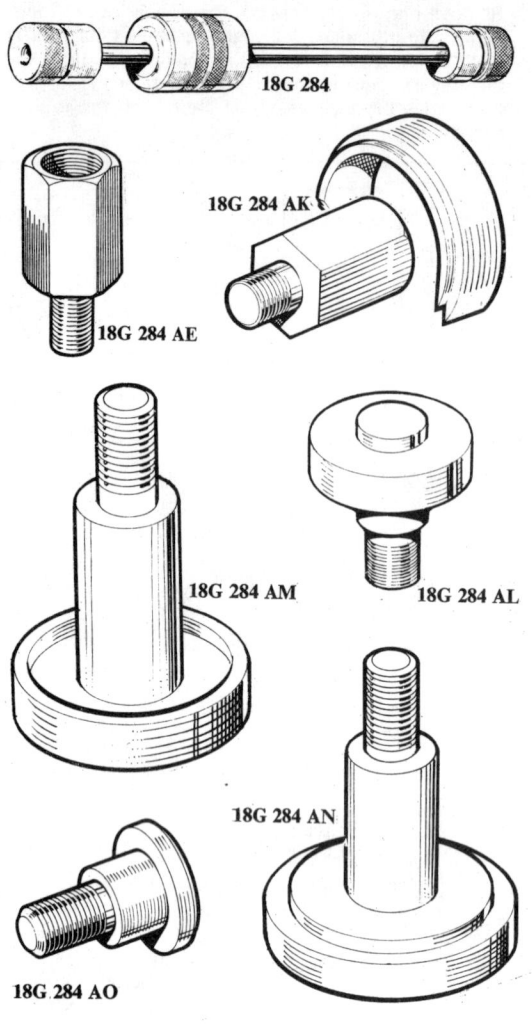

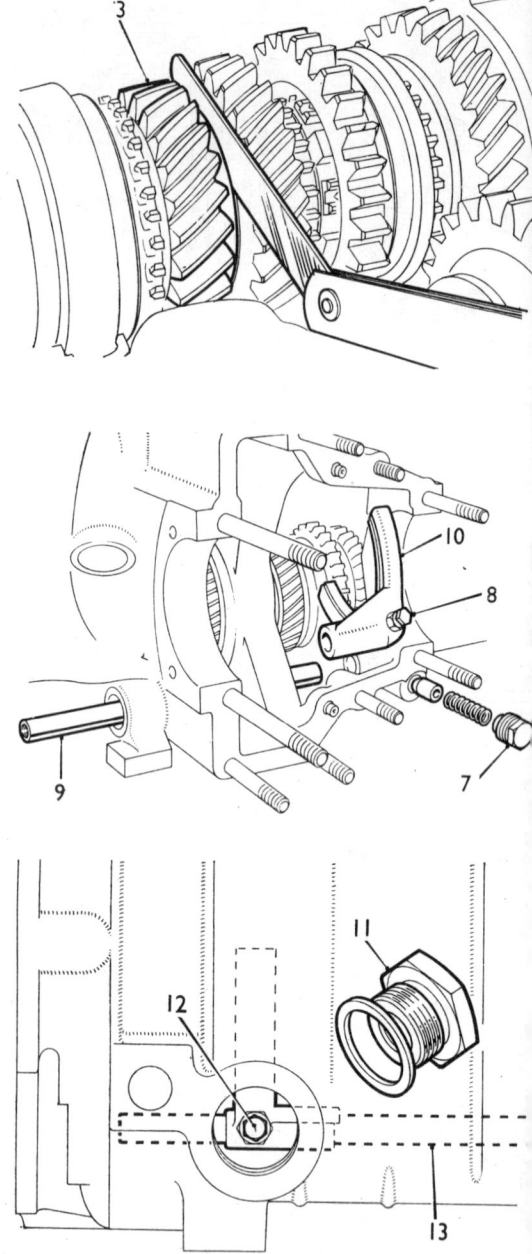

FIG 6:13   Service Tool 18G.284 is an impulse extractor and is the basic tool

Key to Fig 6:13   18G.284.AE is layshaft remover adapter
18G.284.AK is first motion shaft and bearing remover
18G.284.AL is layshaft ballbearing remover/replacer
18G.284.AM is third motion shaft ballbearing remover/replacer
18G.284.AN is third motion shaft roller bearing outer race replacer
18G.284.AO is idler gear roller bearing remover/replacer

4   Remove the first motion shaft 10 complete with bearings and the outer race of the roller bearing. Use Service Tools 18G.284 and 18G.284.AK, as illustrated in **FIG 6:13**.

Refitting:

Using a large-diameter drift, fit the roller bearing outer race 11. Reverse the rest of the dismantling procedure, using new lockwashers and gaskets. Refill with the correct quantities of lubricant and coolant.

FIG 6:14   Removing third motion shaft (see a᷿ FIG 6:15). Top view shows feeler gauge checking e᷿ float of first- and second-speed gears

Key to Fig 6:14   3 Checking end float (third-speed a᷿ first- and second-speed gears)   7 Detent plug (first- a᷿ second-speed)   8 Fork retaining screw (first/seco᷿ selector)   9 First/second selector rod   10 First/seco᷿ selector fork   11 Access plug (third/fourth selector fo᷿ 12 Retaining screw (third/fourth selector fork)   13 Selec᷿ rod

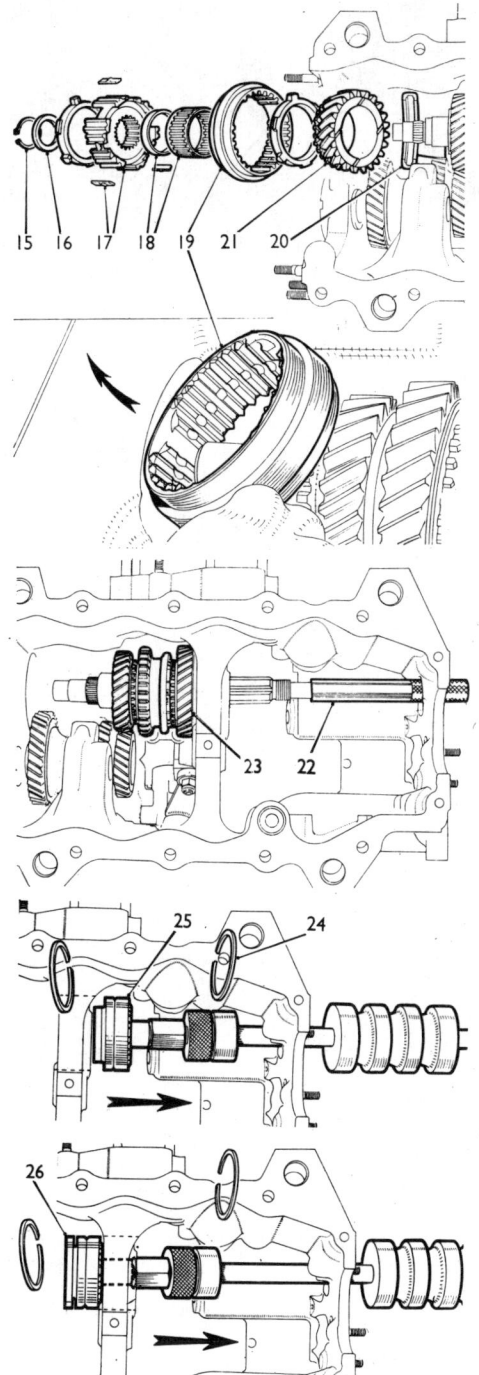

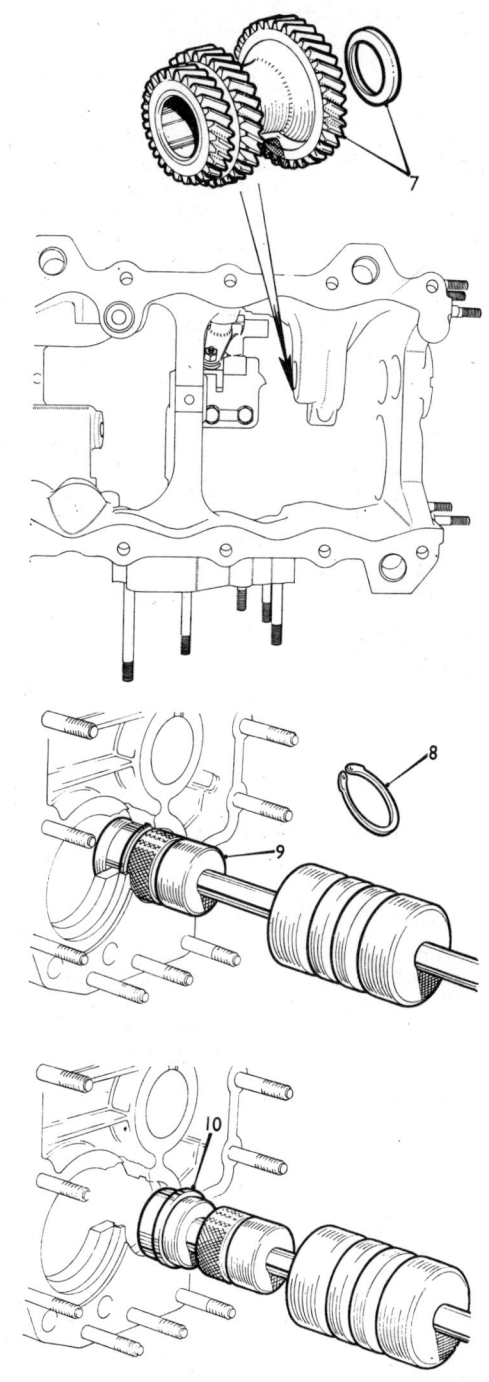

FIG 6:15 Removing and refitting third motion shaft

Key to Fig 6:15   15 Circlip   16 Spacer
17 Synchronizer hub and keys   18 Spacer and bearing
29 Synchronizer collar or sleeve   20 third/fourth selector
fork   21 Third-speed gear   22 Service Tool 18G.1155
23 First-/second-speed synchronizer and gears   24 Bearing
circlip   25 Impulse extractor removing bearings
26 Refitting bearings

**FIG 6:16   Removing and refitting laygear and layshaft
rear bearing**

Key to Fig 6:16   7 Laygear and spacer   8 Circlip
(layshaft rear bearing)   9 Impulse extractor withdrawing
bearing   10 Refitting bearing

6:8 Removing and refitting the third motion shaft
Removing:

1 Remove the power unit (see **Chapter 1**). Remove the transmission assembly (see **Section 6:2**). Refer to **FIG 6:14**.

2 Check the end float between the third-speed gear 3 and the shoulder on the shaft. The correct end float is .005 to .008 inch. Note that the illustration shows end float checking of the first- and second-speed gears.

3 Remove the reverse idler gear (see **Section 6:5**). Remove the layshaft (see **Section 6:6**). Remove the first motion shaft (see **Section 6:7**).

4 Remove the first-/second-speed detent plug 7. Unlock and slacken the first/second fork retaining screw 8. Pull out the selector rod 9 with the tool shown in **FIG 6:6**. Remove the fork 10.

5 Remove the third/fourth selector fork access plug 11 and slacken the retaining screw 12. Remove the third/fourth selector rod and check the end float of the first- and second-speed gears as shown.

6 Refer to **FIG 6:15** and remove circlip 15 from the end of the shaft. Withdraw spacer 16. Withdraw hub 17, collecting the three synchronizer keys. Look out for the plungers and springs. Withdraw the spacer and bearing 18 from inside gear 21.

7 Turn and tilt collar or sleeve 19 until one of the internal cut-aways permits removal over the end of the shaft. Remove fork 20 and gear 21.

8 Drive the shaft rearwards from the casing using Service Tool 18G.1155 as shown at 22. The tool is illustrated in **FIG 6:10**. Remove the first-/second-speed synchronizer and gears 23.

9 Remove circlip 24 which retains the third motion shaft bearings 25. Extract the bearings by using Service Tools 18G.284 and 18G.284.AM as illustrated in **FIG 6:13**.

Refitting:

1 Refit the bearings and circlip as shown at 26. Use Service Tools 18G.284, 18G.284.AM and 18G.284.AN as illustrated in **FIG 6:13**.

2 Position the first-/second-speed synchronizer and gears in the casing. Push the third motion shaft through the gears and synchronizers until it enters the bearings. Drive the shaft into the bearings with Service Tool 18G.1156, supporting the shaft with 18G.1157. The tools are shown in **FIG 6:10**.

3 Fit the third-speed gear with its bearing and spacer. Fit the third/fourth selector fork and synchronizer assembly. Select a suitable spacer 16 to eliminate end float of the synchronizer hub 17. Spacers are available as follows:

Spacer thickness	Identification colour
.0965 to .0975 inch	Self-finish
.097 to .098 inch	Black
.099 to .100 inch	Orange
.101 to .102 inch	Blue
.103 to .104 inch	Green

Fit the selected spacer and fit the circlip.

4 Reverse the rest of the dismantling instructions using new lockwashers and gaskets. When the power unit has been refitted, add the required quantities of lubricant and coolant.

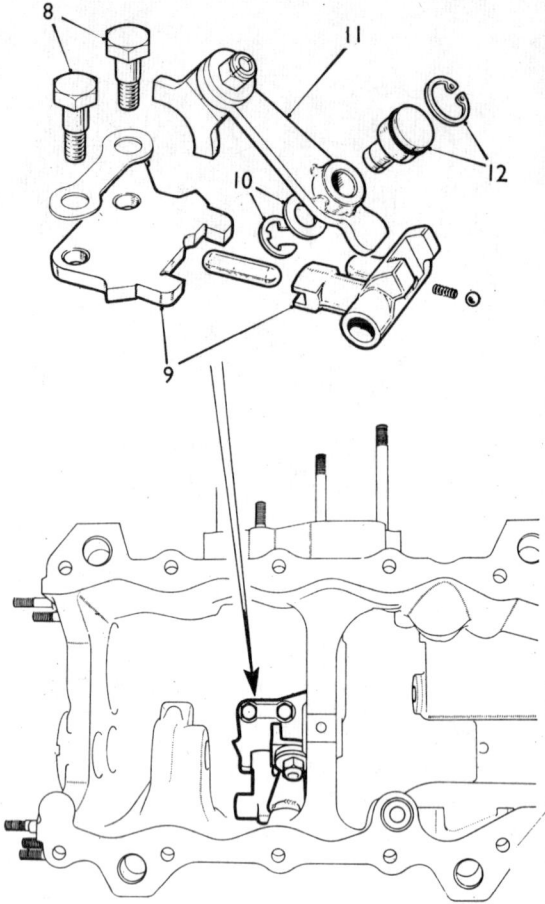

FIG 6:17 Removing and refitting reverse selector assembly

Key to Fig 6:17   8 Securing bolts   9 Interlock plate and interlock assembly   10 Pivot C-clip and washer   11 Selector lever and fork   12 Pivot, circlip and O-ring

6:9 Removing and refitting laygear
Removing:

This may be done after removing the third motion shaft. On rod change models remove the first/second and third/fourth selector forks. On cable change models, withdraw the fifth/reverse selector rod using Tool 18G.1158. Remove the access plug and withdraw the third/fourth selector rod.

Lift out the laygear and spacer 7 in **FIG 6:16**.

Refitting:

Reverse the dismantling sequence, fitting new lockwashers and gaskets. Refill with the correct quantities of lubricant and coolant.

6:10 The layshaft rear bearing
Removing:

Repeat all the operations for removing the laygear and

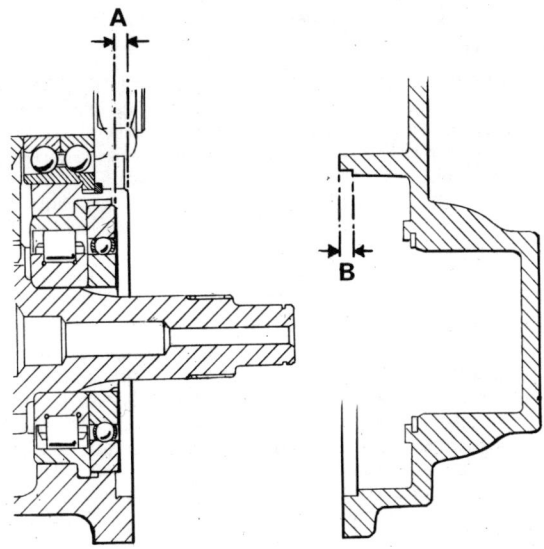

FIG 6:18 Measuring the recesses for the ring dowel which locates the transmission casing and the flywheel housing. **A** is the depth from face of bearing to face of casing, **B** is depth of recess in flywheel housing

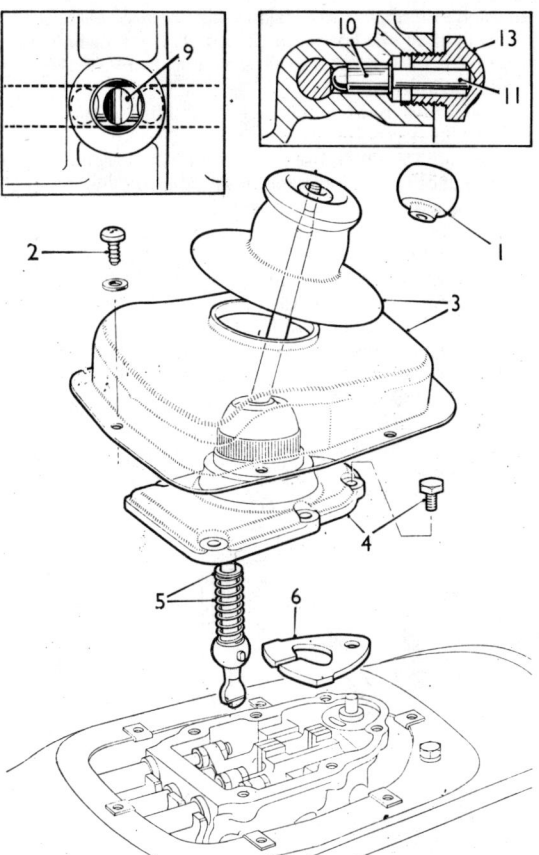

then remove circlip 8 from the layshaft rear bearing as shown in **FIG 6:16**. Withdraw the bearing using Service Tools 18G.284 and 18G.284.AL as indicated at 9. The tools are illustrated in **FIG 6:13**.

Refitting:

Refit the bearing using the same Service Tools, as shown at 10. Reverse all the dismantling operations and refill with the correct quantities of lubricant and coolant when the power unit has been refitted.

6:11 The reverse selector assembly

Removing:

Remove all parts covered by operations 1 and 2 in **Section 6:9**. Refer to **FIG 6:17** and do the following:
1 Remove bolts 8 from the selector assembly. Remove the interlock plate and interlock assembly 9.
2 Remove the C-clip and washer 10 from the selector lever pivot 12. Remove the selector lever and fork 11.
3 Remove the circlip from pivot 12 and withdraw it from the casing together with its O-ring.

Refitting:

Reverse all the dismantling operations using new lockwashers and gaskets. Use Service Tool 18G.1158 (see **FIG 6:6**) to retain the ball and spring in the interlock bore when refitting the selector rod. Refill with the correct quantities of lubricant and coolant.

6:12 The ring dowel (first motion shaft bearing)

The ring dowel is part 24 in **FIG 6:3** and its purpose is to keep the transmission casing and the flywheel housing in correct alignment. When a new or reconditioned trans-

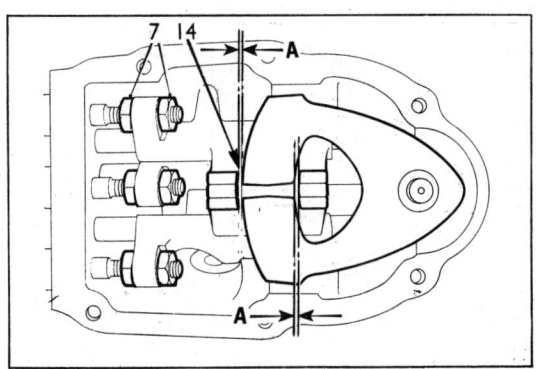

FIG 6:19 Adjusting changespeed cables. **A** indicates equal clearance on either side of interlock

Key to Fig 6:19   1 Gearlever knob   2 Control cover screw   3 Control cover and gaiter   4 Control unit cover and bolt   5 Spring and washer   6 Interlock 7 Cable adjusting nuts   9 Centre (neutral) detent groove in selector rod central in plunger pocket   10 Detent plunger   11 Spacer rod (from 18G.1158)   13 Detent plug   14 Three selector jaws in alignment

mission assembly, transmission casing or flywheel housing is being fitted, the correct thickness of ring dowel must be used. To check for this thickness, refer to **FIG 6:18** and do the following:

1 Make sure that the bearings for the first motion shaft are fully home in their housings.
2 Measure the depth from the face of the bearing to the face of casing as indicated at 'A'. Measure the depth of the recess in the flywheel housing at 'B'.
3 Add 'A' and 'B' together and then add a further .007 inch to allow for the compressed thickness of a new flywheel housing gasket. **It is essential to fit a genuine manufacturer's gasket to ensure that the calculations are accurate.** Then select a dowel which is the same thickness as the three dimensions which have been added together. Dowels are available as follows:
.337 to .339 inch
.339 to .341 inch
.341 to .343 inch
.343 to .345 inch
.345 to .347 inch

6:13 The changespeed control and cables

Adjusting:

If the adjustment of the cables is incorrect it could bring about faulty gear selection and possible damage to the synchronizers and gears. The cables must always be adjusted after any disconnection or removal of the controls or the cables. To adjust, proceed as follows:

1 Refer to **FIG 6:19**. Select neutral and remove knob 1. Turn back the carpet and remove cover screws 2. Remove the cover and gaiter 3.
2 Remove the control unit cover 4. Remove spring and washer 5 from the lever and disengage the lever from interlock 6.
3 Slacken the cable adjusting nuts 7. Remove the gearbox detent plugs, springs and plungers for each selector rod. These are shown in **FIG 6:3**. Move each selector rod until the neutral (or central) detent groove is centrally positioned with respect to the plunger pocket as indicated at 9. Fit the plungers 10 followed by spacer rods 11. These are part of Service Tool

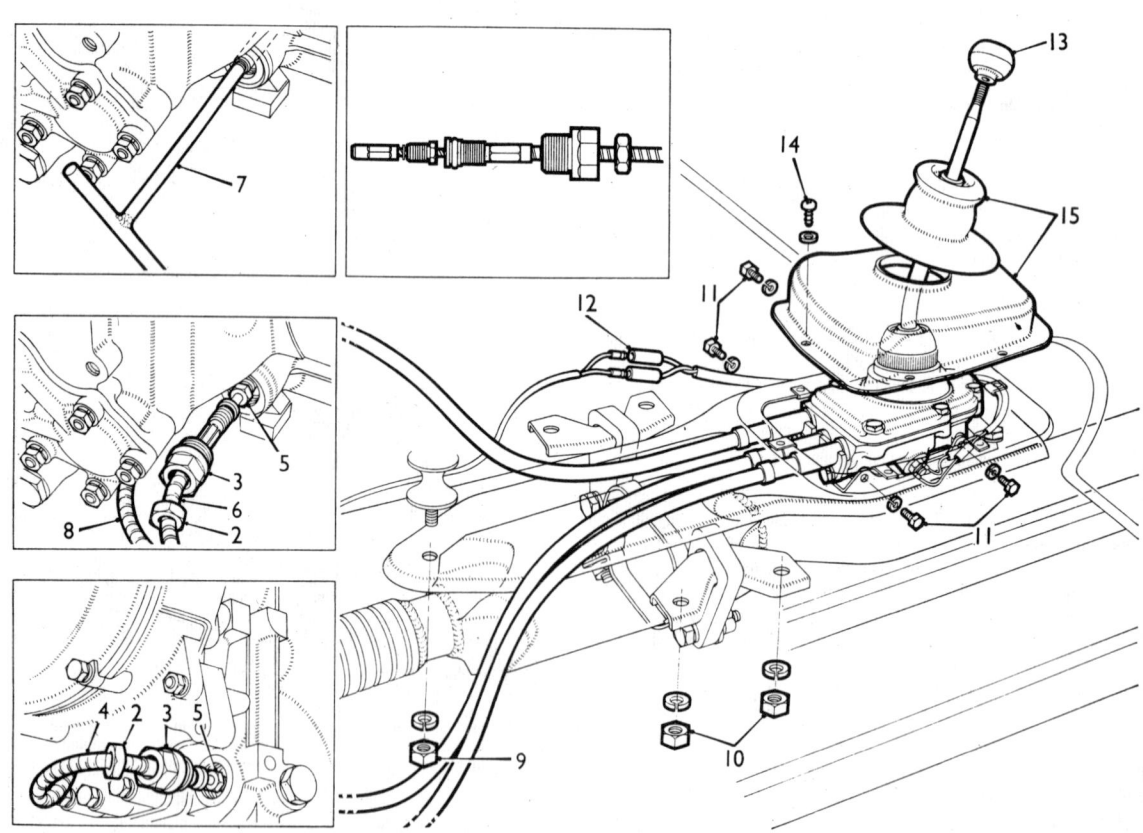

FIG 6:20 Removing and refitting changespeed control and cables

Key to Fig 6:20   2 Cable locknut   3 Outer cable gland nut   4 Fifth/reverse cable   5 Inner cable gland nut
6 First/second cable   7 First/second selector rod in neutral (18G.1158)   8 Third/fourth cable   9 Front nut (heat shield)
10 Silencer mounting nuts   11 Bolts (control to heat shield)   12 Reverse light switch cables   13 Knob
14 Control cover screw   15 Control cover and gaiter

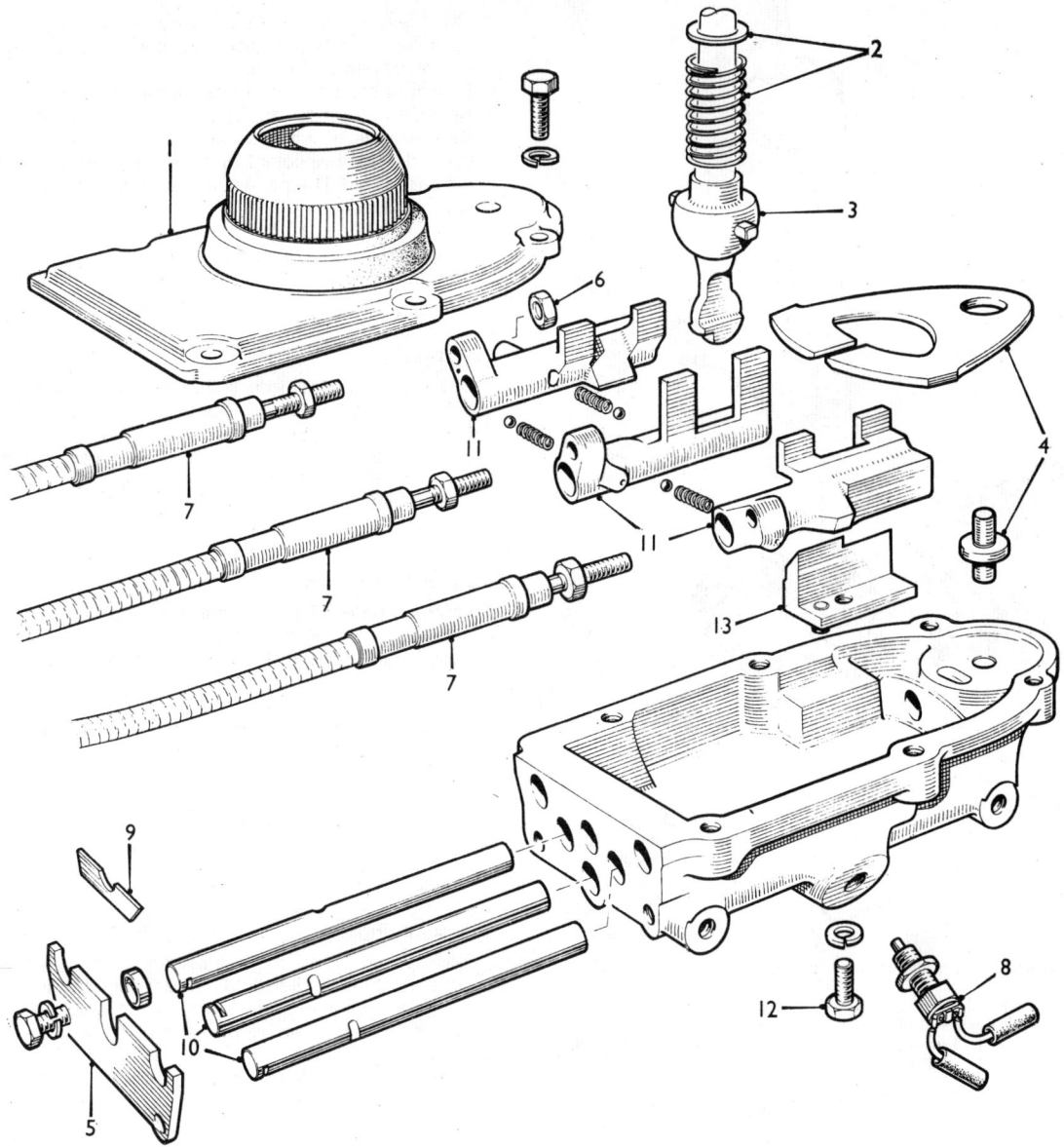

FIG 6:21 Dismantling changespeed control assembly

Key to Fig 6:21   1 Control unit cover   2 Spring and washer   3 Gearlever   4 Interlock and pivot
5 Cable retaining plate   6 Cable inner nuts   7 Cables   8 Reverse light switch   9 Selector shaft retaining plate
10 Selector shafts   11 Selector jaws   12 Bolt for reverse selector stop   13 Reverse stop and dowel

18G.1158 and are $\frac{1}{4}$ inch diameter and 1 inch long. Remove the washers from plugs 13 and screw the plugs in fingertight, thus holding the selector rods accurately in the neutral position.

4 Turn the adjusting nuts 7 until the selector jaws are in line as at 14 and the clearance at 'A' is the same on both sides of the interlock plate. When satisfied, restore all the parts in the reverse sequence to dismantling.

Removing:

1 Refer to **FIG 6:20**. Drain the transmission and unscrew the locking nut 2 from each cable. Unscrew each outer cable gland nut 3.

2 Pull the fifth/reverse cable 4 out of the transmission and unscrew the inner gland nut 5 to detach the cable. Repeat this operation on the first-/second-speed cable 6.

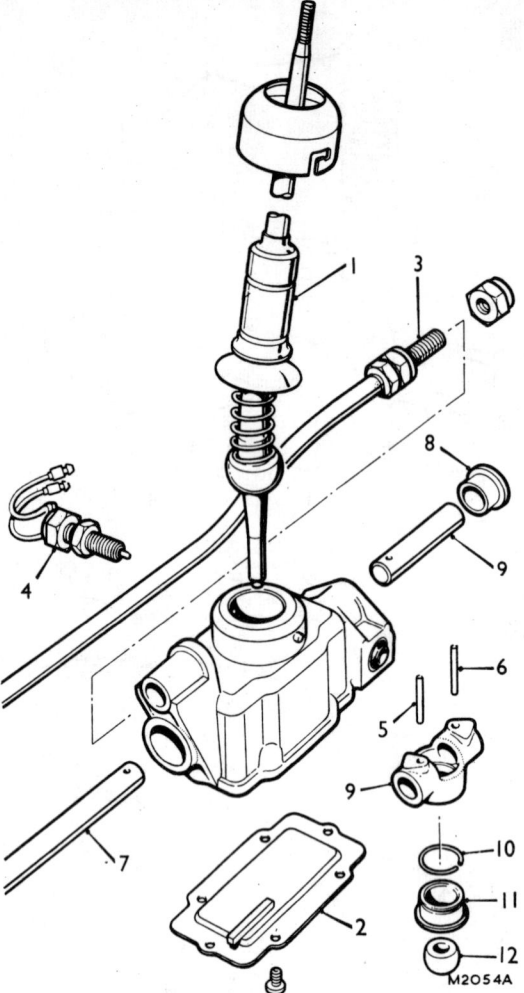

3 Using Service Tool 18G.1158 as illustrated in **FIG 6:6**, push the first-/second-speed selector rod back into the neutral position as indicated at 7.

4 Repeat operation 2 on the third-/fourth-speed cable.

5 Remove nut 9 from the heat shield front mounting. Remove nuts 10 which secure the silencer brackets to the body. Remove bolts 11 which secure the control to the heat shield. Disconnect wiring 12 from the reverse light switch.

6 Remove the knob 13, peel back the carpet and remove cover screws 14. Remove the cover and gaiter 15. Withdraw the control assembly complete with cables.

Refitting:

Reverse operations 1 to 5 and the last sentence of operation 6. Use the Service Tool to pull out each selector rod when connecting the inner cables. When reassembly is complete, adjust the cables as described earlier in this Section and then refill the transmission with the correct quantity of lubricant.

Dismantling the control:

Refer to **FIG 6:21** and do the following:

1 Remove cover 1. Remove spring and washer 2 from the lever. Disengage lever 3 from the interlock, then remove the interlock and pivot 4.

2 Remove cable retaining plate 5 and remove nuts 6 from the inner ends of the cables. Withdraw the cables 7.

3 Remove the reversing light switch 8. Remove the selector shaft retaining plate 9. Withdraw the shafts, collecting the balls and springs shown between the selector jaws 11. Remove the latter.

4 Remove the reverse selector stop 13 by unscrewing bolt 12. Note the dowel.

Reassembling:

Reverse the dismantling procedure, using part of Service Tool 18G.1158 to hold the balls and springs in the selector jaws while the rods are refitted. A short piece of bar of the same diameter as the selector rod would make an effective substitute.

When assembly is completed, adjust the cables as instructed earlier in this Section.

6:14 Remote control (rod gearchange)

This is illustrated in **FIG 6:22** and may be dismantled as follows:

Release the changespeed lever 1. Remove the bottom cover 2, the steady rod 3 and the reverse light switch 4.

Move the extension rod eye to the rear and remove the pin 5.

Move the extension rod eye forwards and remove the pin 6, then withdraw the extension rod 7.

Remove the plug 8 then withdraw the support rod and the extension rod eye 9. Release the circlip 10. Remove the ball-end bearing seat 11 and the ball end bearing 12.

Reassembly is the reverse of the above, noting that the bottom cover is fitted with the reverse stop towards the front. Always use new pins 5 and 6.

FIG 6:22 Components of rod gearchange remote control

Key to Fig 6:22 1 Lever 2 Bottom cover 3 Steady rod 4 Reverse light switch 5, 6 Pins 7 Extension rod 8 Plug 9 Extension rod eye 10 Circlip 11 Ball-end bearing seat 12 Ball-end bearing

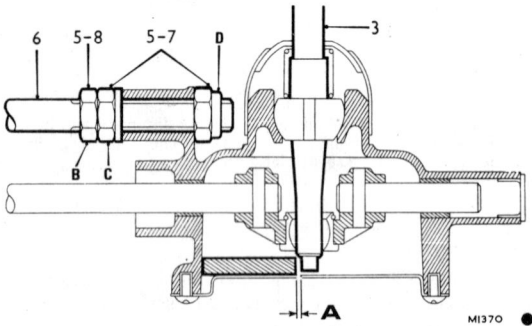

FIG 6:23 Adjusting rod gearchange remote control

Key to Fig 6:23 3 Gearlever A .03 inch (.76 mm) B Front locknut C Rear locknut D Adjusting nut 6 Steady rod

Adjustment (see Fig 6:23):

Disconnect the wiring and slacken the reverse light switch, then hold the gearlever in the neutral position between fifth and reverse gear position 3.

Check the free movement at A by gently pulling the lever to the rear until contact with the reverse stop is felt. This should be .030 inch, corresponding to a knob movement of $\frac{3}{8}$ to $\frac{1}{2}$ inch.

Slacken the steady rod nuts 5 and adjust the length of the steady rod to obtain the correct free movement. Increasing the length of the steady rod will reduce free movement and vice versa. Tighten the two nuts C and D to a torque of 25 lb ft and the front locknut B to 35 lb ft, not forgetting to hold nut C while tightening nut B.

Adjusting reverse light switch:

This should be done either if the switch fails to operate correctly or if the controls have been reset.

Select reverse gear and disconnect the wiring to the switch. Slacken the locknut, screw in the switch as far as possible then unscrew for two complete turns and reconnect the wires.

Switch on the ignition and screw the switch in until the reversing lights are lit, then screw in for one more complete turn. Tighten the locknut and switch off the ignition.

6:15 Reverse selector assembly (rod gearchange)

This is slightly different from that fitted when cable gearchange is used as will be seen from **FIG 6:24**. Dismantling is carried out as follows:

Remove from the gearbox casing the reverse idler gear, layshaft, first and third motion shafts, first/second and third/fourth selector forks and the laygear and spacer.

Rotate the fifth/reverse selector rod 180 deg. so that the flat face will clear the reverse arm 9.

With tool 18G.1158 behind the plain end of the selector rod 10, press the retainer into the interlock 11 so that the ball and spring are retained by the tool, then withdraw the selector rod.

Remove the two bolts 12 securing the selector assembly. Remove the plate and interlock assembly 13. Then remove the C-clip and washer 14 and withdraw the selector lever 15, complete with fork.

Remove the circlip 16 and withdraw the selector pivot.

Reassembly is a reversal of the above procedure not omitting to use new gaskets and lockwashers as applicable.

6:16 Interlock spool and bellcrank levers

These items are perculiar to the rod gearchange installation and are shown in the exploded diagram of **FIG 6:25**.

Dismantle the gearbox up to the selector forks (see **Section 6:15**) then remove the nut 8 and rotate the interlocking spool anticlockwise and lift off the bellcrank levers assembly 9.

Remove the bush 10 and the retaining collar 11, when the spool 12 can be withdrawn from inside the transmission. The pivot post 13 and O-ring are removed by means of a drift.

Reassembly is the reverse of the above, with particular attention to the following points:

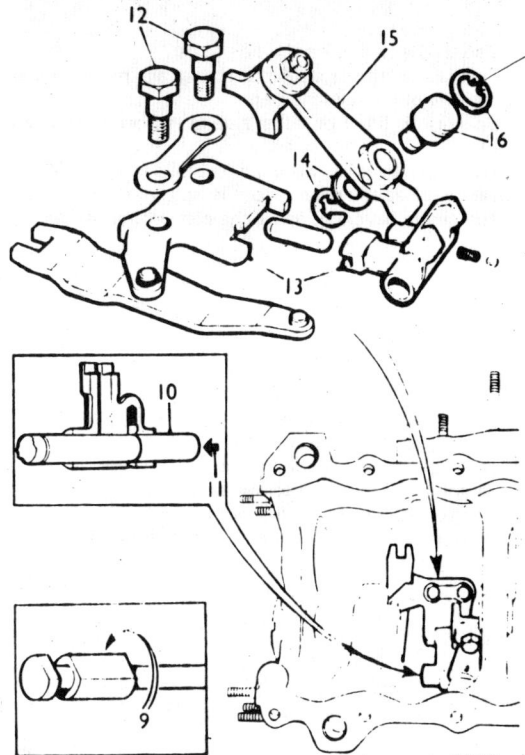

FIG 6:24 Reverse selector assembly, rod gearchange

Key to Fig 6:24   9 5th/Reverse selector rod   10 18G.1158   11 Interlock   12 Bolts   13 Plate/Interlock assembly   14 C-clip and washer   15 Selector lever   16 Pivot and circlip

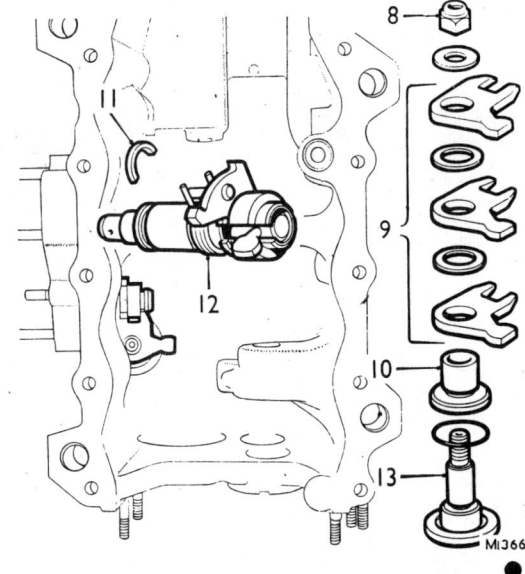

FIG 6:25 Interlock spool and bellcrank levers, rod gearchange

Key to Fig 6:25   8 Nut   9 Interlocking spool and bellcrank assembly   10 Bush   11 Retaining collar   12 Spool assembled   13 Pivot post

Use a new O-ring on the pivot post.

Ensure that the legs of the spring are positioned on either side of the locating peg.

Spacers are fitted on either side of the centre bellcrank lever.

The upper lever has the chamfer on its top face and the lower lever has the chamfer on its bottom face.

The centre bellcrank has a chamfer on both faces.

6:17 Fault diagnosis

(a) Jumping out of gear

1 Broken spring behind selector rod ball
2 Worn grooves in selector rod
3 Worn synchromesh coupling dogs
4 Selector fork securing screw loose
5 Control cable out of adjustment
6 Worn selector fork or synchromesh sleeve

(b) Noisy transmission

1 Insufficient lubricant or wrong grade
2 Excessive end float of gears on third motion shaft
3 Excessive end float of third/fourth synchronizer
4 Excessive end float and wear of primary gearing
5 Worn gears, shafts or bearings
6 Incorrect thickness of ring dowel

(c) Difficulty in engaging gears

1 Check (a)
2 Worn synchromesh cones or baulk rings
3 Incorrect clutch adjustment

(d) Oil leaks

1 Oil feed O-ring out of position
2 Damaged joint washers
3 Faulty joint faces
4 Ineffective oil seals
5 Leaking cable glands

CHAPTER 7

THE FINAL DRIVE AND DRIVE SHAFTS

7:1 Description
7:2 Removing and refitting drive shafts
7:3 Servicing the differential assembly

7:4 Servicing drive shafts
7:5 Fault diagnosis

7:1 Description

Examination of **FIG 6:1** in the preceding chapter will show that the final drive pinion 31 meshes with a crownwheel which is not identified but which is carried by bearings on a centre line coincident with the top line of numbering. From this it will be readily understood how **FIG 7:1** stands in relation to the final drive pinion. Here the crownwheel is part 11. Seen in perspective in **FIG 7:2** the crownwheel is part 6.

Bolted to the crownwheel is differential cage 10, this assembly being carried on ballbearings 4 in housing 1. Inside the differential cage are small bevel pinions 7 freely mounted on pin 5 and meshing with larger bevel gears 9 which are splined to drive shafts 13. When both road wheels offer the same resistance to traction, the differential assembly turns as a unit and both drive shafts transmit equal power at equal speeds. If one wheel must turn at a different speed from the other, as it does when cornering or skidding, the difference in relative speeds of gears 9 is accommodated by the turning of pinions 7.

The short drive shafts 13 end in pot joints in housings 15. These are the inner universal joints for the outer drive shafts 26. The outer shafts also carry constant velocity joints 19 to 24 to permit angular displacement of the front hubs and road wheels when steering deflections are required.

7:2 Removing and refitting drive shafts

Removing:

1 Refer to **FIG 7:3**. Remove the front hub as instructed in the next chapter.
2 Disengage the drive shaft 3 from the differential by using Service Tool 18G.1146. The illustration shows the tool and also the position 2 which it occupies when in use.
3 Withdraw the drive shaft assembly.

Refitting:

Reverse the dismantling order, ensuring that the shaft fully engages the differential gear circlip 12 in **FIG 7:1**. Then refit the hub.

7:3 Servicing the differential assembly

Removing:

Remove the power unit as described in **Chapter 1**, refer to **FIG 7:4** and do the following:

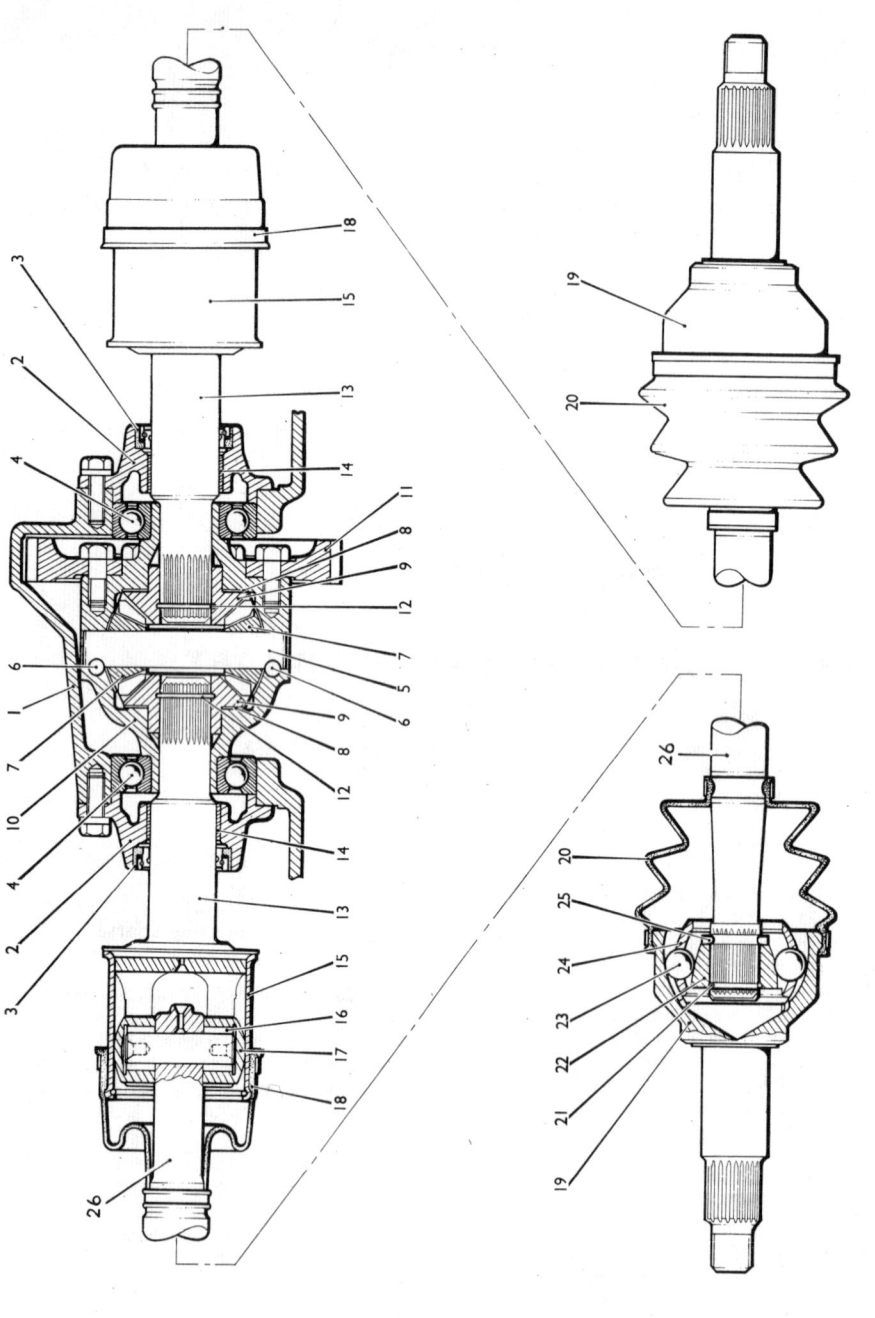

FIG 7:1   A section through the final drive. Crownwheel **11** picks up the drive from the gearbox

Key to Fig 7:1

1 Differential housing	2 Differential side cover	3 Oil seal	4 Differential support bearing	5 Differential pin	6 Roll pin
7 Differential pinion	8 Thrust washer	9 Differential gear	10 Differential cage	11 Crownwheel	12 Circlip	13 Drive shaft	14 Bush
15 Pot joint housing	16 Needle bearing	17 Bearing cap	18 Bearing cap	19 Constant velocity joint housing	20 Boot for constant velocity joint
21 Circlip	22 Inner race	23 Bearing balls	24 Cage	25 Circlip	

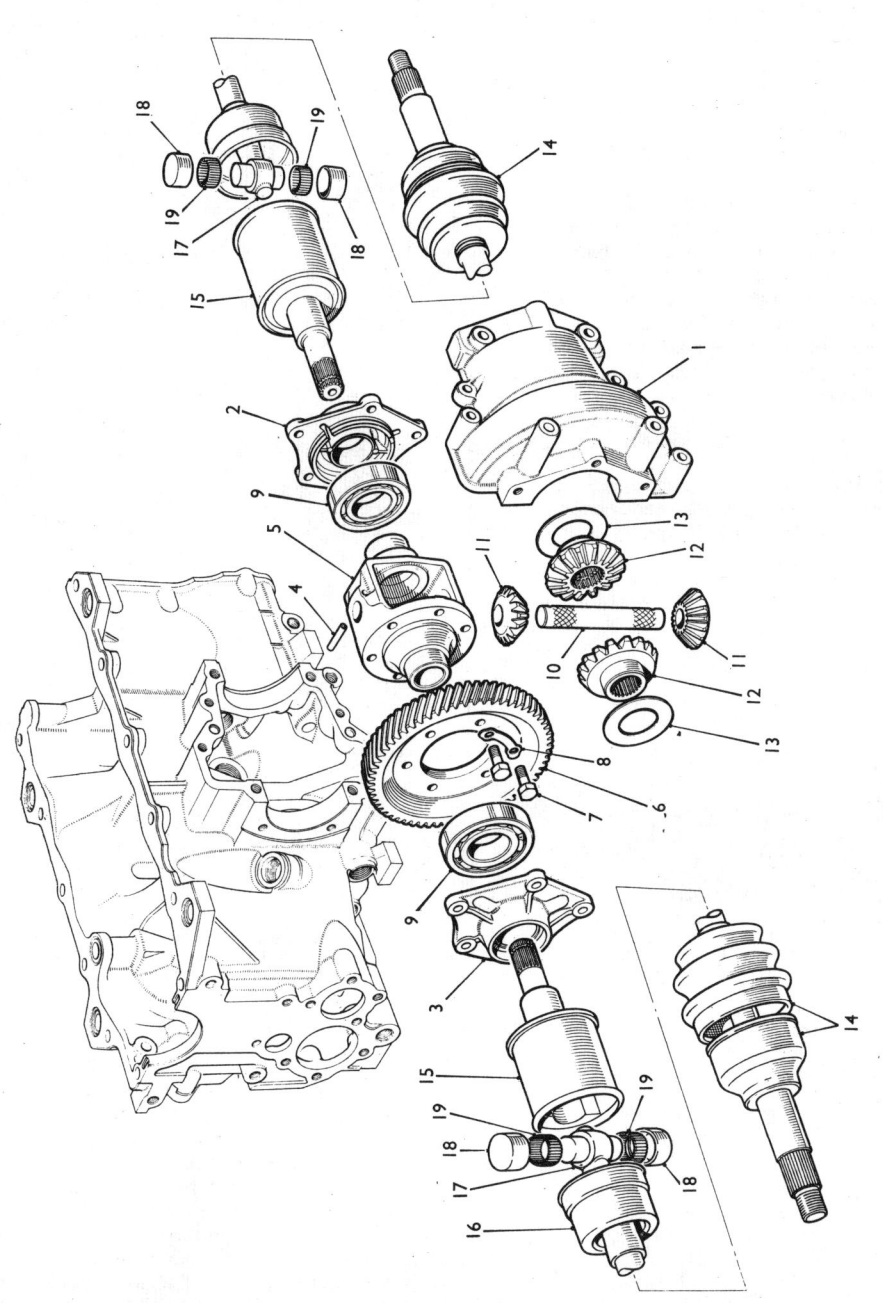

FIG 7:2 Components of the final drive. Note that there are dished thrust washers behind differential pinions 11

Key to Fig 7:2 1 Differential housing 2 Differential side cover—RH 3 Differential side cover—LH 4 Roll pin for differential pin 5 Differential cage
6 Crownwheel 7 Bolt for crownwheel 8 Lockwasher for bolt 9 Differential carrier bearing 10 Differential pin 11 Differential pinion 12 Differential gear
13 Thrust washer 14 Constant-velocity joint 15 Pot joint housing 16 Boot for pot joint 17 Shaft 18 Bearing cap 19 Needle bearing

1 Remove both side covers 2, being careful to collect any shims which may be fitted under the lefthand cover.
2 Unlock and remove the differential housing nuts 3. Remove the housing 4.
3 Withdraw the differential assembly 5, which will come away complete with bearings.

Dismantling:

1 Refer to **FIG 7:2** and withdraw the differential carrier bearings 9 with a suitable puller. Mark the crownwheel 6 and cage 5 for correct reassembly.
2 Unlock and remove the crownwheel bolts 7. Remove the crownwheel.
3 Drive out the two roll pins 4, followed by the pin 10. Remove the pinions 11, the gears 12 and thrust washers 13. Although not illustrated, there are part-spherical thrust washers behind the two pinions 11.

Clean and dry the bearings an check for slackness and roughness. Check the gear teeth and if worn, renew in mated pairs. Renew worn thrust washers and gears with worn splines. Renew the seals in the side covers if oil leakage has been troublesome.

Reassembling:

1 Using Service Tool 18G.1163, fit new circlips into the differential gears. Press a circlip 9 into the ring and then use the drift to push the circlip into its groove in the splines, as shown in **FIG 7:5**.
2 Reverse the dismantling procedure but note that the larger diameter ballbearing is fitted on the crownwheel side of the differential assembly.

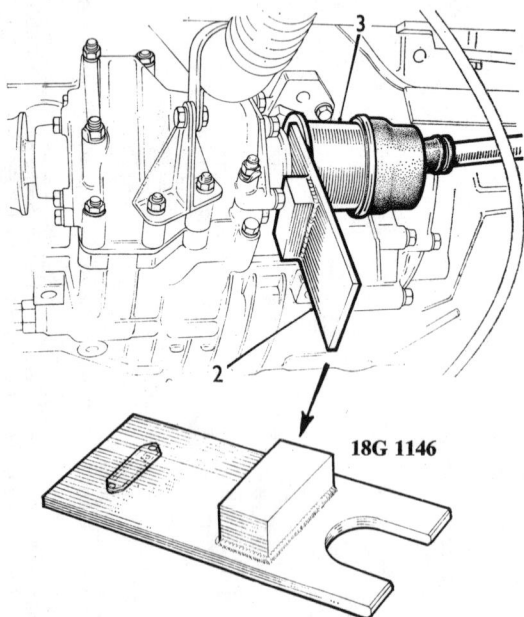

FIG 7:3 Removing a drive shaft from the differential using Service Tool 18G.1146. The tool is in use at 2, the drive shaft assembly is 3

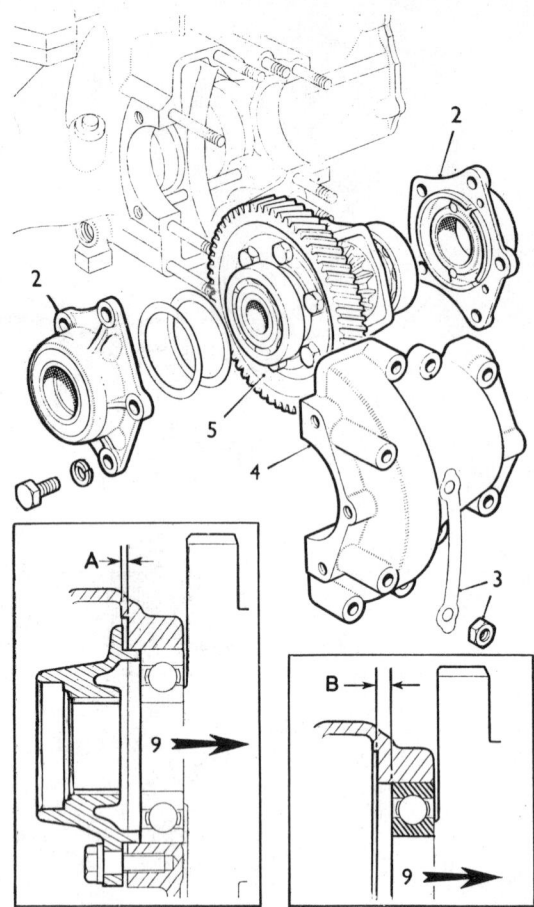

FIG 7:4 Removing the differential assembly. The insets show two methods for determining bearing preload

Key to Fig 7:4   2 Differential side cover
3 Differential housing nut and lockwasher   4 Differential housing   5 Crownwheel and differential assembly
9 Direction for drifting outer race of lefthand bearing

Refitting:

1 Refit the assembly into the transmission casing, but positioned slightly towards the righthand side. Fit the housing and the nuts and lockwashers, but tighten the nuts only just enough to hold the bearings firmly in place. It is essential that the differential assembly can move laterally when the righthand side cover is being fitted.
2 Use a new gasket and refit the righthand side cover, tightening the nuts to a torque of 18 lb ft.
3 With a tubular drift which will press on the outer race of the lefthand bearing, drive the differential assembly fully to the right to ensure that the righthand bearing is in complete contact with the righthand side cover, as indicated by the arrow at 9 in the insets.
4 Check the bearing preload as follows:

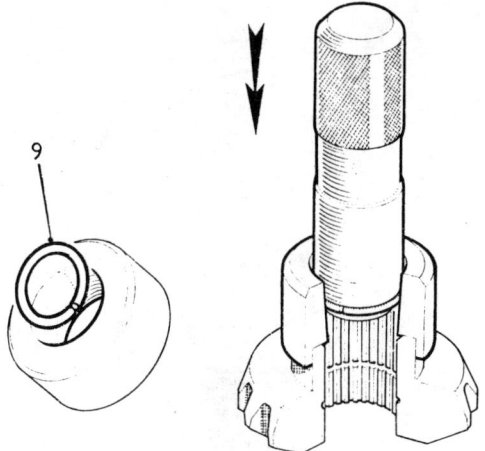

FIG 7:5 Service Tool 18G.1163 in use when fitting a circlip **9** into a differential gear

First method:

1 Fit the lefthand side cover without a gasket. Tighten the cover bolts very carefully a little at a time in a diagonal sequence. The object is to ensure full contact of the spigot on the cover with the outer race of the bearing without applying any preload. The cover must not be distorted.

2 Refer to the lower lefthand inset and use feeler gauges to check the gap between the cover flange and the differential housing as indicated at 'A'. If the gap varies, adjust by means of the fixing bolts but do so without distorting the cover flange. The readings should be taken in three places and should be the same. If no gap exists, remove the cover and add a known thickness of shims in order to produce a clearance. This thickness of shims is used in the calculations for preload.

3 The compressed thickness of the side cover gasket is .008 inch. The required preload on the bearings is .001 to .002 inch. To achieve this, the clearance between the cover flange and the casing must be the sum of the two dimensions. This is .008 inch + .001 or .002 inch which gives .009 inch or .010 inch. Thus, if the measured clearance is .007 inch, the shim thickness required will be .002 or .003 inch. Shims are available in these two thicknesses.

4 After the lefthand cover has been secured by tightening the nuts to a torque of 18 lb ft, tighten the housing nuts to a torque of 18 lb ft for the $\frac{5}{16}$ inch nuts and 25 lb ft for the $\frac{3}{8}$ inch nuts and lock them.

Second method:

1 Refer to the lower righthand inset in **FIG 7:4** and measure distance 'B' with a depth gauge. This is the distance between the lefthand side cover face of the differential housing and the face of the bearing outer race.

2 Compare this measurement with that in the following table and select the appropriate shims.

Measured depth	Shim thickness
.271 to .272 inch	.004 inch

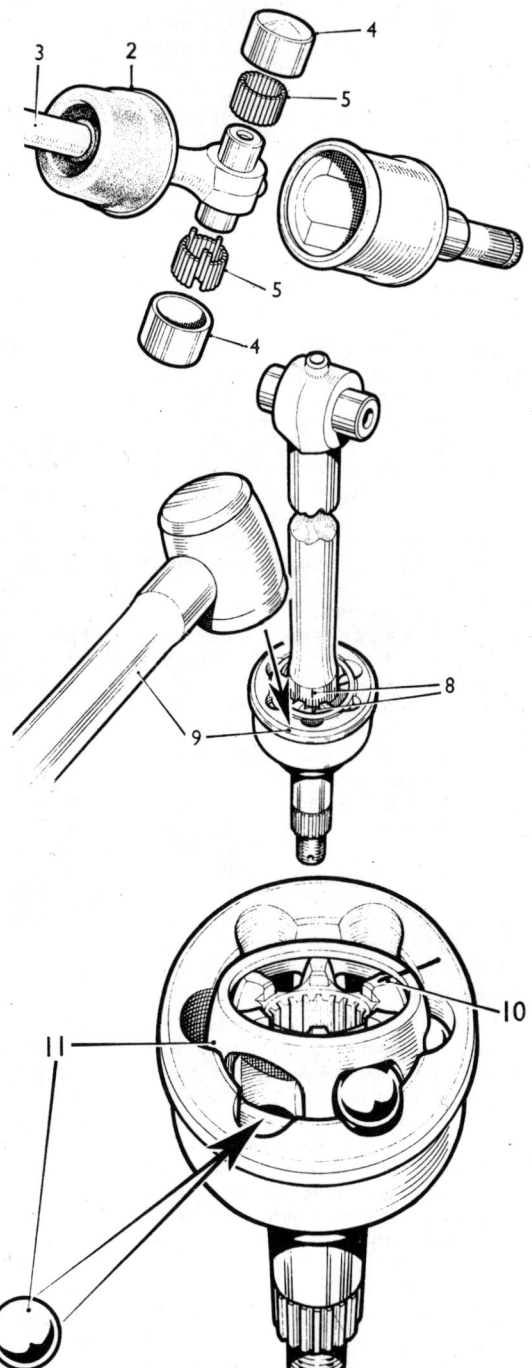

FIG 7:6   Dismantling drive shafts (see also FIG 7:7)

Key to Fig 7:6   2 Rubber boot   3 Drive shaft
4 Bearing cap   5 Needle rollers   8 Alignment marks
on constant-velocity joint   9 Striking outer race to free
shaft from retainer ring   10 Alignment marks on inner and
outer race and cage   11 Tilting cage and inner race to
remove balls

.273 to .274 inch	.006 inch
.275 to .276 inch	.008 inch
.277 to .278 inch	.010 inch
.279 to .280 inch	.012 inch
.281 to .282 inch	.014 inch
.283 inch	.016 inch

3 Fit the shims against the bearing. Tighten and lock the housing nuts to the torque figures given in the preceding operation 4. Finish by fitting the lefthand side cover, using a new gasket. Tighten the nuts to 18 lb ft.

7:4 Servicing the drive shafts

Dismantling:

Having removed the drive shafts as described in **Section 7:2**, proceed as follows:

1 Remove the wire or clip from the rubber boot on the inner pot joints. Refer to **FIG 7:6**. Turn back the boot 2 to expose the joint and mark it for correct reassembly.

2 Withdraw the shaft 3 from the pot joint housing. Remove the bearing caps 4 from the shaft cross-piece and remove the needle rollers 5.

3 Remove the rubber boot. At the outer constant-velocity joint, remove the wire or clip from the rubber boot. Turn back the boot and mark the joint for correct assembly, as indicated at 8.

4 Hold the shaft with the cross-piece uppermost and give the edge of the outer race a sharp tap with a soft-faced hammer as shown at 9. This should free the shaft from its retainer ring. Heavy blows are not necessary.

5 Marks 10 in the lower view are a guide for correct reassembly. After marking, tilt and swivel the cage and inner race as indicated at 11 to remove the balls.

6 Refer to **FIG 7:7** and turn the cage into line with the axis of the joint as at 12 in the top view. Then position it so that two opposite windows coincide with two lands of the joint housing as indicated by the arrows.

7 Turn the inner race at right angles to the cage with two of the lands opposite the cage openings and withdraw it (see 13 in central view).

Inspecting:

Clean all the parts in petrol, shake off the surplus and leave to dry. Examine the balls, races and bearing surfaces for damage or excessive wear. The maximum permissible end float of the assembled joint is .025 inch. Check the shafts for wear of the splines and also for possible cracks. Make sure the square-sectioned circlip is firmly in its groove. **Inspect the rubber boots and renew them if the slightest splitting or deterioration can be seen. Never take a chance with rubber boots in a doubtful condition.**

Reassembling:

1 First reassemble the pot joint in the reverse order of dismantling. Smear all parts with Shell Tivella 'A' grease. This is available as Pack No. AKF.1910, which contains 100 cc, and this is enough for one joint. Fill the joint with all the grease in the pack.

2 Position the rubber boot over the joint so that the large rib is over the locating ridge in the housing and the small rib is over the groove in the shaft.

3 The clip which is shown being fitted at 22 in the lower view has the number 18G.1099. Operation (a) is to

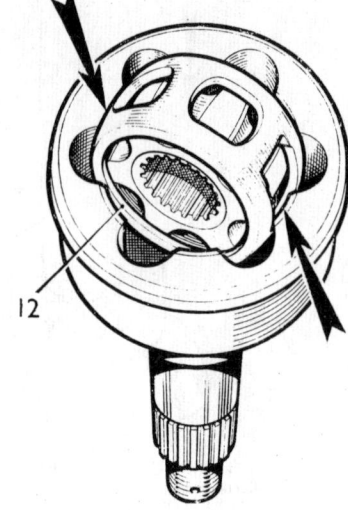

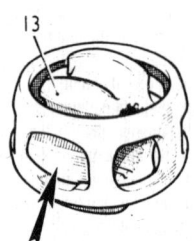

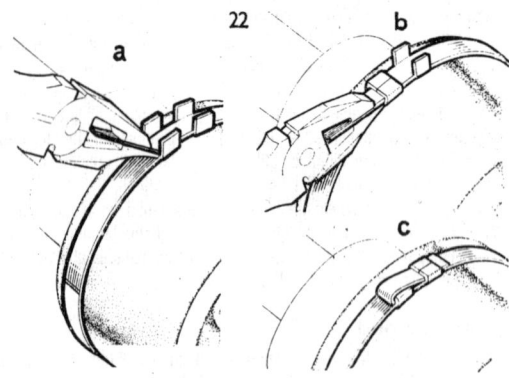

FIG 7:7 Dismantling drive shaft (see also FIG 7:6). The lower view shows how to fit a clip round the rubber boot

Key to Fig 7:7   12 Cage swivelled to remove inner race
13 Inner race positioned for removal   22a Free end of clip pulled tight between tabs   22b Front tabs secured
22c Clip folded back and secured by rear tabs

pull the free end of the clip tightly between the tabs. Holding the end thus, the next step (b) is to bend over the front tabs. Operation (c) is to fold the free end back over the front tabs and secure it with remaining tabs.

4 Reassemble the outer constant-velocity joint in the reverse order of dismantling, smearing the parts with Duckham's Bentone Grease No. Q.5795. 2 oz. of grease are required for one joint so that two packs will be needed. Pack No. AKF.1457 contains 1.1 oz. After assembling the joint, pack it with the remainder of the grease.

5 Position the rubber boot as in operation 2. Fit the clip as in operation 3.

7:5 Fault diagnosis

(a) Excessive backlash

1 Wear in differential assembly
2 Worn pot- or constant-velocity joints
3 Worn splines

4 Worn teeth of crownwheel and pinion
5 Loose crownwheel bolts

(b) Pulling to one side

1 Excessive preload of differential bearings
2 One drive shaft not fully engaged with circlip
3 Joint on one side unlubricated or worn

(c) Knocking when on steering lock

1 Wear in constant-velocity joints
2 Worn pot joints
3 Worn splines
4 Lack of lubricant in joint

(d) Oil leakage, loss of grease

1 Defective gaskets at joint faces
2 Faulty oil seals in side covers
3 Split or deteriorated rubber boots on joints

CHAPTER 8

FRONT SUSPENSION, WHEELS AND TYRES

8:1 Description

The independent front suspension system is based on the now famous Hydrolastic unit. The units can be seen as parts 1 and 2 in **FIG 7:1** and they are mounted horizontally in a cross-tube in the front subframe. Each unit acts as a rubber spring and a fluid displacer, the fluid side being connected by a pipe to the rear displacer unit on the same side of the car. Thus, any fluid displaced by the front unit causes a rise in the height of the rear suspension to give a level ride. From the illustration it can be seen that the lower suspension arm 26 is widely based on bearings 27 and 30 to give great rigidity. At the outer end of the arm is a ball joint 18 which forms the lower pivot for the swivel flange and steering lever 23. At the top of the flange is another ball joint 18 which is connected to the outer end of upper arm 4. This is like a bellcrank mounted on bearings 7. Any upward push on the outer arm causes the short inner arm to move towards the centre line of the car, pressing on knuckle joint 5 and compressing the rubber spring inside the displacer unit. Swivel flange 23 carries bearing 35 which supports the outer section of the drive shaft 33, and the brake disc and driving flange assembly 39 and 40.

8:2 Cautionary note before dismantling

It must be understood that the normal owner has no facilities for pressurizing the Hydrolastic system. There is also a procedure known as 'Evacuating' which draws air out of the system under vacuum and this must be done if any part of the system has been disconnected.

It is possible for the amateur to have the system depressurized so that he can work on many of the components. Having completed any work he is capable of doing with the system depressurized, the owner must take his car to a Service Station which has the necessary equipment to evacuate and pressurize it. The car may be safely driven at speeds not exceeding 30 mph on good roads, as the suspension arms will be contacting the bump rubbers. This is also worth remembering if there is suspension trouble on the road.

8:3 Trim height

This simple check must be carried out if it is suspected that the suspension system is faulty. Refer to **FIG 8:2** for the location of the checking points.

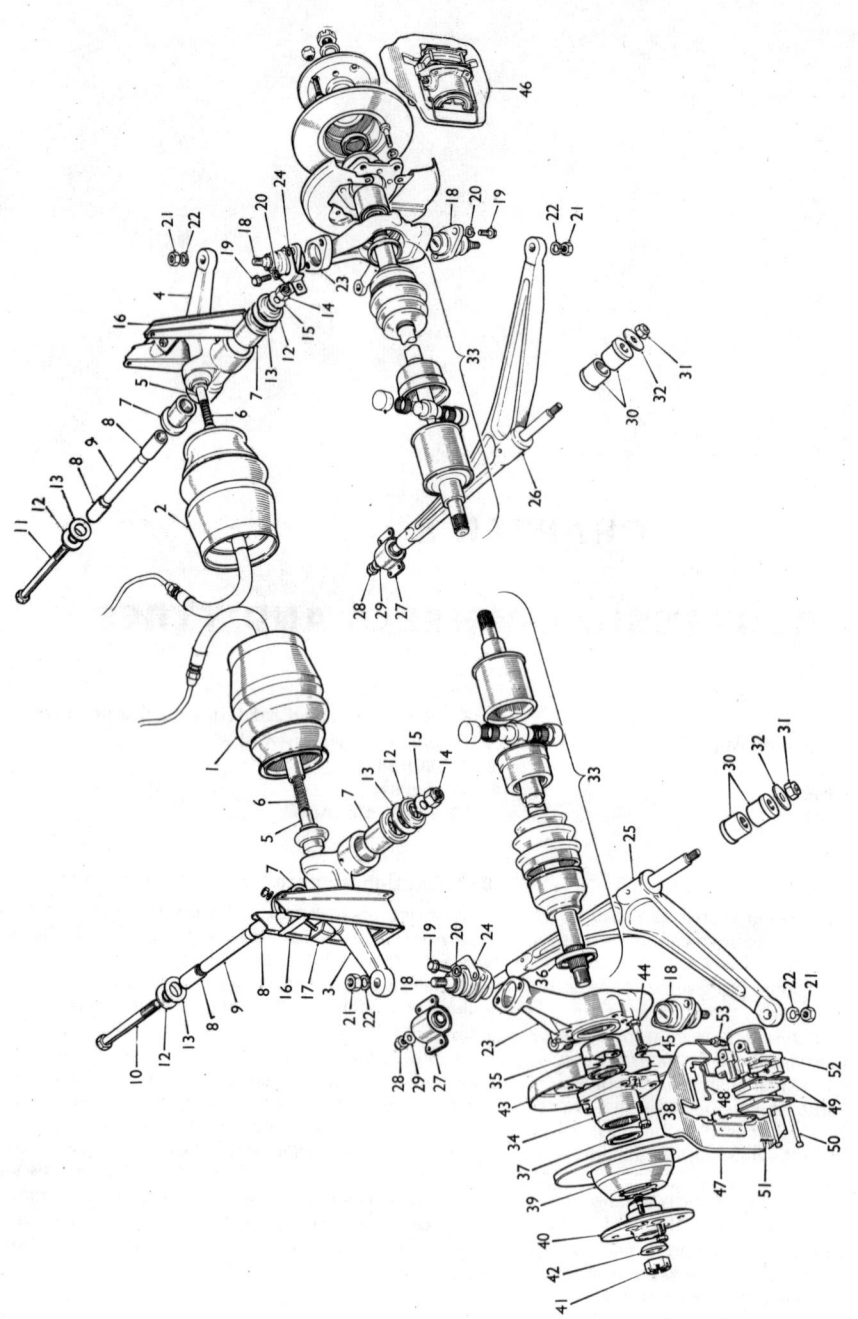

FIG 8:1 The components of the front suspension system

Key to Fig 8:1 1 Displacer unit—RH 2 Displacer unit—LH 3 Upper suspension arm—RH 4 Upper suspension arm—LH 5 Knuckle joint 6 Spring
7 Bearing bush (rubber) 8 Sleeve for bush 9 Pivot tube 10 Pivot bolt—RH 11 Pivot bolt—LH 12 End cap for bearing 13 Washer for bearing
14 Nut for pivot bolt 15 Washer for nut 16 Bump and rebound bracket 17 Rebound rubber 18 Ball joint 19 Bolt for ball joint 20 Washer for bolt
21 Nut for ball joint 22 Washer for nut 23 Swivel flange and steering lever 24 Bracket for brake pipe 25 Lower suspension arm—RH
26 Lower suspension arm—LH 27 Bearing for suspension arm—rear 28 Nut for bearing 29 Washer for nut 30 Bearing for suspension arm—front
31 Nut for bearing 32 Washer for nut 33 Drive shaft 34 Hub bearing housing 35 Hub bearing 36 Oil seal—inner 37 Oil seal—outer
38 Bolt for bearing housing 39 Brake disc 40 Drive flange 41 Nut for hub 42 Spacer for nut 43 Mud shield 44 Bolt for mud shield
45 Washer for bolt 46 Brake caliper assembly 47 Yoke 48 Spring for yoke 49 Friction pads 50 Retaining pins for pads 51 Clip for pins
52 Piston assembly 53 Bleed screw

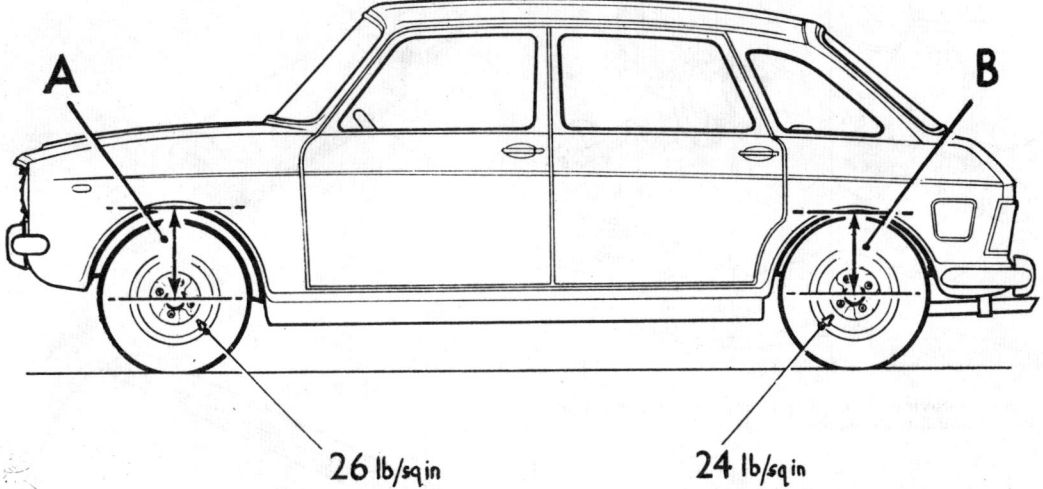

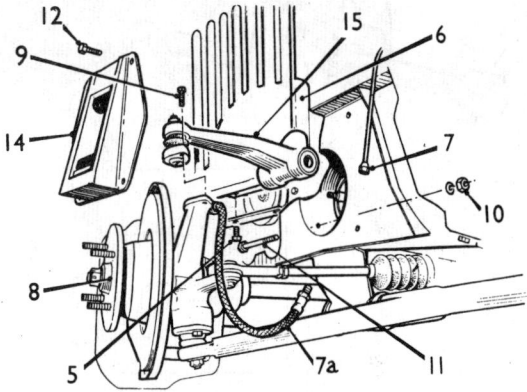

FIG 8:2 Checking the trim height, unladen and on level ground. Correct tyre pressures are also indicated. Distance **A** (from hub centre to wheel arch) should be 14.1 ± .25 inch and distance **B** should be 14.6 ± .25 inch

Stand the car on a level surface. It must be unladen and the tyres must be inflated correctly. Pressure is 26 lb/sq in for the front tyres and 24 lb/sq in for the rear. Roll the car and bounce the suspension. Check the trim height from the centre of each wheel hub to the wheel arch as shown. The front dimension should be 14.1 ± .25 inch and the rear 14.6 ± .25 inch.

Alterations to trim height are made by increasing or decreasing the pressure in the system. If the correct trim figures cannot be obtained the cause must be traced and the faulty component or displacer unit renewed.

8:4 Servicing lower arms

Removing:

1 Raise the front of the car and remove the road wheel. Refer to **FIG 8:3** and remove bolts 3 from the ball joint.

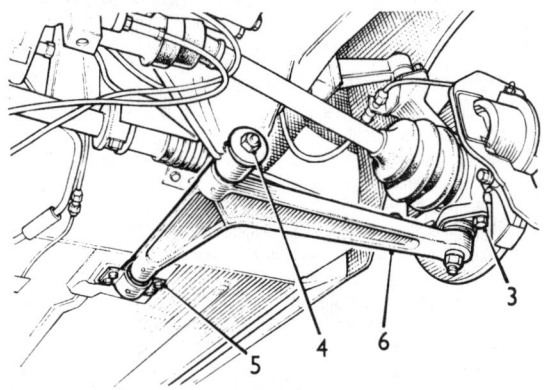

FIG 8:3 Removing the lower suspension arm

Key to Fig 8:3   3 Bolts securing lower ball joint
4 Nut—suspension arm shaft   5 Bolts securing rear bearing   6 Suspension arm

FIG 8:4 Removing the upper suspension arm

Key to Fig 8:4   5 Bolts—engine-to-radiator bracket
6 Radiator moved to give clearance   7 Metal brake pipe
7a Flexible hose   8 Hub assembly   9 Bolts securing upper ball joint   10 Pivot bolt nut   11 Pivot bolt
12 Bolts securing plate 14   14 Bump and rebound plate
15 Upper suspension arm

2 Remove nut 4 and the special washer from the front end of the bearing shaft. Remove securing bolts 5 from the rear bearing housing.

3 Withdraw the lower arm 6 from the subframe housing. To remove the ball joint refer to operation 1 in **Section 8:7**.

Check the condition of the rubber bushes 30 in **FIG 8:1** and the Metalastic assembly 27. Renew any faulty parts. An arm which has been bent in an accident must be renewed. Never attempt to straighten it.

Refitting:

1 Fit one front bush, flange first and position the arm in the housing on the subframe. Fit the second bush.

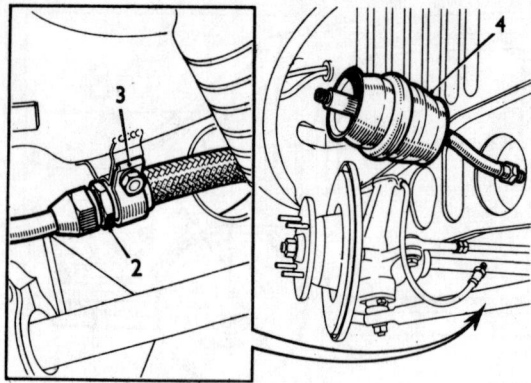

FIG 8:5 Removing a front displacer unit **4**. **2** is the hose connection and **3** the hose clip

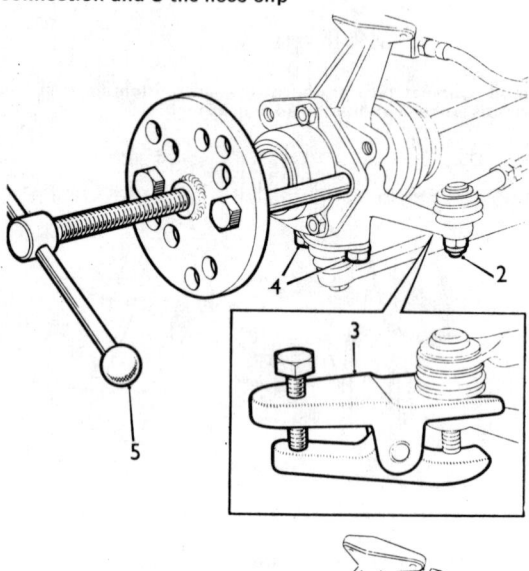

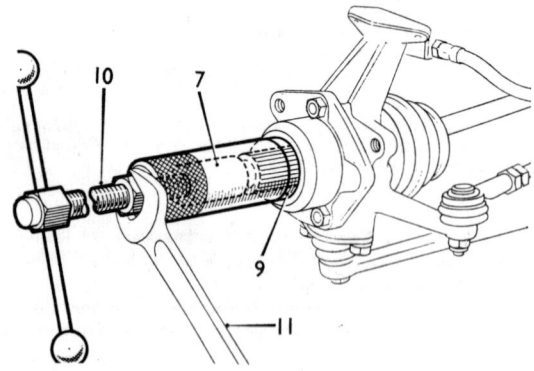

FIG 8:6 Removing and refitting a front hub

Key to Fig 8:6   2 Nut securing steering ball joint
3 Service Tool 18G.1063 for removing ball joint   4 Bolts
securing lower arm ball joint   5 Service Tools 18G.304
and 304.B withdrawing hub   7 Guide of Service Tool
18G.1104.A   9 Collar of Service Tool 18G.1104.A
10 Service Tool 18G.1104   11 Pressing hub assembly
onto drive shaft

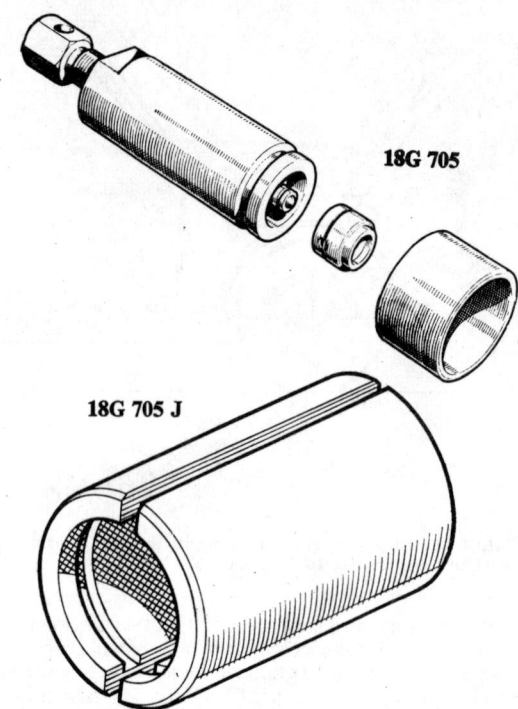

18G 705

18G 705 J

FIG 8:7 Service Tool 18G.705 is the basic remover for bearing centre races. Service Tool 18G.705.J is an adapter for the removal of the front hub bearing centre race

2 Fit the rear bearing but do not tighten the rear nut or the securing bolts. Fit and tighten the bolts securing the ball joint.

3 Refit the wheel, lower the car to the ground and let it stand in a normal unladen condition. Fit the front bearing washer and tighten the nut. Tighten the rear bearing nut and the housing securing bolts. By adopting this procedure, the rubber bushes will be evenly stressed in both directions when the arm deflects on the road.

8:5 Servicing upper arms

Removing—lefthand side:

1 Remove the engine-to-radiator top bracket bolts from the radiator cowl.

2 Raise the front of the car and remove the road wheel. Depressurize and evacuate the relevant side of the suspension.

3 Remove the engine-to-radiator lower bracket bolts 5 from the radiator cowl. Move the radiator enough to allow the upper arm pivot bolt to be withdrawn as shown at 6 in **FIG 8:4**.

4 Disconnect brake pipe 7 from flexible hose 7a. Support hub assembly 8.

5 Remove securing bolts 9 from the upper ball joint. Remove nut 10 from the pivot bolt 11. Withdraw the pivot bolt.

6 Release the bump and rebound plate 14 by unscrewing bolts 12. Lower the hub assembly to remove the plate. Withdraw the upper arm 15.

Check the rubber bushes in the arm and have them

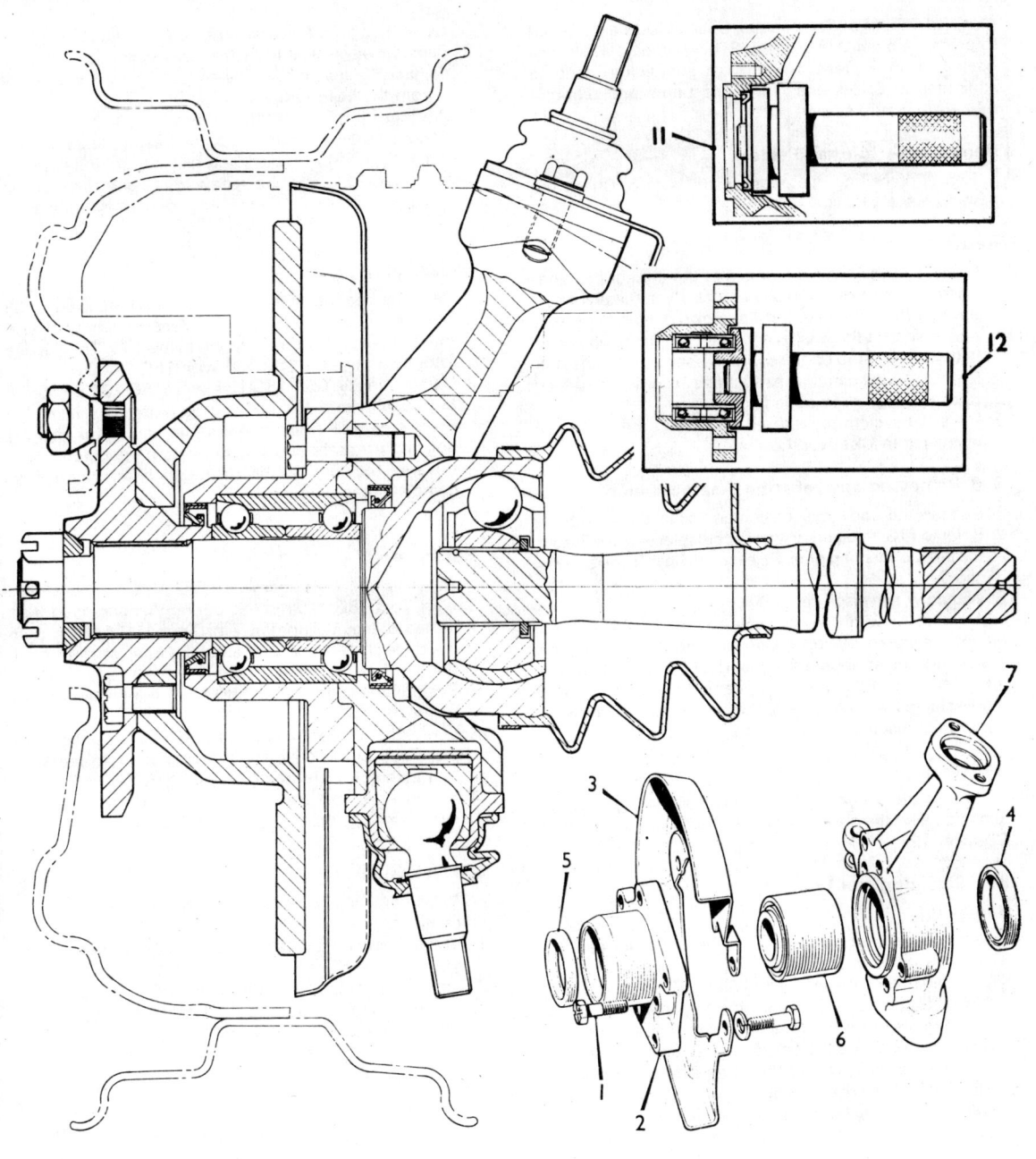

FIG 8:8   A section through the front hub with details of dismantling operations

Key to Fig 8:8   1 Bolts securing bearing housing to swivel flange   2 Bearing housing   3 Brake disc shield
4 Oil seal   5 Oil seal   6 Bearing   7 Swivel flange   11 Fitting oil seal   12 Fitting bearing

renewed if worn or deteriorated. Special tools are needed to press the bushes into place. Renew an arm which has been bent in a crash. No attempt should be made to straighten it. Check and renew the bump and rebound rubbers in plate 14.

Removing—righthand side:

Repeat preceding operations 2 and 4 to 6. Check the parts as just explained.

Refitting:

1 Check that the displacer unit is in the correct position. Fit the arm and align the pivot holes. Push the pivot bolt through the subframe and the arm but do not press it right home. Fit the washer and nut, line-up the bolt head flats with the stop on the subframe and tighten the nut.
2 Reverse the dismantling instructions according to which hand is being reassembled.
3 Have the system pressurized and bleed the brakes as instructed in **Chapter 12**.

8:6 Removing and refitting displacer units

1 Remove the upper suspension arm as in **Section 8:5**.
2 Refer to **FIG 8:5** and disconnect displacer hose 2 from the interconnecting pipe. Release the hose from its body clip 3.
3 Withdraw the displacer unit 4.

Any deterioration in the suspension system which cannot be cured by repressurizing and evacuating the system may be attributable to failure of one or both of the displacer units. If the trim height cannot be corrected by a modest increase in pressure or the suspension bottoms on bumps, the displacer unit must be renewed.

Refitting:

Reverse the dismantling sequence, pressurize the system and bleed the brakes. The last operation is covered in **Chapter 12**.

8:7 Servicing front hubs

Removing:

1 Remove the brake disc as described in **Chapter 11**. Remove nut 2 in **FIG 8:6** from the steering arm ball joint and detach the joint using Service Tool 3, which is 18G.1063. Never hammer on the threaded end of the pin in an attempt to start the tapers as they will be very tight. If a heavy steel block is held against one side of the steering arm eye and the other side given a smart blow with a hammer, it may jar the tapers loose.
2 Remove securing bolts 4 from the lower arm ball joint. Using a puller 5, withdraw the hub assembly from the drive shaft. The Service Tool illustrated is 18G.304 with adapter bolts 18G.304.B.
3 If the inner race of the hub bearing remains on the drive shaft, remove it with Service Tools 18G.705 and 18G.705.J as illustrated in **FIG 8:7**.

Dismantling:

FIG 8:8 shows a section through the front hub assembly and the parts will be recognized from the components in **FIG 8:1**. To dismantle the hub do the following:
1 Unscrew bolts 1 and withdraw bearing housing 2 from

swivel flange 7. Remove brake disc shield 3.
2 Remove oil seal 4 from the swivel flange. This will damage the seal so be prepared to renew it. Remove seal 5 from the bearing housing.
3 Press bearing 6 out of the housing.
Clean all the parts and check the bearing in a dry condition. If the bearing is slack and feels rough due to pitted balls or races it must be renewed. Check the bearing housing and the swivel flange for wear, damage or cracks.

Reassembling:

1 Pack the bearing with a recommended grease. Dip oil seals in oil before pressing into place. Fit a new oil seal into the swivel flange as shown in inset 11. The Service Tool being used is 18G.134 with 18G.134.DE.
2 Using Service Tool 18G.134 with 18G.134.DF, press the bearing into the housing as shown by inset 12. Press a new oil seal into the outer end of the bearing housing using the tools mentioned in operation 1.
3 Reverse the rest of the dismantling instructions to complete reassembling.

Refitting:

Refer to the lower view in **FIG 8:6** which shows Service Tool 18G.1104 in use during this operation.
1 Screw the guide portion 7 of Tool 18G.1104.A onto the drive shaft thread and enter the drive shaft through the hub bearing.
2 Position the collar part of 18G.1104.A in the drive plate recess as at 9.
3 Screw the centre screw 10 of 18G.1104 into the guide just fitted to the drive shaft. Turn nut 11 to press the hub assembly right home on the shaft.
4 Remove the tool and reverse the rest of the removal instructions at the beginning of this Section.

8:8 Wheels

When removing or refitting wheels take the following precautions:
1 Fit the wheel nuts with their tapered faces towards the wheel.
2 Tighten the nuts to a torque of 42 lb ft.
3 Clean and repaint the rims if a tyre is removed.
4 Check the face and flanges of the wheel for excessive runout if there is any difficulty in balancing.

8:9 Tyres

1 Replacement tyres must be of the radial-ply type. These are standard equipment (e.g. Dunlop SP68).
2 Fit and remove tyres over the inner rim of the wheel. Lubricate tyre beads and rims with Dunlop Tyre Bead Lubricant or a vegetable oil soap.
3 Be very careful not to damage the beads of the tyre.
4 The higher air pressure used to seat a tyre must not exceed 50 lb/sq in. Reduce this to normal running pressure before refitting a wheel to the vehicle.
5 Vulcanize all puncture repairs. **Repairs by inserting a plug must be regarded as a temporary measure.**
6 For all conditions, inflate to 26 lb/sq in for front tyres and 24 lb/sq in for rear.

8:10 Fault diagnosis

(a) Wheel wobble

1 Incorrect tracking (see Chapter 10)
2 Worn hub or suspension bearings
3 Defective displacer units
4 Worn swivel flange ball joints
5 Loose wheel fixings
6 Wheel and tyre unbalanced

(b) Bottoming of suspension

1 Check 3 in (a)
2 Incorrect pressurizing
3 Bump rubbers worn or missing

(c) Heavy steering

1 Check 1 in (a)
2 Wrong suspension geometry (see appended note)
3 Incorrect trim height on one side

(d) Excessive tyre wear

1 Check 1 and 6 in (a) and 2 in (c)
2 Under-inflation

(e) Rattles

1 Worn ball joints
2 Worn bearings on upper and lower arms
3 Loose bearing and ball joint fixings

(f) Excessive rolling

1 Check 3 in (a) and 2 in (b)
2 Unbalanced tyre pressures

Note:

If the Hydrolastic suspension system is damaged and the fluid is lost, the radius arms on the damaged side will contact the bump rubbers. In this condition the car may be driven with safety over good roads at speeds not in excess of 30 mph.

The mention of suspension geometry in item (c) of Fault Diagnosis might lead an owner to think that there is adjustment for incorrect angles. These angles are given in Technical Data, but they are for checking purposes only. With the exception of front wheel alignment, the angles are not adjustable, but might be incorrect due to accident damage. **The only cure is to fit new parts.** When checking the angles the vehicle must be standing unladen on a level surface, and at its correct trim height.

CHAPTER 9

REAR SUSPENSION

9:1 Description

The layout of the rear suspension system can be seen in **FIG 9:1**, this being viewed from the front of the car looking rearwards. The trailing radius arms 1 and 2 carry stub axles 47 and hub and brake drum assemblies 53. The outer end of each radius arm is carried in a Metalastic bonded rubber bearing 3 which is bolted to the body.

The inboard end of each arm is bolted to a reaction lever 10 which is machined with sockets on opposite sides. The top one, which can be seen in the illustration, locates on pivot joint 13, which is secured to the fixed support 18. In this way, any turning moment on the reaction lever causes it to pivot about the top joint and the lower pivot on the rear face of the lever forces displacer strut 41 to the rear. This action is transmitted to the rubber spring and displacer units 39 and 46, which are mounted on the body and are hydraulically connected to the displacers of the front suspension.

Bolted to the inner flange of the radius arm is a reaction plate 34 which carries the inner end of trim bar 30. The outer end of the bar is secured to the body by U-bolt 31. Thus, any partial rotation of the inner end of the radius arm will subject the trim bar to a torsional load, giving useful anti-sway and helper spring effects.

In the event of suspension failure with loss of pressure, the arms will contact the arch spring assemblies 60. **In this position it is quite safe to travel at up to 30 mile/hr on good roads.**

9:2 Cautionary note before dismantling

If the owner will read the warning made in **Section 8:2** of the preceding chapter he will understand that depressurizing, evacuating and pressurizing the Hydrolastic system is not within the scope of amateur equipment. He must therefore entrust such operations to a Service Station, or have the system depressurized before he can work on it.

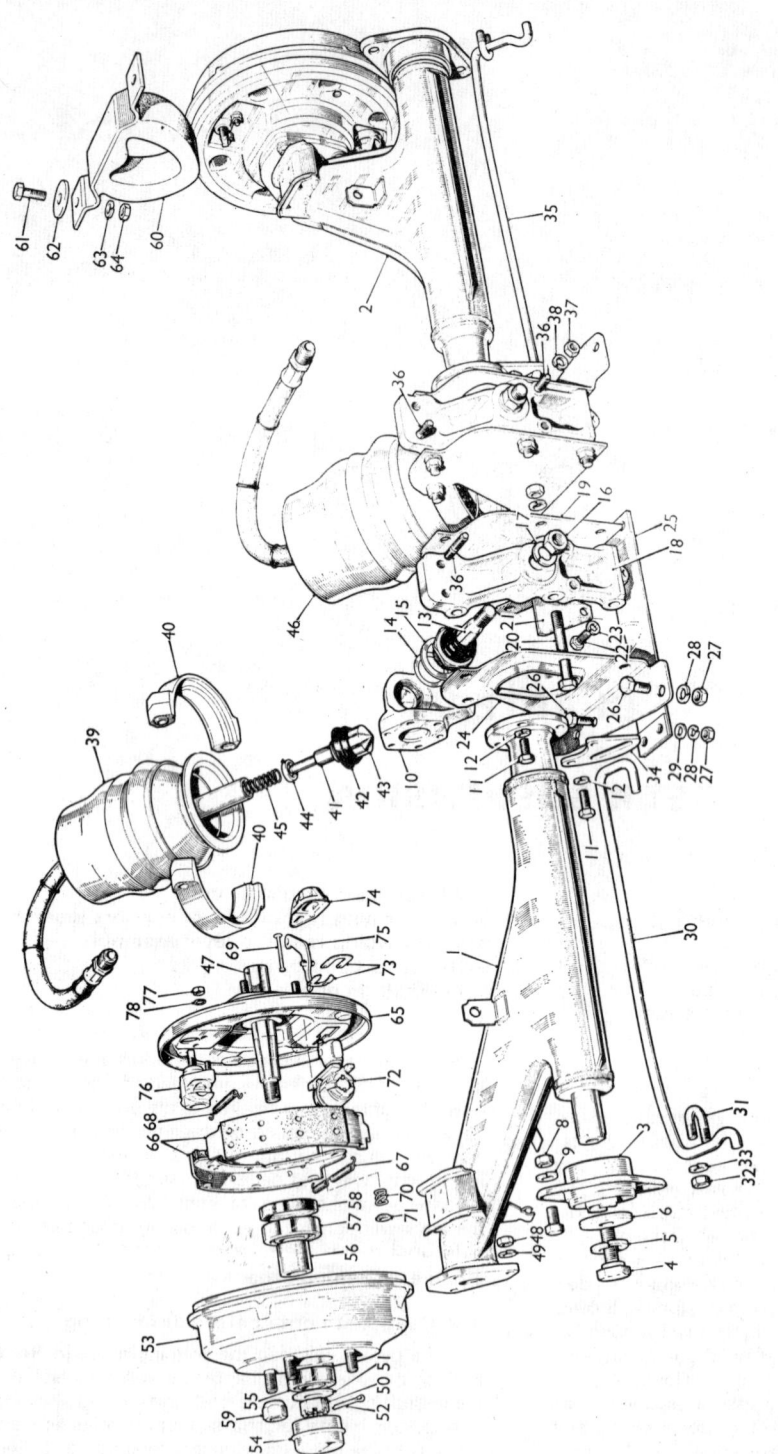

FIG 9:1   Components of the rear suspension as seen when looking from the front of the car

Key to Fig 9:1   1 Radius arm—RH   2 Radius arm—LH   3 Rubber bearing for radius arm   4 Bolt for radius arm   5 Spring washer for bolt
6 Locking washer—radius arm to bearing   7 Bolt for bearing   8 Nut for bolt   9 Spring washer for bolt   10 Reaction lever   11 Bolt—arm to lever
12 Spring washer for bolt   13 Pivot joint   14 Shim for pivot joint   15 Lockwasher for pivot joint   16 Nut for pivot joint   17 Spring washer for nut
18 Support for pivot joint   19 Support housing—LH   20 Bolt for support   21 Rebound buffer   22 Bolt for buffer   23 Spring washer for bolt
24 Support housing—RH   25 Support plate   26 Bolt for supports   27 Nut for bolt   28 Spring washer for bolt   29 Spacer for bolt   30 Trim bar—RH
31 U-bolt for trim bar   32 Nut for bolt   33 Spring washer for bolt   34 Reaction plate for trim bar   35 Trim bar—LH   36 Stud for support   37 Nut for stud
38 Spring washer for stud   39 Displacer unit—RH   40 Support for displacer unit   41 Displacer strut   42 Rubber boot for strut   43 Nylon cap for strut
44 Spacer for strut   45 Spring washer for stud   46 Displacer unit—LH   47 Stub axle   48 Nut for axle   49 Spring washer for nut   50 Nut for hub
51 Washer for nut   52 Splitpin for nut   53 Hub and brake drum assembly   54 Cap for hub   55 Bearing for hub—outer   56 Spacer for bearings
57 Bearing for hub—inner   58 Oil seal   59 Nut for road wheel   60 Arch spring assembly   61 Bolt for arch spring   62 Washer for bolt   63 Spring washer for bolt
64 Nut for bolt   65 Brake backplate   66 Brake shoes   67 Pull-off spring—cylinder side   68 Pull-off spring—adjuster side   69 Brake-shoe retainer
70 Spring for retainer   71 Cup for retainer   72 Wheel cylinder   73 Retainer for cylinder   74 Rubber boot for cylinder   75 Handbrake lever
76 Brake-shoe adjuster   77 Nut for adjuster   78 Washer for nut

102

9:3 Servicing rear hubs

Removing:

1 Raise the rear of the car with the front wheels chocked fore and aft. Remove the road wheel and release the handbrake.
2 Locate the squared adjuster on the brake backplate (see **Chapter 11**) and turn it anticlockwise to slacken the adjustment.
3 Refer to **FIG 9:2** and remove dust cap 4. Remove split-pin 5 and nut 6. **Note that the nut on the lefthand side has a lefthand thread and on the righthand side a righthand thread.**
4 Withdraw the brake drum and hub assembly 7. If it is tight use a puller.

Dismantling:

When the hub is withdrawn it is possible for the inner bearing inner race to remain behind on the stub axle. This can be pulled off using Service Tools 18G.705 and 705.D as shown in **FIG 6:7** and **FIG 9:3**. Then proceed as follows:

1 Refer to **FIG 9:4** and extract oil seal 3. This will damage it so be ready to renew it. Drive out the inner race 4 of the inner bearing, if it is in the hub.
2 Remove spacer 5, making a careful note of its fitted position.
3 Drive out the inner race 6 of the outer bearing. Drive out the two outer races 7, keeping them square all the way.

Inspection:

Clean all the parts and examine the bearings when dry. The races and balls must be free from cracks and pitting. Check the hub and drum for excessive wear, damage or cracks and carry out a similar inspection on the stub axle. If the fit of the races in the hub and on the stub axle has been impaired by frequent extraction, so that there has been relative movement, renew the faulty parts.

Reassembling:

1 Pack the bearings with the recommended grease. Dip the new oil seal in oil before fitting.

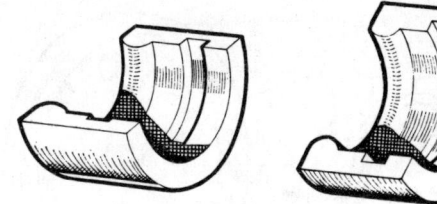

FIG 9:3 Service Tool 18G.705.D. An adapter for removing the rear hub bearing inner race, in conjunction with basic tool 18G.705 as shown in FIG 6:7

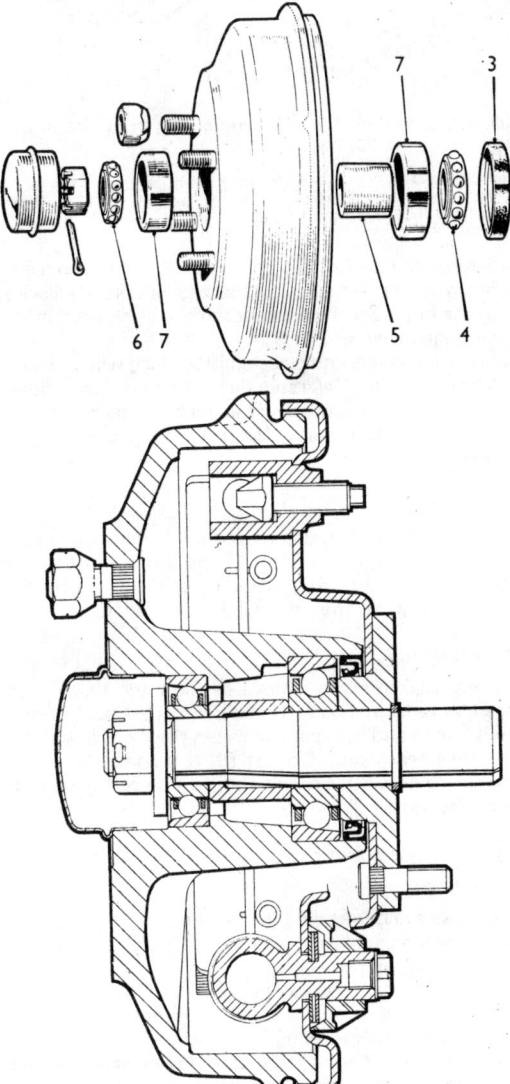

FIG 9:4 Rear hub assembly (top). A section through the brake drum and hub, showing the axle shaft and bearings (bottom)

Key to Fig 9:4   3 Oil seal   4 Inner race of inner bearing   5 Spacer   6 Inner race of outer bearing   7 Outer races of bearings

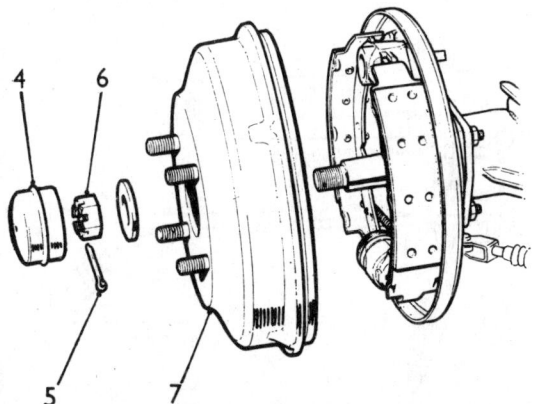

FIG 9:2 The rear hub dismantled

Key to Fig 9:2   4 Dust cap   5 Splitpin   6 Hub nut   7 Brake drum and hub

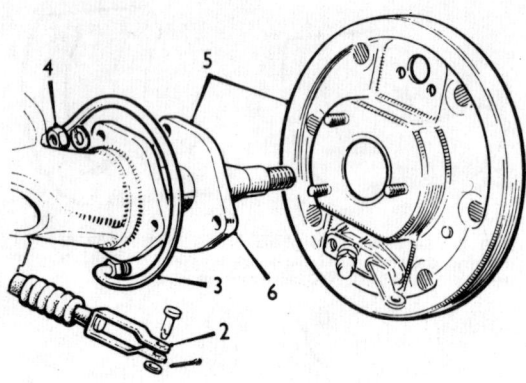

FIG 9:5 Removing a rear axle shaft from the radius arm

Key to Fig 9:5   2 Handbrake cable   3 Brake pipe
4 Nuts securing axle shaft   5 Axle shaft and brake
backplate   6 Axle shaft flange

2 Reverse the dismantling sequence. When the spacer is being fitted make sure that the smaller bore is adjacent to the outer bearing. This position can be seen in the sectioned view of **FIG 9:4**.
3 Press the oil seal into place until it is flush with the inner face of the hub. Make sure that it is square when fitted.
4 There will be enough grease in the bearings to lubricate them for 12,000 miles. **Do not put grease in the dust cap.**

Refitting:

Reverse the dismantling procedure. Tighten the retaining nut to a torque of 60 lb ft. **If the splitpin holes do not line-up, do not slacken off but continue tightening until they do.** Fit a new splitpin.

Maintenance:

Every 12,000 miles, remove the hub and brake drum assembly as instructed at the start of this Section. Repack the bearings and the space between the oil seal with the recommended grease. **Do not fill the space between the bearings with grease and do not put grease in the dust cap.**

9:4 Removing and refitting rear hub axles

Removing:

Remove the hub as described in the preceding Section. Then proceed as follows, referring to **FIG 9:5** for a view of the axle when removed:
1 Disconnect the handbrake cable 2. Disconnect the brake pipe 3. It is a good plan to plug the pipe to prevent dirt from entering.
2 Remove nuts 4 which secure the backplate and hub axle to the radius arm. Using a drift inside the socket at the outer end of the arm, drive out the axle shaft. Separate the backplate and axle.

Inspecting:

Clean and examine the axle. Renew it if the fit in the socket in the radius arm has been impaired. This must also
be done if the bearing inner races have been turning on the shaft, or if the surface which the oil seal contacts is rough or damaged. Renew the axle shaft and the nut if the threads are damaged or strained. **Remember that the lefthand axle has a lefthand thread and the righthand shaft a righthand thread.**

Refitting:

This is a simple reversal of the dismantling procedure, but be very careful to fit each shaft to its correct radius arm if both shafts were removed. The last sentence in the preceding instructions gives the necessary information about the threads. When assembling is completed, bleed the brakes. **Section 9:3** gives the torque for the axle nut.

9:5 Removing and refitting trim bars

Removing:

Refer to **FIG 9:6** and do the following:
1 Chock the front wheels fore and aft and raise the rear of the car, fitting supports for safety. Remove the road wheel on the side to receive attention.
2 Depressurize and evacuate the relevant side of the suspension.
3 Raise the hub with a jack until the plate on top of the radius arm compresses the bump stop on the wheel arch.
4 Release U-bolt 5 from the body at the outer end of the trim bar. Remove bolts 6 which secure the reaction plate and trim bar 7 to the inner flange of the radius arm. Take away the trim bar and plate.

Inspection:

Clean the parts and examine for damage or cracks. It is important not to mark the trim bar with a file or centre punch for identification purposes. Any such marking might lead to premature failure. Wear caused by relative movement of the trim bar, reaction plate or U-bolt calls for renewal of the defective parts.

Refitting:

Refit in the reverse order and pressurize the suspension system on the side affected.

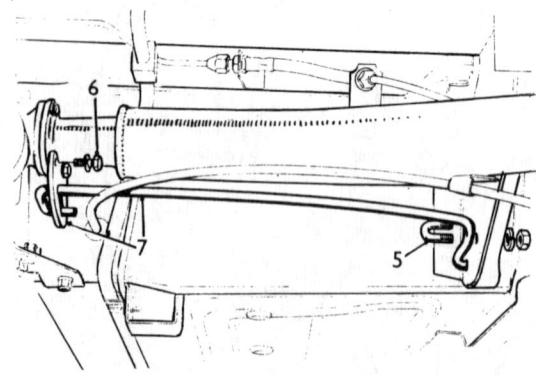

FIG 9:6   Removing a trim bar

Key to Fig 9:6   5 U-bolt fixing to body   6 Bolt for
reaction plate   7 Trim bar and reaction plate

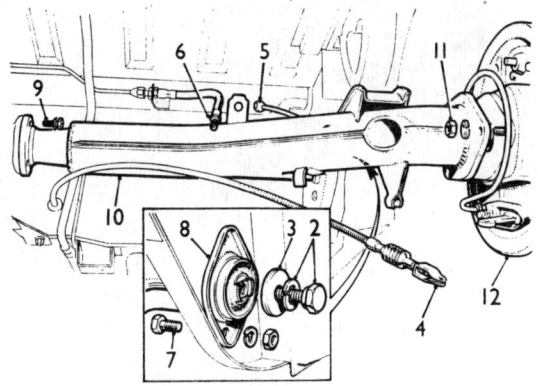

FIG 9:7 Removing a radius arm. The inset is a view of the outer end bearing

Key to Fig 9:7   2 Outer bearing retainer bolt and spring washer   3 Locating washer   4 Handbrake cable 5 Brake pipe   6 Brake hose   7 Bolt for outer bearing 8 Bearing   9 Bolt—radius arm to reaction lever 10 Radius arm   11 Nut securing axle shaft   12 Hub, shaft and backplate assembly

9:6 Removing and refitting radius arms

Removing:

1 Remove the trim bar as just instructed. Refer to **FIG 9:7**.
2 The outer pivot bearing is shown in the inset of the illustration. Remove bolt and spring washer 2. Remove locating washer 3.
3 Disconnect the handbrake cable 4 and the brake pipe 5. Plug the end of the pipe and keep it clean. This also applies to the flexible hose 6, which is next removed from the radius arm clips.
4 Remove bolts 7 which secure the outer bearing 8. Drive the bearing and housing assembly outwards away from the body.
5 At the inner end, remove bolts 9 from the radius arm flange where it is secured to the reaction lever. Remove the radius arm complete with hub. Remove nuts 11 and drive the axle shaft and hub assembly out of the radius arm housing socket.

Inspection:

Renew the arm if it is bent or otherwise damaged. Make no attempt to straighten it. If the rubber bush in the outer bearing has deteriorated or shows signs of cracking, renew the assembly.

Refitting:

Reverse the removal sequence. The only point which calls for extra care is that the flat-sided boss at the outer end of the arm must be aligned with the lugs on the outer bearing before the locating washer, spring washer and bolt are fitted. The correct assembly is clearly shown in the inset to **FIG 9:7**.

9:7 Servicing displacer units

The central mounting of the displacer units can be seen in **FIG 9:8** and an exploded view of the related parts is given in **FIG 9:1**.

Removing:

1 Have the relevant side of the suspension system depressurized and evacuated. Remember that the right-hand displacer unit at the rear is connected to the right-hand front displacer, and the two lefthand units are connected in the same way.
2 Chock the front wheels fore and aft. Raise and support the rear of the car. Remove bolts 3 in **FIG 9:8**. These retain the displacer unit supports.
3 Remove the tie-plate 4. From the rear end of the displacer unit remove the knuckle joint assembly, spacer, nylon cap and spring 5.
4 Remove displacer hose clip 6 and disconnect the hose from the suspension pipe at 7. Remove the displacer unit 8.

Inspection:

Clean the parts and examine assembly 5 for damage or excessive wear. Renew the displacer unit if there has been continued trouble with the suspension system, even though it is known that the front end is in good order and care with pressurizing has not cured the problem.

Refitting:

Reassemble in the reverse order. Before refitting the knuckle joint into the reaction lever, fit the rubber boot to the nylon cap as shown at 5.

9:8 Servicing the reaction lever support assembly

Removing:

Remove the radius arm as described in **Section 9:6** and the displacer unit as described in **Section 9:7**. Then proceed as follows:
1 Refer to **FIG 9:9** and remove the nut from the outer support plate bolt 3. Raise the rear seat cushion for access to the next fixings.
2 Remove retaining nuts 5. Remove the support plate and reaction lever assembly 6 complete.

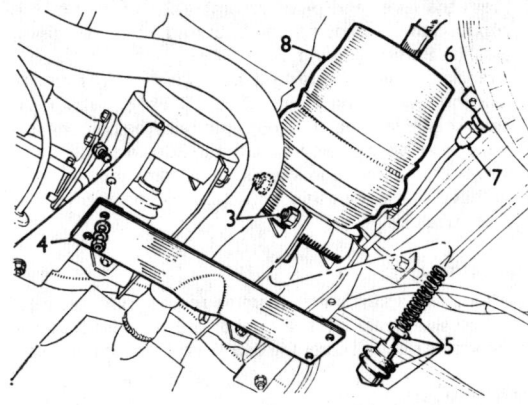

FIG 9:8   Removing a displacer unit

Key to Fig 9:8   3 Bolts for displacer unit supports 4 Tie plate   5 Assembly of knuckle joint   6 Displacer hose clip   7 Hose to suspension pipe connector 8 Displacer unit

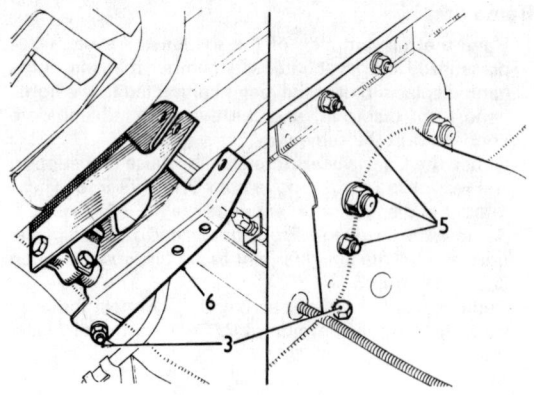

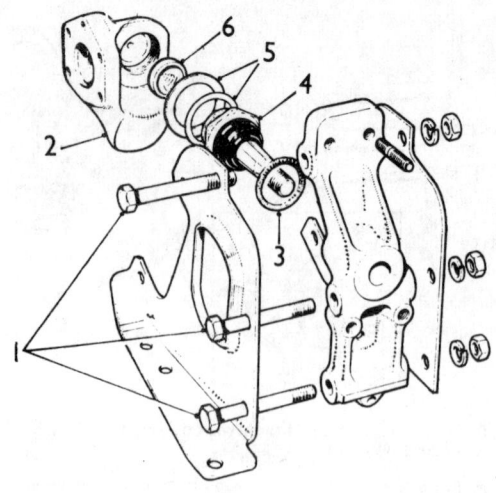

FIG 9:9   Removing a reaction lever assembly

Key to Fig 9:9   3 Fixing for outer support plate (under car on left) (inside car)   5 Retaining nuts for reaction lever assembly   6 Reaction lever and support plate assembly

Inspection:

Check the condition of the rebound buffer, which is part 21 in **FIG 9:1**. Also check pivot 13 for security.

Refitting:

Reverse all the dismantling operations, tightening the support plate fixings securely. Refit the displacer unit and radius arm according to the appropriate instructions.

9:9 Servicing the reaction lever assembly

Dismantling:

Having removed the assembly as instructed in the preceding Section, proceed as follows:

1 Refer to **FIG 9:10** and remove bolts 1 to separate the support plates from the reaction lever assembly.
2 Press the lever and pivot assembly 2 to 6 out of the support after removing the securing nut and spring washer. Remove spring 3.
3 Unlock the pivot housing 4 and unscrew it from the reaction lever, using Service Tool 18G.1164 which is a deep socket spanner, or a box spanner. The ball pin and top socket will come away with the housing. The lower view in the illustration shows the assembly in section.
4 Remove the lockwasher and shims 5 and extract the bottom socket 6.

Inspecting:

After cleaning the parts, examine the ball pin assembly for excessive wear. If the rubber boot is cracked or deteriorated, dirt will enter the pivot and cause rapid wear.

Refitting:

The first step is to determine the correct amount of shimming required to give a smooth action to the ball pin without end float. This is done in the following way:

1 Fit the bottom socket 6, followed by the ball pin, top socket and the housing. Do not fit the lockwasher or shims.

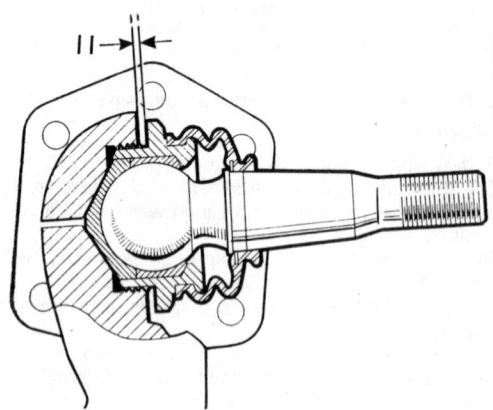

FIG 9:10   Reaction lever assembly dismantled (top), pivot joint for lever in section (bottom)

Key to Fig 9:10   1 Bolts—support plates to pivot joint support   2 Reaction lever   3 Pivot joint spring   4 Pivot joint housing   5 Lockwasher and shims   6 Bottom socket   11 Gap between pivot joint housing and reaction lever

2 Screw the housing into the reaction lever until the pin can be moved about, but without end float. Measure the gap at 11 with feeler gauges.
3 Remove the ball pin assembly and calculate the thickness of shims needed to produce the desired preload on the ball pin. The first step is to take away from the width of the gap, the thickness of the lockwasher. This is .036 inch. From the resultant figure take away .009 to .013 inch to give the required preload. Select suitable shims of the correct thickness.
4 Fit a new lockwasher and replace the ball pin assembly. Tighten the housing to a torque of 70 to 80 lb ft using Service Tool 18G.1164.
5 Complete the reassembling by following the dismantling instructions in reverse.

9:10 Wheels and tyres

Refer to the information given in **Sections 8:8** and **8:9** in the preceding Chapter. Tyre pressure for the rear wheels is 24 lb/sq in.

9:11 Fault diagnosis

(a) Bottoming of suspension

1 Defective displacer units
2 Incorrect pressurizing
3 Bump rubbers worn or missing
4 Fluid leakage from Hydrolastic connections
5 Broken trim bars or fixings

(b) Rattles

1 Check 5 in (a)
2 Faulty outer bearing for radius arm
3 Reaction lever assembly fixings loose

(c) Oil leakage

1 Defective oil seal in hub
2 Dust cap missing from hub

(d) Wear and backlash in reaction lever assembly

1 Loose reaction lever fixings
2 Worn nylon caps in reaction lever
3 Entry of dirt through faulty rubber boots
4 Too much end float in pivot joint of reaction lever

CHAPTER 10

THE STEERING GEAR

10:1 Description

The layout of the steering gear can be seen from the exploded view of the components in **FIG 10:1**. Rack housing 33 is bolted transversely to the body behind the power unit. Sliding inside it is rack 36, the outer ends of the rack carrying ball joints 55 to 58, the actual ball being part of tie rod 59. Each tie rod ends in a ball joint 63, the pin of the joint being secured to a steering arm which is part of the swivel flange carrying the axle and front hub. Meshing with the helical teeth of the rack is a pinion 43 carried in bearings 44 and 47 mounted in the housing. The top splined end of the pinion shaft carries one flange 12 of a flexible joint or coupling 6, the top flange being part of inner steering column 5. This column carries the steering wheel and runs in bushes in outer column 15. The outer column is located by plates 18 and 19 at the lower end and a bracket 22 under the facia. A spring-loaded damper 37 prevents too much free movement of the rack and ensures correct tooth contact of the rack and pinion.

10:2 Lubrication maintenance

There is no provision for regular lubrication of the steering gear, the oil which is injected during assembly being normally sufficient. If there is evidence of loss of lubricant from the housing or rubber gaiters it is possible to replenish the supply in the following way:

1 First check the condition of the gaiters, to make sure there is no split or deterioration. If there is, this will be the cause of the loss and the defective gaiter(s) must be renewed at once. Not only is lubricant being lost but dirt can enter and cause rapid wear.
2 Remove gaiter clip 61 from the pinion end of the rack housing (see **FIG 10:1**). Turn the steering to the straightahead position.
3 Fill a pressure-type oil can with the recommended EP.90 oil and insert the nozzle into the end of the rack housing. Inject not more than $\frac{1}{3}$ pint.
4 Replace the gaiter and tighten the clip. Turn the steering from lock to lock to distribute the oil throughout the housing.

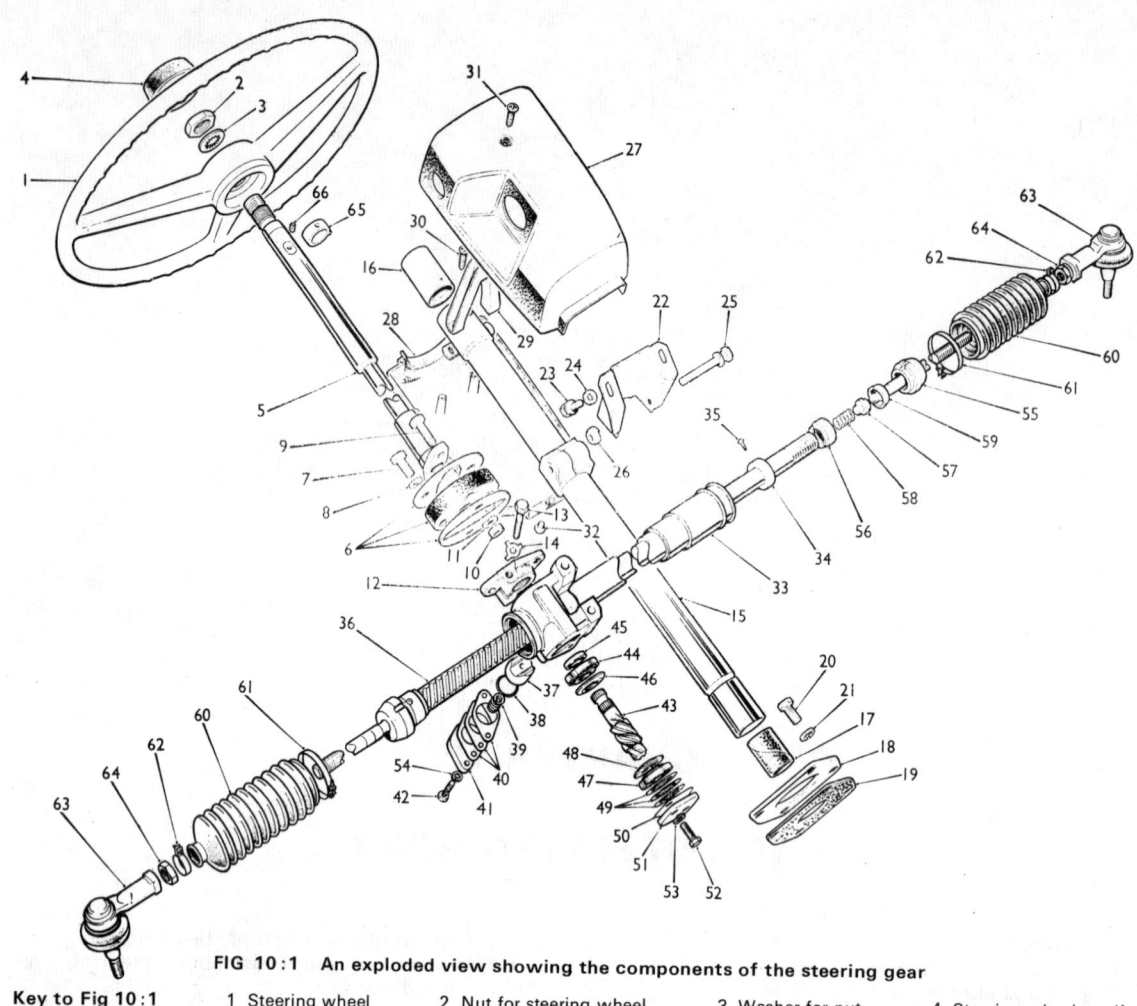

FIG 10:1 An exploded view showing the components of the steering gear

Key to Fig 10:1 1 Steering wheel 2 Nut for steering wheel 3 Washer for nut 4 Steering wheel motif 5 Steering column—inner 6 Coupling 7 Bolt—coupling to pinion flange 8 Washer for bolt 9 Bolt—column flange to coupling 10 Nut for bolt 11 Washer for nut 12 Pinion flange 13 Pinch bolt 14 Lockwasher for bolt 15 Steering column—outer 16 Bush for column (plastic) 17 Bush for column (felt) 18 Toe-plate 19 Gasket for plate 20 Bolt for plate 21 Washer for bolt 22 Bracket for column 23 Bolt for bracket (shear) 24 Washer for bolt 25 Bolt for column (shear) 26 Nut for bolt (captive) 27 Cowl for column—upper 28 Cowl for column—lower 29 Bracket for cowl 30 Screw for bracket 31 Screw for cowl 32 Screw for cowl 33 Rack housing 34 Bush for housing 35 Screw for bush 36 Rack 37 Damper yoke 38 O-ring for yoke 39 Damper spring 40 Shims 41 Cover for damper 42 Bolt for cover 43 Pinion 44 Bearing for pinion—upper 45 Oil seal 46 Thrust washer 47 Bearing for pinion—lower 48 Thrust washer 49 Shims 50 Gasket 51 Cover for pinion housing 52 Bolt for cover 53 Washer for bolt 54 Washer for bolt 55 Ball housing 56 Locking ring 57 Seat 58 Spring for seat 59 Tie rod 60 Gaiter 61 Clip for gaiter—large 62 Clip for gaiter—small 63 Ball joint assembly 64 Locknut 65 Trip for direction indicator switch 66 Screw for trip

10:3 Wheel alignment

Checking:

The following points must be observed when checking the front wheel alignment:

1 The car must be unladen, with tyres at the correct pressure and the steering wheel set in the straightahead position.

2 Measurements must be taken on the side walls of the tyres, 10.5 inch above the ground surface.

3 If a base-bar type of gauge is used, take a measurement in front of and behind the wheel centre. Mark the points with chalk, roll the car forward for half a revolution of the road wheels and take two more readings at the same points on the tyres. This will eliminate error due to uneven tyre mounting. Take an average of the two sets of readings.

The correct toe-in on very early models was $\frac{1}{4}$ inch and if these cars are fitted with new bushes when servicing this remains the correct setting. On later cars, or on early cars with original bushes, the toe-in should be set to $\frac{1}{16}$ inch.

4 When an optical gauge is used, two readings must be taken with the car wheels rolled forward 180 deg. and

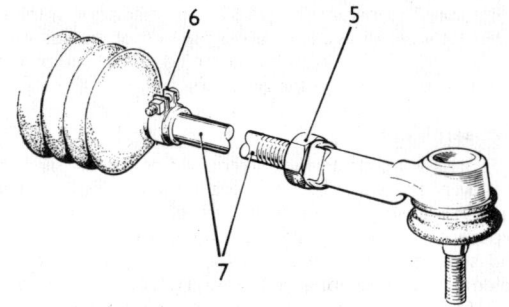

FIG 10:2 The tie rod parts concerned in adjustments to front wheel tracking. Locknut 5 secures the outer ball joint, clip 6 secures the rack housing gaiter and 7 is the tie rod

three readings with the wheels rolled 120 deg. Calculate the average figure from the readings.

Adjusting:

Refer to **FIG 10:2** and proceed as follows:

1 Slacken the tie rod locknuts 5, one on each side. Slacken both small gaiter clips 6.
2 The tie rods both have righthand threads. Turn each rod

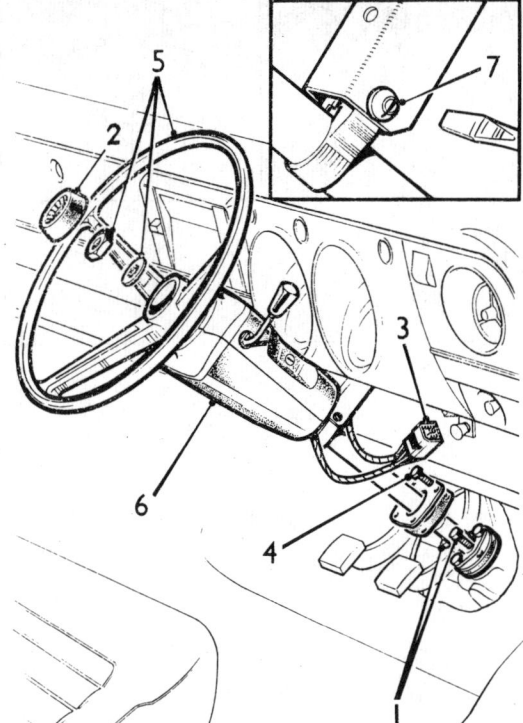

FIG 10:3 Removing the steering column. The inset shows the column bracket shear bolt slotted for removal

Key to Fig 10:3 1 Bolts for coupling 2 Finisher
3 Multipoint wiring plug 4 Toeplate bolts
5 Steering wheel, nut and washer 6 Switch cowl
7 Shear bolt

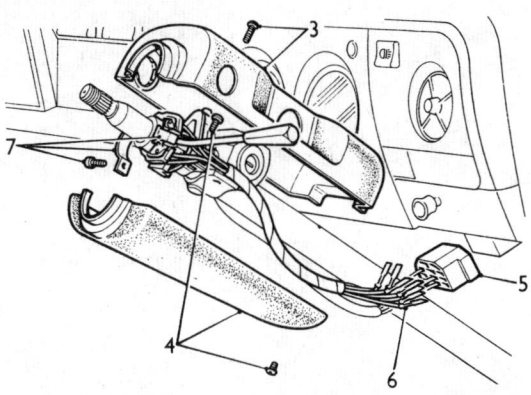

FIG 10:4 Removing the direction indicator switch assembly

Key to Fig 10:4 3 Cowl upper half and screw
4 Cowl lower half and screws 5 Multipoint wiring socket
6 Wiring plugs 7 Indicator switch and fixings

in the required direction to correct the alignment. **When the toe-in is properly set, check the lengths of the tie rods. It is most important that they are equal.** Turning one in and the other out by equal amounts will make no difference to the tracking and will enable both tie rods to be correctly set. Measuring the amount of thread exposed is an easy way of checking the length.

3 When satisfied, tighten the ball joint locknuts to a torque of 35 to 40 lb ft, tighten the gaiter clips and recheck the wheel alignment.

10:4 Servicing the steering column

Removing wheel:

1 Withdraw finisher 2 from the wheel hub (see **FIG 10:3**). Remove nut and washer 5.
2 With hand pressure under the hub and spokes it should be possible to withdraw the wheel from the column splines.

Removing column:

1 Remove bolts 1 which secure the pinion flange to the coupling. Disconnect the battery and disconnect the multipoint plug 3 from under the facia.
2 Remove the toe plate bolts 4. Remove the steering wheel as in the preceding instructions.
3 Remove the top half of the cowl 6, followed by the lower half (see **FIG 10:4**). The column is secured to its bracket by a shear bolt 7 as shown in the inset to the illustration. This bolt cannot be removed until a screwdriver slot is cut in the head of it. The nut for this bolt is secured to the bracket and cannot be turned.
4 Having removed the shear bolt, the steering column can be removed, complete with coupling.

Dismantling:

Although **FIG 10:4** shows the steering column installed, removal of the column and switchgear is possible because of the multipoint plug 6. The top and bottom

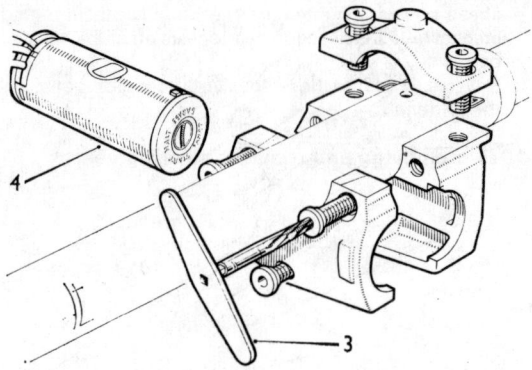

FIG 10:5 Removing the combined steering lock and ignition switch. An extractor 3 is unscrewing a drilled shear bolt, 4 is the lock assembly

halves of the cowl have been removed to reveal the horn, direction indicator, and headlamp flasher switch. Remove the clip indicated at 7 and lift away the switch complete with wiring.

The next step is to remove the combined steering lock and ignition switch shown in FIG 10:5. To prevent tampering with the lock, the bracket is secured by shear screws, so that removal is impossible without a drilling operation. It involves either drilling centrally down the head of each screw with a drill of the top diameter of the screw, so that the head breaks away, or drilling a smaller hole and using an Ezy-out or similar extractor as at 3. The latter is probably the easier method. Once the screw heads or screws are removed the housing and lock assembly 4 are released. Now follow the next instructions, using FIG 10:6 for reference purposes:

1 Make marks 3 so that the inner column and the trip for the direction indicator switch can be correctly re-assembled.
2 Remove grub screw 4 and withdraw trip ring 5.
3 Pull the inner column downwards and out of the outer

column. The lower felt bush 6 will be displaced. If there has been excessive play at the top end of the column, renew the plastic bush 7. This can be drifted and prised out of its housing in the outer column.

Reassembling:

Fit a new top plastic bush if required. A new felt bush at the lower end should be well soaked in oil. Fit the inner column, leaving about 3 inches of the thinner part exposed at the bottom. Wrap the felt bush round this part and slide it up until it enters the housing in the outer column. Press both inner column and felt bush right home.

Refit the switch trip ring and grub screw and tighten the screw when the marks made during dismantling have been aligned. Fit the steering lock and ignition switch assembly, using new shear screws. These must be tightened until the heads shear off at the waisted part. Refit the combined direction indicator switch after checking the contacts and wiring for possible defects.

Refitting:

Before positioning the column in the car, turn the front wheels to the straightahead position. Then proceed as follows:

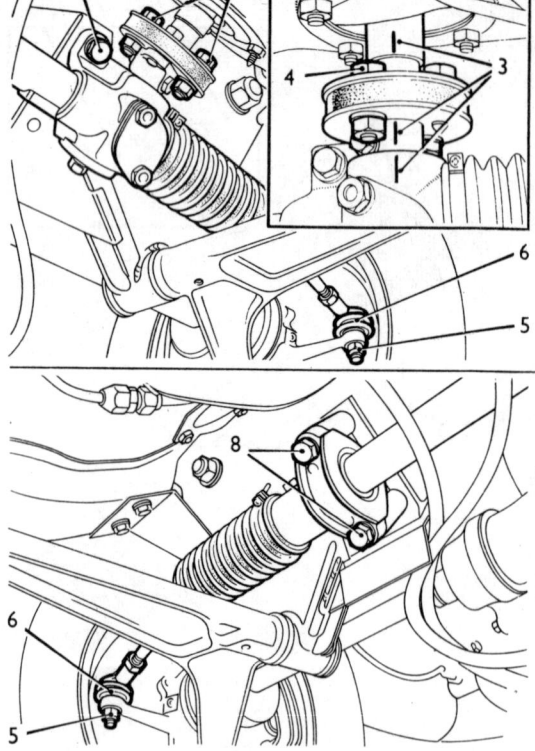

FIG 10:7 Removing the steering gear. The inset shows the flexible coupling and alignment marks

Key to Fig 10:7   3 Alignment marks   4 Bolts for column flange   5 Nut for ball joint   6 Ball joint
7 Bolt—pinion housing to body   8 Bolts—rack housing to body

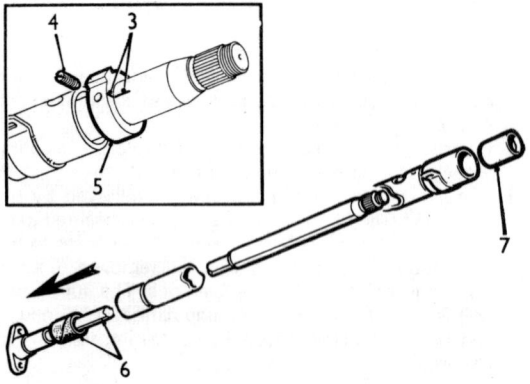

FIG 10:6   Dismantling the steering column

Key to Fig 10:6   3 Alignment marks—switch trip to inner column   4 Grub screw   5 Trip ring
6 Inner column and lower felt bush   7 Upper bush (plastic)

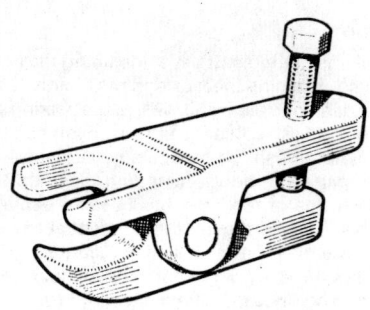

FIG 10:8 Service Tool 18G.1063. Used for removing the ball pin of steering arm and swivel flange ball joints

1 Turn the inner column to the straightahead position by referring to the trip ring and indicator switch. Fit the columns to the car and use a new shear bolt in the mounting bracket. Do not tighten the shear bolt yet.

2 Fit the steering wheel, tightening the retaining nut to a torque of 50 lb ft. Check that the front wheels, inner column and steering wheel are aligned in the straight-ahead position. Tighten the shear bolt in the mounting bracket until the hexagon head shears off at the waisted part.

3 Reverse the rest of the removal instructions to complete the refitting.

10:5 Removing and refitting steering gear

Removing:

This operation must be carried out under the car, so jack-up the front end and support it in such a way that it cannot roll off the jack. Refer to **FIG 10:7** and do the following:

1 Turn the steering into the straightahead position. Refer to the inset in the top view and mark the pinion housing, coupling and column flange for correct reassembly.

2 Remove the bolts 4 from the coupling flange.

3 Remove nuts 5 from the pins of ball joints 6 at the steering arms. Do not hammer on the threaded pins in an attempt to start the tapers. Use Service Tool 18G.1063 as illustrated in **FIG 10:8**. Failing this, the tapers may be jarred loose by striking a smart blow on one side of the steering arm eye while holding a heavy steel block on the opposite side.

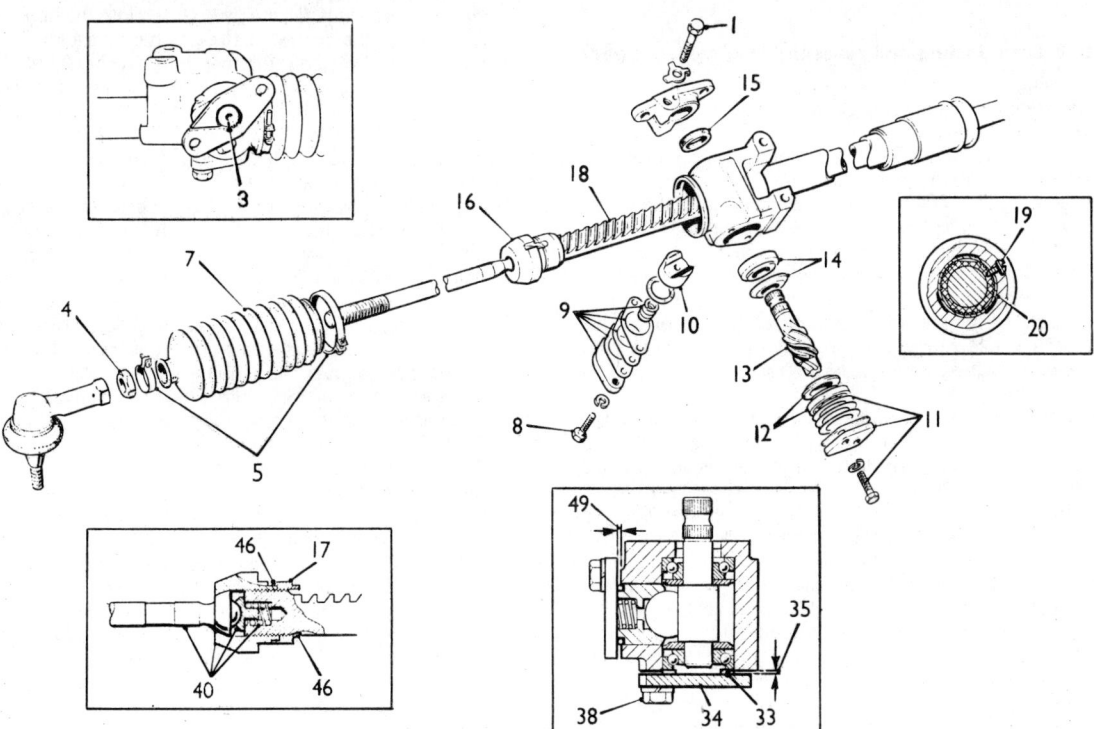

FIG 10:9   Dismantling and adjusting the steering gear

Key to Fig 10:9   1 Pinch bolt—pinion flange   3 Pinion shaft marking   4 Ball joint locknut   5 Gaiter clips
7 Gaiter   8 Damper cover bolt   9 Damper coverplate, shims and spring   10 Damper yoke
11 Pinion housing cover, bolt, shims and gasket   12 Lower bearing and thrust washer   13 Pinion
14 Upper bearing and thrust washer   15 Pinion shaft oil seal   16 Ball housing   17 Ball housing locking ring
18 Rack   19 Bush securing screw   20 Rack housing bush   33 Pinion housing shims   34 Cover
35 Clearance between housing and cover   38 Cover retaining bolt   40 Tie rod, housing, seat and spring
46 Punched locking of ball housing and locking ring   49 Clearance between damper cover and damper housing

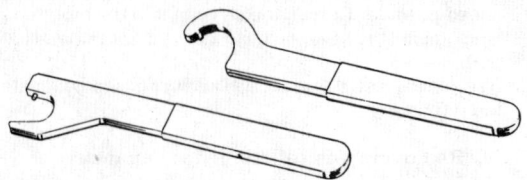

FIG 10:10 Service Tools 18G.707. Spanners for the steering rack ball joint housing and locking ring

4 Remove bolts 7 and 8 to release the gear assembly from the body. Move the assembly to the left enough to disengage it from between the righthand lower suspension arm and the subframe. Then withdraw the assembly from below the righthand side of the body.

Refitting:

This is accomplished by reversing the removal sequence of operations. Before fitting the coupling bolts 4, make sure that the pinion flange, pinion housing, and steering column marks are aligned in the straight-ahead position.

10:6 Dismantling and reassembling steering gear

Having removed the steering gear from the car as instructed in the preceding Section, proceed to dismantle it as follows:

1 Refer to **FIG 10:9** and unlock and remove pinchbolt 1 from the pinion flange. Set the rack in the central position. The total travel is 6.36 inch so that the return of the rack by half that distance from a full-lock position will be the correct setting. This can be checked by observing the slot or arrow marking on the end of the pinion shaft as indicated at 3 in the top inset. This should be pointing downwards at the damper. Also make a note of the position of the pinion flange with respect to the centre line of the rack, so that it can be correctly reassembled.

2 Slacken locknuts 4 on each tie rod and unscrew the ball joints. Slacken the four gaiter retaining clips 5 and drain out the lubricant from the rack housing. Remove the rubber gaiters 7.

3 Unscrew the damper coverplate bolts 8. Remove the plate, shims and spring 9. Withdraw the damper yoke 10 complete with O-ring.

4 The tail bearing 12 of pinion 13 is retained in the housing by plate and bolts 11. Remove these and the gasket and shims. Withdraw the pinion.

5 Remove the upper bearing and thrust washer 14. Remove the pinion shaft oil seal 15.

6 Prise up the locking indentations on the ball joint housing 16 and the locking ring 17 just inboard. Unscrew the parts from the rack, using Service Tools 18G.707 as illustrated in **FIG 10:10**. Removal of the housing will release the tie rod, ball seat and spring (see parts 40 in the bottom lefthand inset).

7 Pull out the rack from the pinion end of the housing, taking care not to damage the bush fitted into the other end. Remove securing screw 19 and extract the bush 20.

Inspection:

Clean all the component parts, including the bore of the rack housing. Examine the rack and the pinion, looking for cracked or damaged teeth and wear of the bearing surfaces. Rattling, or excessive float in the end bush can be cured by fitting a new bush. Be particularly careful to check all the rubber gaiters or boots, including those on the outer ball joints. If one of the latter has been so damaged that road grit has entered the joint it is essential to renew the complete assembly. Faulty gaiters which lead to a loss of lubricant and the entry of grit can lead to rapid wear of the rack, pinion and housing. Check the pinion shaft bearings and the tie rod seatings for wear and renew all defective parts. Renew the pinion shaft oil seal if lubricant has been leaking past it.

Reassembling:

1 Fit the bush 20 into the rack housing with the flats offset to the hole for the retaining screw 19. Use a $\frac{7}{64}$ inch drill through the retaining-screw hole and drill the bush. Clean away all swarf from the bush and housing. Coat the screw with sealing compound and screw it into the bush. As a final check, make sure the screw does not project into the bore.

2 Fit the upper bearing and thrust washer 14 after applying some lubricant. Oil the rack, slide it into the housing and set it in the central or straightahead position.

3 Fit the pinion, making sure that the arrow or slot on the end is pointing downwards at the damper housing. This is shown by 3 in the top inset. Fit the lower thrust washer and bearing. The pinion shaft bearings are preloaded by .001 to .003 inch, and the required shimming is determined by fitting enough shims 33 to give an approximate clearance of .010 inch between the cover 34 and the housing as indicated at 35 in the bottom righthand inset. Tighten cover bolts 38 just enough to hold the cover firmly and check the gap with feeler gauges. Remove the cover and adjust the amount of shimming so that the gap is .007 to .009 inch. As the compressed thickness of the cover gasket is .006 inch, the difference gives the required preload. Arrange the shims so that a .060 inch shim is next to the cover. Use a new gasket and fit the cover. Put sealing compound on the bolt which is nearest to the damper cover and tighten down to a torque of 12 to 18 lb ft.

4 Refer to the lower lefthand inset and screw a new locking ring 17 onto the rack as far as it will go. Using lubricant, fit the spring, ball seat, ball housing and tie rod 40 and tighten the ball housing until the tie rod is just nipped. Run the locking ring up to the ball housing and check that the tie rod is still nipped. Slacken the ball housing by one-eighth of a turn, in which position the tie rod should be free to articulate. Hold the housing firmly so that it cannot turn and tighten the locking ring to it, using a torque of 33 to 37 lb ft. If the adjustment is correct it should require a torque of 32 to 52 lb in to articulate the tie rod. Lock both the ball housing and the locking ring by punching the ring flanges into the rack and housing slots as shown at 46.

5 Fit the damper yoke 10 without O-ring, spring, or shims. Tighten the cover bolts gradually and evenly whilst turning the pinion shaft backwards and forwards through 180 deg. Use a bearing preload gauge set at 15 lb in and continue tightening until it is just possible

to turn the pinion with the required preload setting. At this point measure the clearance between the cover and the housing face as indicated at 49 in the bottom right-hand inset. Select shims to the figure determined plus .002 to .005 inch. Fit the O-ring, spring, shims and cover and tighten the bolts to a torque of 12 to 18 lb ft.

6 With the damper assembled, check the torque required to start movement of the pinion. Fit a new pinion shaft oil seal 15. Refit the gaiters and secure the clips at the housing ends. Secure the small outer clip on the tie rod farthest from the pinion.

7 Inject $\frac{1}{3}$ pint of recommended EP.90 oil between the tie rod and the gaiter at the pinion end and secure the remaining clip. Work the rack to and fro to distribute the oil.

8 Set the rack in the central position. As the total travel of the rack is 6.36 inch or 3.18 inch on each lock, this is a matter for simple measurement. As a check, there should be 3.9 turns of the pinion shaft from lock to lock, and in the central position the marking on the end of the shaft must be in the position indicated at 3 in the top inset.

9 Refit the ball joints to the tie rods, screwing them on so that equal lengths of thread are exposed. Tighten the locknuts just enough to stop the joints turning before the assembly is refitted in the car. Refit the steering gear by following the instructions at the end of **Section 10:5**.

10:7 Fault diagnosis

(a) Wheel wobble

1 Unbalanced wheel and tyre assembly
2 Slackness in steering ball joints
3 Incorrect steering geometry caused by damage
4 Excessive play in steering gear
5 Faulty suspension
6 Worn hub bearings

(b) Wander

1 Check (a)
2 Uneven tyre pressures
3 Uneven tyre wear

(c) Heavy steering

1 Check 3 and 5 in (a)
2 Very low tyre pressures
3 Neglected lubrication
4 Front wheels out of track
5 Rack damper too tight
6 Excessive pinion bearing preload
7 Inner steering column bent
8 Steering column bushes tight

(d) Lost motion

1 Loose steering wheel, worn splines
2 Worn rack and pinion teeth or housing bush
3 Worn ball joints
4 Worn suspension joints
5 Slack pinion bearings
6 Damper pressure insufficient
7 Worn flexible coupling in column

(e) Steering wheel off-centre, unequal locks

1 Tie rod lengths not equal

(f) Direction indicator trip not working

1 Trip ring displaced on inner column

CHAPTER 11

THE BRAKING SYSTEM

11 :1 Description

Under the parcel shelf is a mounting plate attached to the body, and this carries the pedal assembly together with the clutch master cylinder, and the brake servo cylinder to which the brake master cylinder is secured. This assembly can be seen in **FIG 11 : 24** which gives an inside view at the top and a view under the bonnet at the bottom. Note how the brake pedal 17 is carried on pivot bolt 16. Below this can be seen the fork and clevis pin which connect the pedal arm to the servo unit operating rod. On the bonnet side of the bulkhead can be seen the servo unit and master cylinder assembly 1. The vacuum pipe from the servo unit terminates at connection 6 which screws into the inlet manifold. The master cylinder is connected to the brake-operating cylinders by metal and flexible pipes.

The front brakes have discs which are secured to the hubs and driving flanges, as shown in **FIG 11 :13**. Adjacent to the inner face of the disc is a single cylinder carrying two pistons which face outwards. One piston presses on a friction pad bearing directly on the disc face adjoining. The other piston presses on a yoke which transmits the pressure to another pad bearing on the outer face of the disc. Thus, hydraulic pressure on the piston heads produces a balanced braking effect on the disc as it revolves between the pads. This action is clearly shown in the lower view of **FIG 11 :6**. The point to remember is that the arrows would face in the opposite directions when braking, so that pistons 6 and 8 would be moving apart. Piston 8 would apply pad 9 and piston 6 would apply pad 10 through the agency of yoke 7.

The rear brakes are of the drum type, the internal parts being shown in **FIG 11 :7**. At the top is an adjuster 6 which fixes the position of the ends of brake shoes 5 and 8 and is secured to a backplate bolted to the suspension radius arm. The lower ends of the shoes are expanded inside the brake drum by hydraulic cylinder 7. The piston in the cylinder presses on the righthand shoe, and the cylinder, which is free to slide in the backplate presses on the lefthand shoe. A lever mounted on the cylinder will mechanically expand the shoes when operated by a cable connected to the handbrake lever. This lever can be seen in **FIG 11 :11**.

The brake pedal operates the brakes by fluid pressure generated in the master cylinder, the pressure being boosted by a vacuum-operated servo unit to which the master cylinder is bolted. **FIG 11 :16** shows the master cylinder parts exploded. The flange of the cylinder is bolted to the lefthand end of the servo unit shown in section in **FIG 11 :1**. The brake pedal is connected to the fork at the opposite end. Pedal pressure is transmitted by way of operating rod assembly 17 to pushrod 4 which in turn presses on master cylinder piston 4 in **FIG 11 :16**. In this way, fluid in front of the master cylinder piston is forced under pressure out of outlet 12 into the system of

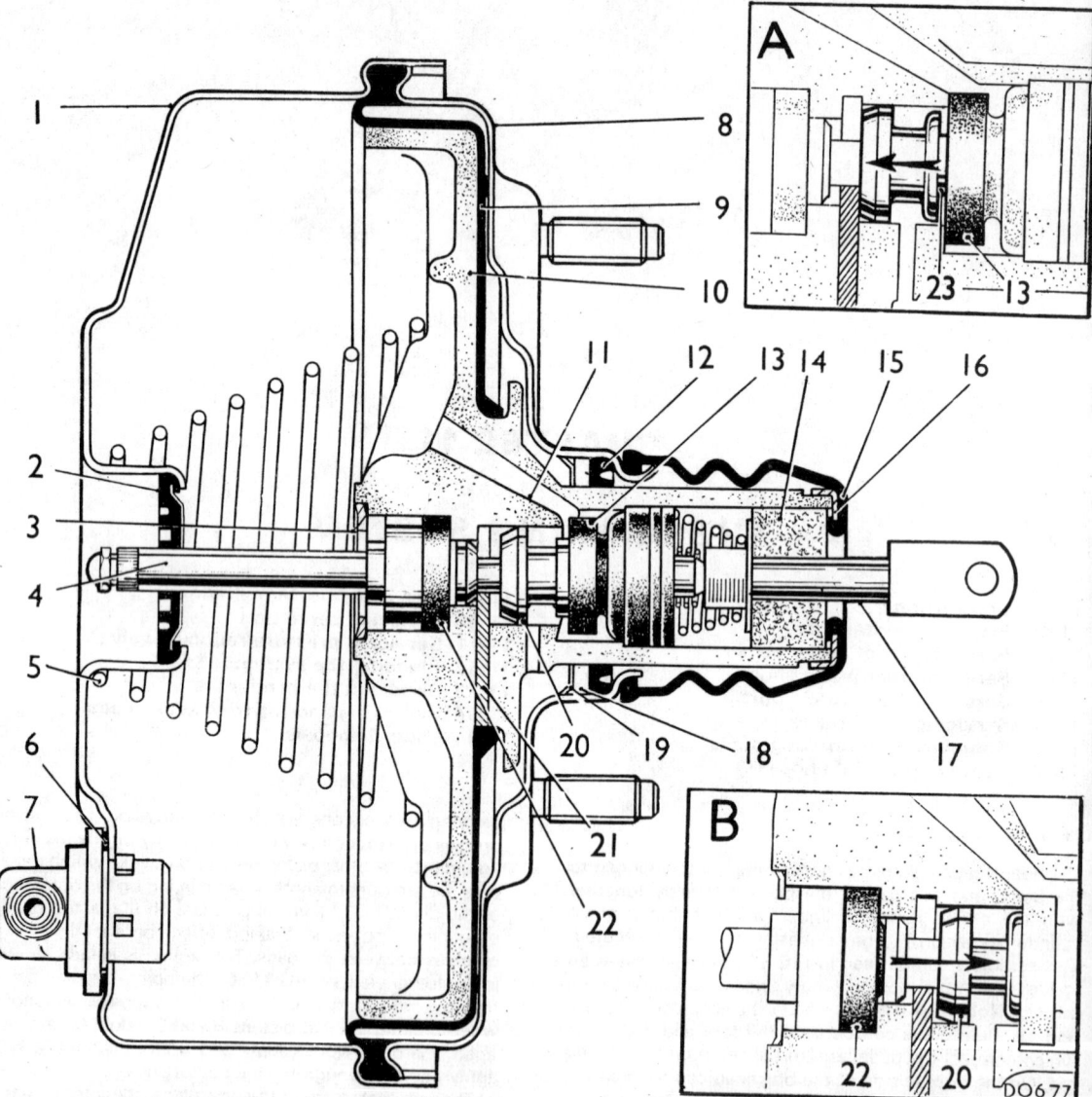

FIG 11 :1   A section through the servo unit (Girling 'Super Vac'). Inset **A** shows the control valve **13** closed, the control piston moved forward and the atmospheric port **23** open. Inset **B** shows how pressure of the diaphragm plate causes reaction disc **22** to bulge into the bore, pressing control piston **20** back and closing the atmospheric port

Key to Fig 11 :1　　1 Front shell　　2 Seal and plate assembly　　3 Retainer (sprag washer)　　4 Pushrod—hydraulic　　5 Diaphragm return spring　　6 O-ring　　7 Non-return valve　　8 Rear shell　　9 Diaphragm　　10 Diaphragm plate　　11 Vacuum port　　12 Seal　　13 Control valve　　14 Filter　　15 Dust cover　　16 End cap　　17 Valve operating rod assembly　　18 Bearing　　19 Retainer　　20 Control piston　　21 Valve retaining plate　　22 Reaction disc　　23 Atmospheric port

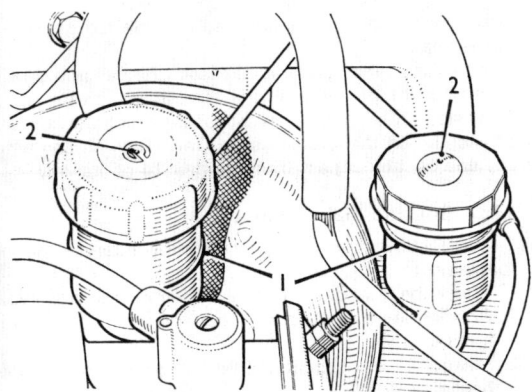

FIG 11:2 The brake master cylinder reservoir is on the left. The smaller one is for the clutch. Fluid level must not fall below the marks indicated at 1. Cap vents 2 must be kept clear

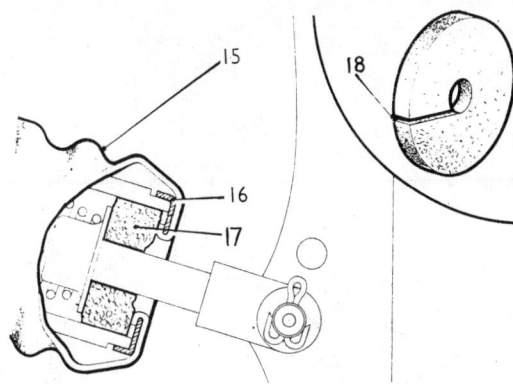

FIG 11:5 Fitting a new servo filter 17. 15 is the dust cover and 16 the end cap. The inset shows how the filter is cut 18

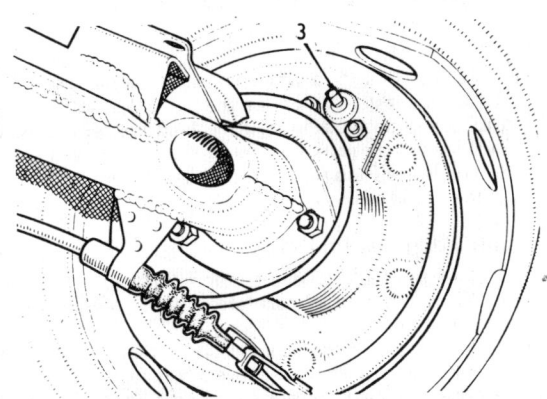

FIG 11:3 The squared adjuster for the rear brake is indicated at 3

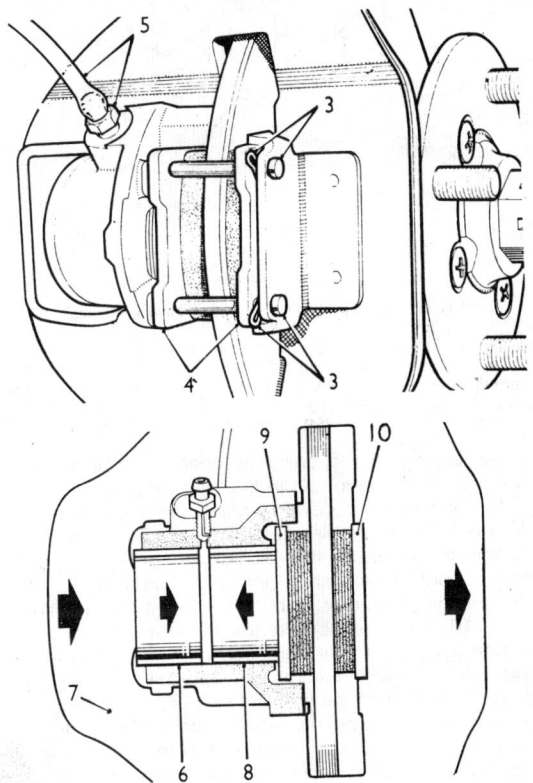

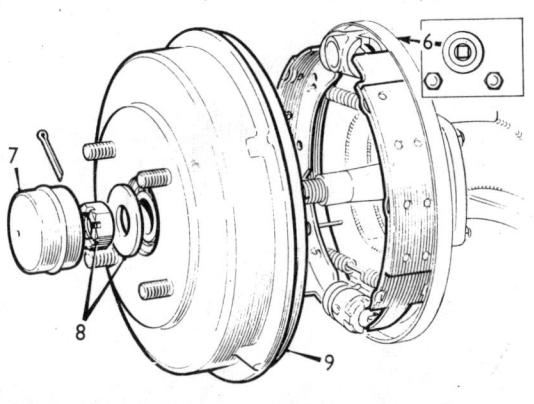

FIG 11:4 Withdrawing the rear hub and brake drum

Key to Fig 11:4

	6 Brake adjuster	7 Dust cap
8 Retaining nut and washer	9 Hub and brake drum	

FIG 11:6 Removing and refitting front brake friction pads. The small arrows show how the pistons 6 and 8 are pressed into the cylinder bore. The large arrows show the movement of the yoke 7 to give clearance for removing indirect pad 10

Key to Fig 11:6

		3 Wire clips and retaining pins
4 Friction pads		5 Tube fitted to bleed screw
6 Indirect piston	7 Yoke	8 Direct piston
9 Direct pad	10 Indirect pad	

MAXI1

119

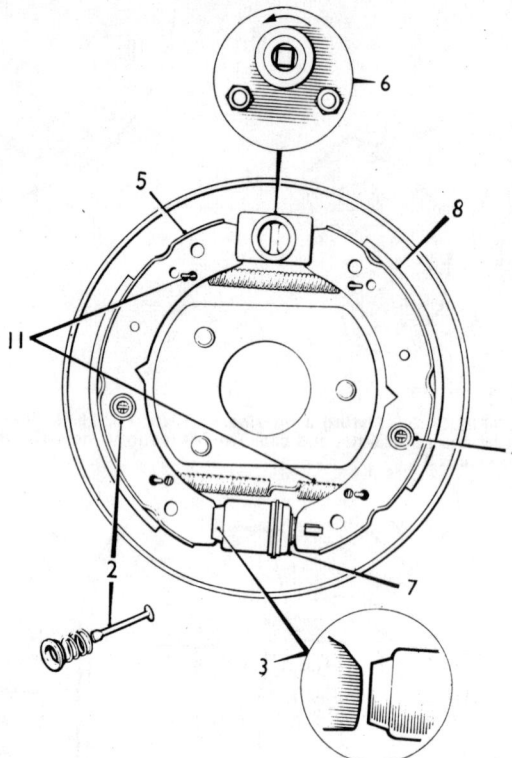

FIG 11 : 7   Removing the rear brake shoes

Key to Fig 11 : 7   2 Steady pin, spring, and cup washer
3 Trailing shoe abutment on cylinder   4 Steady pin for
leading shoe   5 Trailing shoe   6 Adjuster (arrow
shows direction to slacken)   7 Wheel cylinder
8 Leading shoe   11 Return springs

pipes leading to the brake cylinders. The pressure is boosted by the servo unit in the following way:

Movement of the operating rod assembly 17 to the left (see **FIG 11 : 1**) presses control valve 13 onto its seat. Further movement of the rod pushes control piston 20 forward until atmospheric port 23 is uncovered. There are then two factors at work on the diaphragm assembly 9 and 10. On the lefthand side of the assembly, shell 1 is connected to the inlet manifold by way of non-return valve 7. If the engine is running, the closing of vacuum port 11 means that the lefthand side of the diaphragm is subject to the same depression (or vacuum) as that prevailing in the inlet manifold. At the same time, opening port 23 allows atmospheric pressure to act on the right-hand side of the diaphragm. This powerful action is transmitted to the master cylinder piston by pushrod 4. Holding pressure on the brakes, without a continuous rise in effort from the servo unit is achieved by deflection of reaction disc 22. Pressure on this disc by the diaphragm plate causes it to bulge into the bore on its right as shown by the inset 'B'. This bulge pushes control piston 20 to the right to close the atmospheric port. Any further increase in brake pedal pressure will again open this port and give added gain to the boost from the servo unit. If the servo unit fails or the engine is not running, unboosted action

of the master cylinder is possible through the operating rod and pushrod.

When the brake pedal is released, the vacuum port i opened and connection to the atmosphere on the right hand side of the diaphragm causes the complete collaps of vacuum on the lefthand side. Only clean air can ente the unit as it must pass through filter 14 on its way.

11 : 2 Routine maintenance

Every 3,000 miles or at three-monthly intervals, do th following:
1 Check the level of fluid in the master cylinder reservoir
2 Check free travel of brake pedal and adjust rear brake if necessary.
3 Make a visual inspection of the brake pipes and flexible hoses.
Every 6,000 miles or at six-monthly intervals:
1 Inspect the pads in the front disc brakes.
Every 12,000 miles or at twelve-monthly intervals:
1 Remove the rear brake drums, blow out the dust anc inspect the linings.
Every three years, fit a new servo filter.

Topping up:

Refer to **FIG 11 : 2** which shows the larger reservoir o the brake master cylinder on the left. Clean all round the cap before unscrewing it. If the fluid is below the leve indicated by the mark 1 on the outside, top up with Castro Girling Brake Fluid Amber. Make sure that the vent hole 2 in the cap is clear.

Adjusting rear brakes:

Refer to **FIG 11 : 3** and do the following:
1 Chock the front wheels fore and aft and jack-up the rear of the car.
2 Release the handbrake and check that the cables are not pulling on the brake levers behind the backplates. Locate squared adjuster 3 and turn it clockwise until the drum is locked. Slacken the adjuster until it is possible to turn the wheel by hand without the brake rubbing.
3 Repeat this operation on the other brake. **Never adjust only one.** Check that the handbrake operates, giving

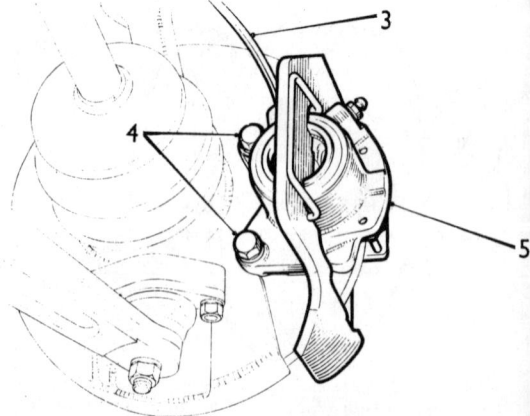

FIG 11 : 8   Removing front caliper unit. 3 is the brake pipe, 4 are the securing bolts and 5 is the unit

120

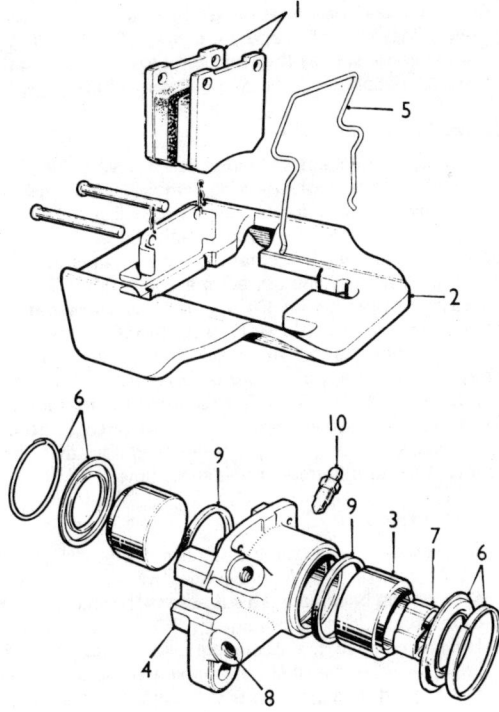

FIG 11 : 9   Dismantling a caliper unit

Key to Fig 11 : 9   1 Friction pads   2 Yoke
3 Indirect piston   4 Cylinder body   5 Yoke spring
6 Dust cover and retaining ring   7 Bias ring
8 Fluid inlet port   9 Piston seal   10 Bleed screw

equal resistance to turning from each brake. If the handbrake is still ineffective, refer to **Section 11 : 13** for instructions on rectification.

Adjusting front brakes :

There is no provision for adjustment of the front disc brakes. The necessary clearance of the pads is automatically achieved and is maintained at all stages of wear.

Removing rear brake drums :

To inspect the rear brake linings and clean out the drums, refer to **FIG 11 : 4** and proceed as follows:

1 Chock the front wheels fore and aft and jack-up the rear of the car. Remove a road wheel. Release the handbrake.
2 Release the brake shoe adjuster 6 by turning it anti-clockwise. Prise off dust cap 7 and remove the splitpin from the nut. Remove the nut and bearing retaining washer 8.
3 Withdraw the hub and drum assembly 9 with a suitable puller.
4 Inspect the linings for wear. The thickness must be such that the brakes will continue to work until the next check is due. Blow out the dust from the drum and backplate.

5 Repack the bearings and the oil seal with grease. **Do not fill the space between the bearings with grease, and do not put grease in the cap.**
6 Refit the hub and drum, tightening the nut to a torque of 60 lb ft. If the splitpin holes do not line-up, tighten still more. **Do not slacken off the nut.**
7 Adjust the brake shoe clearance as described earlier in this Section. Refit the road wheel and repeat the operation on the other side.

Checking front disc pads :

If one pad of a brake is worn more than the other, change over their position. The minimum thickness of pad material is $\frac{1}{16}$ inch, and it is preferable to renew them before they reach that stage to ensure that they will last until the next inspection. The correct material is FERODO 2430F.

Renewing servo filter :

Refer to **FIG 11 : 5** :

1 Under the parcel tray and behind the brake lever will be found the dust cover 15. Pull this back and release the end cap 16. Extract the old filter 17.
2 Take a new filter and cut it diagonally as shown at 18. Slip this over the pushrod and press it into the neck of the servo cylinder.
3 Refit the end cap and dust cover.

11 : 3 Servicing front brake pads

Removing :

Refer to **FIG 11 : 6** and do the following:

1 Apply the handbrake and jack-up the front of the car. Remove the road wheel.
2 Remove the wire clips and extract the retaining pins 3.
3 Withdraw the pads 4. Refer to the preceding Section for instructions on pad renewal.

Refitting :

1 Fit a length of rubber or plastic tubing 5 to the bleed screw. Immerse the end in fresh brake fluid in a container. Slacken the bleed screw by one turn.
2 Press the indirect piston 6 back into its bore and push the yoke 7 in the same direction so that clearance can be obtained for fitting the indirect pad 10. Press the direct piston 8 back into its bore and tighten the bleed screw. Fit the direct pad 9.

FIG 11 : 10   Removing a rear brake backplate

Key to Fig 11 : 10   2 Handbrake cable end   3 Brake pipe   4 Backplate securing nuts   5 Axle and backplate

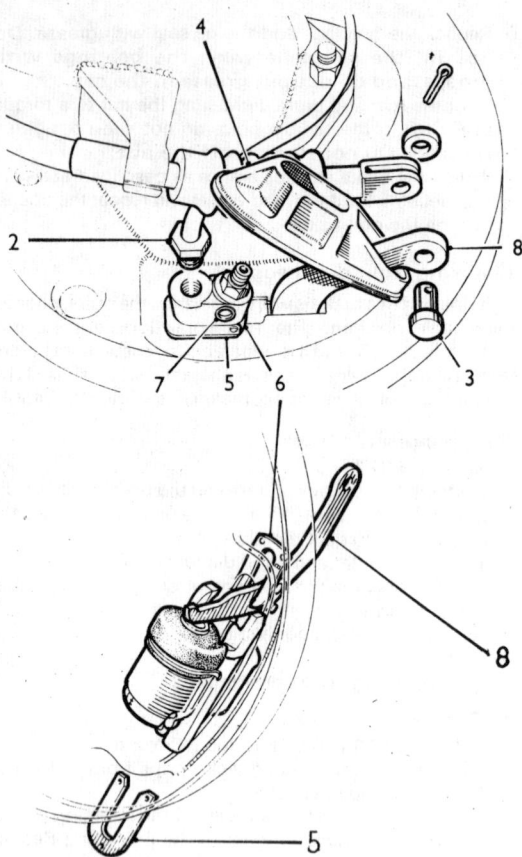

cylinder end of the leading shoe off the handbrake lever. Make sure the operating links are retained in the adjuster housing as they may tend to fall out. Also note the correct position of the brake shoe return springs 11.

Brake lining renewal:

Although replacement linings can be riveted to the old shoes, the best way of renewing linings is to obtain ready-lined shoes on an exchange basis. This will ensure that the linings make complete contact with the shoes and are ground concentrically so that they fit the curvature of the drum at all points. The correct material is MINTEX M79. **Always renew brake linings in complete sets, or there may be trouble with unbalanced braking.**

Do not handle the linings with greasy fingers and keep oil, grease, paint and other contaminants off the linings at all times. If the linings are soaked in oil it is useless to try to clean them with a solvent.

If brake shoes and linings are renewed it is advisable to renew the return springs at the same time.

Refitting:

1 Slacken off all adjustment by turning adjuster screw 6 anticlockwise. Check that wheel cylinder 7 is free to slide on the backplate. This is essential if the full action of the brake is to be obtained.
2 Having cleaned the backplate with Girling Cleaning Fluid, use a smear of Girling Brake Grease on the shoe steady platforms, both ends of the brake shoes and also the adjuster links. **Do not let grease come into contact with rubber parts or the linings.**
3 Before fitting the shoes, check that the adjuster links are correctly positioned in the housing so that the angle of each link rests on the adjuster wedge.
4 Reverse the removal sequence, making sure that the return springs are fitted in the correct holes in the shoe webs as shown in the illustration. Note that the interrupted spring is at the wheel cylinder end.
5 Adjust the brakes as instructed in **Section 11:2** and check the operation of the handbrake.

FIG 11:11   Removing and refitting a rear wheel cylinder

Key to Fig 11:11

	2 Brake pipe	3 Clevis pin
4 Rubber boot	5 Retaining plate	6 Spring plate
7 Wheel cylinder	8 Handbrake lever	

3 Refit the retaining pins and wire clips. Top up the master cylinder with the correct fluid as specified in **Section 11:2**. Apply the brake pedal several times to settle the pads and to reach the normal running clearance.

11:4 Servicing the rear brake shoes

Removing:

1 Remove the hub assembly as instructed in **Section 9:3**.
2 Refer to **FIG 11:7** and remove the steady pin assembly 2 from the trailing shoe 5. The shoe can be identified by the position of the lining on the shoe and the abutment of the lower end 3 against the wheel cylinder. Note how the linings are offset on both shoes. Press and turn the cup washer on the steady pin to release the spring and remove the parts.
3 Disengage the trailing shoe from the wheel cylinder abutment 3 and from the link in the adjuster housing.
4 Remove the steady pin assembly 4 from the leading shoe 8. Remove the two shoes and springs, easing the

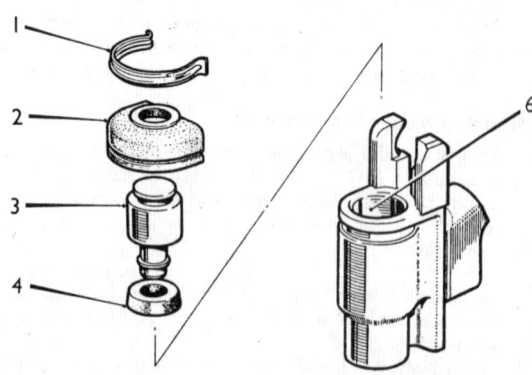

FIG 11:12   Dismantling a rear wheel cylinder

Key to Fig 11:12

	1 Retaining ring	2 Dust cover
3 Piston	4 Piston seal	6 Cylinder bore

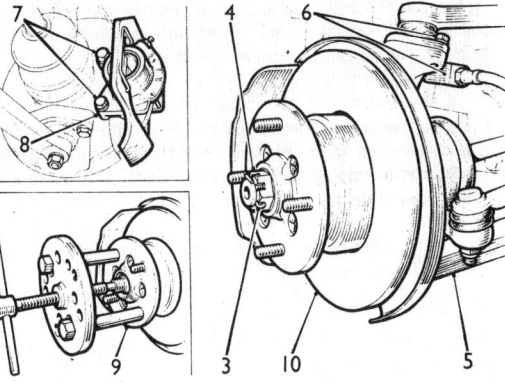

FIG 11 :13   Removing a front brake disc

Key to Fig 11 :13   3 Splitpin   4 Hub nut
... Lower suspension arm   6 Upper ball joint securing
...olts and brake pipe bracket   7 Caliper unit securing bolts
... Caliper unit   9 Driving flange   10 Disc

1 :5 Servicing a front brake unit

Removing :

Apply the handbrake, raise the front of the car and remove a road wheel.

2 Refer to **FIG 11 :8** and disconnect brake pipe 3 from the caliper unit.

3 Remove securing bolts 4 and lift the unit clear of the disc.

Dismantling :

It is always advisable to renew all seals during an overhaul. These are available in kit form. Observe the highest degree of cleanliness when at work on the internal parts of hydraulic mechanisms to ensure that dirt is not the cause of brake failure on the road, with possibly disastrous results. Refer to **FIG 11 :9** and proceed as follows:

1 Remove the friction pads as described in **Section 11 :3**. Clamp yoke 2 between soft jaws in a vice. Press indirect piston 3 fully into cylinder 4.

2 Press the cylinder down, note the position of yoke spring 5 and remove both parts.

3 Remove the dust covers and retaining rings 6 from the cylinder. Withdraw the bias ring 7 from the indirect piston. Apply gentle air pressure to inlet port 8 to blow the pistons out of the cylinder.

4 Remove the piston seals 9 from the cylinder bore with a piece of wood, taking care not to scratch the bore. Remove bleed screw 10. **Do not disturb the setting of the adjusting screw in the cylinder body.**

Cleaning and inspection :

Wash all the parts in Girling Cleaning Fluid. **Never let any of the rubber seals come into contact with petrol or similar solvents, or with engine oil.** Check the pistons and cylinder bore for scores, corrosion or pitting and renew defective parts. Renew all seals.

Reassembling :

During this operation, all parts must be absolutely free from dirt and grit. Before fitting, wet the pistons and seals with Castrol Girling Brake Fluid Amber. Then proceed as follows:

1 Fit a **new** bias ring into the indirect piston. The radiused end must enter the piston first.

2 Fit the wetted seals into their grooves in the cylinder. Push the pistons into the cylinder. The indirect piston goes into the end farthest from the friction pads.

3 Fit the dust covers and retaining rings. Note that the wider ring is at the righthand end in the illustration and this is also the end farthest from the pads. Position the yoke spring on the yoke.

4 **Do not lubricate the cylinder grooves or the sliding edges of the yoke.** Fit the cylinder to the yoke, engaging the tongue of the yoke into the bias ring inside the indirect piston. Settle the legs of the spring into the sliding grooves of the cylinder. The angled leg of the spring must engage in the cylinder groove which is opposite the bleed screw.

5 Fit the bleed screw and the pads.

Refitting :

Simply reverse the removal operations and then bleed the brakes as instructed in **Section 11 :12**.

11 :6 Servicing rear brakes

Removing :

This operation begins with the removal of the hub assembly as described in **Section 9 :3**. It then continues as follows:

1 Refer to **FIG 11 :10** and disconnect the handbrake cable 2. Disconnect the brake pipe 3.

2 Remove nuts 4. These secure the backplate and axle plate 5 to the radius arm.

3 Insert a drift in the socket in the radius arm and drive out the axle. Withdraw the axle from the backplate.

Dismantling :

Remove the brake shoes as detailed in **Section 11 :4**. Refer to **FIG 11 :11** and remove the wheel cylinder as follows:

1 Disconnect brake pipe 2 from the cylinder. Remove rubber boot 4.

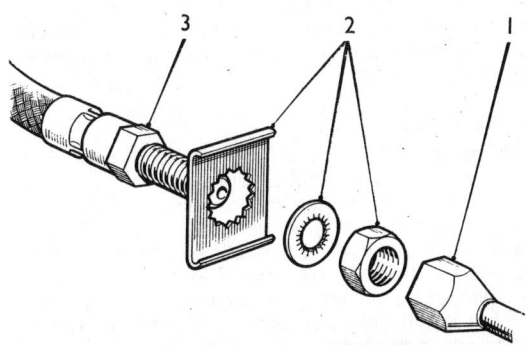

FIG 11 :14   Removing a brake flexible hose correctly. 1 is the metal pipe union nut, 2 are the locking plate parts and 3 is the inner hexagon on the flexible hose

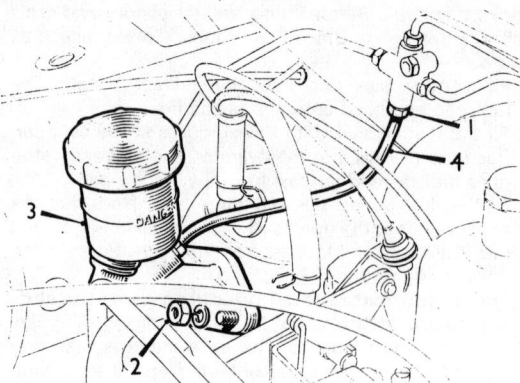

FIG 11 :15 Removing the master cylinder **3. 1** is the union nut of pipe **4** and **2** is a securing nut

2 Tap retaining plate 5 and spring plate 6 from the neck of the cylinder where it protrudes through the backplate. The cylinder will now be free to be removed. Disengage the handbrake lever 8 from the cylinder.

3 Unscrew two nuts to release the adjuster from the backplate, taking care to retrieve the two links if they fall out. Note the angled ends where the links locate on the adjusting wedge. Screw the wedge out of the housing.

To dismantle the wheel cylinder, refer to **FIG 11 :12** and do the following:

1 Remove dust cover retaining ring 1. Remove dust cover 2.

2 Tap out piston 3 or blow it out with **gentle** air pressure. Remove seal 4 from the piston.

Cleaning and inspection :

Wash all the components of the wheel cylinder in Girling Cleaning Fluid or methylated spirit. **Do not use petrol or similar solvents as they will ruin the rubber seals. It is also important not to let mineral oil contact the seals.** Check the piston and cylinder bore for scoring, pitting or corrosion and renew defective parts. Always renew seals at every overhaul.

Clean the adjuster links, wedge and housing and lubricate with Girling Brake Grease. Clean up the backplate and ensure that the sliding surfaces of the plate and the wheel cylinder are clean and free from rust. Renew rubber boots and dust covers which are cracked or show signs of deterioration.

Reassembling :

Fit the wedge into the adjuster housing, screwing it fully home in an anticlockwise direction as viewed from behind the backplate. Refit the housing. Leave the links until the shoes are being refitted so that they cannot be lost. Reassemble the wheel cylinder by immersing all parts and seals in Castrol Girling Brake Fluid Amber and fitting them wet. Using the fingers only, press the seal onto the piston with its flat face against the piston. When inserting into cylinder 6 be careful not to trap or turn back the lip of the seal. Fit the dust cover and retaining ring, settling the outer end of the cover into the locating groove in the piston. Reassemble the backplate as follows.

1 Refer to **FIG 11 :11**. Smear the slot in the backplate and the wheel cylinder face with Girling Brake Grease. Locate the handbrake lever spindle in the recesses in the cylinder arms.

2 Pass the lever and the neck of the wheel cylinder through the slot in the backplate. Slide the spring plate 6 between the cylinder neck and the backplate. From the opposite side, introduce the retaining plate between the spring plate and the wheel cylinder and tap it home so that the pips in the spring plate engage in the holes in the retaining plate. Check that the cylinder can slide in the backplate slot.

3 Reverse the rest of the dismantling instructions, refitting the shoes as described in **Section 11 :4**. Do not forget to fit the adjuster links, correctly angled against the adjusting wedge.

4 Refit the backplate assembly and axle shaft to the radius arm, connect the brake pipe and handbrake cable, refit the hub, and bleed the brakes according to **Section 11 :12**.

11 :7 Removing and refitting discs

To remove a hub and disc assembly it is necessary to apply the handbrake, jack-up the front of the car and remove the road wheel. Then refer to **FIG 11 :13** and carry out the following operations:

1 Withdraw splitpin 3 and remove nut 4. Support the lower suspension arm 5 with a jack.

2 Remove the bolts securing the upper swivel ball joint and disengage the brake pipe bracket 6.

3 From inside the unit, remove the caliper securing bolts 7. Lift clear the caliper unit 8, supporting it so that the flexible brake hose is not strained.

4 Use a puller to withdraw the disc 10 and driving flange 9. Remove four screws to release the disc from the flange.

If the disc is cracked, pitted or deeply scored it must be renewed. Light, concentric scoring is not detrimental to braking efficiency.

Refitting :

Before reversing the dismantling sequence, check that the mating surfaces of the disc and flange are clean and free from burrs. Tighten the securing screws and check the runout of the disc face near the periphery with a dial gauge. Repositioning the disc on the flange may effect an improvement if runout is thought to be excessive. Tighten the hub nut to a torque of 150 lb ft.

11 :8 Removing flexible hoses

This operation needs care to avoid straining the hose by twisting. The correct procedure is to start at the bracket end, referring to **FIG 11 :14** for details of the assembly. First unscrew union nut 1 which secures the metal pipeline. Remove the locknut, lockwasher and locking plate 2 from the bracket, holding the adjacent hexagon of hose 3 to prevent it from twisting. At the outer end of the hose, use the other hexagon to unscrew the hose from the cylinder. In this way, the hose is not subjected to twisting. Refit in the reverse order, making sure that the hose is not strained while the locknut is tightened. Such a strain may alter the run of the hose and cause rubbing, which might lead to failure.

11 :9 Servicing the master cylinder

Removing:

The master cylinder is bolted to the front face of the servo cylinder as depicted in **FIG 11 :15**. Remove it by unscrewing union nut 1 to detach pipe 4 from the four-way connector. Remove two nuts 2 and withdraw the master cylinder. The pipe can then be detached.

Dismantling:

This operation and the one of reassembling demand absolute cleanliness. It must be impossible for dirt or grit to adhere to any of the internal parts, so begin by plugging the outlet port and cleaning the outside of the assembly with Girling Cleaning Fluid or methylated spirits, after pouring off any fluid in the reservoir. Discard this fluid. Refer to **FIG 11 :16** and carry on dismantling in the following way:

1 Pressing the pushrod slightly inwards to relieve the pressure, remove circlip 1. Take away the pushrod and dished washer 2.
2 Tap out the complete piston assembly 3 or use gentle air pressure at the outlet port 12 with a finger over the vent hole in the reservoir cap.
3 Lift the leaf 21 of thimble 7 and withdraw the piston stem from the thimble. Remove seal 5 from the piston.
4 Press on the end of valve stem 6 to compress the spring and disengage the stem from the elongated hole in the

thimble. Pull the thimble out of the spring.
5 Remove valve spacer and curved washer 8 from the valve stem and remove seal 9 from the valve head.

Cleaning and inspecting:

Wash all the components in Girling Cleaning Fluid or methylated spirit. **Do not use petrol or any similar solvent. These, and mineral oil, have a bad effect on rubber seals.** Check the condition of the piston and cylinder bore. These must be free from scoring, ridges, pitting or corrosion. Renew all defective parts and always fit new seals. Check that the reservoir and outlet ports are free from obstruction.

Reassembling:

All internal parts must be dipped in Castrol Girling Brake Fluid Amber and assembled whilst wet. Proceed as follows:

1 Refer to the section of the valve head shown in the top righthand corner of the illustration. This shows how to fit the valve seal 14 correctly, so that its smallest diameter is back against the valve head.
2 Fit curved washer 15 with its domed face against the valve shoulder, then fit spacer 16 with the legs towards the valve seal. Fit the spring centrally on the spacer. Insert the thimble in the other end of the spring.
3 Press on the thimble to compress the spring and insert

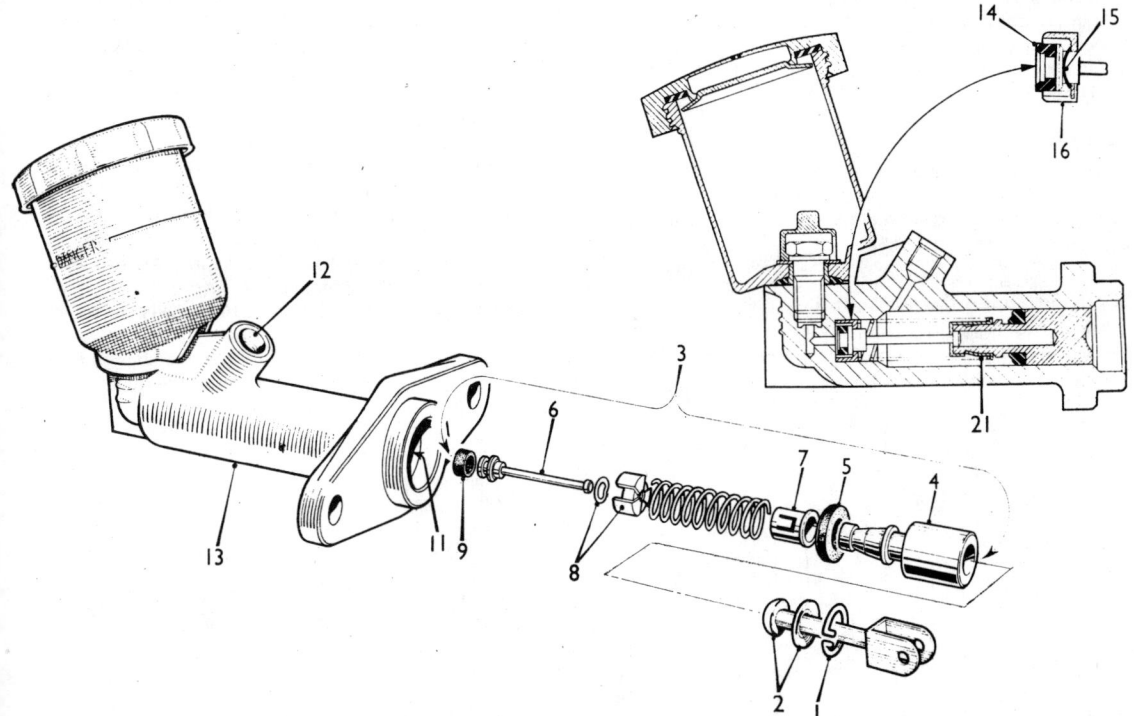

FIG 11 :16 Component parts of a master cylinder. The inset shows the correct assembly of the valve seal parts

Key to Fig 11 :16   1 Circlip   2 Pushrod and dished washer   3 Piston assembly   4 Piston   5 Piston seal
6 Valve stem   7 Thimble   8 Spacer and curved washer   9 Valve seal   11 Master cylinder bore   12 Outlet port
13 Master cylinder and reservoir   14 Valve seal on valve head   15 Curved washer   16 Spacer   21 Leaf on thimble

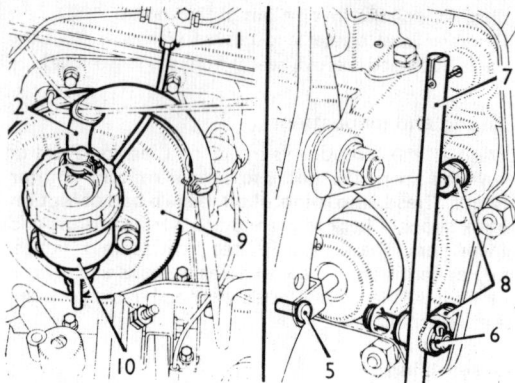

FIG 11 :17 Removing the servo assembly. On the left a view under the bonnet and on the right a view inside the car

Key to Fig 11 :17
2 Vacuum hose	1 Brake pipe union nut
6 Accelerator pedal pivot pin	5 Brake pedal clevis pin
8 Servo securing nuts	7 Accelerator pedal
10 Master cylinder	9 Servo assembly

the valve stem in the elongated hole in the thimble, moving the stem into a central position last of all.

4 Fit a new seal to the piston with its flat face against the piston shoulder. Insert the stem of the piston into the thimble until the spring leaf can be pressed inwards behind the shoulder as shown at 21.

5 Fit the pushrod and dished washer, press inwards slightly and fit the circlip.

Refitting :

This is a reversal of the removal procedure. Make sure the pipe is free from obstruction before connecting it. When installation is complete, bleed the brakes as explained in **Section 11 :12.**

11 :10 Servicing the servo unit

The unit is shown in section in **FIG 11 :1** and the components are illustrated in **FIG 11 :18**. Refer to **FIG 11 :17** to remove the servo unit as follows:

1 Unscrew the union nut 1 to disconnect the fluid pipe from the four-way connector. Release the clip and disconnect the vacuum hose 2 from the unit.

2 Working inside the car, remove the securing screws from the parcel shelf. Raise the shelf enough to reach the brake pedal mountings. Remove the clevis pin 5 from the pedal.

3 Remove the splitpin and washer 6 from the accelerator pedal pivot pin. Move the accelerator pedal so that it is possible to put a spanner on the servo securing nuts 8. Remove the four nuts to release the unit. From under the bonnet, withdraw the servo unit 9 complete with master cylinder 10. Unscrew the two nuts from the fixing flange to remove the master cylinder.

Dismantling :

The Girling 'Super Vac' servo unit is normally serviced by obtaining a replacement unit rather than by fitting new parts. The following notes on dismantling will, however, be found useful, but it will be necessary to make up the tools shown in **FIG 11 :19**. It is useless to try to carry out the dismantling without these tools. Note that top plate 2 picks up the four studs at the rear of the unit and drilled channel 2a locates the two master cylinder studs. Hold the channel in a vice and carry out the following operations, using **FIGS 11 :18** and **11 :19** for reference purposes:

1 Make alignment marks 1 across the two shells of the assembly. Secure the front shell to the channel by nuts on the master cylinder studs. Secure lever 2 to the studs on the rear shell.

2 Connect a vacuum hose from the non-return valve 16 to the inlet manifold, start the engine and prepare to separate the shells. The vacuum will draw the two shells together to make this possible.

3 Turn lever 2 anticlockwise until the indentations in the front shell line-up with the recesses in the rim of the rear shell.

4 Apply downward pressure on the top shell and detach the vacuum hose at the same time. Also depress the operating rod to release the vacuum. This should result in the two shells coming apart, but it might be necessary to tap the front shell with a hide mallet to break the bond.

5 Switch off the engine. Lift off the rear shell 8. Remove diaphragm return spring 9. Remove the dust cover, end

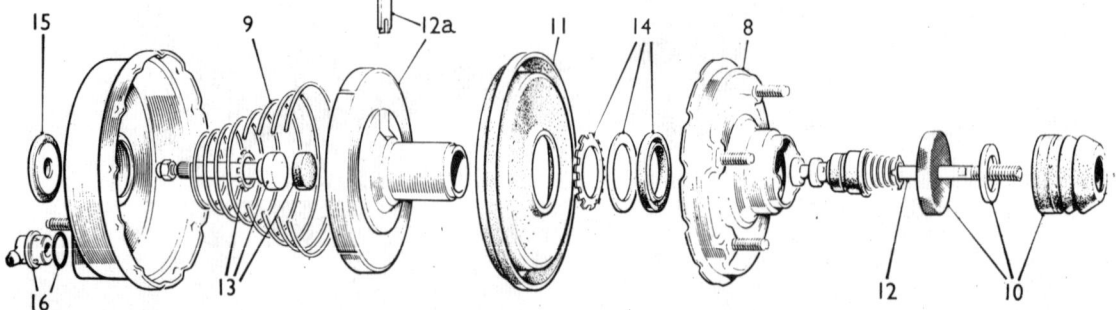

FIG 11 :18 Components of the servo unit. Valve **16** is connected to the vacuum hose and valve rod **12** to the brake pedal

Key to Fig 11 :18
8 Rear shell   9 Diaphragm return spring   10 Dust cover, end cap and filter   11 Diaphragm
12 Valve rod assembly   12a Valve retaining plate and diaphragm plate   13 Hydraulic pushrod, reaction disc and retaining washer
14 Seal, bearing and retainer   15 Seal and plate   16 Non-return valve and grommet

cap and filter 10.

6 Remove diaphragm 11. Depress valve rod 12 and shake out the valve retaining plate from the diaphragm plate 12a. Pull out the valve rod assembly.

7 Ease the retaining washer from the diaphragm plate, and withdraw the hydraulic pushrod and reaction disc 13. Moving to the rear shell 8, ease out the retaining washer and press out the bearing and seal 14. Be careful not to damage the sealing surface of the shell. From the front shell, press out the seal and plate assembly 15. Remove the non-return valve and grommet 16 if considered necessary.

Cleaning and inspection:

Clean all the parts in Girling Cleaning Fluid and no other. Check the sealing surfaces at the rear end of the long neck on the diaphragm plate and those in the rear shell. They must be undamaged and free from corrosion. Renew all working parts by obtaining an official major repair kit. **The two kinds of grease contained in this kit are not interchangeable. The unit will be seriously damaged if the greases are not used as directed.**

Reassembling:

1 Smear seal and bearing 14 with Girling Grease No. 64949008 and fit to the rear shell. Make sure that the flat face of the seal registers against the bearing, as can be seen by parts 12 and 18 in **FIG 11 :1**. Press the bearing and seal firmly into position. Fit the retainer.

2 Smear the reaction disc and pushrod 13 with Girling Grease No. 64949008. Fit them to the diaphragm plate. Press in the large retaining washer and discard the small one included in the kit. **Do not attempt to alter the length of the hydraulic pushrod, as any movement of the adjustment will strip the threads.**

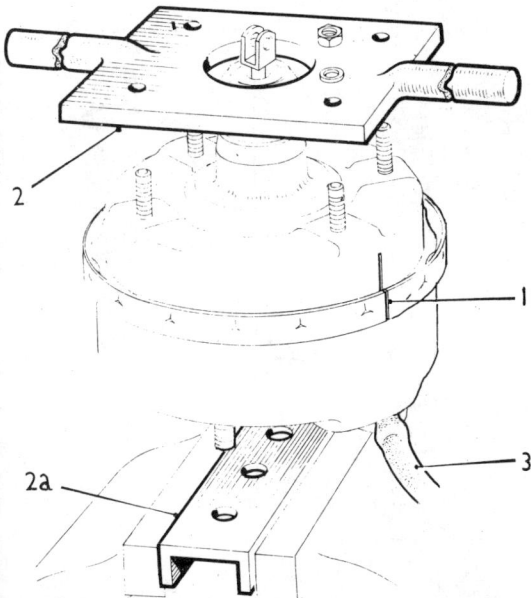

FIG 11:19   Tools for servicing servo unit shells

Key to Fig 11:19   1 Alignment marks   2 Lever
(secured to rear shell studs)   2a Base plate
3 Vacuum hose

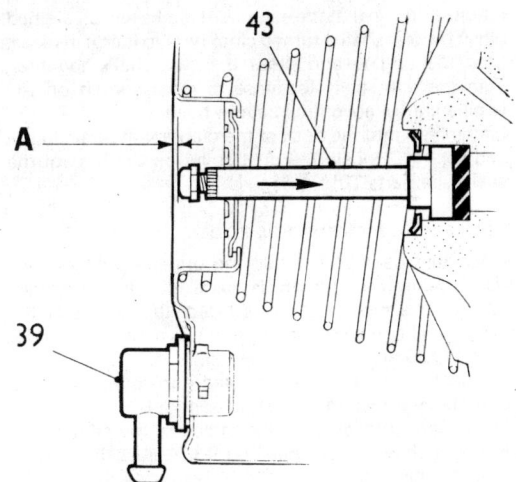

FIG 11 : 20   Adjusting servo unit hydraulic pushrod. Clearance at **A** should be .011 to .016 inch. **39** is the non-return valve and **43** is the pushrod

A new pushrod can be adjusted for length and this procedure will be covered at the end of this set of instructions.

3 Smear the outer surface of the diaphragm plate neck and the working surface for the valve plunger with Girling Grease No. 64949008. Insert the valve rod assembly into the neck and secure with retaining plate 12a.

4 Fit the diaphragm. If the non-return valve was removed, lubricate the grommet with Girling Grease No. 64949008 and fit it to the front shell, followed by the valve.

5 Smear the seal and plate assembly 15 with Girling Grease No. 64949008 and press into the front shell with the plate facing inwards.

6 Secure the front shell to the channel held in a vice and bolt the lever to the rear shell. Connect a vacuum hose between the non-return valve and the inlet manifold.

7 Locate the diaphragm return spring in the front shell. Smear the outer bead of the diaphragm with Girling Grease No. 64949009 and fit the diaphragm assembly into the rear shell. Locate the rear shell assembly on the

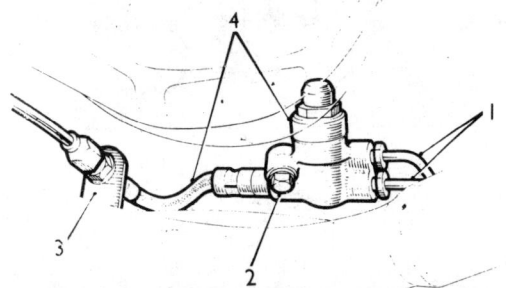

FIG 11 : 21   Removing the pressure reducing valve

Key to Fig 11 : 21   1 Brake pipes   2 Valve securing bolt
3. Radius arm bracket for hose   4 Valve and flexible hose

return spring so that the alignment marks will be aligned when the rear shell is turned clockwise to lock it in place.

8 Start the engine and press the two shells together. Turn the rear shell clockwise to lock. Switch off the engine and remove the vacuum hose.

9 Fit the filter into the neck of the diaphragm plate, fit the end cap, and locate the dust cover on the lugs of the shell (see parts 10).

Fitting a new hydraulic pushrod:

It has just been stated that the original pushrod will suffer damage if an attempt is made to alter the adjustment. When a new pushrod is fitted, the height of the adjusting bolt can be set after the unit is assembled. Refer to **FIG 11:20** and do the following:

1 Connect a vacuum hose between non-return valve 39 and the inlet manifold. Start the engine.

2 Put Loctite (grade B) on the thread of the adjustment bolt and screw it into pushrod 43. Adjust the bolt so that its face is .011 to .016 inch below the face of the front shell as indicated at 'A'. Leave the Loctite for 24 hours to let it set.

3 Switch off the engine and detach the vacuum hose.

Refitting:

Follow the removal instructions in reverse but note that the clevis pin for the pushrod goes into the lower of the two holes in the pedal arm. When all is secure, bleed the brakes as specified in **Section 11:12**.

11:11 Servicing the pressure reducing valve

This is located adjacent to one of the radius arms as shown in **FIG 11:21**. Its function is to limit the pressure on the rear brakes under heavy braking to minimize skidding.

Removing:

1 Disconnect the two brake pipes 1. Remove the valve securing bolt 2.

2 Disconnect flexible hose 3 from the bracket on the radius arm, using the method described in **Section 11:8**.

3 Remove the valve complete with hose.

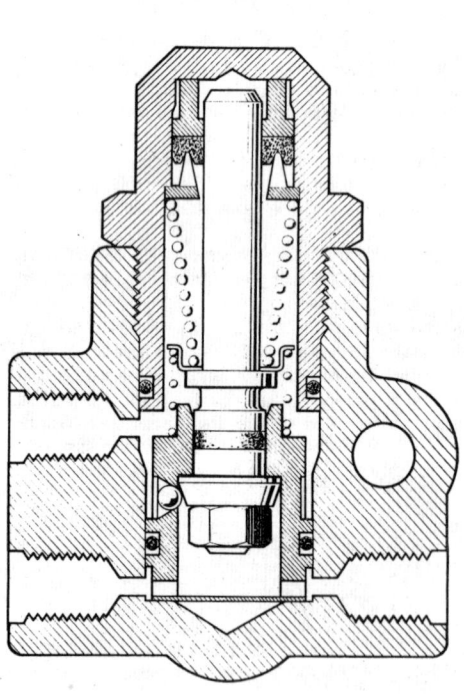
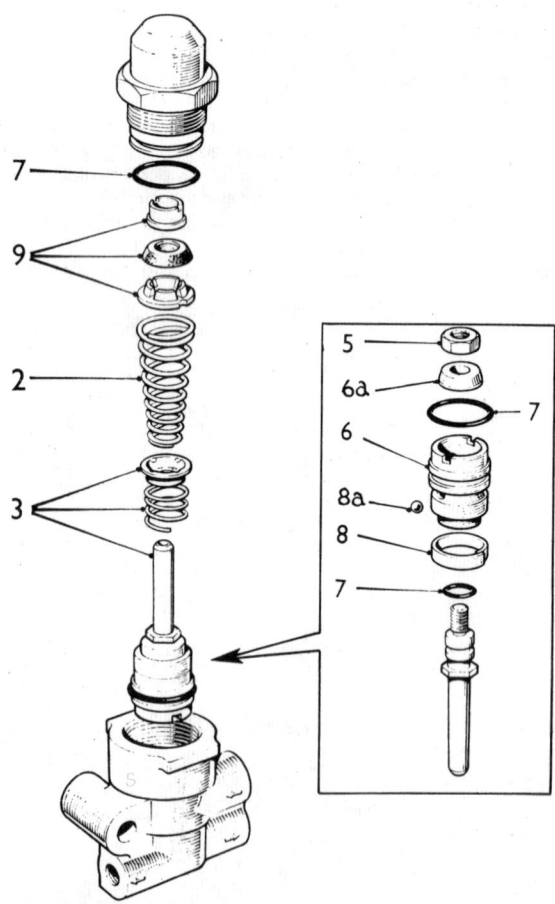

FIG 11:22   Components of brake pressure reducing valve on the right. A section through the valve on the left

Key to Fig 11:22   2 Tapered spring   3 Spring seat, light spring, and piston assembly   5 Valve sleeve nut
6 Valve sleeve   6a Valve plate   7 Seals   8 Bias clip   8a Ball   9 Rod guide, seal, and seal spacer

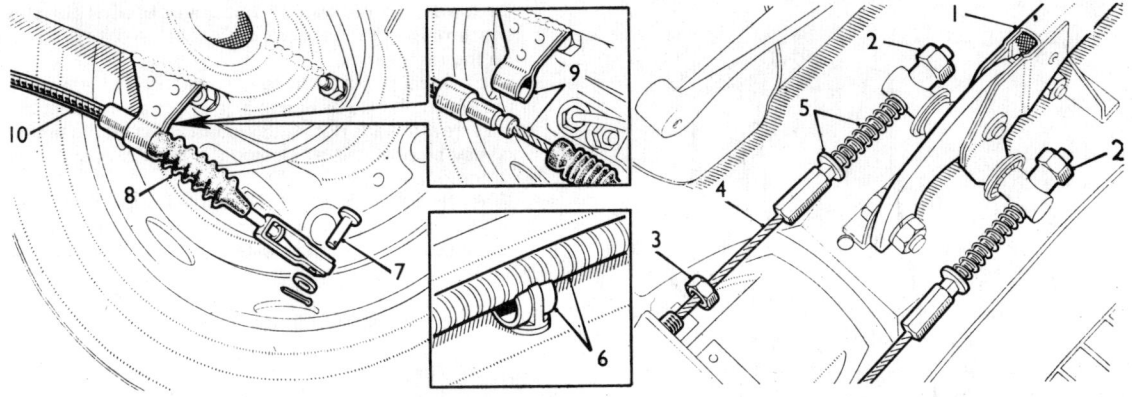

FIG 11 : 23   Removing handbrake cables

Key to Fig 11 : 23   1 Handbrake lever   2 Adjusting nuts   3 Outer cable nut   4 Inner cable   5 Plain washer and spring
6 Outer cable and body clip   7 Clevis pin   8 Rubber boot   9 Cable and radius arm clip   10 Cable

Dismantling:

Refer to **FIG 11 : 22** which shows a section through the valve and the components. Take the valve to pieces in the following way:

1 Clamp the valve in a vice fitted with soft jaws. The end plug must be uppermost.
2 Remove the plug and withdraw the tapered spring 2.
3 Withdraw the piston assembly 3, separating the spring seat and light spring afterwards. Clamp the piston assembly between soft jaws in a vice with the sleeve end uppermost as shown in the righthand inset.
4 Remove the securing nut 5, lift off the sleeve 6 and shake out the valve plate 6a. Remove the three seals 7 from the piston, sleeve and end plug.
5 Slide bias clip 8 off the sleeve and shake out ball 8a. From the end plug, remove the seal spacer, gland seal, and rod guide 9.

Cleaning and inspection:

Clean the parts in Girling Cleaning Fluid or Castrol Girling Brake Fluid Amber. **Do not use petrol or similar solvents as these will damage the seals.** If the bore is ridged, scored or corroded, renew the unit. Renew the end plug seal if there has been leakage.

Reassembling:

Take all the components and dip them in Castrol Girling Brake Fluid Amber. Assemble them wet, as follows:

1 Fit the rod guide into the end plug, small end first. Follow with the gland seal, small diameter first. Drop the seal spacer onto the seal with the flat surface facing outwards. Parts 9 in the central view show this assembly clearly.
2 Fit the large O-ring into the groove in the end plug and the smaller ones to the sleeve and piston.
3 Drop the valve plate into the sleeve, large diameter first, insert the threaded end of the piston from the opposite end of the sleeve, pass it through the valve plate and fit the nut. Tighten the nut to a torque of 3 to 4 lb ft.
4 Fit the ball into the port in the sleeve and hold in place by sliding the bias clip over the ball. Insert the piston and sleeve assembly into the bore of the body.

5 Fit the light spring into the sleeve and position the spring seat. Slide the small end of the tapered spring over the piston so that it registers in the spring seat. Refit the end plug and tighten it to a torque of 25 to 35 lb ft.

11 :12 Bleeding the system

This operation is necessary if air has entered the hydraulic system. This occurs when pipes are disconnected or cylinders dismantled. A 'spongy' feel at the brake pedal is commonly due to air in the system because air is compressible. This air can be eliminated as follows:

1 First check that the rear wheel cylinder is free to slide in the slot in the backplate. Check all pipe connections for tightness and make sure all bleed screws are closed.
2 Release the handbrake and fill the master cylinder reservoir with fresh Castrol Girling Brake Fluid Amber. **As fluid is used during the process of bleeding the system, keep inspecting the level in the reservoir and top up when necessary.** If the fluid level is allowed to drop so low that the bottom of the reservoir is exposed it is likely that more air will be drawn into the system and this necessitates a fresh start.
3 Use about two feet of rubber or plastic tubing which is a tight fit on the bleed screw. Clear plastic tubing is best because the air bubbles can be seen travelling along it. Attach the tubing to the bleed screw on the front brake caliper farthest from the master cylinder. Immerse the free end of the tube in a little brake fluid in a clean glass jar.
4 Open the bleed screw about half a turn and secure the services of an assistant to pump the brake pedal. There should be a full slow stroke of the pedal, followed by three short rapid strokes, the pedal then being allowed to fly back freely. Watch the immersed end of the tube for emerging air bubbles. Continue the operation of pumping the pedal until no air bubbles are seen and then close the bleed screw during a last slow stroke of the pedal.
5 Repeat the process on the other front brake and then do the rear brakes. Do not overtighten the bleed screws.

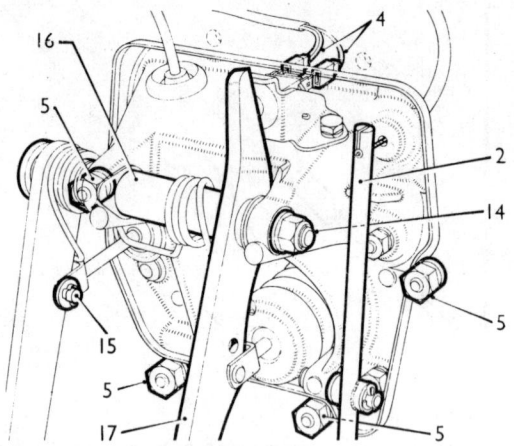

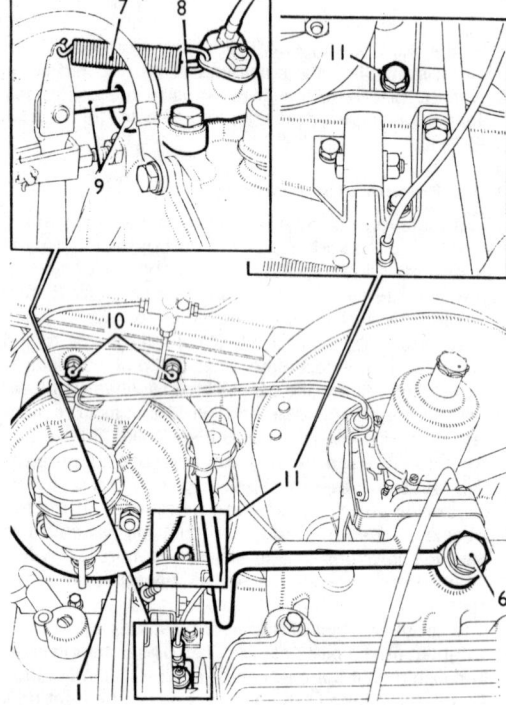

FIG 11:24 Removing the brake pedal. The top view is from inside the car. The central insets are of the slave cylinder and mounting bracket and the lower view is from under the bonnet

Key to Fig 11:24 1 Servo and master cylinder assembly
2 Accelerator pedal 4 Wiring from brake light switch
5 Nuts securing pedal mounting bracket 6 Connection of servo pipe to inlet manifold 7 Return spring
8 Slave cylinder bolt 9 Slave cylinder and pushrod
10 Top bolts (mounting bracket) 11 Bolt (mounting bracket to subframe) 14 Pedal pivot nut 15 Clevis pin (clutch pedal) 16 Pivot 17 Brake pedal

Discard all fluid which has been bled from the system. Being aerated it is unfit to be used for topping up the reservoir.

If air bubbles continue to emerge without apparent improvement, it may be due to air being drawn in past the bleed screw threads during the return stroke of the pedal. This may be obviated by closing the bleed screw during each return stroke.

When the whole system has been bled, apply the brakes hard and check all pipe connections and bleed screws for possible leaks. Top up the master cylinder to the required level.

11:13 Servicing the handbrake

Adjustment:

Normally there is no need for handbrake adjustment because the correct shoe clearance in the rear brakes automatically sets the handbrake. If handbrake movement is excessive and it is known that the rear brakes are properly adjusted, with linings which are not excessively worn, it is likely that the handbrake cables have stretched. Take up this stretch as follows:

1 Refer to **FIG 11:23.** Pull up the handbrake lever to engage the third notch. Chock the front wheels fore and aft and jack-up the rear end of the car.
2 Adjust nuts 2 until the rear wheels can just be turned by heavy hand pressure. Both wheels should offer equal resistance.
3 Release the handbrake lever and check that both rear wheels will turn freely. If not, check that the return springs in the binding brake are not broken, that the piston is not seized in the wheel cylinder and that the cylinder is free to slide in the backplate.

Removing lever:

Disconnect the cables from the lever by unscrewing nuts 2. Remove the two bolts securing the lever ratchet plate to the floor tunnel and lift away the assembly.

Refitting lever:

Reverse the dismantling sequence and then adjust the cables as just instructed.

Removing cables:

1 Release the handbrake and remove the cable nuts 2. Remove the outer cable abutment nuts 3.
2 Disengage the cables 4 from the lever and remove springs and washers 5.
3 Release the outer cables from the body clips 6. Behind the rear brakes, remove clevis pins 7 to disconnect the cable forks from the brake levers.
4 Detach rubber boots 8 and disengage the outer cable abutments from the radius arm clips 9. Withdraw the cables 10 rearwards from the body grommet.

Refitting cables:

Reverse the order of dismantling and then adjust the cables as instructed at the beginning of this Section.

11:14 Removing and refitting brake pedal

Removing:

1 Remove the master cylinder and servo assembly 1 in **FIG 11 : 24**, as described in **Section 11 : 10**. Remove the accelerator pedal 2 by uncoupling the cable from the top end, removing the pivot pin washer and splitpin and then tapping out the pivot pin enough to enable the pedal to be removed.

2 Disconnect the speedometer cable from the instrument. Disconnect wiring 4 from the brake stoplight switch. Remove the nuts 5 which secure the pedal mounting bracket.

3 Detach servo pipe 6 from the inlet manifold. Unhook the clutch lever return spring 7 from the slave cylinder. Remove bolts 8 and pull the slave cylinder 9 off the pushrod.

4 From under the bonnet, remove the two top mounting bolts 10. Remove bolt 11 which secures the mounting bracket to the subframe. Disconnect the speedometer cable from the transmission.

5 Manoeuvre the mounting bracket assembly from the body aperture.

6 Remove the nut and washer 14 from the pedal pivot. Remove clevis pin 15 from the clutch pedal. Keeping an eye on the return spring, drive the pivot and clutch pedal 16 from the mounting bracket and remove the brake pedal.

Refitting:

When refitting the brake pedal in the reverse sequence, ensure that the flat on the pivot shoulder abuts the stop on the bracket. Finally, bleed the brakes as in **Section 11 : 12**.

11:15 Fault diagnosis

(a) 'Spongy' brake pedal

1 Leak in the hydraulic system
2 Worn master cylinder
3 Leaking wheel cylinders
4 Air in the brake fluid
5 Gaps between rear brake shoes and linings

(b) Excessive pedal movement

1 Check 1 and 4 in (a)
2 Excessive rear brake lining wear
3 Very low fluid level in reservoir

(c) Brakes grab or pull to one side

1 Distorted or badly worn discs or drums
2 Wet or oily pads or linings
3 Disc loose on hub flange
4 Worn suspension or steering connections
5 Mixed linings, wrong grade, differing thicknesses
6 Unequal tyre pressures
7 Broken shoe return springs
8 Seized handbrake cable
9 Seized piston in wheel cylinder
10 Loose caliper fixings

(d) Excessive pedal pressure needed

1 Leak in vacuum hose to servo unit
2 Defective servo unit
3 Servo filter blocked
4 Rear linings water soaked
5 Incorrect pad or lining material
6 Rear linings glazed, out of adjustment

(e) Loss of pedal pressure

1 Defective master cylinder, worn bore, piston or seals
2 Leaking wheel cylinder or servo unit
3 Leaking brake pipes and connections

CHAPTER 12

THE ELECTRICAL SYSTEM

12:1 Description

The 12-volt electrical system has the negative terminal of the battery earthed. Generator output to the battery is controlled by a unit containing a voltage regulator, a current regulator and a cut-out. The first two devices control the charging rate at all states of battery charge. The cut-out connects or disconnects the generator and the battery at a certain engine speed which ensures that the battery cannot discharge through the generator when the engine is running slowly. There are some adjustments which can be made to the control box, but we must stress that the operations require the use of accurate meters. **It is useless to attempt the adjustments with cheap and unreliable instruments.**

The lights are controlled by a rocker-type switch and the headlamp dipping and flashing switch is mounted on the steering column. This switch assembly includes the horn control and the direction indicator switch. There are also rocker-type switches for the two-speed wiper motor and two-speed heater blower. There are warning lights on the panel for ignition and oil pressure, two for the direction indicators, and a main beam warning light. A printed circuit board provides connections behind the instrument panel.

The fuel and temperature gauges are of the bi-metal resistance type and are wired to a tank unit and a thermal transmitter respectively. The operating voltage is kept at a constant 10-volts by a stabilizer.

Although this chapter gives instructions on the servicing of the electrical equipment, it is not sensible to try to repair items which are seriously defective, electrically or mechanically. These should be replaced by new units which can be obtained on an Exchange basis.

The wiring diagram included in Technical Data at the end of this manual will enable those with electrical experience to trace and rectify faults.

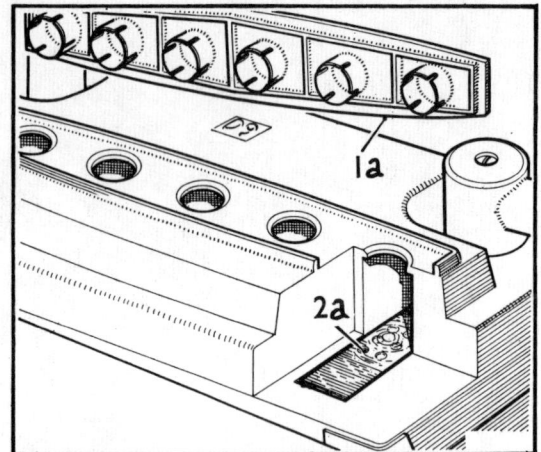

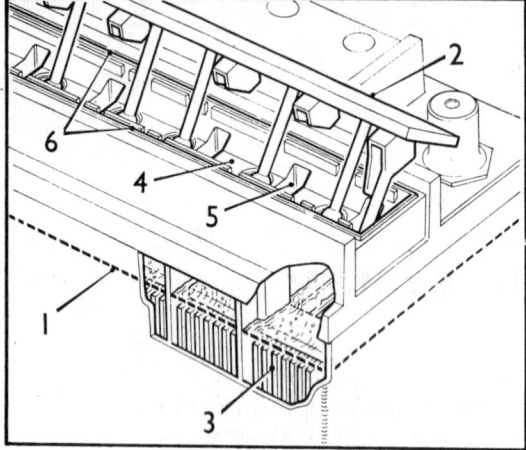

FIG 12:1 Topping up the battery, type D9 and DZ9 (top) and type A9, AZ9 or A11, AZ11 (bottom)

Key to Fig 12:1
1 Electrolyte level	1a Manifold	2a Separator guards
4 Trough	2 Vent cover	3 Separator plates
seating grooves	5 Rectangular filling slots	6 Cover

12:2 The battery

This is a 12-volt lead/acid type of 40 amp hr capacity at the 20-hour rate. It is located behind the engine, under the bonnet. The heavy drain on a battery, particularly in the winter, calls for extra care to see that it is properly maintained.

Routine maintenance:

Keep the top of the battery dry and clean, as dampness can cause electrical leakage, and corrosion through the spreading of electrolyte. Clean off all signs of corrosion from the battery and its mountings. Use dilute ammonia, dry off and then paint any affected parts with anti-sulphuric paint. Make sure the contact surfaces of the terminals are clean and bright, smear them with petroleum jelly and see that the terminal screws are tight. Poor contact at the terminals is a frequent cause of trouble because

high resistance prevents the discharge of current from the battery. This is particularly noticeable on equipment which takes a heavy current such as the starter motor, and may be the reason why the motor will not deliver full power.

Topping up:

Every 3,000 miles, check the level of the electrolyte in the battery and top up if necessary. **Do not use a naked light when checking.** Use the following instructions according to the type of battery installed (the car must be standing on level ground):

Type D9 and DZ9:

Refer to the top view in **FIG 12:1**. Remove manifold 1a and check the level in each cell. The separator guards 2a must be just covered. Top up with distilled water if necessary. Do not overfill, and after topping up wipe the top of the battery dry.

'Pacemaker' (type A9, AZ9 and A11, AZ11):

Refer to the bottom view in **FIG 12:1**. The levels 1 can be seen through the translucent battery case or by fully raising the vent cover 2 and tilting it to one side. The electrolyte should just cover the separator plates 3. To avoid flooding, do not top up within half an hour of charging from any source other than the generator on the car.

To top up, raise the vent cover and pour distilled water into trough 4 until all the rectangular slots 5 are full and the bottom of the trough is just covered. Wipe dry the cover seating grooves 6 and press the cover firmly into position. The correct quantity of distilled water will automatically be distributed to each cell. In extremely cold weather, run the engine immediately after topping up to mix the electrolyte.

Electrolyte:

Never add neat acid to a battery. If electrolyte has been accidentally lost, add fresh electrolyte of the correct specific gravity. If any attempt is made to prepare such electrolyte, always add the sulphuric acid to the distilled water. **It is highly dangerous to add water to acid.**

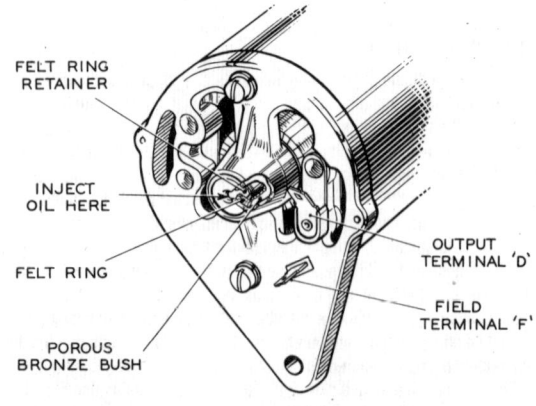

FIG 12:2 Details of the commutator end bracket of the generator showing lubricating point and terminal tags

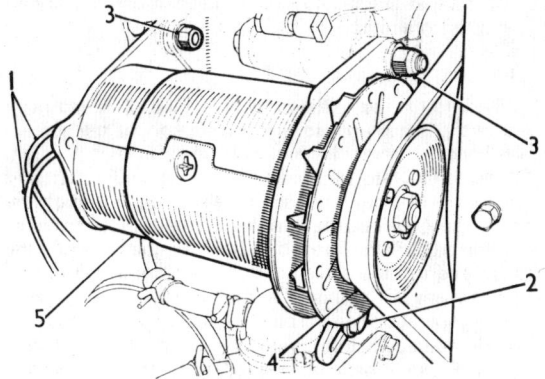

FIG 12:3 The generator fixings

Key to Fig 12:3 1 Leads 2 Adjusting link bolt
3 Mounting bolts 4 Belt 5 Generator

After topping up, check each cell with an hydrometer. Squeeze the rubber bulb of the hydrometer and suck up enough electrolyte to float the indicator. The readings should be as follows:

For climates below 27°C or 80°F:

Cell fully charged	1.270 to 1.290
Cell half-discharged	1.190 to 1.210
Cell discharged	1.110 to 1.130

For climates frequently above 27°C or 80°F:

Cell fully charged	1.210 to 1.230
Cell half-discharged	1.130 to 1.150
Cell discharged	1.050 to 1.070

These figures are correct for an electrolyte temperature of 16°C or 60°F. For every 3°C or 5°F above that temperature add .002. For every 3°C or 5°F below that temperature subtract .002.

All cells should read approximately the same. If one cell differs radically from the rest it may be due to an internal fault or to spilling or leakage of the electrolyte

If the battery is in a low state of charge, take the car for a long daylight run. Alternatively, put it on a charger at 4 amps (9 cell) or 5 amps (11 cell) until all cells are gassing freely and evenly. The gas is inflammable, so keep naked lights away. During the charge, check the level of the electrolyte but always keep the vent closed during actual charging or the electrolyte will flood. Add distilled water to keep the level to the top of the separator guard. Never detach the vent cover from the battery.

A battery which stands unused for long periods must be given a freshening-up charge every month. A discharged battery will be ruined if left in that condition.

Removing the battery:

Remove the screws from the terminal posts and lift off the terminals. Release the hook bolts and remove the strap. Lift out the battery.

To remove the battery tray, undo the securing bolts. Clean all parts free from corrosion and give a coat of anti-sulphuric paint. Reassemble in the reverse order. Do not overtighten the screws securing the terminals.

12:3 Routine maintenance

Details which concern the battery are given in the preceding Section.

The generator:

Check the tension of the driving belt and adjust it according to the instructions in **Section 4:2.**

Every 6000 miles, add a few drops of oil through the centre hole in the rear bearing housing as shown in **FIG 12:2.** Do not overlubricate or there may be trouble with oil on the commutator. Make sure the cable connections are tight.

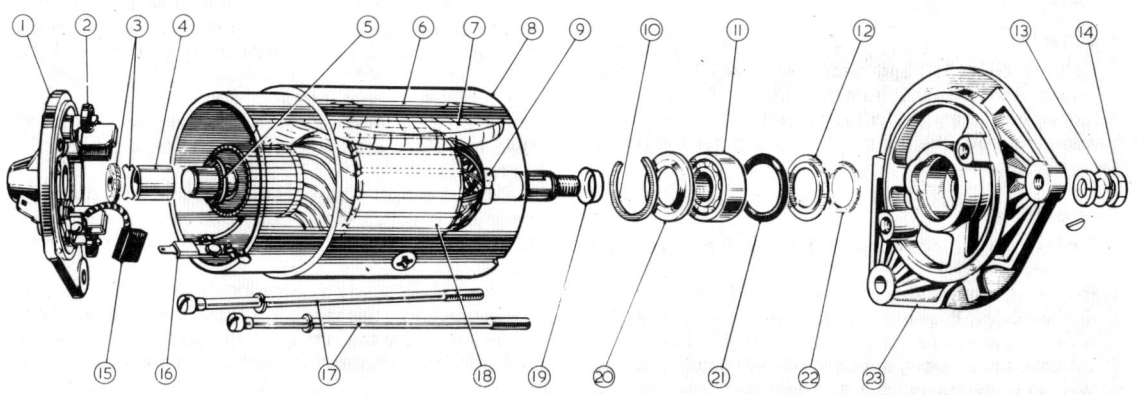

FIG 12:4 The component parts of Lucas generator, type C40/1

Key to Fig 12:4 1 Commutator end bracket 2 Brush springs 3 Oiling felt and retainer 4 Self-lubricating bush
5 Thrust washer 6 Pole piece 7 Field coil 8 Yoke 9 Collar 10 Circlip 11 Ballbearing 13 Washer
14 Nut 15 Brush 16 Field terminal 'F' 17 Through bolts 18 Armature 19 Bearing retainer ring
20 Bearing plate 21 O-ring 22 Felt washer 23 Drive end bracket

The lights:

Every 6000 miles check all bulbs by switching on and observing the effect. Check the action of the dipswitch and flasher, and the direction indicators. Check that the stoplights and rear lights are functioning correctly. Check the alignment of the headlamps and adjust according to the regulations.

12:4 Servicing the generator

Testing without removal:

1 Check the armature and brushgear for electrical continuity using a 0–20-volt moving coil meter. Refer to **FIG 12:2** and remove the cables from the output and field terminals by pulling them off.

2 Connect the positive lead of the voltmeter to the output terminal and the negative lead to a good earth.

3 Run the engine at approximately 1500 rev/min. If the armature and brushgear are satisfactory the meter will register 2- to 4-volts. If there is no reading, remove the generator for detailed examination.

4 Having passed the armature and brushgear as satisfactory, test the field coils. Leave the voltmeter connected to the generator output terminal and earth. Connect a 0 to 10 or 0 to 20 amp moving coil meter between the output and field terminals. The positive lead must go to the larger terminal to which the voltmeter is already connected.

5 Start the engine and run it at increasing speed until the voltmeter reads 12-volts. The ammeter should then read about 2 amp.

6 If the ammeter shows no reading there is a break in the field winding. If the reading is high it indicates a short-circuit in the field winding. A low reading shows that there is a high-resistance connection in the field winding. With any of these faults it is necessary to remove the generator for further examination.

7 There is one cause of apparent failure which might be missed. If a radio suppression capacitor is fitted between the generator output terminal and earth, a defective capacitor might be the cause of the trouble.

Removal:

Refer to **FIG 12:3** and disconnect leads 1 from the generator. Remove bolt 2 from the adjusting link. Slacken mounting bolts 3 and lower the generator. The belt 4 can now be lifted off, the mounting bolts removed and the generator lifted away.

Dismantling:

Refer to the exploded view in **FIG 12:4** and proceed as follows:

1 Remove the nut and spring washer and withdraw the driving pulley. Prise out the Woodruff key if bracket 23 is to be removed for attention to the ballbearing.

2 Unscrew the two long through bolts 17. Gentle tapping will now release bracket 1, which will come away complete with brushes. Tapping bracket 23 off the other end will release it from the yoke 8, but it will also bring armature 18 with it.

3 If the armature or the ballbearing need renewal, push the armature shaft out of the bearing with a hand press.

Check that there is no key in the shaft before carrying out this operation.

Checking brushes:

Refer to the top lefthand view in **FIG 12:5** and push the two brushes up into their boxes so that the springs will bear on their sides and hold them in that position. Fit the commutator end bracket to the armature shaft and release the brushes. Lift each brush spring in turn off the brush. Pull gently on the flexible lead to the brush to check that the brush is free in the box. If it is sluggish, remove the brush and rub the sides lightly on a smooth file until it moves easily but without too much shake.

In all operations on the brushes, make sure that they are always refitted in the correct boxes and the right way round. Brushes become bedded-in to the commutator and a change of position may lead to poor contact.

The minimum permissible length of a brush is $\frac{9}{32}$ inch. New brushes must be bedded-in by making the contact face of the same curvature as the commutator. This is achieved by threading a strip of fine glasspaper over the commutator and under the new brush. Drawing the strip to and fro under the brush with the abrasive side in contact, will quickly shape the end of the brush to the correct curve.

It will be appreciated that the spring pressure on a very short brush is much less than that on a new one. If a sensitive spring balance, reading in ounces is available, hook one end under the end of the spring nearest a new brush and check the pull required at the moment the spring begins to deflect. The pull of the balance must be in line with the brush, which is radial to the commutator. The reading should be approximately 30 ozf. Any reading which is appreciably above or below that figure calls for renewal of the spring.

The commutator:

This must be smooth, only slightly discoloured, and free from scoring, pitting or burned spots. Burnt segments indicate a break in the armature windings.

Clean the commutator with a fuel-moistened cloth and polish it with fine glasspaper. **Never use emery cloth as the grains of abrasive become embedded in the copper to cause rapid wear of the brushes.** If the condition of the commutator demands drastic treatment it is possible to skim it in a lathe, between centres. First check that the finished diameter is not going to be less than 1.430 inch. Below that diameter, the armature must be renewed.

When the machining operation is completed, polish the commutator with fine glasspaper and clean all the grooves between the segments. These must be free of copper and carbon.

There is no need to undercut the insulation between the segments as this is of such a depth that the insulation is always below the surface of the commutator provided that the latter is not machined below the diameter just given.

The armature:

The simplest check for an apparently faulty armature is to replace it with one of known performance. Electrical

METHOD OF TRAPPING BRUSH IN RAISED POSITION WITH SPRING

METHOD OF RELEASING BRUSH ON TO COMMUTATOR

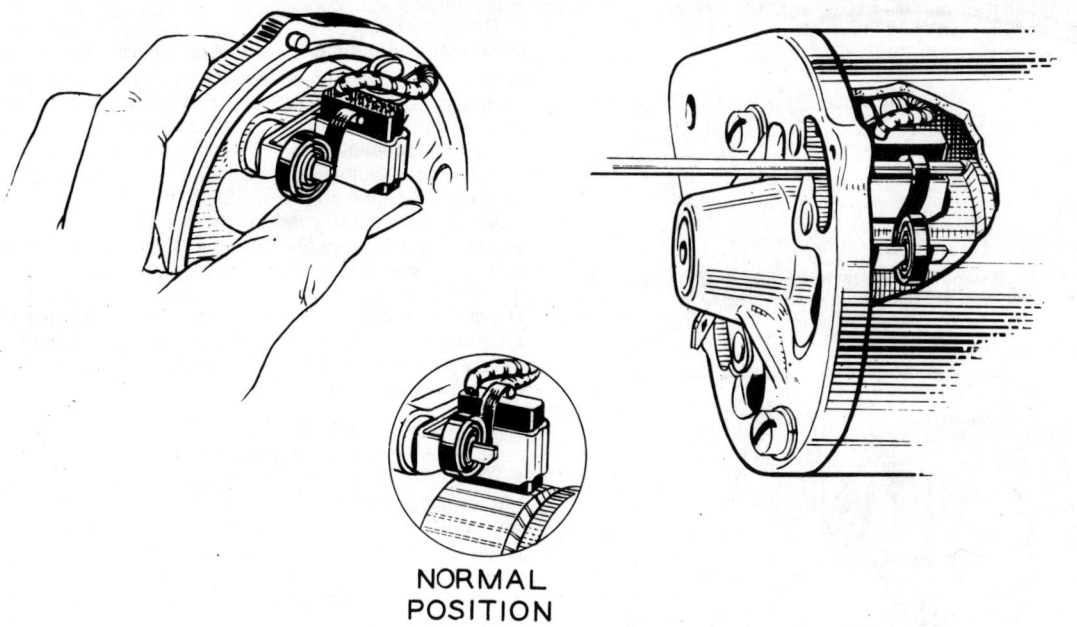

NORMAL
POSITION

FIG 12:5   Positions of the brush springs during generator reassembly. In the top lefthand view the spring can be seen bearing on the side of the brush

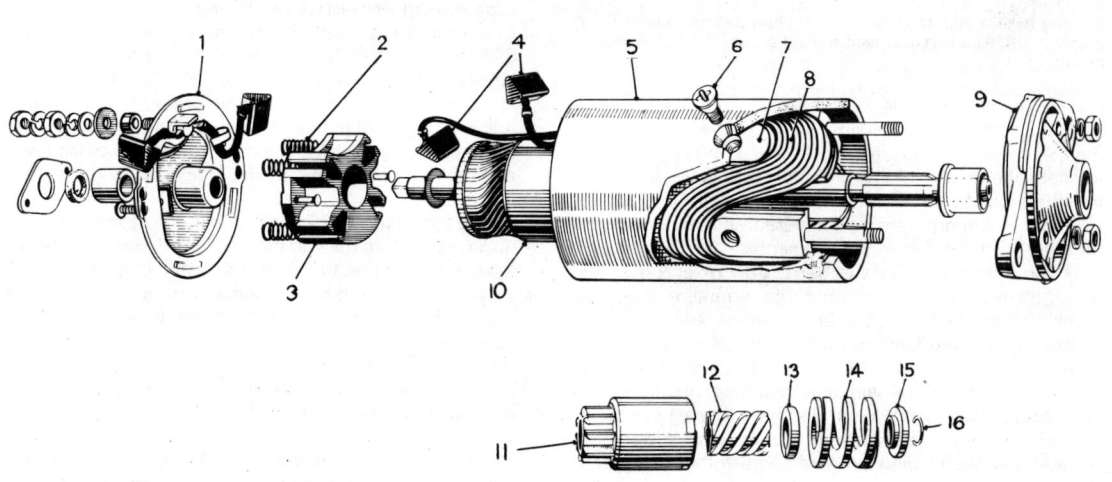

FIG 12:6   Components of the Lucas starter motor, type M35.J. The drive pinion assembly is shown underneath

Key to Fig 12:6   1 Commutator end bracket   2 Brush springs   3 Brushbox housing   4 Brushes   5 Yoke
6 Screw for pole piece   7 Pole piece or shoe   8 Field coil winding   9 Drive end bracket   10 Armature
11 Pinion and barrel   12 Screwed sleeve   13 Buffer washer   14 Main spring   15 Spring cup   16 Jump ring or circlip

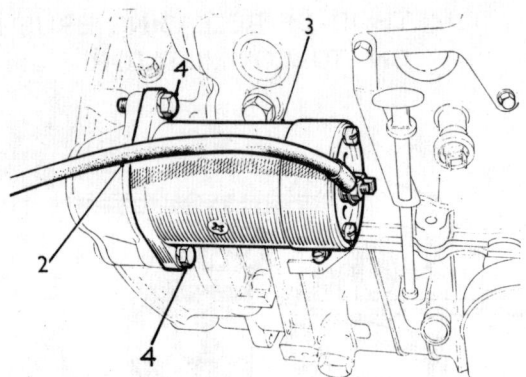

FIG 12:7 Removing the starter motor **3**. The cable is **2** and the securing bolts **4**

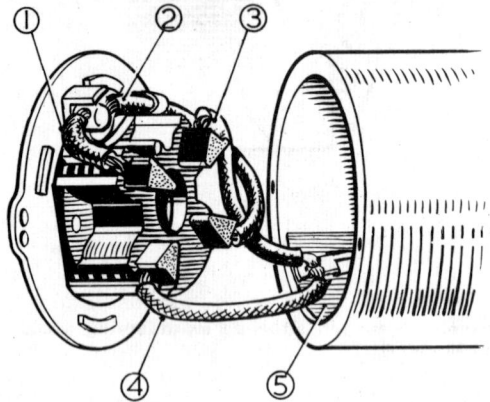

FIG 12:8 The starter brushgear

Key to Fig 12:8   1 Short flexible lead to brush
2 Long flexible lead to brush   3 Long flexible lead to field
brush   4 Short flexible lead to field brush   5 Insulation
piece

testing for shortcircuits or breaks in the windings is beyond the scope of most amateurs and it is best to give the job to authorized agents. A visual inspection may indicate the cause of the trouble. Breaks in armature windings lead to burnt commutator segments, and short-circuited windings are discoloured by overheating, together with burning of the segments.

If the armature shaft is bent, do not attempt to straighten it. Neither should the armature core be machined in order to obtain clearance between the stampings and the field coil polepieces 6 in **FIG 12:4**.

The correct way to fit a new armature to the driving end bracket 23 is to use a 4-inch length of steel tubing which will accept the armature shaft and bear against the inner race of the ballbearing. With the tubing firmly supported, the armature shaft can be pressed home without stressing the end bracket.

The field coils:

The original electrical testing will give some indication of a fault in the field system. A further test is to measure the resistance of the coils with an ohmmeter. Connect the

instrument between the field terminal 16 and the yoke 8, making sure to contact bright metal on the yoke. The meter should read 6 ohms. If such a meter is not available, connect a 12-volt battery between the field terminal and the yoke with an ammeter in series. The meter should read approximately 2 amperes.

There is a break in the field coil windings if the ohm-meter reads 'Infinity' or the ammeter records zero. If the ohmmeter reading is much below 6 ohms or the ammeter reading is much more than 2 amperes it shows that there is an insulation breakdown in the field coil circuit.

It is not recommended to try to fit new field coils, the best cure for a faulty yoke assembly being to exchange it for a reconditioned one.

Although an unlikely defect, it sometimes happens that a generator refuses to charge because the residual mag-netism has been destroyed or reversed in polarity, usually by shortcircuiting the battery through the generator. The cure in this case is to connect the negative terminal of a 12-volt battery to the yoke. The positive cable from the battery should then be stroked quickly across the field terminal several times.

Bearings:

The bearing bush 4 is pressed into the commutator end bracket 1 by means of a shouldered pilot. If such a tool is not available, entrust the operation to a Service Station. If the tool can be made, it is necessary to use the same dia-meter of steel bar as the bush. One end is then turned down the same diameter as the armature shaft at the commutator end and long enough to extend to the full length of the bush. This part must be parallel and highly polished. The object of this pilot is to press the bush into the bracket without the bore size contracting below the diameter of the armature shaft, so that a good running fit will be obtained. This is the only way in which the bush can be fitted. **On no account fit the bush and then reamer it out to the required bore size or the self-lubricating properties will be lost.**

Before fitting a new bush, immerse it for 24 hours in SAE engine oil so that the pores will become filled with lubricant.

To remove the old bush, screw in a $\frac{5}{8}$ inch tap squarely into the bush and pull on the tap. Withdraw the oiler parts 3 and clean them. Put a few drops of engine oil on the felt and refit it, followed by the metal retainer, and then press in the bush.

The ballbearing 11 is held in place by circlip 10 which fits in a groove in the end bracket 23. To renew the bearing if wear is such that the armature shaft can be moved side-ways or the bearing feels rough, insert a screwdriver under the circlip and prise it out. There is a recess in the housing which is provided for this purpose. Remove the retaining plate and press out the bearing from the pulley side. It is not necessary to remove any more parts. Ensure that the new bearing is packed with high-melting point grease.

Press the new bearing squarely into place and make sure it is fully home. Replace the retaining plate and the circlip. Press the whole assembly into the housing until the circlip settles properly into its groove.

Reassembling the generator:

With all parts reconditioned, proceed to reassemble as

follows:

1 Fit the driving end bracket to the armature shaft using the method described under 'The armature'. Fit the assembly to the yoke, ensuring that the dowel on the bracket engages the groove in the yoke.

2 Push the brushes up into their boxes and hold them there by letting the springs bear on the sides as shown in **FIG 12:5**. Fit thrust washer 5 (when fitted) to the armature shaft and feed the commutator end bracket into place. Take care not to trap the flexible connectors to the brushes. Locate the dowel correctly as instructed for the other end bracket. Refer to the illustration again and lift the brush springs with a piece of rod or a screwdriver until the brushes can be restored to their correct positions, with the spring pressing on top as shown in the lower view.

3 Refit the two through bolts. Fit the shaft key and the pulley spacer, press the pulley into place and secure with the nut and spring washer. Finish off by injecting a few drops of SAE 30 engine oil into the hole in the end bracket indicated in **FIG 12:2. Do not over-oil.**

Refitting:

This operation is a reversal of the removal instructions. Before fully tightening the mounting and link bolts, check the driving belt tension as instructed in **Section 4:2.**

12:5 Servicing the starter

It will be seen from **FIG 12:6** that there are many improvements in the design of the Lucas starter motor, type M35J. Of the new features, the most noticeable is the face-type commutator at the lefthand end of armature 10. The wedge-shaped brushes 4 are carried in a plastic moulded box 3, the brush springs 2 being captive in the box and providing the requisite pressure to hold the brushes against the commutator. The brushes each have a keyway to ensure correct fitting.

The field coils 8 are one continuous winding without joins. One end is earthed to yoke 5 by a soldered connection or a riveted eyelet, while the other end terminates at two of the brushes.

The yoke has no windows and the end brackets are secured independently without the use of through bolts. The commutator end bracket 1 is secured by two screws into the end face of the yoke. Early starters had the drive end bracket 9 secured by threaded studs and nuts, but later models have bolts which screw into two of the pole pieces.

Routine maintenance:

There is no need for regular maintenance, but make an occasional check for tightness of the terminal nuts. During a major engine overhaul the starter should be dismantled and new brushes and bearings fitted. The pinion drive may also receive attention.

Starter checking without removal:

In cases of starter trouble, first check the condition of the battery, and in particular, the cleanliness and tightness of the cable connections. Poor contact at the battery terminals and a poor earth are common causes of starter problems because any high resistance at these points will not permit the passage of the heavy current required. If the starter motor just hums and fails to get up speed, then check the connections first.

If the battery and cables are known to be working satisfactorily, switch on the lights and try the starter. If the lights go dim but the starter does not run it shows that current is reaching the starter. The probable cause of failure in this case is that the pinion is jammed. This can be released by using a spanner on the squared end of the armature shaft. This can be seen at the lefthand end in **FIG 12:6**. If there is initial effort required to turn the shaft and then it comes free, the pinion has been released. Another method worth trying is to engage a gear **with the ignition switched off**. If the car is now rocked backwards and forwards, the jammed pinion will free itself.

If the lights do not go dim, check the starter switch and the solenoid. Also check all connections and cables in the switch, solenoid and starter circuits (see the Wiring Diagram in Technical Data at the end of this manual). If the starter still fails to work, remove it for a more detailed examination.

Removing the starter motor:

Refer to **FIG 12:7**. Remove the battery leads, and cable 2 from the terminal on the end of the starter. Remove the two securing bolts 4 and pull the motor 3 out of the flywheel housing and away.

Checking:

A running test can be made by clamping the starter motor in a vice. Connect up a 12-volt battery, taking one lead to a 100 amp moving coil meter and the other lead from the meter to the starter input terminal. The other battery lead should go to a clean metallic part of the yoke. Heavy cable must be used to carry the required current. The motor should run at high speed. The current consumption will be 65 amperes at 8000 to 10,000 rev/min. This high-speed, no-load test can also be made without the meter. If the motor does not run or is obviously at fault, proceed to dismantle it.

Dismantling the starter:

Before taking the motor entirely to pieces it is wise to check the brushgear and commutator. Refer to **FIG 12:6**.

1 Remove the two screws and pull the end plate 1 away from yoke 5. Check that the brushes move freely in the brushbox moulding 3.

2 Any brush which sticks can usually be freed by cleaning with a fuel-moistened cloth. The minimum length is $\frac{3}{8}$ inch.

3 Clean the commutator with the fuel-moistened cloth and refit the end plate. Check the motor as suggested in the preceding section.

Brushes:

If the motor still does not run properly, dismantle it by removing the endplate as before and then service the brushgear as follows:

1 If the brushes are worn to $\frac{3}{8}$ inch or less, they must be renewed as a set of four. Refer to **FIG 12:8** which shows the disposition of the two brushes with short leads and the two with long leads.

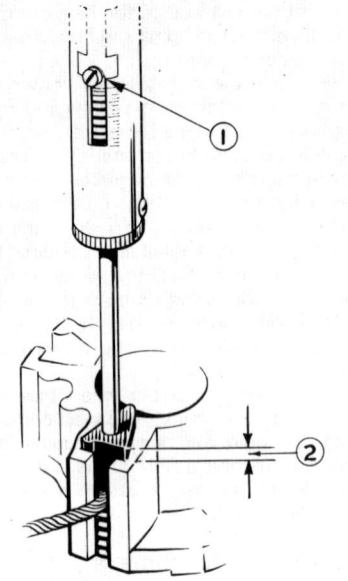

FIG 12:9 Checking spring pressure of starter brush. The push-type spring gauge is **1**, dimension **2** is $\frac{1}{16}$ inch

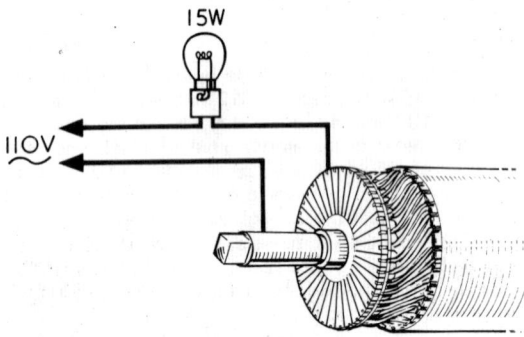

FIG 12:10 Testing the insulation of a starter armature using 110-volt AC current and a 15W bulb

2 Cut brush flexible leads 1 and 2 from the terminal post. With a file or a hacksaw, make a groove in the head of the terminal deep enough to take the two new leads.
3 Make sure that the insulating sleeving on the new leads will give the maximum coverage consistent with satisfactory soldering. Solder the long and short leads into the terminal groove.
4 Cut the brush flexible leads 3 and 4 about $\frac{1}{4}$ inch from the joint with the field winding. Make sure the insulation piece 5 is undamaged.
5 Again check the insulating sleeving and then solder the new long and short leads to the ends of the original leads.

Brush springs:

To measure the brush spring pressure, refer to **FIG 12:9**. Place a new brush in its correct slot in the brush box and press on it with a push-type gauge. When the brush is about $\frac{1}{16}$ inch from the face of the moulding as indicated at 2, the gauge should read approximately 28 ozf. If the spring pressures are appreciably incorrect, the bracket assembly complete with springs and moulding must be renewed.

Armature and commutator:

To remove the armature proceed as follows:
1 Release the driven end bracket 9 by removing the two nuts (or bolts).
2 Tap the bracket off the yoke, bringing with it the pinion assembly and the armature. Note that there is a thrust washer on the shaft at the commutator end .

If the commutator is worn, or is pitted and burnt, it may be skimmed. This operation must not reduce the thickness of the commutator below .080 inch. Clean up the segments in a lathe and then polish the working face with very fine glasspaper. **Do not use emerycloth. The insulation between the copper segments must not be undercut.**

Check that the armature core has not been fouling the field pole shoes 7. If there has been contact it may be due to a bent armature shaft or to worn bearings. **Do not attempt to straighten a bent shaft.**

Check the armature insulation with a 110-volt AC test lamp of 15 watts as shown in **FIG 12:10**. A step-down transformer can be used on a normal town supply. Connect one of the prods to each commutator segment in turn and the other to the shaft. The lamp will light if there is a breakdown of the insulation. Renewal of the armature is the only cure.

Breaks or shortcircuits in the armature winding can be detected by using a 'growler', but this equipment is not normally available to the car owner and he is advised to consult a Service Station.

The field winding:

FIG 12:11 shows how to test the field winding for continuity. Use a 12-volt battery and test lamp, connecting the prods between each brush in turn and a clean part of the yoke. If the lamp lights then continuity may be considered satisfactory.

To check the insulation, make an initial observation of the inside of the yoke. This may reveal signs of an insulation breakdown. Again, if no-load speed was low and current consumption high on test, it might be due to faulty field winding insulation. These checks, if they suggest field winding trouble, will justify disconnecting the earthed end of the winding. This is done where the winding terminates in a soldered (or riveted) connection at the yoke. It is important not to disturb the hot-pressed joint of the copper link to the field winding.

Having disconnected the end of the winding at the yoke, connect a 110-volt AC, 15 watt lamp across the disconnected end of the winding and a clean earth on the yoke. Take care that the brushes and flexible leads do not contact the yoke during this test. The lamp will light if the insulation is not satisfactory.

To renew a faulty field winding it is necessary to remove screws 6 in **FIG 12:6. These are exceedingly tight** and require the use of a wheel-operated screwdriver which cannot slip out of engagement and which will give the leverage needed to start the screws. If this can be done, proceed with the operation as follows:

1 Disconnect the earthed end of the winding at the yoke by unsoldering it or drilling out the rivet (whichever is applicable).

2 Slacken the four pole shoe retaining screws 6. Remove these screws from a diametrically opposite pair of shoes and remove the shoes from the yoke. The remaining pair of shoes need only be slackened enough to permit withdrawal of the winding.

3 Slide the winding out from under the shoulders of the slackened pole shoes and remove from the yoke.

4 Wipe the inside of the yoke and clean the insulating piece which separates the field winding brush joint from the yoke. Loosely fit the new winding and pole shoes into the yoke. Position the insulating piece correctly between the winding brush joint and the yoke.

5 Tighten the pole shoe screws evenly and remake a good earth connection between the winding connector and the yoke.

The commutator end bracket:

After the brushes have been checked as previously instructed, carry out tests on the bracket. Use a 110-volt AC lamp of 15 watts, and refer to **FIG 12:12**. Connect one prod of the test lamp to a clean area of the bracket and the other to each spring in turn. Check the terminal post in the same way. Ensure that the brushes and any exposed part of the flexible leads do not make contact with the end bracket during this test. If the insulation has broken down, the lamp will light up. Renew the assembly if this test shows such a breakdown.

Bearings:

These are of the porous bronze self-lubricating variety in the form of bushes. Renew them when the engine has a major overhaul, as follows:

1 Drill out the two rivets securing the brushbox moulding to the commutator end bracket. This will release the outer retaining plate for the felt seal. These parts can be seen on the extreme left in **FIG 12:6**.

2 Working from the outside of the bracket, insert a $\frac{1}{2}$ inch tap into the bush and pull on the tap to withdraw the bush.

3 The bush in the drive end bracket 9 can be pressed out while the bracket is supported. The pinion assembly must be removed (see 'The pinion drive').

4 Press in new bushes using a stepped and polished pilot mandrel as suggested for the generator bush under the heading 'Bearings' in **Section 12:4**. This will ensure that any closing-in of the bush will not make for a tight bearing. Before fitting new bushes, they must be fully immersed in clean SAE 30 engine oil for not less than 24 hours. **Do not use a reamer to size the bore of these sintered bushes as the pores will be closed and the self-lubricating qualities lost.**

The pinion drive:

The parts of this assembly are shown below the yoke in **FIG 12:6**. When fitted, they occupy the righthand end of the armature shaft where the splines for screwed sleeve 12 can be seen. It is important to note that the pinion and barrel 11, and the screwed sleeve, must not be lubricated. Oil on these parts may cause grit to adhere and this is some-

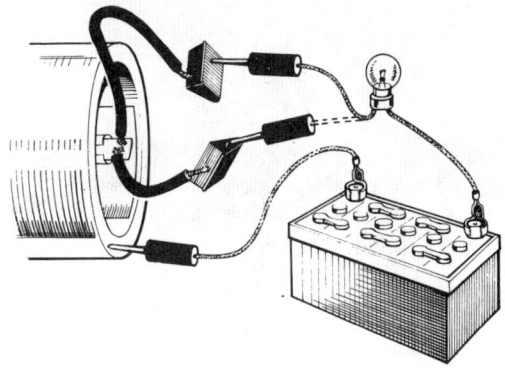

FIG 12:11 Testing continuity of starter field winding using a 12-volt battery and bulb

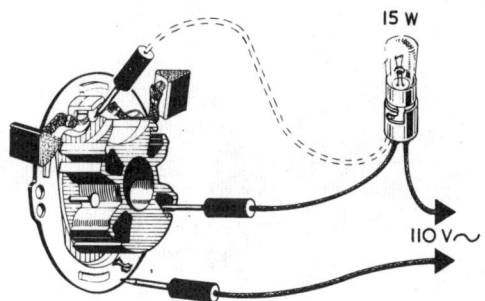

FIG 12:12 Testing insulation of starter brush springs and input terminal using 110-volt AC current and a 15W bulb

times the reason why the pinion fails to engage with the flywheel teeth, though the motor may be running at high speed.

The first step in dealing with the pinion assembly is to check that it is clean and dry. The pinion and barrel should turn freely on the screwed sleeve. Also check that the springs are not broken. If wear is apparent, dismantle the assembly as follows:

1 Exert heavy pressure on cup 15 to compress spring 14. This will reveal the circlip or jump ring 16 which is fitted to a groove in the shaft.

2 Prise out the circlip and relieve the pressure on the spring. Renew the worn parts. Remember that the pinion and barrel assembly is mated to the screwed sleeve and these parts must be renewed as a pair.

3 Reassemble in the reverse order. **Do not lubricate.** Fit the end bracket before the drive is assembled.

Reassembling the starter motor:

In general, this is a reversal of the dismantling procedure. Do not forget the thrust washer which goes on the shaft at the commutator end. When fitting the commutator end bracket to the yoke, make sure that the brushes are correctly positioned and that the flexible leads are not trapped or displaced.

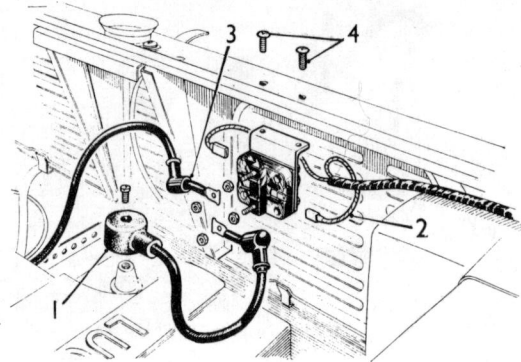

FIG 12:13   Removing the starter solenoid

Key to Fig 12:13
1 Battery terminal and cable
2 Control leads from ignition switch   3 Heavy starter cable
4 Solenoid securing screws

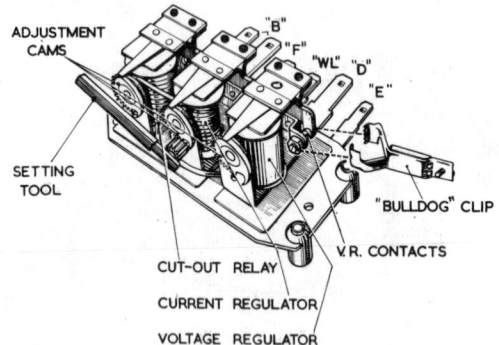

FIG 12:14   Lucas control box RB.340 showing the arrangement for setting the current regulator by using a 'Bulldog' clip on the voltage regulator contacts

Refitting the starter motor:

This, too, is a reversal of the removal procedure. It is important to make a clean tight connection of the cable to the terminal.

12:6 The starter solenoid

This is actuated by light current from the ignition/starter switch to enable it to pass the heavy current required by the starter motor. If it fails, it is best to renew the unit. It can be seen in **FIG 12:13**, which shows how it is removed.

First disconnect the battery at terminal 1. Disconnect the light-duty cables 2 and then the heavy-duty cables 3. Remove screws 4 to release the switch. Replace in the reverse order.

12:7 Servicing the control box

This device is shown in **FIG 12:14** with the cover removed. A description of the functions of it are given in **Section 12:1**. The dispositions of the three units is such that the cut-out is on the left, the current regulator in the middle and the voltage regulator on the right. The 'Bulldog' clip is used when setting the current regulator. Vibrating armatures and contacts are the control mechanisms and

adjustment is effected through the cams by using a special tool obtainable from a Lucas Service Station.

Normally the works settings should be perfectly satisfactory and tinkering is to be deprecated. It is suggested that the following simple tests are made if there is trouble with the charging circuit before disturbing the control box.

Checking the charging circuit:

1 Check that the driving belt is not slipping.
2 Check the battery by substitution, or by using an hydrometer as instructed in **Section 12:2**. A heavy-discharge tester can be used to see how well the battery stands up to a heavy demand.
3 Check the generator by substitution or by testing with a voltmeter. Disconnect the cables from the generator and join the terminals 'D' and 'F' together with wire. Connect the voltmeter between this link and earth. Run the generator up to about 1000 rev/min, when a steadily rising voltage should be indicated.
4 Check all wiring for continuity between the generator, the control box and the ammeter. Make sure all connections are clean and tight.
5 Check all earth connections, particularly those of the control box and the battery.
6 Make certain that the low state of the battery is not just due to under-charging because the running mileage of the car has been very short.

If these tests indicate that the generator and battery are working well, the control box may be at fault and the following adjustments can be made by a reasonably competent person using reliable meters.

Adjusting the voltage regulator:

This is an open-circuit test and the ideal testing conditions are those when the unit is at ambient temperature. The first set of figures in the following table will then apply. If the unit is above ambient temperature and there is no time to let it cool down, use the second set of figures.

Ambient temperature	Open-circuit voltage
0 to 25°C (32 to 77°F)	$14\frac{1}{2}$ to $15\frac{1}{2}$
26 to 40°C (78 to 104°F)	$14\frac{1}{4}$ to $15\frac{1}{4}$

An open-circuit setting that falls outside these limits **by no more than $\frac{1}{4}$ a volt** (and is non-fluctuating) should be reset to the nearest maximum or minimum end of the appropriate limits. For example, a regulator which is checked at 20°C and is found to have an open-circuit voltage between 14 and 14.4-volts should be reset to $14\frac{1}{2}$-volts. It is not advisable to reset a unit when the open-circuit setting departs from the limits given in the second row by more than $\frac{1}{2}$-volt. This extreme deviation from the normal setting indicates a constructional fault in the control box and it must be renewed. To carry out the adjustments, do the following:

1 Withdraw the cables from both terminals 'B' (see **FIG 12:14**). The ignition switch is fed by terminal 'B' so that it will be necessary to join the ignition and battery leads together with wire before the engine can be started.
2 Connect a top-grade 0 to 20-volt moving coil voltmeter between control box terminal 'D' and a good earth. This is conveniently done by withdrawing the cable from terminal 'WL' and clipping the correct polarity lead from the voltmeter to this terminal because it is electrically common with terminal 'D'.

3 Start the engine and run the generator at 3000 rev/min. The voltmeter reading should be steady and lie between the limits given in the table. An unsteady reading may be due to dirty contacts. Cleaning these is covered later. If the reading is steady but lies outside the limits given, adjust the unit as follows:

Stop the engine. Remove the control box cover by pressing the centre core through each of the two plastic rivets which secure it. The cover, with rivets, can then be withdrawn. Restart the engine and run the generator at 3000 rev/min.

Using the Lucas setting tool (Part No. 543.817.42), turn the voltage adjustment cam on the right in **FIG 12 :14**. Turn it clockwise to raise the setting and anticlockwise to lower it. When the reading is correct, stop the engine, restart it and check that the reading is within the limits, running the generator at 3000 rev/min as before.

Finally, restore the connections and refit the cover.

Adjusting the current regulator:

The on-load setting of the current regulator should be the same as the rated output of the generator, which is 22 amperes. The current regulator is the middle unit in the illustration. Check and adjust as follows:
1 The generator must be made to deliver its maximum rated output irrespective of the state of charge in the battery. The voltage regulator must therefore be rendered inoperative by clamping the contacts together with a 'Bulldog' clip. An alternative method is to connect a $\frac{1}{2}$ ohm, 30 amp resistor between the battery terminals.
2 Pull the cables from control box terminal blades 'B'. Connect these cables by wire to the load side of a 0 to 40-ampère moving coil meter. Connect the other side of the meter to one of the control box terminals 'B'. It is important that terminals 'B' carry this one connection only. All other load connections including the ignition coil feed must be made to the battery side of the ammeter.
3 Start the engine and run the generator at 4500 rev/min. The ammeter should indicate a steady reading of 22 amperes. An unsteady reading may be due to dirty contacts. Clean them as instructed later.
4 If the reading is too high or too low, adjust by using the Lucas setting tool mentioned in the instructions for the voltage regulator. Turn the tool clockwise to raise the setting and anticlockwise to lower it. This operation is shown in the illustration.
5 Switch off the engine, restore the connections and refit the cover.

Adjusting the cut-out:

This is the unit on the right in **FIG 12 :16**. Checking the electrical setting of the unit must be completed as quickly as possible to avoid errors due to heating of the operating coil. Check and adjust as follows:

Cut-in adjustment:

1 Connect a reliable 0 to 20-volt moving coil meter between control box terminal 'D' and a good earth. A convenient way to do this is to withdraw the cable from terminal 'WL' and to clip the voltmeter lead of the correct polarity to this terminal as it is electrically common with terminal 'D'.

FIG 12 :15 Setting the armature-to-bobbin core gap on voltage and current regulators using a .058 inch feeler gauge

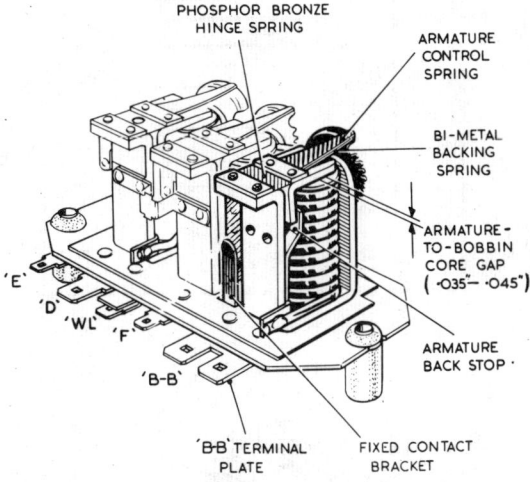

FIG 12 :16 Setting the armature-to-bobbin core gap of the cut-out using a .035 to .045 inch feeler gauge

2 Switch on the headlamps, start the engine and gradually increase its speed. The voltage should rise steadily and then drop slightly at the moment when the cut-out contacts close. The voltage indicated just before this drop is the cut-in voltage. It should lie between 12.7 and 13.3-volts.
3 If outside these limits adjust as follows:

Remove the control box cover as instructed in the section on adjusting the voltage regulator. Use the Lucas setting tool to turn the adjusting cam to alter the setting. Turn it clockwise to raise the setting and anticlockwise to lower it. Repeat the checking procedure until the correct setting is obtained, taking care not to overheat the coil. When satisfied, switch off the engine, restore the connections and refit the cover.

Drop-off adjustment:

To carry out this check, withdraw the cables from control box terminal 'B'. With a piece of wire, join the ignition and battery leads together so that the engine may be started. Then proceed as follows:
1 Connect a first-grade 0 to 20-volt moving coil meter between control box terminal 'B' and a good earth.
2 Start the engine and run it up to about 3,000 rev/min. Slowly decelerate and watch the meter needle. Note the reading when the needle drops to zero.

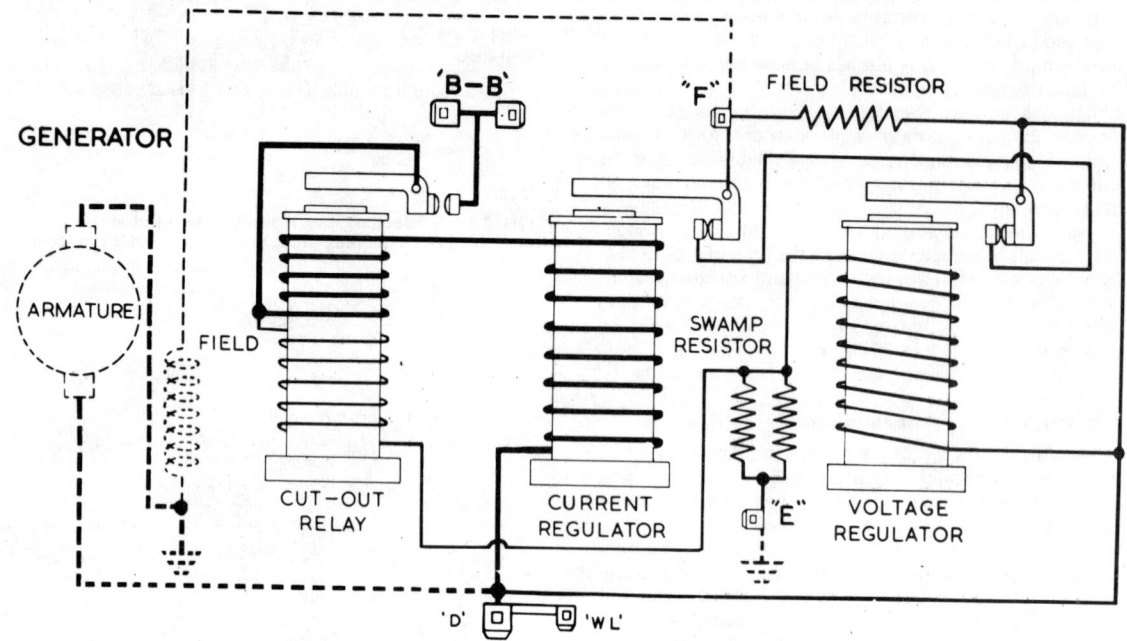

FIG 12:17 Circuit diagram of control box RB.340. Note the twin tags **B** and common tags **D** and **WL**

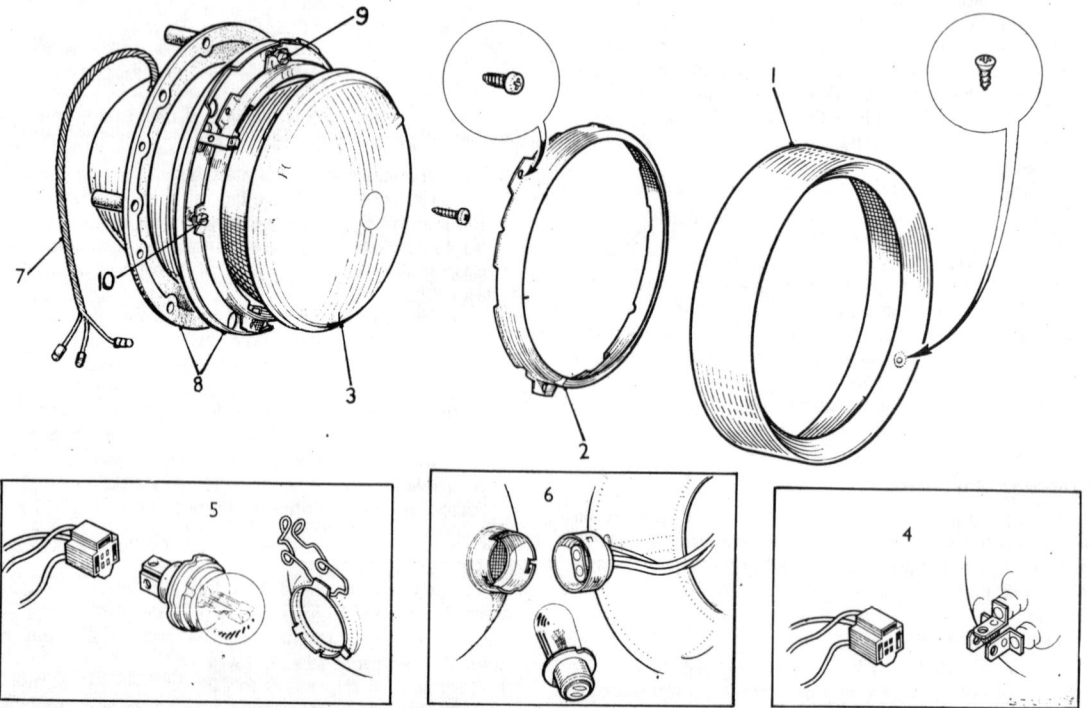

FIG 12:18 The headlamp components. The sealed beam connector is **4**, the separate bulb and spring clip **5** and the separate bulb and bayonet cap **6**

Key to Fig 12:18   1 Outer rim   2 Light unit retaining rim   3 Light unit   7 Wiring   8 Back-shell

3 The needle drops because the cut-out points have opened. This should happen between 9.5 and 11.0-volts. If the drop-off voltage is outside these limits, adjust as follows:

Stop the engine and remove the control box cover (see 'Voltage regulator adjustment'). Locate the contact points. The fixed one is carried on a bracket. Bend this bracket to alter the drop-off voltage, reducing the contact gap to raise it and increasing to lower it. Carry out another test and readjust until the correct drop-off voltage is obtained. Restore the original connections and refit the cover.

Adjustment of air gap settings:

These are accurately set during manufacture and should not need attention. If the original settings have been disturbed readjust as follows:

Armature-to-bobbin core gap of voltage and current regulators:

1 Disconnect the battery. Turn the Lucas adjusting tool fully anticlockwise to give the minimum lift to the armature control spring, as shown in **FIG 12:15**.
2 Slacken the locknut of the adjustable contact and unscrew the contact. Insert a .058 inch feeler between the armature and the core face as indicated. Insert the feeler as far back as the first of the two rivet heads on the underside of the armature. Keep the feeler in position and press down squarely on the armature, which is the flat plate on top of the unit to which the spring tongue is riveted. Holding the armature down, screw in the adjustable contact until it just touches the contact which is riveted to the armature. Tighten the locknut and withdraw the feeler.

After this adjustment it is necessary to carry out the electrical setting procedure, as instructed earlier.

Armature-to-bobbin core gap of cut-out:

This mechanical setting is made as follows:
1 Insert a .015 inch feeler between the armature and the copper separation on the core face. Holding the armature in this position, adjust the fixed contact bracket so that the contacts just touch.
2 Remove the gauge. Adjust the armature back stop to give a core gap of .035 to .045 inch, as shown in **FIG 12:16**.
3 After making this mechanical setting, repeat the electrical checks for cut-in and drop-off voltages.

Cleaning contacts:

Use a fine carborundum stone or some silicon carbide paper to clean the voltage or current regulator contacts. After dressing the points, clean off all dust with methylated spirit.
Do not use carborundum stone or emery cloth on the cut-out contacts. Use a strip of fine glasspaper and clean off all dust with methylated spirit.

Circuit, and resistance values:

The circuit diagram is given in **FIG 12:17** and to make it more useful, the following resistance values are given:
1 Resistance of shunt windings at 20°C or 68°F is 10.8 to 11.8 ohms for the voltage regulator and 9.5 to 10.5 ohms for the cut-out.
2 The field resistor is 55 to 65 ohms.
3 The swamp resistor is 13.25 to 14.25 ohms when measured on the unit, between the centre tag and the base, with terminals 'D', 'F' and 'WL' disconnected.

12:8 The lamps

Headlamps:

The various types of bulb fittings are shown in **FIG 12:18**, where the top view shows the general assembly and the lower views the different bulb fixings according to the regulations prevailing in various countries. The sealed-beam type is shown in inset 4. Remove the three types as follows:
1 Remove the outer rim 1 after unscrewing the cross-head retaining screw.
2 Remove three cross-head screws to release the light unit retaining ring 2.
3 Withdraw the light unit 3. From the back of the unit, remove the sealed beam three-pin connector 4. Alternatively, in the case of the spring-clip type 5, withdraw the three-pin connector, disengage the spring clip and withdraw the bulb. To remove the bulb in type 6, press and turn the bayonet cap and pull out the bulb.

Refitting the unit is a reversal of the removal sequence in the case of the sealed beam type. To fit a new bulb in type 5, ensure that the pip on the flange of the bulb engages the slot in the reflector. Fit the spring clip so that the coils rest on the base of the bulb and the spring legs are fully engaged under the reflector lugs.

When dealing with type 6, fit the new bulb so that the notch in the flange of the bulb engages with the ridge in the reflector housing. Engage the cap lugs in the reflector housing slots, press the cap inwards and turn it clockwise.

To remove the back shell 8, first disconnect the wiring 7.

Headlamp beam setting:

Accurate beam setting is best left to a Service Station with the necessary equipment. The beams are affected by the load on the car and they must be set on a level surface with the car loaded for night driving. The beams must be set slightly below the horizontal or according to the regulations prevailing. **They must never be set above the horizontal.**

Adjustment points are provided on each headlamp and these are shown in **FIG 12:18**. Turn top screw 9 to make vertical adjustments and screw 10 to make horizontal settings.

Side and direction indicator lamps:

To reach the bulbs, remove the two cross-head screws retaining the lens. To remove the unit, disconnect the wiring and remove the nuts securing it inside the body panel.

Stop, tail, and direction indicator lamps:

Remove three cross-head screws to release the lens to gain access to the bulbs. To remove the unit, disconnect the wiring and remove the cross-head screws securing the assembly to the body.

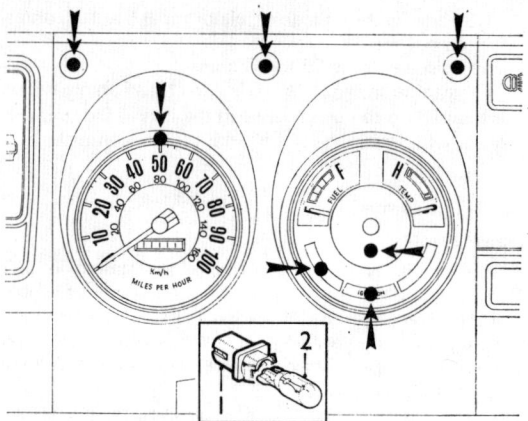

FIG 12:19 The arrows indicate the locations of the panel and warning lights. The bulb holder is **1** and the bulb **2**

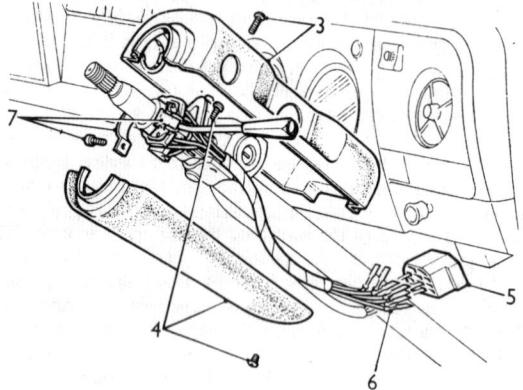

FIG 12:20 Removing the direction indicator, horn, and headlamp flasher switch

Key to Fig 12:20   3 Top half of cowl, and securing screw
3 Bottom half of cowl, and securing screws   5 Connector
block   6 Wiring tags   7 Switch, fixings, and wiring

Direction indicator side repeater lamps:

To reach the bulb remove the single cross-head screw and unclip the lens from the opposite end. To remove the assembly, disconnect the wiring and remove the two nuts inside the body panel.

Number plate and reverse lamp:

Remove the cover (two cross-head screws) and lift off the three lenses to reach the bulbs. To remove the unit, disconnect the wiring and remove the two nuts from underneath.

Interior lamp:

Gently squeeze the sides of the lens to withdraw it from the lamp. The festoon bulb will then be accessible. To remove the unit, disconnect the wiring from the spring clips and remove the two cross-head screws.

Panel and warning light bulbs:

Refer to **FIG 12:19** which shows the location of the bulbs 2. These are a push fit in their holders 1. The holders are accessible from below the instrument panel.

12:9 The switches

Panel switches:

Using some thin packing to prevent damage to the panel, lever up the flange on one side of the switch. Push and lift under the flange on the opposite side of the switch and withdraw it from the panel. Pull the wiring off the back. To remove the switch from the bezel or housing, it is necessary to depress the locating tongues, using Service Tool 18G.1145.

Direction indicator, horn and headlamp flasher switch:

To remove the switch, refer to **FIG 12:20**, and proceed as follows:
1 Disconnect the battery. Remove the steering wheel as instructed in **Chapter 10**.
2 Remove one screw and the top half of the switch cowl 3. Remove the bottom half of the cowl 4.
3 Detach the wiring connector block 5. Disconnect the direction indicator, horn, and headlamp flasher switch wiring 6 from the connector.
4 Remove the switch 7 complete with wiring.

Check the action of the switch and check the continuity of the wiring and contacts with a bulb, battery and test prods. The trip ring for cancelling the switch is secured to the steering column by a grub screw. Failure to cancel properly may be due to a misplaced trip.

To refit the switch adopt the reverse sequence to dismantling.

Ignition switch:

Instructions for removing the combined steering lock and ignition/starter switch will be found in **Chapter 10**.

Brake light switch:

This is secured to the pedal mounting plate inside the car. It is operated by an extension of the brake pedal arm. To remove it, do the following:

1 Disconnect the wiring from the two tags on the back of the switch.
2 Remove the two bolts and spring washers which secure the switch bracket to the top of the pedal plate.
3 Unscrew the switch from the bracket.

To refit the switch, screw it into the bracket until one complete thread of the switch housing is visible on the pedal side of the bracket.

12:10 Instrument panel printed circuit

The removal sequence is shown in **FIG 12:21**. Proceed as follows:
1 Remove the instrument panel as instructed in **Chapter 13**. Remove the fuel and temperature gauges (see **Section 12:11**).
2 Remove the voltage stabilizer (see **Section 12:11**). Remove the three voltage stabilizer terminals 4.
3 Remove the seven bulb holders 5.

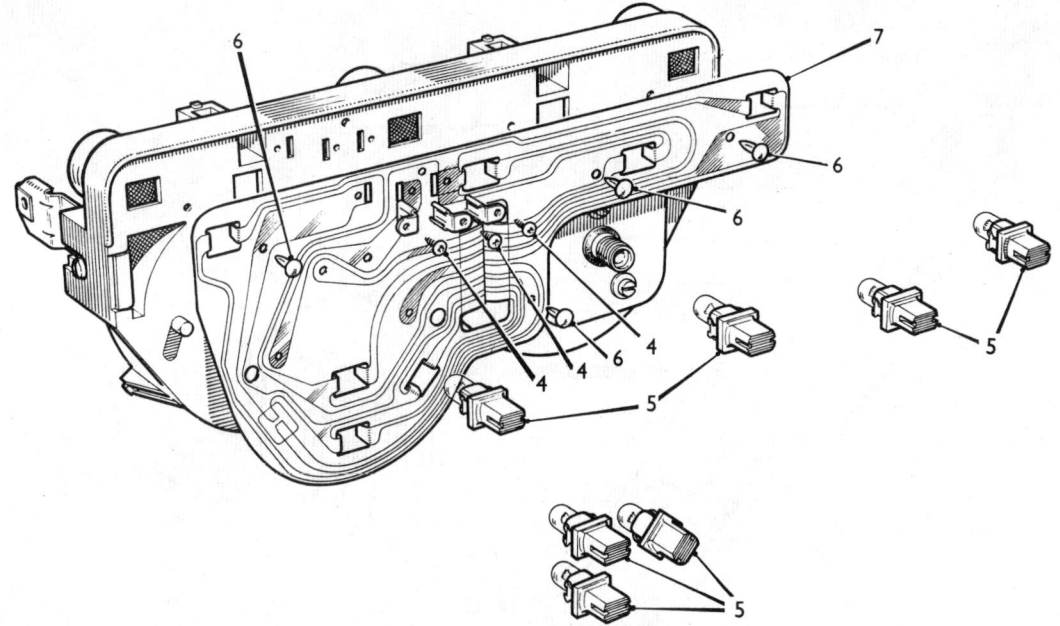

FIG 12:21   Removing the instrument panel printed circuit

Key to Fig 12:21   4 Voltage stabilizer terminal tags   5 Bulb holders   6 Circuit retaining pins   7 Printed circuit

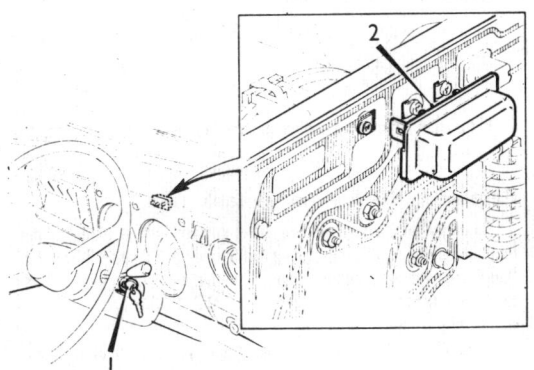

FIG 12:22   Location and removal of voltage stabilizer for bi-metal resistance instrumentation. **1** is the ignition switch, **2** is the stabilizer unit

4 Remove the four pins 6 retaining the printed circuit to the back of the instrument panel. Withdraw the circuit 7. Use a test lamp to check for continuity. Refit in the reverse order.

12:11 Fuel and temperature gauges

The bi-metal resistance equipment for the fuel and temperature gauges consists of an indicator head and transmitter, each unit being connected to a common voltage stabilizer. As the equipment is voltage-sensitive it is necessary to have a stabilizer to ensure a constant supply of the required voltage.

Testing:

The following series of tests will enable a faulty part to be traced. **Do not, at any time during the tests, shortcircuit a gauge to earth.**

Checking battery voltage:

1 Connect a voltmeter to terminal 2 on the fuse block and to earth.
2 With the ignition switched off the meter should read 12-volts. Start the engine and run it at around 1000 rev/min to ensure that the ignition warning light is out.
3 Check the voltage. It should be approximately 12 to 13-volts.

Checking the wiring:

1 Check for continuity between each unit and for a leak to earth, using a test lamp and prods.
2 Check for shortcircuits in the wiring to the transmitters.
3 Ensure that the stabilizer and the transmitters are earthed.

Checking the voltage stabilizer:

1 Switch on the ignition, and after two minutes check the main voltage between output terminal 1 and earth. The reading should be 10-volts. If the stabilizer is faulty, fit a new one. The location is given in **FIG 12:22**.
2 To fit a new stabilizer, switch off the ignition at 1. The stabilizer 2 is behind the instrument panel and is simply pulled out to disengage the terminal tags.
3 Fit the new unit, noting that the tags are offset so that it can be fitted only one way round.

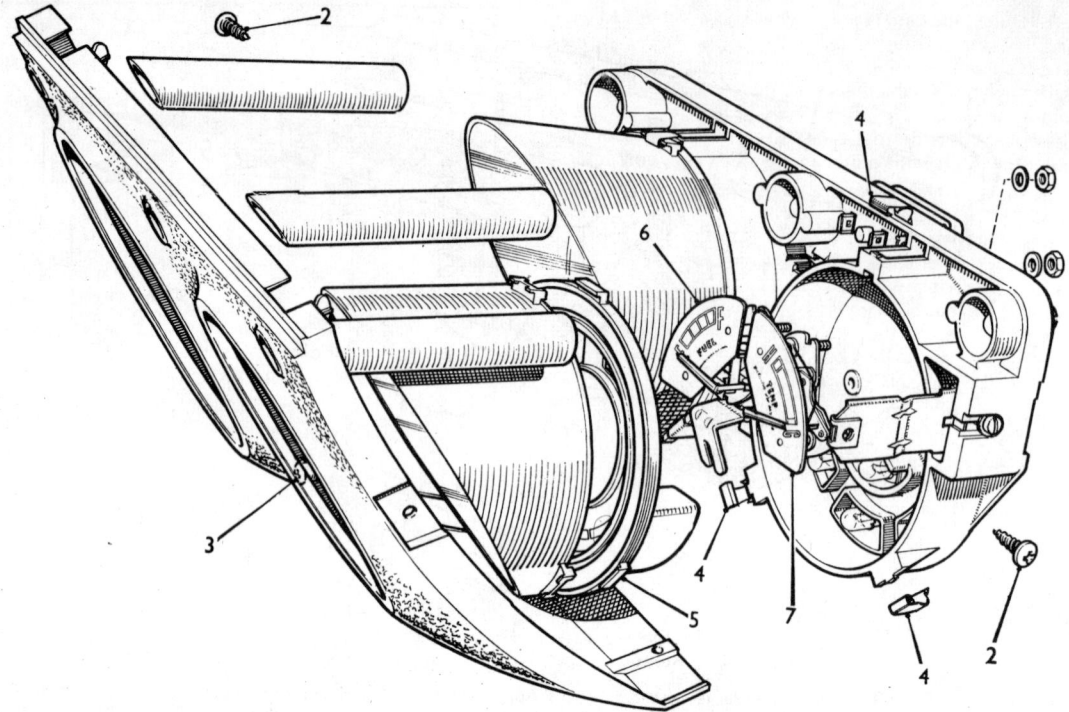

FIG 12:23   Removing the fuel and temperature gauges

Key to Fig 12:23   2 Side screws retaining instrument moulding   3 Central retaining screw   4 Clips retaining lens assembly
5 Seat for lens assembly   6 Fuel gauge   7 Temperature gauge

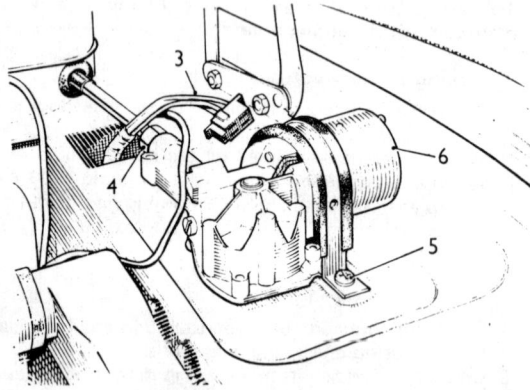

FIG 12:24   Removing the wiper block **6**. **3** is the wiring connector, **4** is the outer cable retaining nut and **5** a motor securing screw

Checking gauges:

1 Check for continuity between the terminals with the wiring disconnected. Again, be careful not to short-circuit a gauge to earth.
2 Fit a new gauge if one proves to be faulty.

Checking the thermal transmitter:

1 Check for continuity between the terminal and the outer casing with the lead disconnected.

2 Fit a new transmitter if the one being tested proves to be faulty.

Removing the fuel gauge tank unit:

Disconnect the battery and remove the access panel from the floor of the luggage compartment. Disconnect the wiring and the fuel pipe. The unit is removed from the tank by means of Service Tool 18G.1001 which consists of a short length of thin-walled steel tubing suitably notched to engage two of the lugs. Refit a new unit in the reverse order.

Removing fuel and temperature gauges:

Use **FIG 12:23** as a guide. Proceed as follows:
1 Remove the instrument panel as instructed in **Chapter 13**. Remove the two side screws 2.
2 Slacken central screw 3 and remove the instrument moulding together with the tubes for the warning lights.
3 Remove the three clips 4 and withdraw the lens assembly. Remove lens seat 5.
4 Remove fuel gauge 6 and temperature gauge 7.
Renew faulty gauges and reassemble in the reverse order.

12:12 Windscreen wiper motor

To remove the motor, refer to **FIG 12:24** and do the following:

1 Disconnect the battery and remove the wiper arms (see instructions in **Chapter 13**).
2 Disconnect the wiring 3 from the motor terminals.
3 Unscrew nut 4 which secures the outer cable to the motor housing.
4 Remove the two cross-head screws 5 to release the motor. Withdraw the motor and gearbox assembly complete with inner cable. The inner cable will turn the wiper spindles as it is withdrawn.

When refitting the motor in the reverse order, make sure that the inner cable engages correctly with the gear teeth in each wiper wheelbox.

If the motor has been giving trouble, check the end float of the armature and the condition of the brushgear. The correct specifications for these items are given in Technical Data at the end of this volume.

12:13 Fuses

The fuses are located inside the car on the righthand side between the facia panel and the parcel shelf as shown in **FIG 12:25**. Block 1 houses four working fuses 2, 3, 4 and 5. Fuses 6 are spares.

The following details indicate which circuits are protected by the individual fuses. These can be checked on the wiring diagram given in Technical Data.

Fuse 2:

This protects the equipment which operates independently of the ignition switch. This is the horn, the interior light and the headlamp flasher circuit. The rating is 35 amp.

Fuse 3:

This protects the righthand panel, side, and tail lamps. The rating is 15 amp.

Fuse 4:

This protects the lefthand panel, side, and tail lamps. The rating is 15 amp.

Fuse 5:

This protects the circuits which operate only when the ignition switch is on. The equipment protected is the windscreen wipers, direction indicators, brake lights, heater fan, heated backlight and cigar lighter (when fitted). The rating is 35 amp.

Blown fuses:

A blown fuse is indicated by failure of the circuits protected by it. Pull out the suspected fuse and check that it has blown. If it has, do not fit a new fuse until the particular circuits have been checked for shortcircuits or other faults, or the new fuse may also blow.

Before fitting the new fuse, check that it has the correct value. This will be found marked on a slip of paper inside the glass tube of the fuse.

12:14 Cars equipped with an alternator

When there is an alternator (instead of the orthodox generator) fitted to the car, take the following precautions to avoid damage to the alternator and its control equipment:

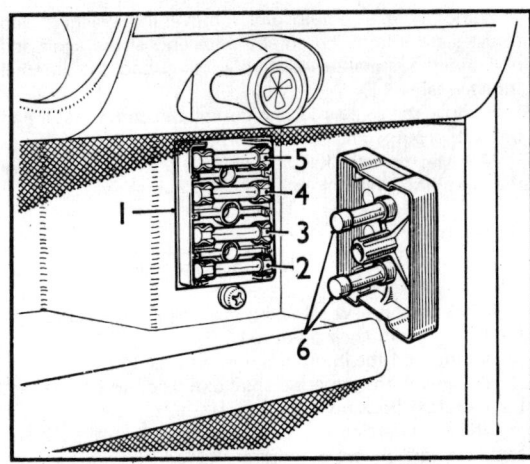

FIG 12:25 Location and rating of fuses

Key to Fig 12:25   1 Fuse block   2 35 amp fuse
3 15 amp fuse   4 15 amp fuse   5 35 amp fuse
6 Spare fuses

1 Ensure that all electrical connections in the generating and charging circuits are always tight.
2 Do not run the engine with the battery or any of the charging circuit cables disconnected. If the engine must be run with the charging circuit incomplete, disconnect the cables from the alternator and join the alternator terminals with a loop of wire.
3 Ensure that the battery negative (or —) terminal is always connected to earth.
4 Disconnect all cables from the alternator and control unit terminals before using electric arc-welding equipment on the car or boosting the battery with a high-rate charger.

12:15 Starter motor type M35JPE

On 1750 models, and some 1500 cars exported to colder territories, this pre-engaged type of starter is fitted. From the cut-away view given in **FIG 12:26** it will be seen that it differs from the earlier model in that the solenoid switch is mounted on the main starter casing and is equipped with an engagement lever by means of which the starter drive pinion is moved into engagement with the starter ring gear before the starting current is applied.

Dismantling:

Disconnect the link 1 between the solenoid STA terminal and the motor terminal, then remove the nuts 2 securing the solenoid 3 to the drive-end bracket 7 and withdraw the solenoid unit.

Lift the solenoid plunger and return spring 4 from the engagement lever 8. Remove the rubber sealing block 5.

Remove the retaining ring (Spire nut) from the engagement lever pivot pin 6 and withdraw the pin.

Unscrew the nuts and withdraw the drive-end bracket. Remove the engagement lever from the drive operating plate.

Withdraw the splitpin and remove the washers and thrust plate 9 from the commutator end of the shaft and pull out the armature assembly 10 noting the internal thrust washer 11.

Remove the screws 12 and detach the commutator end bracket, disengaging the field brushes.

Move the thrust collar clear of the jump ring 14, remove the jump ring and slide off the drive assembly.

Reassembly:

This is the reverse of the above procedure, noting the following:

Always use a new retaining ring (Spire nut) to secure the engagement lever pivot pin.

Do not omit the internal thrust washer 11.

Fit shims to the armature shaft extension to ensure that the end float does not exceed .010 inch.

When assembling the thrust washers and plate 9 see that they are in correct order and are prevented from rotating separately by engaging the cotterpin with the locking piece on the thrust plate.

12:16 Fault diagnosis

(a) Battery discharged

1 Terminal connections loose or dirty
2 Shorts in lighting circuits
3 Generator or alternator not charging
4 Regulator or cut-out units not working properly
5 Battery defective internally

(b) Insufficient charging current

1 Check 1 and 4 in (a)
2 Driving belt slipping

(c) Battery will not hold charge

1 Low electrolyte level
2 Battery plates sulphated
3 Electrolyte leakage from cracked case
4 Plate separators defective

(d) Battery overcharged

1 Regulators need adjusting

(e) Generator output low or nil

1 Belt broken or slipping
2 Regulator unit out of adjustment
3 Worn bearings, loose pole pieces
4 Commutator worn, burned or shorted
5 Armature shaft worn or bent
6 Brushes sticking, springs weak or broken
7 Field coil winding broken, shorted or burned

(f) Starter motor lacks power or will not operate

1 Battery discharged, terminals loose or dirty
2 Starter pinion jammed in flywheel gear
3 Starter switch or solenoid faulty
4 Brushes worn or sticking, leads detached or shorting
5 Commutator dirty or worn
6 Armature shaft bent
7 Engine abnormally stiff, perhaps after rebore

(g) Starter motor runs but will not engage

1 Pinion sticking on screwed sleeve
2 Broken teeth on pinion or flywheel gears

(h) Noisy starter pinion when engine is running

1 Broken pinion drive spring

(j) Starter motor inoperative

1 Check 1 and 4 in (f)
2 Armature or field coils faulty

(k) Starter motor rough or noisy

1 Mounting bolts loose
2 Damaged teeth on pinion or flywheel
3 Main spring on pinion broken

(l) Lamps inoperative or erratic

1 Battery low, bulbs burned out
2 Faulty earthing of lamps or battery
3 Lighting switch faulty, loose or broken connections

(m) Wiper motor sluggish, taking high current

1 Faulty armature
2 Bearings dry or out of alignment
3 Commutator dirty or shortcircuited
4 Wheelbox spindle binding, cable rack tight in outer casing
5 Lack of lubrication
6 No end float to armature spindle

(n) Wiper motor runs but does not drive arms

1 Wheelbox gear and spindle worn
2 Cable rack faulty
3 Gearbox components worn

(o) Fuel or temperature gauges do not work

1 Break in wiring
2 Voltage stabilizer faulty
3 Check instruments and transmitters for continuity

CHAPTER 13

THE BODY AND ACCESSORIES

13:1 Bodywork finish

The large-scale repair of damaged body panels is best left to the expert. Even the elimination of small dents may prove troublesome, as too much hammering can stretch the metal and make matters worse instead of better. Filling minor dents and scratches is the best method of restoring the surface so that it blends perfectly with the original finish. This operation is within the powers of most car owners, particularly as self-spraying cans of paint in the correct colours are also readily available. It must be remembered, however, that paint changes colour with age, so that retouching may not be imperceptible. In this case it is best to spray a complete wing, rather than try to touch-up a small area.

Before setting out to spray paintwork, it is essential to remove all traces of wax polish. This can be done with white spirit unless the polish contains silicones. In this case more drastic treatment is required, involving the use of abrasives.

To fill blemishes, use a primer surfacer or paste stopper according to the amount of filling required. When it is dry, rub it down with 400 grade 'Wet or dry' paper until the surface is smooth and flush with the surrounding area. Time spent in getting the best possible finish will be rewarded by a superior gloss when the paint is applied.

When spraying, keep the central area wet and the outer edges light and dry. After leaving to dry for a few hours, use a cutting compound to remove the dry spray and finish off with a liquid polish.

13:2 The doors and locks

When repairs are needed on the doors, use **FIG 13:1** for views of the components, but refer to **FIG 13:2** for details of the locks.

In most cases, dismantling is a matter of removing self-tapping screws, orthodox screws and nuts or else one of the various forms of spring clip. The door liners or trim panels are hooked under a top finishing strip and held at

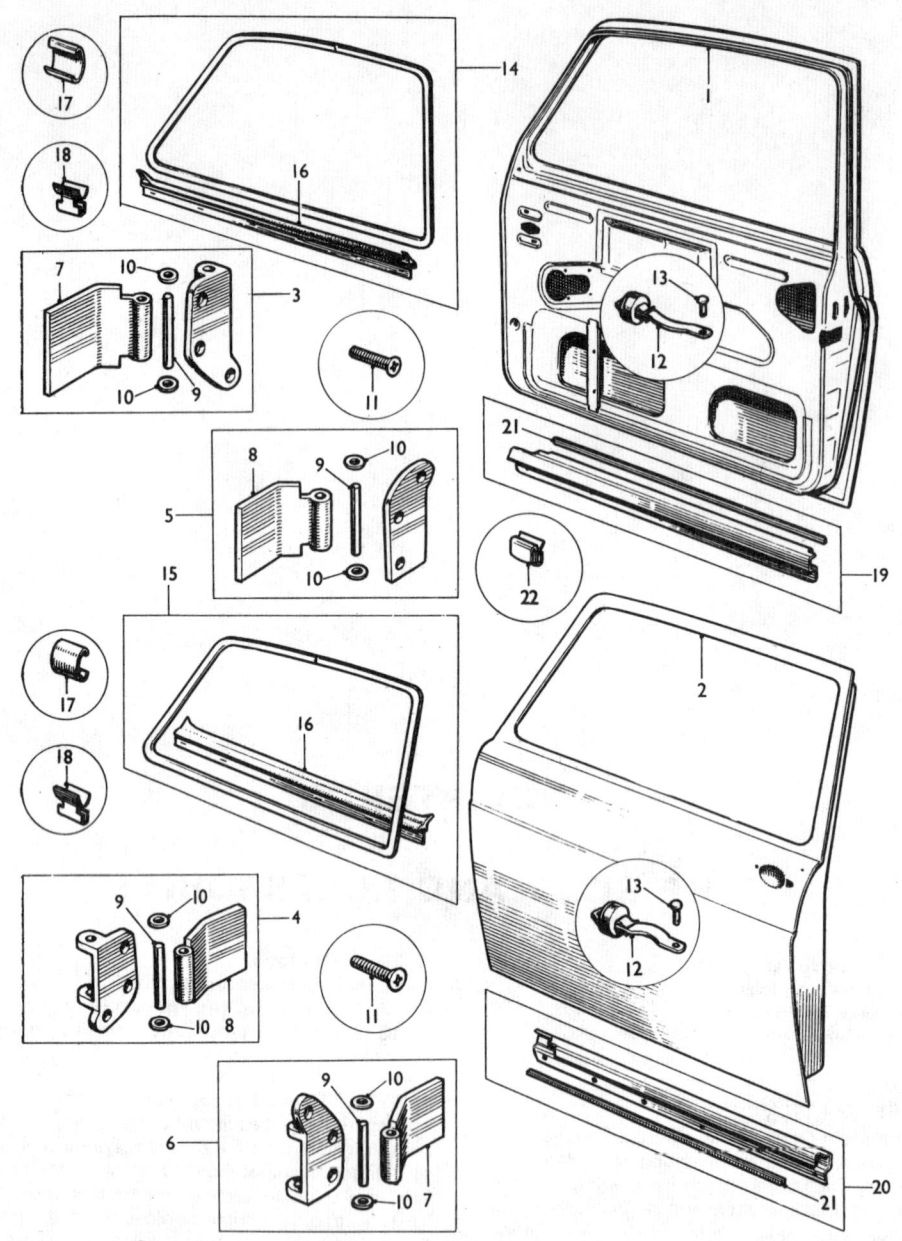

FIG 13:1   Components of the righthand and lefthand front doors

Key to Fig 13:1   1 RH door shell   2 LH door shell   3 RH door upper hinge assembly   4 LH door upper hinge assembly
5 RH door lower hinge assembly   6 LH door lower hinge assembly   7 Hinge leaf   8 Hinge leaf   9 Hinge pin
10 Brass washer   11 Screw   12 Door check arm   13 Clevis pin   14 RH outer moulding assembly
15 LH outer moulding assembly   16 Weatherstrip   17 Moulding capping   18 Clip   19 RH inner waist capping assembly
20 LH inner waist capping assembly   21 Weatherstrip   22 Clip

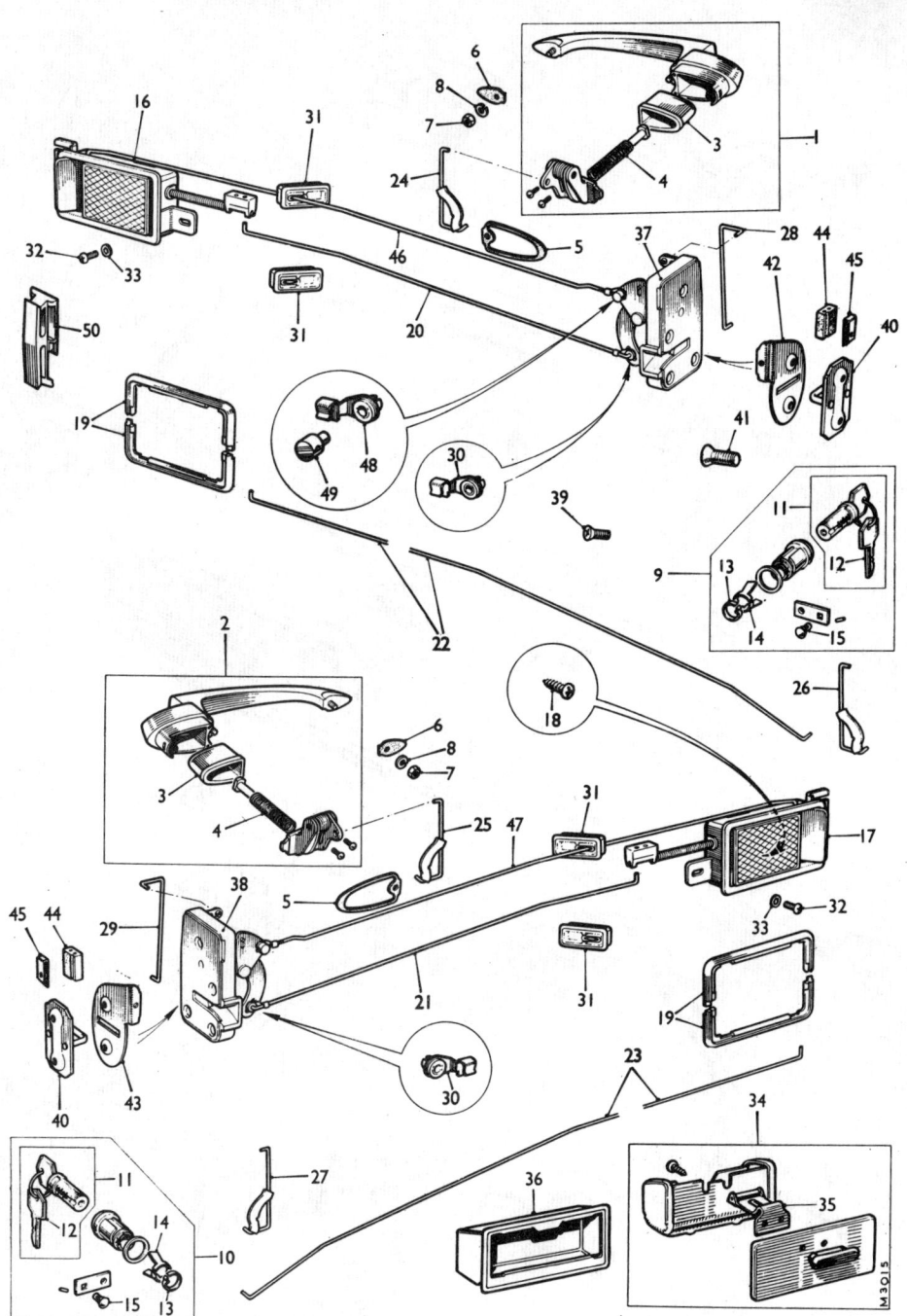

FIG 13:2 Components of the door locks and remote control

Key to Fig 13:2   1 Door handle assembly   2 Door handle assembly   3 Push button   4 Spring   5 Washer
6 Washer   7 Nut   8 Spring washer   9 Door lock assembly   10 Door lock assembly   11 Barrel assembly
12 Key   13 Spring clip   14 Retaining clip   15 Operating stud   16 Remote control   17 Remote control
18 Screw   19 Bezel   20 Remote control rod   21 Remote control rod   22 Remote control rod
23 Remote control rod   24 Handle push button rod   25 Handle push button rod   26 Handle push button rod
27 Handle push button rod   28 Private lock rod   29 Private lock rod   30 Clip   31 Grommet   32 Screw
33 Shakeproof washer   34 Ashtray assembly   35 Spring   36 Ashtray case   37 Door lock   38 Door lock
39 Screw   40 Striker   41 Screw   42 Striker plate   43 Striker plate   44 Seal   45 Retainer
46 Lock operating rod   47 Lock operating rod   48 Clip   49 Adjustment pin   50 Guide link

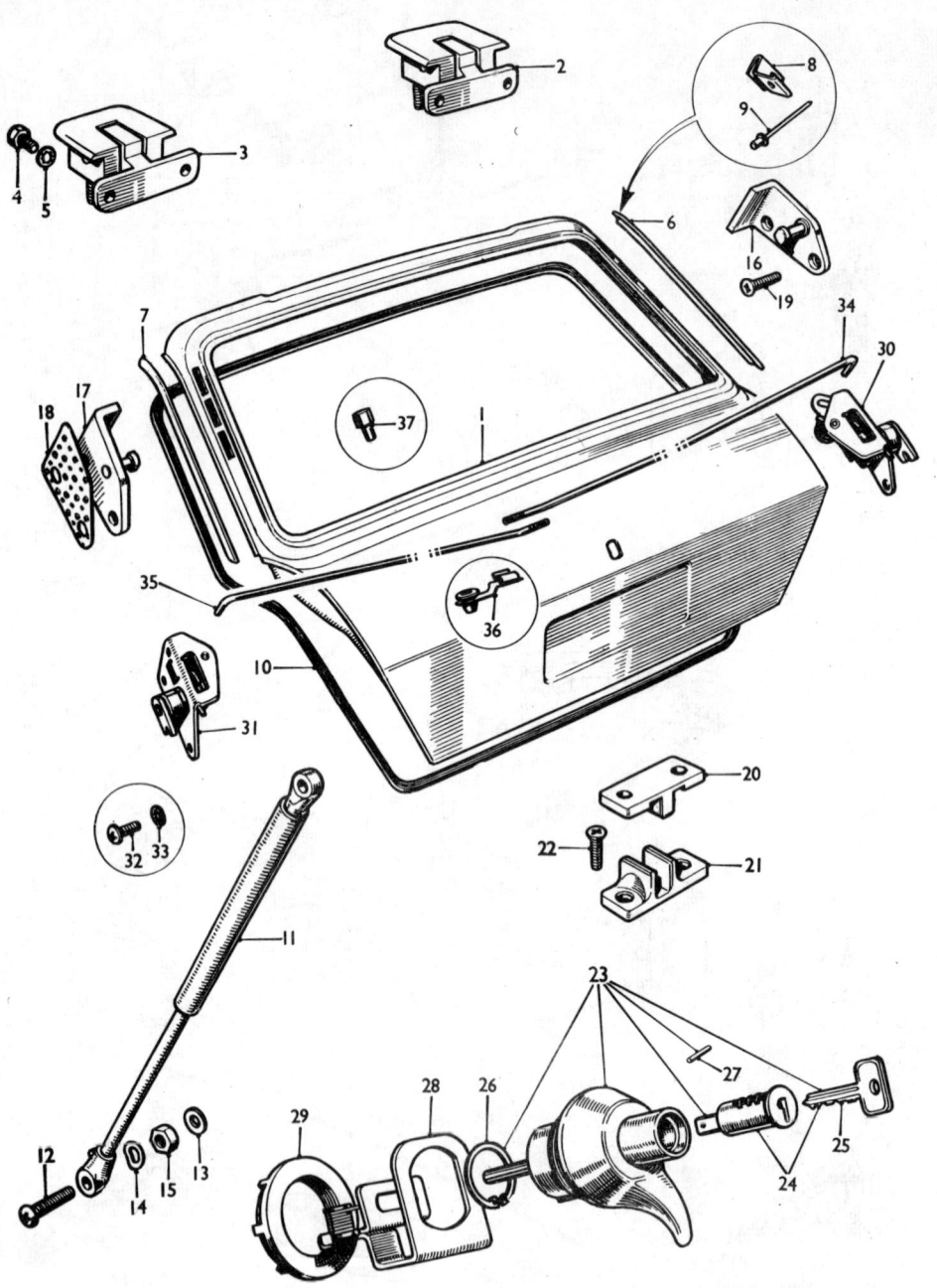

FIG 13:3 Components of the tailgate. There are important precautions to be taken when dealing with rams **11** (see text)

Key to Fig 13:3   1 Tailgate panel   2 RH hinge   3 LH hinge   4 Screw   5 Shakeproof washer   6 RH moulding   7 LH moulding   8 Clip   9 Rivet   10 Seal   11 Ram   12 Screw   13 Plain washer   14 Anti-rattle washer   15 Nut   16 RH striker   17 LH striker   18 Shim   19 Screw   20 Upper dovetail   21 Lower dovetail   22 Screw   23 Tailgate push button assembly   24 Locking barrel assembly   25 Key   26 Circlip   27 Bissel pin   28 Centre plate   29 Push button locknut   30 RH latch   31 LH latch   32 Screw   33 Shakeproof washer   34 RH link rod   35 LH link race   36 Clip   37 Adjustment pin

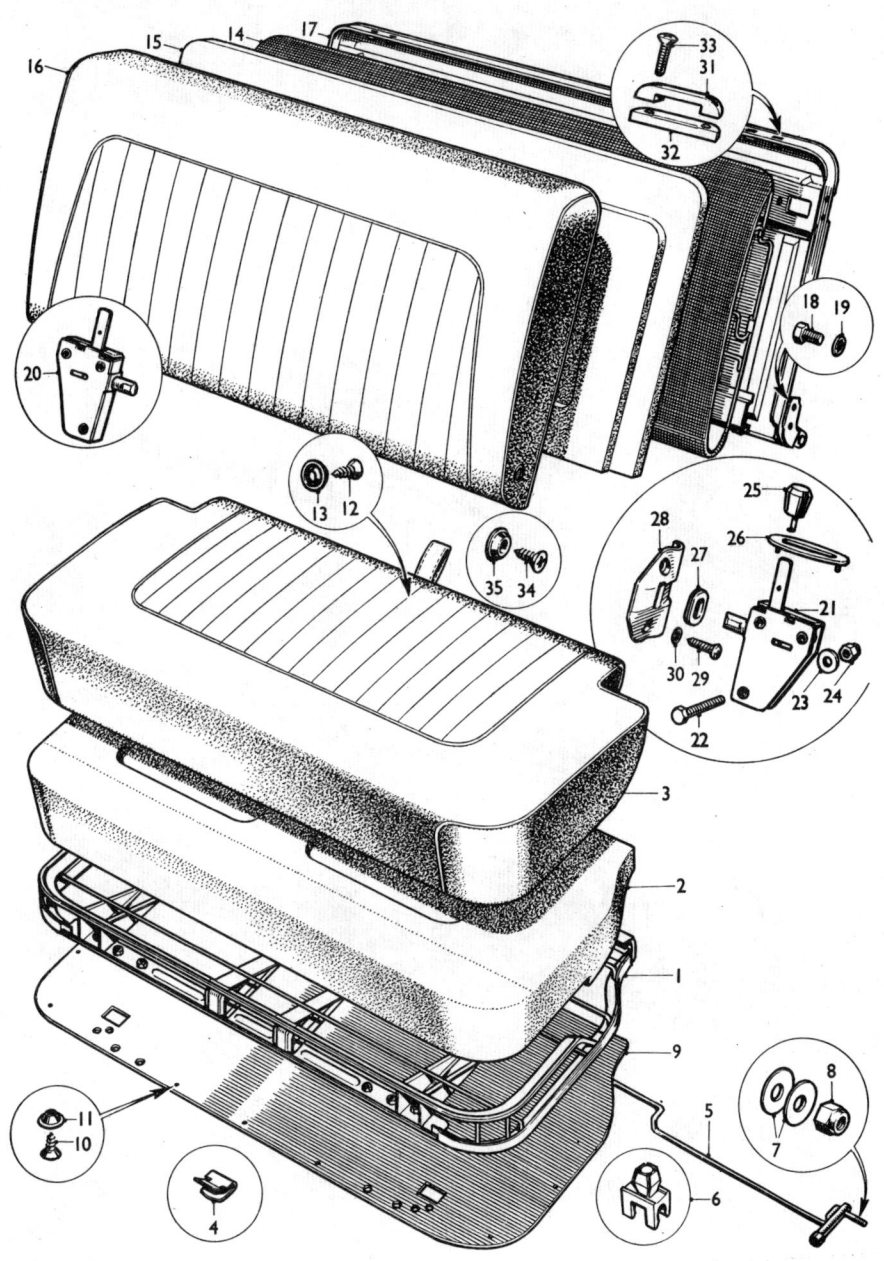

FIG 13:4   Components of the rear seats

Key to Fig 13:4   1 Rear cushion frame   2 Rear cushion pad   3 Rear cushion cover   4 Clip
5 Rear cushion support   6 Clip   7 Plain washer   8 Locknut   9 Rear cushion bottom liner   10 Screw
11 Cup washer   12 Screw   13 Cup washer   14 Rear squab spring case   15 Rear squab pad   16 Rear squab pad cover
17 Squab panel   18 Screw   19 Lockwasher   20 RH squab lock   21 LH squab lock   22 Screw   23 Plain washer
24 Locknut   25 Knob   26 Lock escutcheon   27 Grommet   28 Lock striker plate   29 Screw
30 Lockwasher   31 Squab support hasp   32 Squab hasp backing plate   33 Screw   34 Screw   35 Cup washer

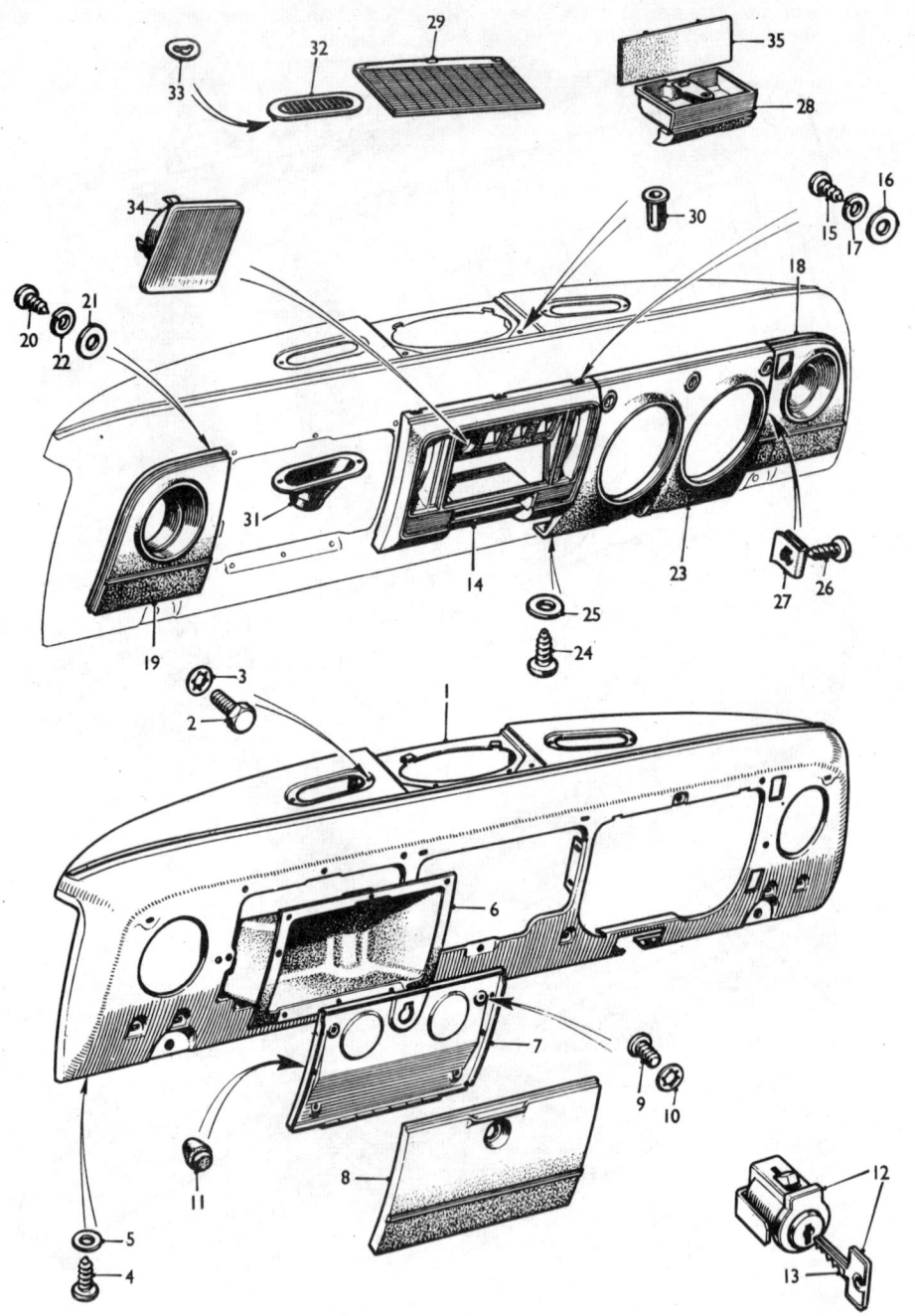

FIG 13:5 Components of the facia

Key to Fig 13:5   1 Facia panel   2 Screw   3 Shakeproof washer   4 Screw   5 Washer   6 Glovebox
7 Glovebox lid inner panel   8 Glovebox lid   9 Screw   10 Shakeproof washer   11 Buffer   12 Glovebox lid catch assembly
13 Key   14 Centre console   15 Screw   16 Plain washer   17 Spring washer   18 Righthand facia outer moulding
19 Lefthand facia outer moulding   20 Screw   21 Washer   22 Spring washer   23 Instrument nacelle moulding
24 Screw   25 Washer   26 Screw   27 Nut   28 Ashtray   29 Radio speaker fret   30 Retainer
31 Demister   32 Demister outlet fret   33 Retainer   34 Cover for cigar-lighter aperture   35 Cover for radio aperture

other places by screws or clips. Use a screwdriver to prise the panel clips out of the locating cups, taking care not to damage the paintwork.

It will be seen from the parts shown in **FIG 13:2** that the door lock assemblies 9 and 10 are held in place by spring clips 13 and retaining clips 14. The removal of the remote control and operating rods is a matter of unclipping items 30 or 48. Note that the lengths of the lock operating rods 46 and 47 can be altered by turning pin 49 on the thread until the correct position is found. The assembly is then secured by pressing the clip over the rod.

13:3 The tailgate

The components are shown in **FIG 13:3** and the illustration is clear on the assembly of the parts. **When dealing with the tailgate rams 11, there are essential precautions to be taken. These are necessary because the rams contain gas under pressure and heat must never be applied near them.** The precautions are as follows:

1 Remove the rams, by undoing the fixings shown in the illustration, if welding or any other repair operation involving heat is to be carried out near them.

2 **Never apply heat to the rams in any circumstances.**

3 **Do not try to dismantle the rams.** If renewal is necessary, obtain complete assemblies.

4 Fit the rams in the position shown. **Never fit them in an inverted position.**

13:4 Seat components

There is little to be said about the reclining front seats as the runner fixings will be readily seen upon examination.

Use **FIG 13:4** when working on the rear seats. The various fixings are clearly shown and the squab locks 20 and 21 should present no difficulty in removing. The locks are serviced as an assembly.

13:5 The facia

The components are shown in **FIG 13:5**. From the enlarged views of the fixings and their positions, removal should present no difficulties.

In association with the removal of the facia, refer to the appropriate Section in **Chapter 12** for details of the

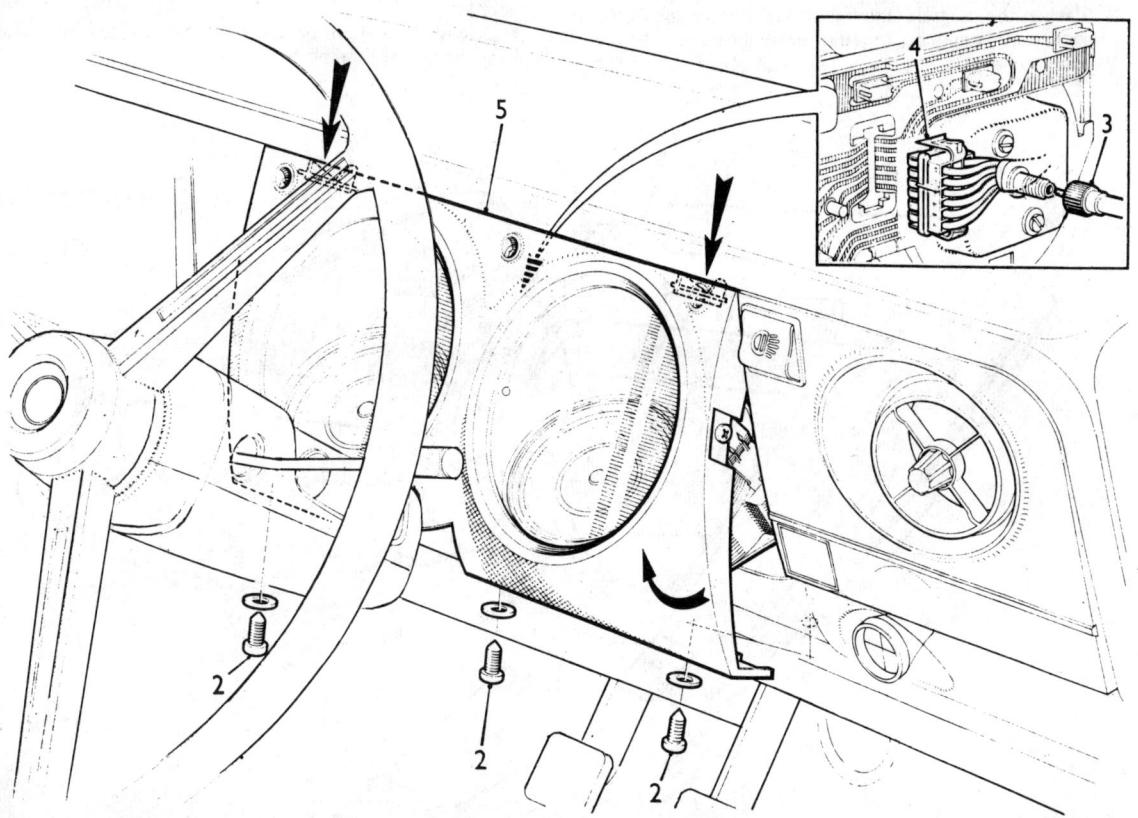

FIG 13:6   Removing the instrument panel. The inset is a view behind the circuit board

Key to Fig 13:6   2 Panel securing screws   3 Speedometer cable   4 Wiring plug   5 Instrument panel

removal of the printed circuit board, and also the removal of the fuel and temperature gauges. To remove the instrument panel and speedometer, refer to **Sections 13:6** and **13:7**.

13:6 The instrument panel

To remove the panel, refer to **FIG 13:6** and do the following:
1 Disconnect the battery. Remove the securing screws 2 from under the instrument panel.
2 Remove the speedometer cable 3 from behind the panel by unscrewing the union nut. Disconnect the wiring plug 4.
3 Pull the panel 5 forward at the bottom to unhook the clips arrowed.

When refitting the instrument panel follow the removal instructions in reverse.

13:7 Removing the speedometer and cable

Refer to **FIG 13:7** and follow these instructions:
1 Remove the instrument panel as described in the preceding Section.
2 Remove the screws 2 from each side of the instrument moulding.
3 Slacken the central retaining screw 3 and remove the instrument moulding together with the tubes for the warning lights.

4 Remove clips 4 and withdraw the lens assembly. Remove the lens assembly seat 5.
5 Remove the two screws and washers 6 from behind the panel and withdraw the speedometer 6a. Remove the speedometer mounting rubber 7.

Use these removal instructions in reverse when refitting the speedometer.

Removing the speedometer cable:

The cable is released from the instrument as shown in the inset to **FIG 13:6**. Release the other end from the transmission in similar fashion. By unclipping the cable from the body, it may be withdrawn.

When refitting a cable, note the following points:
1 Lubricate by withdrawing the inner cable and coating it lightly with grease, except for 8 inches at the speedometer end. Insert the inner cable into the casing and wipe off surplus grease.
2 Check the speedometer end of the cable. The inner cable should project approximately $\frac{3}{8}$ inch beyond the outer casing at this point.
3 Check the run of the cable. There must be no bends within 2 inches of the connecting ends. The run of the cable must be smooth, with no bend of less than 6 inch radius.
4 Do not have sharp bends in the cable at the clips and avoid overtightening the clip fixings.

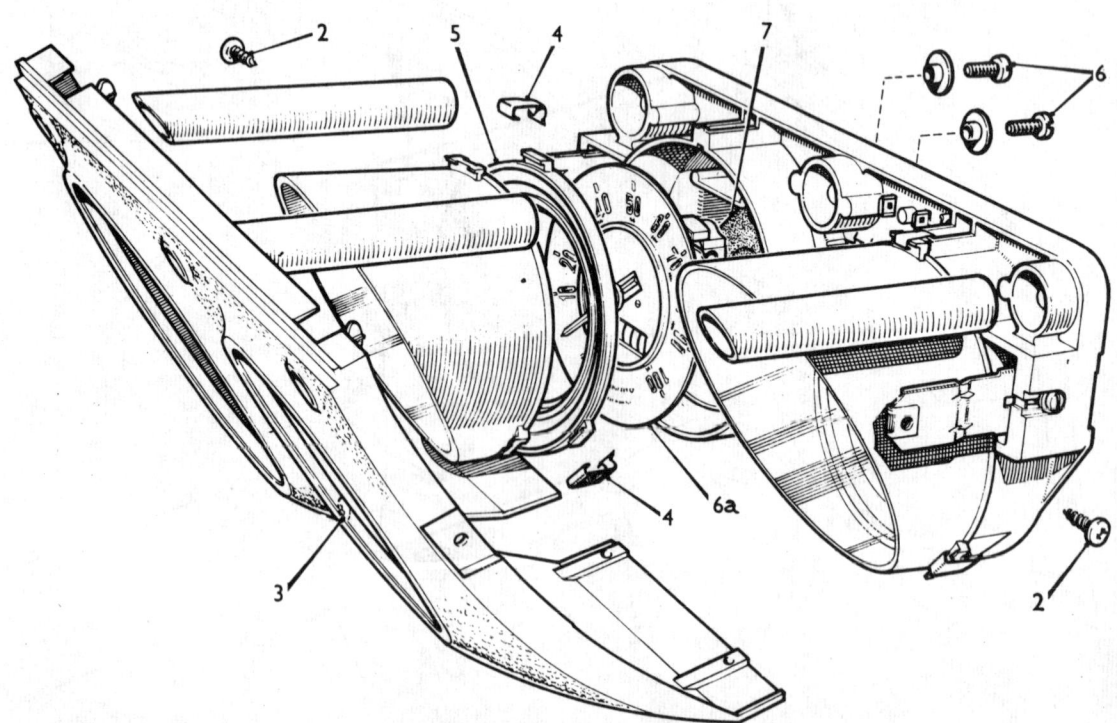

FIG 13:7 Removing the speedometer

Key to Fig 13:7   2 Instrument moulding side screws   3 Central screw   4 Lens clips   5 Lens seat
6 Speedometer securing screws   6a Speedometer   7 Speedometer mounting rubber

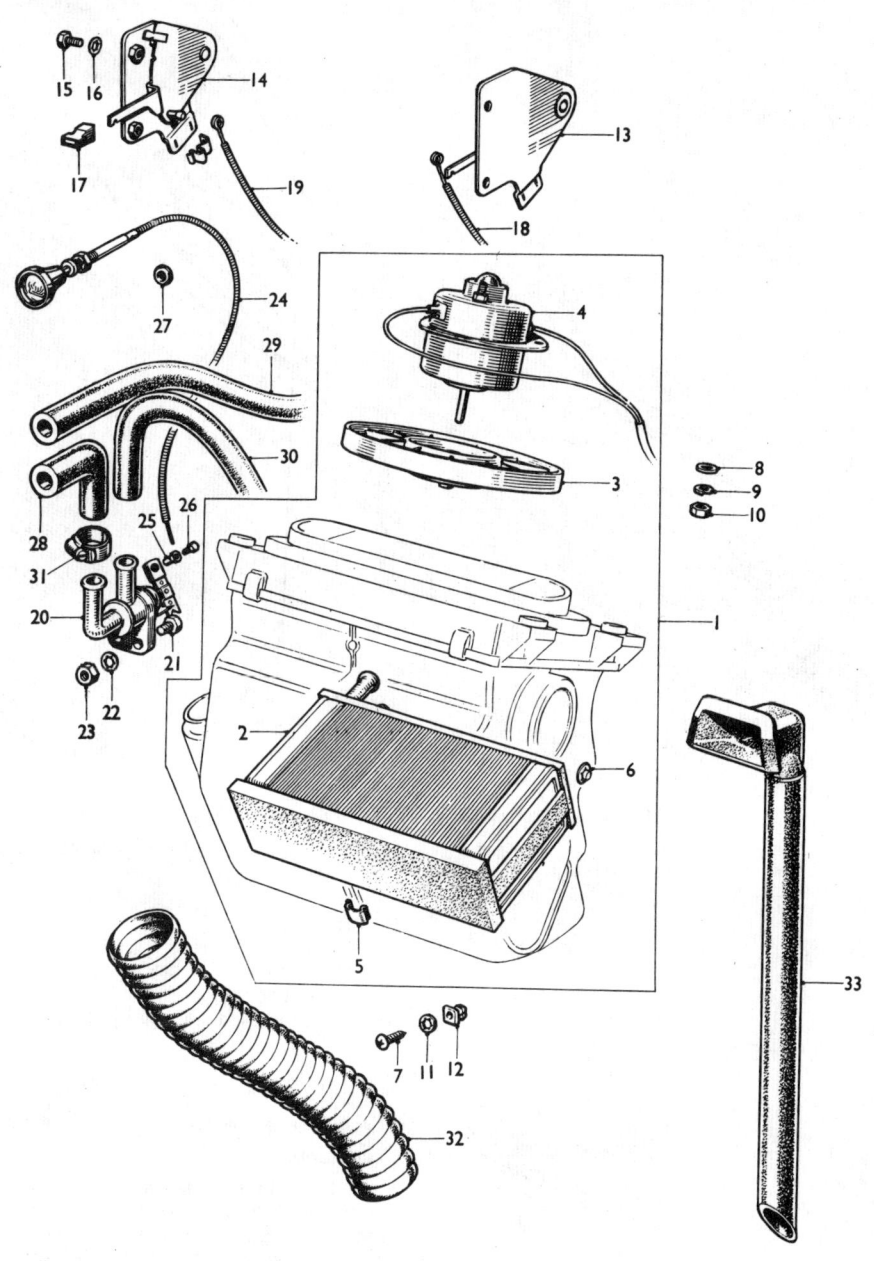

FIG 13:8 Components of the heater

Key to Fig 13:8   1 Heater assembly   2 Heater matrix   3 Fan   4 Motor   5 Clip   6 Clip   7 Screw
8 Plain washer   9 Spring washer   10 Nut   11 Shakeproof washer   12 Locknut   13 Temperature control lever
14 Demister control lever   15 Screw   16 Shakeproof washer   17 Knob for lever   18 Temperature control cable
19 Demister control cable   20 Water control valve   21 Screw   22 Shakeproof washer   23 Nut   24 Water control valve guide
25 Trunnion for cable   26 Screw   27 Grommet   28 Heater to water control valve hose   29 Hose
30 Control valve to water pump hose   31 Hose clip   32 Demister hose   33 Heater intake duct drain tube

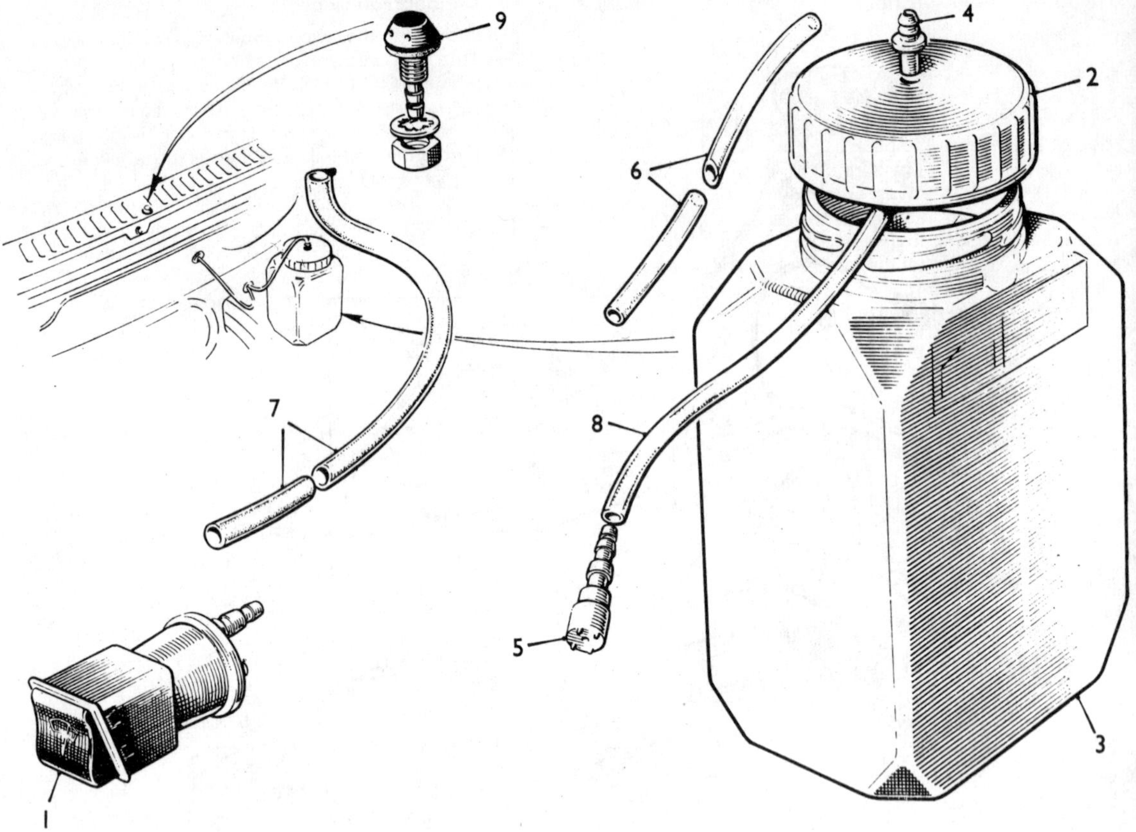

FIG 13:9   Components of the windscreen washer

Key to Fig 13:9   1 Windscreen washer pump   2 Reservoir cap   3 Reservoir   4 Connector   5 Non-return valve
6 Reservoir to pump tube   7 Pump to jet tube   8 Pickup tube   9 Jet

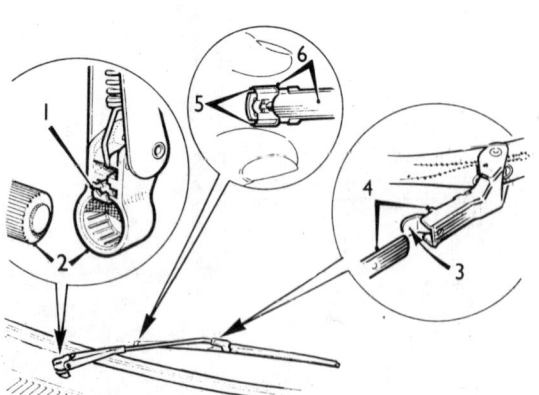

FIG 13:10   Dismantling a wiper arm and blade

Key to Fig 13:10   1 Spring clip   2 Arm and spindle
3 Blade retaining clip   4 Blade and arm   5 Retaining
clip on blade   6 Rubber assembly

5 If it is thought that the cable has too much free movement, fix additional clips.

6 Secure the end connections of the cable by hand tightness only.

13:8 Heater, windscreen washer and wipers

The heater:

The components are shown in **FIG 13:8**, and from
these views there should be no difficulty in dismantling
and renewing any defective parts. In the case of motor 4 it
is best to renew it complete if the bearings, windings, or
brushgear give trouble. Adjustment of the controls is a
matter of moving the outer casings of cables 18 and 19 in
their attaching spling clips. The inner cable of the water
valve control 24 is secured in trunnion 25 so that its
position can be set by releasing screw 26. If the system is
emptied of water, an air lock on refilling might cause
trouble due to an inability to warm up. Run the engine and
release the outlet hose ends in turn until all air is ejected.
Keep the radiator header tank topped up meanwhile.

The windscreen washer:

The components can be seen in **FIG 13:9**. The only point which might affect dismantling is that the pump is screwed into the back of the push. To remove the push from the facia, unscrew the pump after disconnecting the pipes and then ease the push assembly out of the hole in the panel. It is held in by spring tongues.

In cases where the washer fails to deliver fluid, check that the non-return valve 5 seals on the pumping stroke. Check that there are no defects in the piping, that the jets are not blocked and that the pump sucks and blows when reciprocated. Tube 6 must go to the suction side of the pump. Do not use antifreeze in the reservoir.

The windscreen wiper:

Removal of the wiper motor has been covered in **Chapter 12, Section 12:12**. To remove the wiper blades, study **FIG 13:10**. Press down retaining clip 3 and withdraw blade 4 from the arm. To renew the rubber assembly, squeeze retaining clip 5 until it can be withdrawn from the blade, then withdraw the rubber assembly from the clips on the blade.

To remove the wiper arm from the operating spindle, lift spring clip 1 clear of the retaining groove in the spindle. The arm 2 can then be pulled off the spindle splines. These splines enable some adjustment of the arm position in cases where the wiper does not cover the correct area. Refit all parts in the reverse order of dismantling.

APPENDIX

TECHNICAL DATA

        Engine   Fuel system   Ignition system   Cooling system
        Clutch   Transmission   Suspension system   Steering
        Brakes   Electrical equipment   Capacities   Dimensions
        Torque wrench settings

WIRING DIAGRAM

        FIG 14:1 Austin Maxi

HINTS ON MAINTENANCE AND OVERHAUL

GLOSSARY OF TERMS

INDEX

TECHNICAL DATA

Dimensions are in inches unless otherwise stated

Engines:

Type 1500	14H
Capacity	1485 cc
Bore and stroke	76.2 x 81.28 mm
Compression ratio	9.0:1
Type 1750	17H
Capacity	1748 cc
Bore and stroke	76.2 x 95.75 mm
Compression ratio	8.75:1
Cranking pressure	170 to 195 lb/sq in
Idling speed	500 rev/min
Firing order	1, 3, 4, 2

Crankshaft:

Type	SG iron, 5 main bearings
Main journal diameter	2.2505 to 2.2510
Crankpin journal diameter	1.8759 to 1.8764
End float	.002 to .003
End float adjustment	Selective thrust washers
Main bearing length	.811 to .821
Main bearing diametrical clearance	.002 to .0035
Main bearing material	Steel-backed, reticular tin
Undersizes (main and crankpin)	—.010, .020, .030 and .040

Connecting rods:

Type	Big-end split horizontally, small-end solid
Big-end bearing material	Steel-backed, reticular tin
Length between centres	5.828 to 5.832
Small-end bore	.811 to .8115
End float on crankpin (nominal)	.006 to .01

Gudgeon pin:

Type	Press-fit in small-end
Outside diameter	.8123 to .8125

Pistons:

Type	Aluminium, solid skirt-slotted
Oversize	.020
Clearance in cylinder:	
Top (below oil control groove)	.0018 to .0024
Bottom	.001 to .0016
Width of ring grooves:	
Top, second and third	.064 to .065
Oil control	.1565 to .1575

Piston rings:

Number of rings 1500	3 compression 1 oil control
1750	2 compression 1 oil control
Type:	
Top	Plain chrome, sintered alloy
Second and third	Tapered, sintered alloy
Oil control	Two chrome-faced rings with expander
Width:	
Top, second and third	.0615 to .0625
Oil control	.100 to .105
Ring to groove clearance:	
Top, second and third	.0015 to .0035
Fitted gap:	

Top, second and third	.012 to .022
Oil control	.015 to .045

Camshaft:

Type	Single, overhead, three-bearing, chain driven

Journal diameters:

Front	1.9355 to 1.9365
Centre	1.9668 to 1.9678
Rear...	1.998 to 1.999
End float	.002 to .007
End thrust taken	On front locating plate
Adjustment	Renew locating plate
Drive	Chain, .375 pitch x 108 pitches
Bearings	3 direct in aluminium carrier

Tappets:

Type	Bucket, spherical base, internal shims for adjustment

Valves:

Seat angle	45¼ deg.

Head diameter:

Inlet...	1.5
Exhaust	1.216 to 1.220

Stem diameter, before engine Nos. 14H/283EH/39163 and 14H/288EH/1102

Inlet	.3110 to .3115
Exhaust	.3100 to .3105

Stem to guide clearance:

Inlet	.002
Exhaust	.003

Stem diameter, later engines:

Inlet	.3115 to .3120
Exhaust	.3115 to .3120

Stem to guide clearance:

Inlet	.0015
Exhaust	.0015
Valve lift	.36

Running clearance (adjust only if less than .012):

Inlet...	.016
Exhaust	.020

Valve timing clearance:

Inlet and exhaust	.021

Valve springs:

Free length	1.797
Fitted length	1.38
Load at fitted length	52 lb
Load at top of lift	96 lb
Valve timing marks	On boss of camshaft sprocket and camshaft housing. On flywheel

Oil pump:

Type	Concentric (serviced as a unit)

Oil filter:

Type	Purolator fullflow

Oil pressure:

Idling	15 lb/sq in
Running	60 lb/sq in

FUEL SYSTEM

Carburetter:

Type	SU HS.6 horizontal
Needle 1500	KP
1750	BAR
Jet size	.10
Piston spring	Red

Fuel pump:

Type	SU mechanical, type AUF.702
Suction (min.)	6 in. Hg
Pressure (min.)	3 lb/sq in

IGNITION SYSTEM

Sparking plugs:

Type	Champion N.9Y
Gap	.024 to .026

Coil:

Type	Lucas 11C.12

Distributor:

Type	Lucas 25D4
Rotation of rotor	Anticlockwise
Contact points gap	.014 to .016
Capacitor (condenser) capacity	.18 to .24 mF
Serial No.	41246
Timing 1500	By stroboscope on flywheel marks. 12 deg. BTDC at 650 rev/min
1750	13 deg. BTDC

COOLING SYSTEM

Type	Pressurized. Spill-return to expansion tank. Pump- and fan-assisted
Pressure in system	15 lb/sq in

Thermostat:

Type	Non-pressure sensitive, wax
Opening temperature:	
Standard	82°C or 180°F
Hot countries	74°C or 165°F
Cold countries	88°C or 190°F

CLUTCH

Clutch:

Type	7¾ diameter Borg and Beck. Diaphragm spring. Hydraulic operation
Friction material	Raybestos WR.7
Driven plate damper springs:	
Number	6
Colour	Pink/Grey (2), Red/Grey (2), Yellow/Grey (1), Blue/Grey (1)
Release bearing	Ball journal

Hydraulic operation:

Fluid ... ... Castrol Girling Brake Fluid Amber

Master cylinder bore ... ... .625

Slave cylinder bore ... ... .875

TRANSMISSION

Gearbox:

Type ... ... Manual (with cable selection). Five forward ratios and reverse. Overdrive ratio on fifth speed

Synchromesh ... ... All forward speeds

Ratios (overall):

	1500	1750
Fifth...	3.34:1	3.38:1
Fourth	4.20:1	3.89:1
Third	5.76:1	5.33:1
Second	8.42:1	7.79:1
First...	13.54:1	12.45:1
Reverse	14.56:1	13.49:1

Road speed in top at 1000 rev/min ... ... 20.92 mile/hr

Final drive:

Ratio 1500 ... ... 3.94:1

1750 ... ... 3.65:1

SUSPENSION SYSTEM

Front suspension:

Type ... ... Independent. Swivel axles ball-jointed to upper and lower arms. Hydrolastic units crosswise in subframe

Trim height (unladen):

Hub centre to wheel arch ... ... $14.1 \pm .25$

Rear suspension:

Type ... ... Independent. Trailing arms, rubber and ball-joints to Hydrolastic units

Trim height (unladen):

Hub centre to wheel arch ... ... $14.6 \pm .25$

Suspension pressure (approx.) ... 245 lb/sq in

Tyres:

Type ... ... 155—13 Dunlop SP68 tubeless or Goodyear tubeless, radial ply

Pressure (all conditions):

Front ... ... 26 lb/sq in

Rear... ... ... 24 lb/sq in

STEERING

Steering:

Type ... ... Rack and pinion. Rubber-joint in column, with lock

Lock (side to side) ... ... 3.9 turns of steering wheel

Turning circle ... ... 30.5 feet

Steering angles:

Camber angle ... ... 1 deg.

Castor angle ... ... 4 deg.

Swivel hub inclination... ... ... 12 deg.

Toe-in ... ... $\frac{1}{4}$ early cars $\frac{1}{16}$ later cars

BRAKES

Brakes:
Type (front)	Disc, hydraulic, 9.68 dia. Single-cylinder caliper
Type (rear)	Drum, hydraulic, 8 dia., but cable operated for handbrake
Operation	Hydraulic by pedal. Vacuum-servo assisted. Valve limits pressure to rear brakes

Brake lining material:
Front	Ferodo 2430F
Rear	Mintex M79
Brake fluid	Castrol Girling Brake Fluid. Amber
Rear wheel cylinder bore	.75

ELECTRICAL EQUIPMENT

System	12-volt negative earth

Battery:
Type	Lucas A9/AZ9 or A11/AZ11
Capacity at 20-hour rate	40 amp-hr or 50 amp-hr (cold countries)

Generator (dynamo)
Type	Lucas C40/1
Maximum output	22 ± 1 amp
Cut-in speed	1585 rev/min at 13.5 volts
Field resistance	6.0 ohms at 20°C or 68°F.
Brush spring tension	20 to 34 oz
Brushes (minimum length)	$\frac{1}{4}$

Starter motor:
Type	Lucas M35J or M35JPE
Light running current	45 to 60 amps at 8500 to 10,000 rev/min
Brush spring tension	30 to 40 oz
Brushes (minimum length)	$\frac{5}{16}$

Control box:
Type	Lucas RB.340
Setting at 20°C or 68°F	14.5 to 15.5 volts at 3000 rev/min generator speed
Cut-in voltage	12.7 to 13.3 volts
Drop-off voltage	9.5 to 11.5 volts

Wiper motor:
Type	Lucas 14W, 2-speed, self-switching
Armature end float	.004 to .008
Running current (light)	1.5 amps at 13.5 volts
Brushes (minimum length)	$\frac{3}{16}$
Brush spring tension	5 to 7 oz

Horns:
Current consumption	$3\frac{1}{2}$ amps
Fuses	See Section 12:13 in Chapter 12

CAPACITIES (approx.)

Fuel tank	10 gallon

Engine sump:
Including filter	$9\frac{1}{2}$ pints
Filter	1 pint
Between 'MAX' and 'MIN' marks	1.5 pints

Cooling system:
... ...	9 pints
Without heater...	$7\frac{1}{4}$ pints

DIMENSIONS

Overall length ...	...	...	...	...	...	13 ft $2\frac{1}{4}$ inch
Overall width ...	...	...	...	...	...	5 ft $4\frac{1}{4}$ inch

Track (static and unladen):

Front ...	...	...	...	...	...	4 ft $5\frac{3}{4}$ inch
Rear ...	...	...	...	...	...	4 ft $5\frac{1}{4}$ inch
Turning circle ...	...	...	...	...	...	30 ft 6 inch

TORQUE WRENCH SETTINGS
Figures are in lb ft unless otherwise specified

Engine:

Cylinder head bolts	60
Oil filter bolt	20
Lifting bracket setscrews	30
Camshaft carrier to cylinder head	20
Camshaft sprocket	35
Camshaft cover	6
Thermostat housing to head	8 to 10
Water outlet elbow to head	8 to 10
Manifold to cylinder head	18 to 20
Adaptor plugs	30
Carburetter studs	6 to 8
Water pump setscrews	18 to 20
Water pump body plug	35
Water pump pulley nut	18
Front cover studs	6
Front cover nuts	18
Fuel pump studs	6
Fuel pump nuts	15 to 18
Flywheel housing studs	6
Flywheel housing nuts	18
Crankshaft pulley bolt	60 to 70
Timing cover, chain guides and pivot pin	18 to 20
Big-end bolts	30
Main bearing bolts	70
Flywheel bolts	60

Clutch:

Clutch cover	15 to 18
Clutch to pressure plate	35 to 38
Clutch thrust plate screw	8 to 10
Slave cylinder bolts	18 to 20

Transmission:

Magnetic drain plug	40 to 50
Transmission case to block ($\frac{5}{16}$ inch bolts)	20 to 25
Transmission case to block ($\frac{3}{8}$ inch bolts)	30
Detent plug (small)	15 to 20
Detent plug (large)	35 to 40
Access plug (third and fourth fork)	55 to 60
First motion shaft nut	120
Layshaft nuts	120
Third motion shaft nut	150

Final drive:

Differential cover ($\frac{5}{16}$ inch nuts)	18
Differential cover ($\frac{3}{8}$ inch nuts)	25
Differential end cover setscrews	18
Final drive pinion nut	150

Electrical:

Generator mounting bolts	...	...	...	...	18 to 20
Generator pulley nut	...	...	...	...	25 to 28
Distributor retaining bolts	...	...	...	...	8 to 10
Distributor clamp bolt ...	...	...	...	...	2.5
Starter bolts	...	...	...	...	30

Steering:

Steering wheel nut	...	...	...	...	50
Column coupling to pinion	...	...	...	...	15
Ball joints to steering arms	...	...	...	...	25
Rack coverplate	...	...	...	...	12 to 18

Suspension:

Front:

Upper and lower swivel hub nuts	...	...	...	45
Lower arm to body ...	...	...	...	15
Lower arm pivot nuts	...	...	...	50
Subframe to body	...	...	...	25
Subframe to lower dash panel	...	...	...	15
Hub nut	...	...	...	150 (align onwards to next splitpin hole)
Ball pin assembly to swivel hub	...	...	...	38 to 45
Cap nut—ball joints	...	...	...	70 to 80

Rear:

Support brackets to body	...	...	...	25
Suspension pivot nuts	...	...	...	50
Pivot joint to body ...	...	...	...	65
Rear arch springs to body	...	...	...	15
Outer bearing retainer bolt ...	...	...	...	60
Outer bearing to body fixing bolts	...	...	...	30
Hub nut	...	...	...	60 (align onwards to next splitpin hole)
Pivot joint and reaction lever assembly	...	...	70 to 80

Brakes:

Caliper to hub ...	...	...	...	...	40 to 50
Disc to driving flange ...	...	...	...	...	38 to 45
Shield to swivel hub	...	...	...	...	17 to 25
Bleed screws ...	...	...	...	...	4 to 6
Brake adjuster nuts	...	...	...	...	4 to 6
Master cylinder to servo	...	...	...	17
Tipping valve securing nut	...	...	...	35 to 45
Pressure reducing valve, end plug	...	...	...	25 to 35
Pressure reducing valve, piston locknut	...	...	3 to 4

Exhaust:

Shield to body...	...	...	...	...	15

Road wheels:

Wheel nuts	...	...	...	...	50

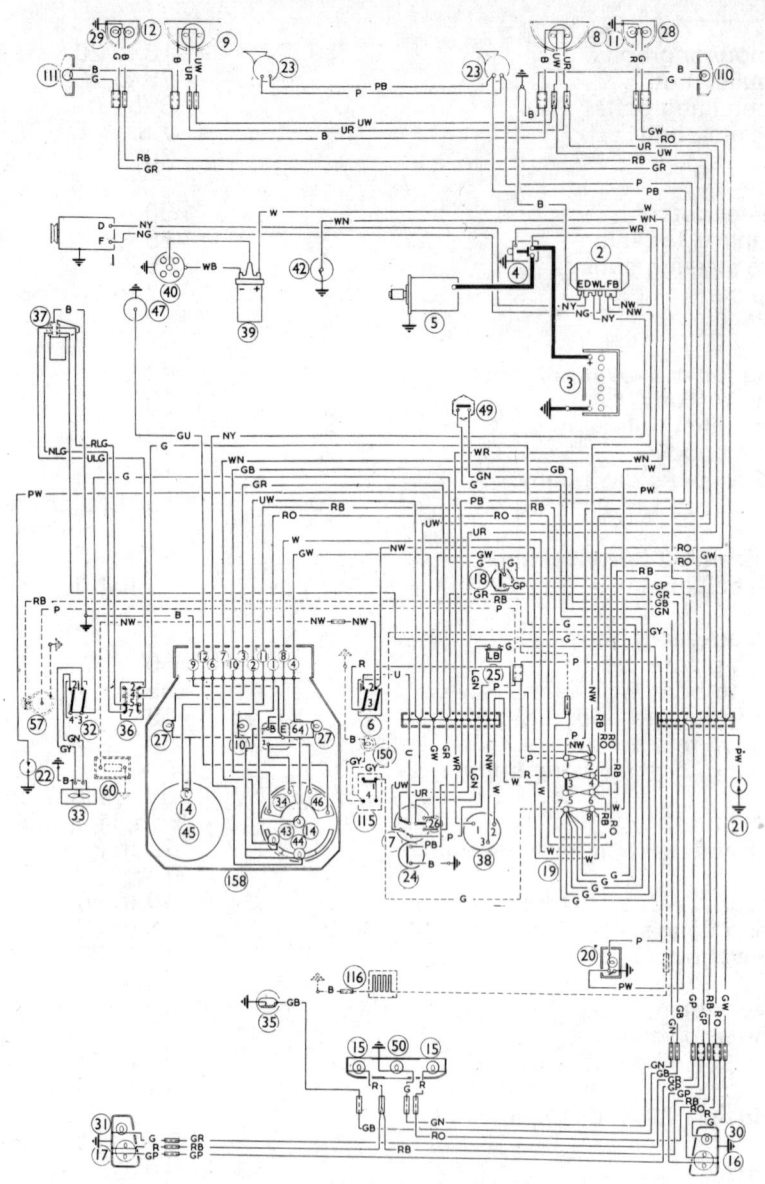

FIG 14:1   Wiring diagram for Austin Maxi

Key to Fig 14:1   1 Generator   **2** Control box   **3** Battery   **4** Starter solenoid   **5** Starter motor   **6** Lighting switch   **7** Headlamp dipswitch   **8** Righthand headlamp   **9** Lefthand headlamp   **10** Main-beam warning lamp   **11** Righthand sidelamp   **12** Lefthand sidelamp   **14** Panel lamps   **15** Number-plate lamps   **16** Righthand stop/tail lamp   **17** Lefthand stop/tail lamp   **18** Stop lamp switch   **19** Fuse block   **20** Interior lamp   **21** Righthand door switch   **22** Lefthand door switch   **23** Horn   **24** Horn-push   **25** Flasher unit   **26** Direction indicator and headlamp flasher switch   **27** Direction indicator warning lamps   **28** Righthand front flasher lamp   **29** Lefthand front flasher lamp   **30** Righthand rear flasher lamp   **31** Lefthand rear flasher lamp   **32** Heater blower switch*   **33** Heater blower motor*   **34** Fuel gauge   **35** Fuel gauge tank unit   **36** Windscreen wiper switch   **37** Windscreen wiper motor   **38** Ignition/starter switch   **39** Ignition coil   **40** Distributor   **42** Oil pressure switch   **43** Oil pressure warning lamp   **44** Ignition warning lamp   **45** Speedometer   **46** Water temperature gauge   **47** Water temperature transmitter   **49** Reverse lamp switch   **50** Reverse lamp   **57** Cigar lighter*   **60** Radio*   **64** Bi-metal instrument voltage stabilizer   **110** Righthand repeater flasher   **111** Lefthand repeater flasher   **115** Rear window demist switch*   **116** Rear window demist unit*   **150** Rear window demist warning lamp*   **158** Printed circuit instrument panel
Accessory or optional extra

CABLE COLOUR CODE:
  N Brown   O Orange   W White   U Blue   G Green   Y Yellow   R Red   LG Light green   B Black
  When a cable has two colour code letters the first denotes the main colour and the second denotes the tracer colour

Inches	Decimals	Milli-metres	Inches to Millimetres		Millimetres to Inches	
			Inches	mm	mm	Inches
1/64	.015625	.3969	.001	.0254	.01	.00039
1/32	.03125	.7937	.002	.0508	.02	.00079
3/64	.046875	1.1906	.003	.0762	.03	.00118
1/16	.0625	1.5875	.004	.1016	.04	.00157
5/64	.078125	1.9844	.005	.1270	.05	.00197
3/32	.09375	2.3812	.006	.1524	.06	.00236
7/64	.109375	2.7781	.007	.1778	.07	.00276
1/8	.125	3.1750	.008	.2032	.08	.00315
9/64	.140625	3.5719	.009	.2286	.09	.00354
5/32	.15625	3.9687	.01	.254	.1	.00394
11/64	.171875	4.3656	.02	.508	.2	.00787
3/16	.1875	4.7625	.03	.762	.3	.01181
13/64	.203125	5·1594	.04	1.016	.4	.01575
7/32	.21875	5.5562	.05	1.270	.5	.01969
15/64	.234375	5.9531	.06	1.524	.6	.02362
1/4	.25	6.3500	.07	1.778	.7	.02756
17/64	.265625	6.7469	.08	2.032	.8	.03150
9/32	.28125	7.1437	.09	2.286	.9	.03543
19/64	.296875	7.5406	.1	2.54	1	.03937
5/16	.3125	7.9375	.2	5.08	2	.07874
21/64	.328125	8.3344	.3	7.62	3	.11811
11/32	.34375	8.7312	.4	10.16	4	.15748
23/64	.359375	9.1281	.5	12.70	5	.19685
3/8	.375	9.5250	.6	15.24	6	.23622
25/64	.390625	9.9219	.7	17.78	7	.27559
13/32	.40625	10.3187	.8	20.32	8	.31496
27/64	.421875	10.7156	.9	22.86	9	.35433
7/16	.4375	11.1125	1	25.4	10	.39370
29/64	.453125	11.5094	2	50.8	11	.43307
15/32	.46875	11.9062	3	76.2	12	.47244
31/64	.484375	12.3031	4	101.6	13	.51181
1/2	.5	12.7000	5	127.0	14	.55118
33/64	.515625	13.0969	6	152.4	15	.59055
17/32	.53125	13.4937	7	177.8	16	.62992
35/64	.546875	13.8906	8	203.2	17	.66929
9/16	.5625	14.2875	9	228.6	18	.70866
37/64	.578125	14.6844	10	254.0	19	.74803
19/32	.59375	15.0812	11	279.4	20	.78740
39/64	.609375	15.4781	12	304.8	21	.82677
5/8	.625	15.8750	13	330.2	22	.86614
41/64	.640625	16.2719	14	355.6	23	.90551
21/32	.65625	16.6687	15	381.0	24	.94488
43/64	.671875	17.0656	16	406.4	25	.98425
11/16	.6875	17.4625	17	431.8	26	1.02362
45/64	.703125	17.8594	18	457.2	27	1.06299
23/32	.71875	18.2562	19	482.6	28	1.10236
47/64	.734375	18.6531	20	508.0	29	1.14173
3/4	.75	19.0500	21	533.4	30	1.18110
49/64	.765625	19.4469	22	558.8	31	1.22047
25/32	.78125	19.8437	23	584.2	32	1.25984
51/64	.796875	20.2406	24	609.6	33	1.29921
13/16	.8125	20.6375	25	635.0	34	1.33858
53/64	.828125	21.0344	26	660.4	35	1.37795
27/32	.84375	21.4312	27	685.8	36	1.41732
55/64	.859375	21.8281	28	711.2	37	1.4567
7/8	.875	22.2250	29	736.6	38	1.4961
57/64	.890625	22.6219	30	762.0	39	1:5354
29/32	.90625	23.0187	31	787.4	40	1.5748
59/64	.921875	23.4156	32	812.8	41	1.6142
15/16	.9375	23.8125	33	838.2	42	1.6535
61/64	.953125	24.2094	34	863.6	43	1.6929
31/32	.96875	24.6062	35	889.0	44	1.7323
63/64	.984375	25.0031	36	914.4	45	1.7717

UNITS	Pints to Litres	Gallons to Litres	Litres to Pints	Litres to Gallons	Miles to Kilometres	Kilometres to Miles	Lbs. per sq. In. to Kg. per sq. Cm.	Kg. per sq. Cm. to Lbs. per sq. In.
1	.57	4.55	1.76	.22	1.61	.62	.07	14.22
2	1.14	9.09	3.52	.44	3.22	1.24	.14	28.50
3	1.70	13.64	5.28	.66	4.83	1.86	.21	42.67
4	2.27	18.18	7.04	.88	6.44	2.49	.28	56.89
5	2.84	22.73	8.80	1.10	8.05	3.11	.35	71.12
6	3.41	27.28	10.56	1.32	9.66	3.73	.42	85.34
7	3.98	31.82	12.32	1.54	11.27	4.35	.49	99.56
8	4.55	36.37	14.08	1.76	12.88	4.97	.56	113.79
9		40.91	15.84	1.98	14.48	5.59	.63	128.00
10		45.46	17.60	2.20	16.09	6.21	.70	142.23
20				4.40	32.19	12.43	1.41	284.47
30				6.60	48.28	18.64	2.11	426.70
40				8.80	64.37	24.85		
50					80.47	31.07		
60					96.56	37.28		
70					112.65	43.50		
80					128.75	49.71		
90					144.84	55.92		
100					160.93	62.14		

UNITS	Lb ft to kgm	Kgm to lb ft	UNITS	Lb ft to kgm	Kgm to lb ft
1	.138	7.233	7	.967	50.631
2	.276	14.466	8	1.106	57.864
3	.414	21.699	9	1.244	65.097
4	.553	28.932	10	1.382	72.330
5	.691	36.165	20	2.765	144.660
6	.829	43.398	30	4.147	216.990

HINTS ON MAINTENANCE AND OVERHAUL

There are few things more rewarding than the restoration of a vehicle's original peak of efficiency and smooth performance.

The following notes are intended to help the owner to reach that state of perfection. Providing that he possesses the basic manual skills he should have no difficulty in performing most of the operations detailed in this manual. It must be stressed, however, that where recommended in the manual, highly-skilled operations ought to be entrusted to experts, who have the necessary equipment, to carry out the work satisfactorily.

Quality of workmanship:

The hazardous driving conditions on the roads to-day demand that vehicles should be as nearly perfect, mechanically, as possible. It is therefore most important that amateur work be carried out with care, bearing in mind the often inadequate working conditions, and also the inferior tools which may have to be used. It is easy to counsel perfection in all things, and we recognize that it may be setting an impossibly high standard. We do, however, suggest that every care should be taken to ensure that a vehicle is as safe to take on the road as it is humanly possible to make it.

Safe working conditions:

Even though a vehicle may be stationary, it is still potentially dangerous if certain sensible precautions are not taken when working on it while it is supported on jacks or blocks. It is indeed preferable not to use jacks alone, but to supplement them with carefully placed blocks, so that there will be plenty of support if the car rolls off the jacks during a strenuous manoeuvre. Axle stands are an excellent way of providing a rigid base which is not readily disturbed. Piles of bricks are a dangerous substitute. Be careful not to get under heavy loads on lifting tackle, the load could fall. It is preferable not to work alone when lifting an engine, or when working underneath a vehicle which is supported well off the ground. To be trapped, particularly under the vehicle, may have unpleasant results if help is not quickly forthcoming. Make some provision, however humble, to deal with fires. Always disconnect a battery if there is a likelihood of electrical shorts. These may start a fire if there is leaking fuel about. This applies particularly to leads which can carry a heavy current, like those in the starter circuit. While on the subject of electricity, we must also stress the danger of using equipment which is run off the mains and which has no earth or has faulty wiring or connections. So many workshops have damp floors, and electrical shocks are of such a nature that it is sometimes impossible to let go of a live lead or piece of equipment due to the muscular spasms which take place.

Work demanding special care:

This involves the servicing of braking, steering and suspension systems. On the road, failure of the braking system may be disastrous. Make quite sure that there can be no possibility of failure through the bursting of rusty brake pipes or rotten hoses, nor to a sudden loss of pressure due to defective seals or valves.

Problems:

The chief problems which may face an operator are:
1 External dirt.
2 Difficulty in undoing tight fixings.
3 Dismantling unfamiliar mechanisms.
4 Deciding in what respect parts are defective.
5 Confusion about the correct order for reassembly.
6 Adjusting running clearance.
7 Road testing.
8 Final tuning.

Practical suggestions to solve the problems:

1 Preliminary cleaning of large parts—engines, transmissions, steering, suspensions, etc.,—should be carried out before removal from the car. Where road dirt and mud alone are present, wash clean with a high-pressure water jet, brushing to remove stubborn adhesions, and allow to drain and dry. Where oil or grease is also present, wash down with a proprietary compound (Gunk, Teepol etc.,) applying with a stiff brush—an old paint brush is suitable—into all crevices. Cover the distributor and ignition coils with a polythene bag and then apply a strong water jet to clear the loosened deposits. Allow to drain and dry. The assemblies will then be sufficiently clean to remove and transfer to the bench for the next stage.

On the bench, further cleaning can be carried out, first wiping the parts as free as possible from grease with old newspaper. Avoid using rag or cotton waste which can leave clogging fibres behind. Any remaining grease can be removed with a brush dipped in paraffin. If necessary, traces of paraffin can be removed by carbon tetrachloride. Avoid using paraffin or petrol in large quantities for cleaning in enclosed areas, such as garages, on account of the high fire risk.

When all exteriors have been cleaned, and not before, dismantling can be commenced. This ensures that dirt will not enter into interiors and orifices revealed by dismantling. In the next phases, where components have to be cleaned, use carbon tetrachloride in preference to petrol and keep the containers covered except when in use. After the components have been cleaned, plug small holes with tapered hard wood plugs cut to size and blank off larger orifices with greaseproof paper and masking tape. Do not use soft wood plugs or matchsticks as they may break.

2 It is not advisable to hammer on the end of a screw thread, but if it must be done, first screw on a nut to protect the thread, and use a lead hammer. This applies particularly to the removal of tapered cotters. Nuts and bolts seem to 'grow' together, especially in exhaust systems. If penetrating oil does not work, try the judicious application of heat, but be careful of starting a fire. Asbestos sheet or cloth is useful to isolate heat.

Tight bushes or pieces of tail-pipe rusted into a silencer can be removed by splitting them with an open-ended hacksaw. Tight screws can sometimes be started by a tap from a hammer on the end of a suitable screwdriver. Many tight fittings will yield to the judicious use of a hammer, but it must be a soft-faced hammer if damage is to be avoided, use a heavy block on the opposite side to absorb shock. Any parts of the steering system which have been damaged should be renewed, as attempts to repair them may lead to cracking and subsequent failure, and steering ball joints should be disconnected using a recommended tool to prevent damage.

3 It often happens that an owner is baffled when trying to dismantle an unfamiliar piece of equipment. So many modern devices are pressed together or assembled by spinning-over flanges, that they must be sawn apart. The intention is that the whole assembly must be renewed. However, parts which appear to be in one piece to the naked eye, may reveal close-fitting joint lines when inspected with a magnifying glass, and, this may provide the necessary clue to dismantling. Left-handed screw threads are used where rotational forces would tend to unscrew a right-handed screw thread.

Be very careful when dismantling mechanisms which may come apart suddenly. Work in an enclosed space where the parts will be contained, and drape a piece of cloth over the device if springs are likely to fly in all directions. Mark everything which might be reassembled in the wrong position, scratched symbols may be used on unstressed parts, or a sequence of tiny dots from a centre punch can be useful. Stressed parts should never be scratched or centre-popped as this may lead to cracking under working conditions. Store parts which look alike in the correct order for reassembly. Never rely upon memory to assist in the assembly of complicated mechanisms, especially when they will be dismantled for a long time, but make notes, and drawings to supplement the diagrams in the manual, and put labels on detached wires. Rust stains may indicate unlubricated wear. This can sometimes be seen round the outside edge of a bearing cup in a universal joint. Look for bright rubbing marks on parts which normally should not make heavy contact. These might prove that something is bent or running out of truth. For example, there might be bright marks on one side of a piston, at the top near the ring grooves, and others at the bottom of the skirt on the other side. This could well be the clue to a bent connecting rod. Suspected cracks can be proved by heating the component in a light oil to approximately 100°C, removing, drying off, and dusting with french chalk, if a crack is present the oil retained in the crack will stain the french chalk.

4 In determining wear, and the degree, against the permissible limits set in the manual, accurate measurement can only be achieved by the use of a micrometer. In many cases, the wear is given to the fourth place of decimals; that is in ten-thousandths of an inch. This can be read by the vernier scale on the barrel of a good micrometer. Bore diameters are more difficult to determine. If, however, the matching shaft is accurately measured, the degree of play in the bore can be felt as a guide to its suitability. In other cases, the shank of a twist drill of known diameter is a handy check.

Many methods have been devised for determining the clearance between bearing surfaces. To-day the best and simplest is by the use of Plastigage, obtainable from most garages. A thin plastic thread is laid between the two surfaces and the bearing is tightened, flattening the thread. On removal, the width of the thread is compared with a scale supplied with the thread and the clearance is read off directly. Sometimes joint faces leak persistently, even after gasket renewal. The fault will then be traceable to distortion, dirt or burrs. Studs which are screwed into soft metal frequently raise burrs at the point of entry. A quick cure for this is to chamfer the edge of the hole in the part which fits over the stud.

5 **Always check a replacement part with the original one before it is fitted.**

If parts are not marked, and the order for reassembly is not known, a little detective work will help. Look for marks which are due to wear to see if they can be mated. Joint faces may not be identical due to manufacturing errors, and parts which overlap may be stained, giving a clue to the correct position. Most fixings leave identifying marks especially if they were painted over on assembly. It is then easier to decide whether a nut, for instance, has a plain, a spring, or a shakeproof washer under it. All running surfaces become 'bedded' together after long spells of work and tiny imperfections on one part will be found to have left corresponding marks on the other. This is particularly true of shafts and bearings and even a score on a cylinder wall will show on the piston.

6 Checking end float or rocker clearances by feeler gauge may not always give accurate results because of wear. For instance, the rocker tip which bears on a valve stem may be deeply pitted, in which case the feeler will simply be bridging a depression. Thrust washers may also wear depressions in opposing faces to make accurate measurement difficult. End float is then easier to check by using a dial gauge. It is common practice to adjust end play in bearing assemblies, like front hubs with taper rollers, by doing up the axle nut until the hub becomes stiff to turn and then backing it off a little. Do not use this method with ballbearing hubs as the assembly is often preloaded by tightening the axle nut to its fullest extent. If the splitpin hole will not line up, file the base of the nut a little.

Steering assemblies often wear in the straight-ahead position. If any part is adjusted, make sure that it remains free when moved from lock to lock. Do not be surprised if an assembly like a steering gearbox, which is known to be carefully adjusted outside the car, becomes stiff when it is bolted in place. This will be due to distortion of the case by the pull of the mounting bolts, particularly if the mounting points are not all touching together. This problem may be met in other equipment and is cured by careful attention to the alignment of mounting points.

When a spanner is stamped with a size and A/F it means that the dimension is the width between the jaws and has no connection with ANF, which is the designation for the American National Fine thread. Coarse threads like Whitworth are rarely used on cars to-day except for studs which screw into soft aluminium or cast iron. For this reason it might be found that the top end of a cylinder head stud has a fine thread and the lower end a coarse thread to screw into the cylinder block. If the car has mainly UNF threads then it is likely that any coarse threads will be UNC, which are not the same as Whitworth. Small sizes have the same number of threads in Whitworth and UNC, but in the $\frac{1}{2}$ inch size for example, there are twelve threads to the inch in the former and thirteen in the latter.

7 After a major overhaul, particularly if a great deal of work has been done on the braking, steering and suspension systems, it is advisable to approach the problem of testing with care. If the braking system has been overhauled, apply heavy pressure to the brake pedal and get a second operator to check every possible source of leakage. The brakes may work extremely well, but a leak could cause complete failure after a few miles.

Do not fit the hub caps until every wheel nut has been checked for tightness, and make sure the tyre pressures are correct. Check the levels of coolant, lubricants and hydraulic fluids. Being satisfied that all is well, take the car on the road and test the brakes at once. Check the steering and the action of the handbrake. Do all this at moderate speeds on quiet roads, and make sure there is no other vehicle behind you when you try a rapid stop.

Finally, remember that many parts settle down after a time, so check for tightness of all fixings after the car has been on the road for a hundred miles or so.

8 It is useless to tune an engine which has not reached its normal running temperature. In the same way, the tune of an engine which is stiff after a rebore will be different when the engine is again running free. Remember too, that rocker clearances on pushrod operated valve gear will change when the cylinder head nuts are tightened after an initial period of running with a new head gasket.

Trouble may not always be due to what seems the obvious cause. Ignition, carburation and mechanical condition are interdependent and spitting back through the carburetter, which might be attributed to a weak mixture, can be caused by a sticking inlet valve.

For one final hint on tuning, never adjust more than one thing at a time or it will be impossible to tell which adjustment produced the desired result.

GLOSSARY OF TERMS

Allen key Cranked hexagonal bar for turning socket head screws.

Alternator Rotary machine for generating alternating current electricity. Car alternators embody silicon diodes to rectify the AC output to DC for energizing the field and supplying the load.

Ambient temperature Surrounding atmospheric temperature.

Annulus A ring-shaped element. The outer gear of an epicyclic train.

Armature The rotating member, comprising shaft, windings and commutator, of a generator or motor. The moving element of a relay or solenoid.

Axial In line with, or pertaining to, an axis.

Backlash Play between meshing gears.

Balance lever Lever in which the force applied at the centre is divided equally between connections to the ends.

Bendix pinion Self-meshing and disengaging pinion on the shaft of an inertia type starter motor.

Bevel pinion Conical shaped gearwheel designed to mesh with a similar gear whose axis usually is at 90 deg. to its own.

bhp Brake horse power, as measured on a dynamometer.

bmep Brake mean effective pressure. The average pressure exerted on a piston during the working stroke.

Brake cylinder Cylinder with hydraulically operated piston(s) acting on brake shoes or pads.

Brake regulator Control valve fitted to some hydraulic braking systems to limit pressure applied to rear brakes to prevent the rear wheels locking when heavily braking.

Camber Angle at which a front wheel is tilted from the vertical.

Capacitor Modern term for condenser. Used across ignition make-and-break to produce a hot spark at the plug.

Castellated Top face of a nut, slotted across the flats to take a locking pin.

Castor Angle at which the kingpin or swivel pin is tilted from the vertical when viewed from one side.

cc Cubic centimetres. In engine capacity, the area of the bore in sq cm multiplied by the stroke in cm and the number of cylinders.

Clevis Forked connector with pin. Commonly used in handbrake and similar connections.

Collet Ring or collar, usually split, to encircle a groove in a stem or shaft where it is retained by an outer ring or seating. Used to secure the springs to the valves in the cylinder head of a car.

Commutator A segmented collar or faceplate on the armature of a generator or motor through which current is conveyed from or to the windings via the brushes. A current reversing device.

Compression ratio Ratio of total volume (piston at bottom of stroke) to unswept volume (piston at top of stroke) in an engine cylinder.

Condenser See 'Capacitor'.

Core plug Plug for blanking off a core or 'fettling' hole on an iron casting. A 'Welch' plug.

Crown wheel Large ring bevel gear, secured to differential housing in rear axle, transmitting drive from the bevel pinion on the propeller shaft to the rear wheel axles.

C spanner Spanner shaped like a letter C with a handle. Used on screw collars with slots instead of flats for turning.

Damper Modern term for shock absorber.

Depression Lowering of atmospheric pressure as, for example, in the inlet manifold or carburetter.

Dowel Close fitting pin, peg, tube or bolt for locating mating parts accurately.

Drive shaft Output shaft of gearbox transmitting torque to the propeller shaft. Sometimes 'third motion shaft'.

Dry liner Thin walled tube pressed into bored-out engine cylinder.

Dry sump Sump from which all oil collected is immediately scavenged and returned to a separate tank.

Dynamo See 'Generator'.

Electrode Terminal part of an electrical component such as the centre element of a sparking plug.

Electrolyte In car batteries, sulphuric acid diluted with distilled water.

End float Play or movement on a shaft in an axial direction; end play.

EP (Extreme pressure). As applied to lubricants, indicates special grades for heavily loaded bearing surfaces such as gear teeth in a gearbox or crownwheel and pinion in a rear axle assembly.

Field coils Windings on polepieces of motors and generators.

Fullflow filter   Filter in which all the oil pumped around the engine passes for filtering. If the filter element becomes clogged, a bypass valve opens to circulate unfiltered oil.

Gear pump   Pump in which oil is circulated by two meshing gears in a close fitting casing. Oil is carried from one side around the outer periphery of both gears in the spaces between the teeth to the outlet at the other, the meshing teeth in the centre preventing passage back to the inlet.

Gearshaft   Shaft transmitting drive from clutch to layshaft in the gearbox. 'First motion' shaft.

Generator   A machine for generating direct current and incorporating a commutator and brushes. A dynamo.

Grommet   Close fitting ring of rubber or plastic around pipes or cables to protect them from abrasion in passage through bulkheads and to seal the opening against entry of dirt and water.

Grubscrew   Setscrew without a head, threaded full length, with slot for turning, usually for securing a pulley or collar to a shaft.

Gudgeon pin   Shaft connecting piston to the connecting rod; a 'wrist-pin' or 'piston-pin'.

Halfshaft   One of a pair transmitting drive from the differential gearing to the wheel hubs.

Helical   In spiral form. The teeth of helical gears are cut in a spiral at an angle to the side faces of the gearwheel.

Hot spot   Heated area assisting vapourization of fuel on its way to the cylinders. Usually provided by a close contact area between inlet and exhaust manifolds.

HT   High tension. The high voltage output produced by the ignition coil for the sparking plugs.

Hydrometer   Device for checking the specific gravity of battery electrolyte.

Hypoid gear   Form of bevel gear used in rear axle crown and bevel combinations in which the bevel pinion meshes with the crownwheel below its centre line, giving a lower propeller shaft line.

Idler   Device for passing on movement, e.g. a free-running gear between driving and driven gears; a lever transmitting track rod movement to a side rod in a steering gear.

Impeller   Rotating element of a water pump to produce flow.

Intermediate gear   In a gearbox, an idler gear introduced between layshaft and drive shaft to reverse motion.

Journals   Parts of a shaft in intimate contact with bearings.

Kingpin   Main vertical pin around which the front stub axle is turned to provide steering.

Layshaft   In a gearbox, the intermediate shaft, carrying the laygear, transmitting the drive from the gearshaft, or first motion shaft, to the drive shaft, or third motion shaft. The second motion shaft.

lb ft   Pound-feet, a measure of twist or torque; the product of radius and load. A pull of 10 lb at a radius of 1 ft is a torque of 10 lb ft.

Little-end   The small, or piston, end of a connecting rod.

l.s.   The leading shoe in a brake drum, has a tendency to wedge into the drum when applied, so increasing the braking effect.

LT   Low tension. The electrical output from the battery and generator.

Mandrel   Accurately machined bar or rod used for test or centring purposes.

Manifold   Pipe or duct with several branches. In car engines the duct between the cylinder ports and the carburetter or exhaust pipe.

Needle rollers   Bearing rollers whose length is many times their diameter.

Oil bath   Reservoir for lubricating parts by immersion. In air filters a separate oil supply for wetting a wire mesh element to hold the dust.

Overlap   Period during which inlet and exhaust valves are open together.

Pawl   Pivoted catch engaging the teeth of a ratchet to permit rotation in one direction only.

Peg spanner   Spanner with pegs or pins for insertion in holes or slots in a collar or cap for turning.

Pinion   The smaller of a pair of gears; a spur gear.

Piston type damper   Shock absorber in which damping is controlled by a piston working in a closed, oil-filled cylinder.

Preloading   Preset static pressure on ball or roller bearings not due to working loads.

Radial   Radiating from a centre, like the spokes of a wheel.

Radius rod   Pivoted arm confining movement to an arc of fixed radius.

Ratchet	Toothed wheel or rack capable of movement in one direction only. Movement in the other is prevented by a pawl.	**TDC**	Top dead centre. The point of highest travel of a piston in its cylinder.
Ring gear	Large diameter toothed ring secured to the outer periphery of a flywheel for engagement with the pinion of the starter motor.	**Thermostat**	Device for regulating temperature. In cars, used to restrict the circulation of cooling water through the radiator until engine temperature has risen.
Runout	Amount by which a rotating part is out of truth.	**Threequarter floating axle**	Outer end of rear axle halfshaft flanged and bolted to wheel hub which runs in bearing mounted on outside of axle casing. The axle shaft does not bear the vehicle weight.
Semi-floating axle	Outer end of rear axle halfshaft carried on bearing inside the axle casing. Wheel hub is secured to the end of the halfshaft.	**Thrust bearing**	—or washer. Bearings or washers for reducing friction through axial loading on rotating shafts or components.
Servo	Hydraulic or pneumatic device for assisting or augmenting a force applied manually.	**Torque**	Turning or twisting effort.
Setscrew	A screw threaded for the full length of the shank.	**Track rod**	Bar across the front underside of the vehicle coupling the steering arms and maintaining the front wheels in proper alignment.
Shackle	Coupling link in the form of two parallel pins connected by side plates. Used to anchor one end of a leaf spring to take up length variation on deflection.	**Transducer**	Electrical device for converting mechanical or thermal stress into an electrical signal for operating a warning lamp or indicator.
Shell bearing	Thin walled, steel shell lined with anti-friction metal. Usually semi-circular and used in pairs for main and big-end bearings.	**Transmitter**	Electrical device for transmitting the state of a measuring device, such as a fuel gauge, to a suitably scaled indicator.
Shock absorber	Device linked to front and rear suspensions to damp out vertical oscillation due to uneven road surfaces; a damper.	**t.s.**	Trailing shoe in a brake drum, has a tendency to break away from the drum when applied, so reducing the braking effect.
Socket head screw	Screw with hexagonal socket in head for an Allen key.	**UJ**	Universal joint. Coupling between shafts not in alignment permitting stress-free torque transmission.
Solenoid	Coil of wire creating a magnetic field when electric current passes through it. Commonly applied to coil, complete with armature or core, for operating a mechanical device or contacts.	**UNF**	Unified national fine screw thread.
		Vacuum servo	Servo device, usually for brake operation, utilising the difference in pressure between atmospheric and that in the inlet manifold to augment the manually applied braking effort.
Spur gear	Gear with teeth cut axially across the periphery.	**Venturi**	Restriction or 'choke' in a tube, as in a carburetter, to produce a change in velocity and pressure.
Stub axle	Short axle mounted at one end only.		
Steering box	Gearbox at lower end of steering column, containing gearing for translating rotational steering wheel motion into lateral movement for swivelling the front wheels.	**Vernier**	A pair of adjacent scales for determining very small measurements.
		Welch plug	See 'Core plug'.
Sway bar	Bar connected between a fixed point on the chassis or body and an axle to limit sideways movement of the axle.	**Wet liner**	Removable cylinder barrel, sealed at both ends against surrounding coolant in a cylinder block but with coolant circulating around the centre section.
Tachometer	Instrument for the accurate measurement of rotational speed. Usually indicates revolutions per minute.	**Wet sump**	Detachable lower half of a crankcase in which the lubricant is allowed to drain and remain until re-circulated.

INDEX

THE AUTOBOOK SERIES OF WORKSHOP MANUALS

Make				Author	Title
ALFA ROMEO					
1600 Giulia TI 1962–67	..	..	..	Ball	Alfa Romeo Giulia 1962–70 Autobook
1600 Giulia Sprint 1962–68	..	..	..	Ball	Alfa Romeo Giulia 1962–70 Autobook
1600 Giulia Spider 1962–68	..	..	..	Ball	Alfa Romeo Giulia 1962–70 Autobook
1600 Giulia Super 1965–70	..	..	..	Ball	Alfa Romeo Giulia 1962–70 Autobook
ASTON MARTIN					
All models 1921–58	..	..	..	Coram	Aston Martin 1921–58 Autobook
AUSTIN					
A30 1951–56	..	..	..	..	Ball	Austin A30, A35, A40 Autobook
A35 1956–62	..	..	..	..	Ball	Austin A30, A35, A40 Autobook
A40 Farina 1957–67	..	..	..	Ball	Austin A30, A35, A40 Autobook
A40 Cambridge 1954–57	..	..	..	Ball	BMC Autobook Three
A50 Cambridge 1954–57	..	..	..	Ball	BMC Autobook Three
A55 Cambridge Mk 1 1957–58	..	..	Ball	BMC Autobook Three
A55 Cambridge Mk 2 1958–61	..	..	Smith	BMC Autobook One
A60 Cambridge 1961–69	..	..	..	Smith	BMC Autobook One
A99 1959–61	..	..	..	..	Ball	BMC Autobook Four
A110 1961–68	..	..	..	Ball	BMC Autobook Four
Mini 1959–70	..	..	..	..	Ball	Mini 1959–70 Autobook
Mini Clubman 1969–70	..	..	..	Ball	Mini 1959–70 Autobook
Mini Cooper 1961–70	..	..	..	Ball	Mini Cooper 1961–70 Autobook
Mini Cooper S 1963–70	..	..	..	Ball	Mini Cooper 1961–70 Autobook
1100 Mk 1 1963–67	..	..	..	Ball	1100 Mk 1 1962–67 Autobook
1100 Mk 2 1968–70	..	..	..	Ball	1100 Mk 2, 1300 Mk 1, 2, America 1968–70 Autobook
1300 Mk 1, 2 1968–70	..	..	..	Ball	1100 Mk 2, 1300 Mk 1, 2, America 1968–70 Autobook
America 1968–70	..	..	..	Ball	1100 Mk 2, 1300 Mk 1, 2, America 1968–70 Autobook
1800 Mk 1, 2 1964–70	..	..	..	Ball	1800 1964–70 Autobook
1800S 1969–70	..	..	..	Ball	1800 1964–70 Autobook
Maxi 1969	..	..	..	Ball	Austin Maxi 1969 Autobook
AUSTIN HEALEY					
100/6 1956–59	..	..	..	Ball	Austin Healey 100/6, 3000 1956–68 Autobook
Sprite 1958–70	..	..	..	Ball	Sprite, Midget 1958–70 Autobook
3000 Mk 1, 2, 3 1959–68	..	..	..	Ball	Austin Healey 100/6, 3000 1956–68 Autobook
BEDFORD					
CA Mk 1 and 2 1961–69	..	..	..	Ball	Vauxhall Victor 1, 2 FB 1957–64 Autobook
Beagle HA 1964–66	..	..	..	Ball	Vauxhall Viva HA 1964–66 Autobook
BMW					
1600 1966–70	..	..	..	..	Ball	BMW 1600 1966–70 Autobook
1600–2 1966–70	..	..	..	..	Ball	BMW 1600 1966–70 Autobook
1600TI 1966–70	..	..	..	..	Ball	BMW 1600 1966–70 Autobook
1800 1964–70	..	..	..	..	Ball	BMW 1800 1964–70 Autobook
1800TI 1964–67	..	..	..	..	Ball	BMW 1800 1964–70 Autobook
2000 1966–70	..	..	..	..	Ball	BMW 2000, 2002 1966–70 Autobook
2000A 1966–70	..	..	..	..	Ball	BMW 2000, 2002 1966–70 Autobook
2000TI 1966–70	..	..	..	..	Ball	BMW 2000, 2002 1966–70 Autobook
2000CS 1967–70	..	..	..	..	Ball	BMW 2000, 2002 1966–70 Autobook
2000CA 1967–70	..	..	..	..	Ball	BMW 2000, 2002 1966–70 Autobook
2002 1968–70	..	..	..	..	Ball	BMW 2000, 2002 1966–70 Autobook
CITROEN					
DS19 1955–65	..	..	..	..	Ball	Citroen DS19, ID19 1955–66 Autobook
ID19 1956–66	..	..	..	..	Ball	Citroen DS19, ID19 1955–66 Autobook

Make					Author	Title

COMMER

Cob Series 1, 2, 3 1960–65	..	..		..	Ball	Hillman Minx 1 to 5 1956–65 Autobook
Imp Vans 1963–68	..	..	..	..	Smith	Hillman Imp 1963–68 Autobook
Imp Vans 1969–71	..	..	..	..	Ball	Hillman Imp 1969–71 Autobook

DE DION BOUTON

One-cylinder 1899–1907	..	..		..	Mercredy	De Dion Bouton Autobook One
Two-cylinder 1903–1907	..	..		..	Mercredy	De Dion Bouton Autobook One
Four-cylinder 1905–1907	..	..		..	Mercredy	De Dion Bouton Autobook One

DATSUN

1300 1968–70	..	..	..	..	Ball	Datsun 1300, 1600 1968–70 Autobook
1600 1968–70	..	..	..	..	Ball	Datsun 1300, 1600 1968–70 Autobook

FIAT

500 1957–61	..	..	..	..	Ball	Fiat 500 1957–69 Autobook
500D 1960–65	..	..	..	..	Ball	Fiat 500 1957–69 Autobook
500F 1965–69	..	..	..	..	Ball	Fiat 500 1957–69 Autobook
500L 1968–69	..	..	..	..	Ball	Fiat 500 1957–69 Autobook
600 633cc 1955–61	..	..		..	Ball	Fiat 600, 600D 1955–69 Autobook
600D, 767cc 1960–69	..	..		..	Ball	Fiat 600, 600D 1955–69 Autobook
850 Sedan 1964–70	..	..		..	Ball	Fiat 850 1964–70 Autobook
850 Coupé 1965–70	..	..		..	Ball	Fiat 850 1964–70 Autobook
850 Roadster 1965–70	..	..		..	Ball	Fiat 850 1964–70 Autobook
850 Family 1965–70	..	..		..	Ball	Fiat 850 1964–70 Autobook
850 Sport 1968–70	..	..		..	Ball	Fiat 850 1964–70 Autobook
124 Saloon 1966–70	..	..		..	Ball	Fiat 124 1966–70 Autobook
124S 1968–70	..	..	..	..	Ball	Fiat 124 1966–70 Autobook

FORD

Anglia 100E 1953–59	..	..		..	Ball	Ford Anglia Prefect 100E Autobook
Anglia 105E 1959–67	..	..		..	Smith	Ford Anglia 105E, Prefect 107E 1959–67 Autobook
Anglia Super 123E 1962–67	..	..		..	Smith	Ford Anglia 105E, Prefect 107E 1959–67 Autobook
Capri 109E 1962					Smith	Ford Classic, Capri 1961–64 Autobook
Capri 116E 1962–64	..	..		..	Smith	Ford Classic, Capri 1961–64 Autobook
Capri 1300, 1300GT 1968–69		..		..	Ball	Ford Capri 1968–69 Autobook
Capri 1600, 1600GT 1968–69		..		..	Ball	Ford Capri 1968–69 Autobook
Classic 109E 1961–62		..		..	Smith	Ford Classic, Capri 1961–64 Autobook
Classic 116E 1962–63		..		..	Smith	Ford Classic, Capri 1961–64 Autobook
Consul Mk 1 1950–56		..		..	Ball	Ford Consul Zephyr, Zodiac 1, 2 1950–62 Autobook
Consul Mk 2 1956–62		..		..	Ball	Ford Consul, Zephyr, Zodiac 1, 2 1950–62 Autobook
Corsair V4 3004E 1965–68		..		..	Smith	Ford Corsair V4 1965–68 Autobook
Corsair V4 GT 1965–66		..		..	Smith	Ford Corsair V4 1965–68 Autobook
Corsair V4 1663cc 1969–70		..		..	Ball	Ford Corsair V4 1969–70 Autobook
Corsair 2000, 2000E 1966–68		..		..	Smith	Ford Corsair V4 1965–68 Autobook
Corsair 2000, 2000E 1969–70		..		..	Ball	Ford Corsair V4 1969–70 Autobook
Cortina 113E 1962–66		..		..	Smith	Ford Cortina 1962–66 Autobook
Cortina Super 118E 1963–66	..			..	Smith	Ford Cortina 1962–66 Autobook
Cortina Lotus 125E 1963–66	..			..	Smith	Ford Cortina 1962–66 Autobook
Cortina GT 118E 1963–66	..			..	Smith	Ford Cortina 1962–66 Autobook
Cortina 1300 1967–68		..		..	Smith	Ford Cortina 1967–68 Autobook
Cortina 1300 1969–70		..		..	Ball	Ford Cortina 1969–70 Autobook
Cortina 1500 1967–68		..		..	Smith	Ford Cortina 1967–68 Autobook
Cortina 1600 (including Lotus) 1967–68					Smith	Ford Cortina 1967–68 Autobook
Cortina 1600 1969–70		..		..	Ball	Ford Cortina 1969–70 Autobook
Escort 100E 1955–59	..	..		..	Ball	Ford Anglia Prefect 100E Autobook
Escort 1100 1967–70	..	..		..	Ball	Ford Escort 1967–70 Autobook
Escort 1300 1967–70	..	..		..	Ball	Ford Escort 1967–70 Autobook
Prefect 100E 1954–59	..	..		..	Ball	Ford Anglia Prefect 100E Autobook
Prefect 107E 1959–61	..	..		..	Smith	Ford Anglia 105E, Prefect 107E 1959–67 Autobook
Popular 100E 1959–62	..	..		..	Ball	Ford Anglia Prefect 100E Autobook

Make				Author	Title
Squire 100E 1955–59	..	..	..	Ball	Ford Anglia Prefect 100E Autobook
Zephyr Mk 1 1950–56				Ball	Ford Consul, Zephyr, Zodiac 1, 2 1950–62 Autobook
Zephyr Mk 2 1956–62			..	Ball	Ford Consul, Zephyr, Zodiac 1, 2 1950–62 Autobook
Zephyr 4 Mk 3 1962–66			..	Ball	Ford Zephyr, Zodiac Mk 3 1962–66 Autobook
Zephyr 6 Mk 3 1962–66			..	Ball	Ford Zephyr, Zodiac Mk 3 1962–66 Autobook
Zodiac Mk 3 1962–66..				Ball	Ford Zephyr, Zodiac Mk 3 1962–66 Autobook
Zodiac Mk 1 1953–56..				Ball	Ford Consul, Zephyr, Zodiac 1, 2 1950–62 Autobook
Zodiac Mk 2 1956–62..				Ball	Ford Consul, Zephyr, Zodiac 1, 2 1950–62 Autobook
Zephyr V4 2 litre 1966–69			..	Ball	Ford Zephyr V4, V6, Zodiac 1966–69 Autobook
Zephyr V6 2.5 litre 1966–69		..		Ball	Ford Zephyr V4, V6, Zodiac 1966–69 Autobook
Zodiac V6 3 litre 1966–69		..		Ball	Ford Zephyr V4, V6, Zodiac 1966–69 Autobook

HILLMAN

Hunter GT 1966–70	..		..	Ball	Hillman Hunter 1966–70 Autobook
Minx series 1, 2, 3 1956–59	..		..	Ball	Hillman Minx 1 to 5 1956–65 Autobook
Minx series 3A, 3B, 3C 1959–63		..		Ball	Hillman Minx 1 to 5 1956–65 Autobook
Minx series 5 1963–65		..		Ball	Hillman Minx 1 to 5 1956–65 Autobook
Minx series 6 1965–67		..		Ball	Hillman Minx 1965–67 Autobook
New Minx 1500, 1725 1966–70			..	Ball	Hillman Minx 1966–70 Autobook
Imp 1963–68	..	..	..	Smith	Hillman Imp 1963–68 Autobook
Imp 1969–71			..	Ball	Hillman Imp 1969–71 Autobook
Husky series 1, 2, 3 1958–65		..		Ball	Hillman Minx 1 to 5 1956–65 Autobook
Husky Estate 1969–71		..		Ball	Hillman Imp 1969–71 Autobook
Super Minx Mk 1, 2, 3 1961–65		..		Ball	Hillman Super Minx 1, 2, 3 1961–65 Autobook
Super Minx Mk 4 1965–67	..	..		Ball	Hillman Minx 1965–67 Autobook

HUMBER

Sceptre Mk 2 1965–67		..	..	Ball	Hillman Minx 1965–67 Autobook
Sceptre 1967–70	..		..	Ball	Hillman Hunter 1966–70 Autobook

JAGUAR

XK 120 1948–54	..		..	Ball	Jaguar XK120, 140, 150 Mk 7, 8, 9 1948–61 Autobook
XK 140 1954–57	..		..	Ball	Jaguar XK 120, 140 150 Mk 7, 8, 9 1948–61 Autobook
XK 150 1957–61	..		..	Ball	Jaguar XK 120, 140, 150 Mk 7, 8, 9 1948–61 Autobook
XK 150S 1959–61	..			Ball	Jaguar XK 120, 140, 150 Mk 7, 8, 9 1948–61 Autobook
Mk 7, 7M, 8, 9 1950–61		..		Ball	Jaguar XK 120, 140, 150 Mk 7, 8, 9 1948–61 Autobook
2.4 Mk 1, 2 1955–67	..			Ball	Jaguar 2.4, 3.4, 3.8 Mk 1, 2 1955–69 Autobook
3.4 Mk 1, 2 1957–67	..			Ball	Jaguar 2.4, 3.4, 3.8 Mk 1, 2 1955–69 Autobook
3.8 Mk 2 1959–67	..			Ball	Jaguar 2.4, 3.4, 3.8 Mk 1, 2 1955–69 Autobook
240 1967–69	..	..		Ball	Jaguar 2.4, 3.4, 3.8 Mk 1, 2 1955–69 Autobook
340 1967–69	..			Ball	Jaguar 2.4, 3.4, 3.8 Mk 1, 2 1955–69 Autobook
E Type 3.8 1961–65	..			Ball	Jaguar E Type 1961–70 Autobook
E Type 4.2 1964–69	..			Ball	Jaguar E Type 1961–70 Autobook
E Type 4.2 2+2 1966–70		..		Ball	Jaguar E Type 1961–70 Autobook
E Type 4.2 Series 2 1969–70	..		..	Ball	Jaguar E Type 1961–70 Autobook
S Type 3.4 1963–68	..		..	Ball	Jaguar S Type and 420 1963–68 Autobook
S Type 3.8 1963–68	..		..	Ball	Jaguar S Type and 420 1963–68 Autobook
420 1963–68	..		..	Ball	Jaguar S Type and 420 1963–68 Autobook
XJ6 2.8 litre 1968–70 ..				Ball	Jaguar XJ6 1968–70 Autobook
XJ6 4.2 litre 1968–70 ..				Ball	Jaguar XJ6 1968–70 Autobook

JOWETT

Javelin PA 1947–49	..	..	..	Mitchell	Jowett Javelin Jupiter 1947–53 Autobook
Javelin PB 1949–50	..	..		Mitchell	Jowett Javelin Jupiter 1947–53 Autobook
Javelin PC 1950–51	..	..		Mitchell	Jowett Javelin Jupiter 1947–53 Autobook
Javelin PD 1951–52	..	..		Mitchell	Jowett Javelin Jupiter 1947–53 Autobook
Javelin PE 1952–53	..	..		Mitchell	Jowett Javelin Jupiter 1947–53 Autobook
Jupiter Mk 1 SA 1949–52		..		Mitchell	Jowett Javelin Jupiter 1947–53 Autobook
Jupiter Mk 1A SC 1952–53		..	..	Mitchell	Jowett Javelin Jupiter 1947–53 Autobook

Make				Author	Title

LANDROVER

Series 1 1948–58	..	..	..	Ball	Landrover 1, 2 1948–61 Autobook
Series 2 1997 cc 1959–61	..	..	..	Ball	Landrover 1, 2 1948–61 Autobook
Series 2 2052 cc 1959–61	..	..	..	Ball	Landrover 1, 2 1948–61 Autobook
Series 2 2286 cc 1959–70	..	..	..	Ball	Landrover 2, 2A 1959–70 Autobook
Series 2A 2286 cc 1959–70	..	..	..	Ball	Landrover 2, 2A 1959–70 Autobook
Series 2A 2625 cc 1959–70	..	..	..	Ball	Landrover 2, 2A 1959–70 Autobook

MG

TA 1936–39	..	..	..	Ball	MG TA to TF 1936–55 Autobook
TB 1939	..	..	..	Ball	MG TA to TF 1936–55 Autobook
TC 1945–49	..	..	..	Ball	MG TA to TF 1936–55 Autobook
TD 1950–53	..	..	..	Ball	MG TA to TF 1936–55 Autobook
TF 1953–54	..	..	..	Ball	MG TA to TF 1936–55 Autobook
TF 1500 1954–55	..	..	..	Ball	MG TA to TF 1936–55 Autobook
Midget 1961–70	..			Ball	Sprite, Midget 1958–70 Autobook
Magnette ZA, ZB 1955–59	..			Ball	BMC Autobook Three
Magnette 3, 4 1959–68				Smith	BMC Autobook One
MGA 1500, 1600 1955–62	..			Ball	MGA, MGB 1955–68 Autobook
MGA Twin Cam 1958–60	..			Ball	MGA, MGB 1955–68 Autobook
MGB 1962–68	..			Ball	MGA, MGB 1955–68 Autobook
MGB 1969–70	..			Ball	MG MGB 1969–70 Autobook
1100 Mk 1 1962–67	..	..		Ball	1100 Mk 1 1962–67 Autobook
1100 Mk 2 1968	..			Ball	1100 Mk 2, 1300 Mk 1, 2, America Autobook
1300 Mk 1, 2 1968–70	..	..		Ball	1100 Mk 2, 1300 Mk 1, 2, America 1968–70 Autobook

MERCEDES BENZ

190B 1959–61	..	..	..	Ball	Mercedes-Benz 190B, C, 200 1959–68 Autobook
190C 1961–65	..	..	..	Ball	Mercedes-Benz 190B, C, 200 1959–68 Autobook
200 1965–68	..	..	..	Ball	Mercedes-Benz 190B, C, 200 1959–68 Autobook
220B 1959–65	..	..	..	Ball	Mercedes-Benz 220 1959–65 Autobook
220SB 1959–65	..	..	..	Ball	Mercedes-Benz 220 1959–65 Autobook
220SEB 1959–65	..	..	..	Ball	Mercedes-Benz 220 1959–65 Autobook
220SEBC 1961–65	..	..		Ball	Mercedes-Benz 220 1959–65 Autobook

MORGAN

Four wheelers 1936–69	..	..	..	Clarke	Morgan 1936–69 Autobook

MORRIS

Oxford 2, 3 1956–59	..	..	..	Ball	BMC Autobook Three
Oxford 5, 6 1959–69	..	..	..	Smith	BMC Autobook One
Minor series 2 1952–56	..	..	..	Ball	Morris Minor 1952–70 Autobook
Minor 1000 1957–70	..	..	..	Ball	Morris Minor 1952–70 Autobook
Mini 1959–70	..	..	..	Ball	Mini 1959–70 Autobook
Mini Clubman 1969–70	..	..	..	Ball	Mini 1959–70 Autobook
Mini Cooper 1961–70	..	..	..	Ball	Mini Cooper 1961–70 Autobook
Mini Cooper S 1963–70	..	..	..	Ball	Mini Cooper 1961–70 Autobook
1100 Mk 1 1962–67	..	..	..	Ball	1100 Mk 1 1962–67 Autobook
1100 Mk 2 1968–70	..	..	..	Ball	1100 Mk 2, 1300 Mk 1, 2, America 1968–70 Autobook
1300 Mk 1, 2 1968–70	..	..	..	Ball	1100 Mk 2, 1300 Mk 1, 2, America 1968–70 Autobook
1800 Mk 1, 2 1966–70	..	..	..	Ball	1800 1964–70 Autobook
1800S 1968–70	..	..	..	Ball	1800 1964–70 Autobook

OPEL

Kadett 993 cc 1962–65	..	..	..	Ball	Opel Kadett 1962–70 Autobook
Kadett 'B' 1965–70	..	..	..	Ball	Opel Kadett 1962–70 Autobook

PEUGEOT

404 1960–69	..	..	..	Ball	Peugeot 404 1960–69 Autobook

SINGER

Make	Author	Title
Chamois 1964–68	Smith	Hillman Imp 1963–68 Autobook
Chamois 1969–70	Ball	Hillman Imp 1969–71 Autobook
Chamois Sport 1964–68	Smith	Hillman Imp 1963–68 Autobook
Chamois Sport 1969–70	Ball	Hillman Imp 1969–71 Autobook
Gazelle series 2A 1958	Ball	Hillman Minx 1 to 5 1956–65 Autobook
Gazelle 3, 3A, 3B, 3C 1958–63	Ball	Hillman Minx 1 to 5 1956–65 Autobook
Gazelle series 5 1963–65	Ball	Hillman Minx 1 to 5 1956–65 Autobook
Gazelle series 6 1965–67	Ball	Hillman Minx 1965–67 Autobook
New Gazelle 1500, 1725 1966–70	Ball	Hillman Minx 1966–70 Autobook
Vogue series 4 1965–67	Ball	Hillman Minx 1965–67 Autobook
New Vogue 1966–70	Ball	Hillman Hunter 1966–70 Autobook

SKODA

Make	Author	Title
440, 445, 450 1957–69	Skoda	Skoda Autobook One

SUNBEAM

Make	Author	Title
Alpine series 1, 2, 3, 4 1959–65	Ball	Sunbeam Rapier Alpine 1955–65 Autobook
Alpine series 5 1965–67	Ball	Hillman Minx 1965–67 Autobook
Alpine 1969–70	Ball	Hillman Hunter 1966–70 Autobook
Rapier series 1, 2, 3, 3A, 4 1955–65	Ball	Sunbeam Rapier Alpine 1955–65 Autobook
Rapier series 5 1965–67	Ball	Hillman Minx 1965–67 Autobook
Rapier H.120 1967–70	Ball	Hillman Hunter 1966–70 Autobook
Imp Sport 1963–68	Smith	Hillman Imp 1963–68 Autobook
Imp Sport 1969–71	Ball	Hillman Imp 1969–71 Autobook
Stilletto 1967–68	Smith	Hillman Imp 1963–68 Autobook
Stilletto 1969–71	Ball	Hillman Imp 1969–71 Autobook

TOYOTA

Make	Author	Title
Corona 1500 Mk 1 1965–70	Ball	Toyota Corona 1500 Mk 1 1965–70 Autobook
Corona 1900 Mk 2 1969–70	Ball	Toyota Corona 1900 Mk 2 1969–70 Autobook

TRIUMPH

Make	Author	Title
TR2 1952–55	Ball	Triumph TR2, TR3, TR3A 1952–62 Autobook
TR3, TR3A 1955–62	Ball	Triumph TR2, TR3, TR3A 1952–62 Autobook
TR4, TR4A 1961–67	Ball	Triumph TR4, TR4A 1961–67 Autobook
TR5 1967–69	Ball	Triumph TR5, TR250, TR6 1967–70 Autobook
TR6 1969–70	Ball	Triumph TR5, TR250, TR6 1967–70 Autobook
TR250 1967–69	Ball	Triumph TR5, TR250, TR6 1967–70 Autobook
1300 1965–70	Ball	Triumph 1300 1965–70 Autobook
1300TC 1967–70	Ball	Triumph 1300 1965–70 Autobook
2000 1963–69	Ball	Triumph 2000 1963–69 Autobook
Herald 948 1959–64	Smith	Triumph Herald 1959–68 Autobook
Herald 1200 1961–68	Smith	Triumph Herald 1959–68 Autobook
Herald 1200 1969–70	Ball	Triumph Herald 1969–70 Autobook
Herald 12/50 1963–67	Smith	Triumph Herald 1959–68 Autobook
Herald 13/60 1967–68	Smith	Triumph Herald 1959–68 Autobook
Herald 13/60 1969–70	Ball	Triumph Herald 1969–70 Autobook
Spitfire 1962–68	Smith	Triumph Spitfire Vitessse 1962–68 Autobook
Spitfire Mk 3 1969–70	Ball	Triumph Spitfire Mk 3 1969–70 Autobook
Vitesse 1600 and 2 litre 1962–68	Smith	Triumph Spitfire Vitesse 1962–68 Autobook
Vitesse 2 litre 1969–70	Ball	Triumph GT6, Vitesse 2 litre 1969–70 Autobook
GT Six 2 litre 1966–68	Smith	Triumph Spitfire Vitesse 1962–68 Autobook
GT Six 1969–70	Ball	Triumph GT6, Vitesse 2 litre 1969–70 Autobook

VANDEN PLAS

Make	Author	Title
3 litre 1959–64	Ball	BMC Autobook Four
1100 Mk 1 1963–67	Ball	1100 Mk 1 1962–67 Autobook
1100 Mk 2 1968	Ball	1100 Mk 2, 1300 Mk 1, 2, America 1968–70 Autobook
1300 Mk 1, 2, 1968–70	Ball	1100 Mk 2, 1300 Mk 1, 2, America 1968–70 Autobook

MAXI1

Make						Author	Title

PORSCHE

356A 1957–59	..		..	..		Ball	Porsche 356A, 356B, 356C 1957–65 Autobook
356B 1959–63			..	..		Ball	Porsche 356A, 356B, 356C 1957–65 Autobook
356C 1963–65			..	..		Ball	Porsche 356A, 356B, 356C 1957–65 Autobook
911 1964–67	..			..		Ball	Porsche 911 1964–69 Autobook
911L 1967–68						Ball	Porsche 911 1964–69 Autobook
911S 1966–69						Ball	Porsche 911 1964–69 Autobook
911T 1967–69						Ball	Porsche 911 1964–69 Autobook
911E 1968–69			..			Ball	Porsche 911 1964–69 Autobook

RENAULT

					Author	Title
R4L 748cc, 845cc 1961–65	..		..	..	Ball	Renault R4, R4L, 4 1961–70 Autobook
R4 845cc 1962–66	..			..	Ball	Renault R4, R4L, 4 1961–70 Autobook
4 845cc 1966–70	..			..	Ball	Renault R4, R4L, 4 1961–70 Autobook
6 1968–70	..	..			Ball	Renault 6 1968–70 Autobook
R8 956cc 1962–65					Ball	Renault 8, 10, 1100 1962–70 Autobook
8 956cc, 1108cc 1965–70					Ball	Renault 8, 10, 1100 1962–70 Autobook
8S 1108cc 1968–70	..				Ball	Renault 8, 10, 1100 1962–70 Autobook
1100, 1108cc 1964–69					Ball	Renault 8, 10, 1100 1962–70 Autobook
R10 1108cc 1967–69	..				Ball	Renault 8, 10, 1100 1962–70 Autobook
10 1289cc 1969–70					Ball	Renault 8, 10, 1100 1962–70 Autobook
16 1470cc 1965–70	..				Ball	Renault R16 1965–70 Autobook
16TS 1565cc 1968–70			..		Ball	Renault R16 1965–70 Autobook

RILEY

					Author	Title
1.5 1957–65	..				Ball	BMC Autobook Three
4/68 1959–61	..				Smith	BMC Autobook One
4/72 1961–69	..				Smith	BMC Autobook One
Elf Mk 1, 2, 3 1961–70				..	Ball	Mini 1959–70 Autobook
1100 Mk 1 1965–67	..				Ball	1100 Mk 1 1962–67 Autobook
1100 Mk 2 1968		..			Ball	1100 Mk 2, 1300 Mk 1, 2, America 1968–70 Autobook
1300 Mk 1, 2 1968–70			..		Ball	1100 Mk 2, 1300 Mk 1, 2, America 1968–70 Autobook

ROVER

					Author	Title
60 1953–59	..				Ball	Rover 60–110 1953–64 Autobook
75 1954–59	..				Ball	Rover 60–110 1953–64 Autobook
80 1959–62	..				Ball	Rover 60–110 1953–64 Autobook
90 1954–59	..				Ball	Rover 60–110 1953–64 Autobook
95 1962–64	..				Ball	Rover 60–110 1953–64 Autobook
100 1959–62	..				Ball	Rover 60–110 1953–64 Autobook
105R 1957–58					Ball	Rover 60–110 1953–64 Autobook
105S 1957–59					Ball	Rover 60–110 1953–64 Autobook
110 1962–64	..				Ball	Rover 60–110 1953–64 Autobook
2000 SC 1963–69	..				Ball	Rover 2000 1963–69 Autobook
2000 TC 1963–69		..			Ball	Rover 2000 1963–69 Autobook
3 litre Saloon Mk 1, 1A 1958–62		..			Ball	Rover 3 litre 1958–67 Autobook
3 litre Saloon Mk 2, 3 1962–67		..			Ball	Rover 3 litre 1958–67 Autobook
3 litre Coupé 1965–67		..			Ball	Rover 3 litre 1958–67 Autobook
3500, 3500S 1968–70		..	..		Ball	Rover 3500, 3500S 1968–70 Autobook

SIMCA

					Author	Title
1000 1961–68	..	..		..	Ball	Simca 1000 1961–70 Autobook
1000 GL 1963–70	..		..	..	Ball	Simca 1000 1961–70 Autobook
1000 GLS 1964–70	..				Ball	Simca 1000 1961–70 Autobook
1000 GLA 1966–70					Ball	Simca 1000 1961–70 Autobook
1100 LS 1967–70	..				Ball	Simca 1100 1967–70 Autobook
1100 GL, GLS 1967–70					Ball	Simca 1100 1967–70 Autobook
1200 1970	..	..	..	..	Ball	Simca 1100 1967–70 Autobook

Make				Author	Title

VAUXHALL

Victor 1 1957–59	..	..	..	..	Ball	Vauxhall Victor 1, 2 FB 1957–64 Autobook
Victor 2 1959–61	..	..	..	..	Ball	Vauxhall Victor 1, 2 FB 1957–64 Autobook
Victor FB 1961–64	..	..	..	..	Ball	Vauxhall Victor 1, 2 FB 1957–64 Autobook
VX4/90 FBH 1961–64	..	..	..		Ball	Vauxhall Victor 1, 2 FB 1957–64 Autobook
Victor FC 101 1964–67	..	..	/..		Ball	Vauxhall Victor 101 1964–67 Autobook
VX 4/90 FCH 1964–67	..	..	..		Ball	Vauxhall Victor 101 1964–67 Autobook
Victor FD 1599cc 1967–69	..		..		Ball	Vauxhall Victor FD 1600, 2000 1967–69 Autobook
Victor FD 1975cc 1967–69	..		..		Ball	Vauxhall Victor FD 1600, 2000 1967–69 Autobook
Velox, Cresta PA 1957–62	..		..		Ball	Vauxhall Velox Cresta 1957–70 Autobook
Velox, Cresta PB 1962–65	..		..		Ball	Vauxhall Velox Cresta 1957–70 Autobook
Cresta PC 1965–70	..		..		Ball	Vauxhall Velox Cresta 1957–70 Autobook
Viscount 1966–70	..	..			Ball	Vauxhall Velox Cresta 1957–70 Autobook
Viva HA (including 90) 1964–66		..			Ball	Vauxhall Viva HA 1964–66 Autobook
VIva HB (including 90 and SL90) 1966–69		..		Ball	Vauxhall Viva HB 1966–69 Autobook

VOLKSWAGEN

1200 Beetle 1954–67	..	..	..	..	Ball	Volkswagen Beetle 1954–67 Autobook
1200 Beetle 1968–70	..	..	..	..	Ball	Volkswagen Beetle 1968–70 Autobook
1200 Karmann Ghia 1955–65	..	..	..		Ball	Volkswagen Beetle 1954–67 Autobook
1200 Transporter 1954–64		..			Ball	Volkswagen Transporter 1954–67 Autobook
1300 Beetle 1965–67	..	..	..		Ball	Volkswagen Beetle 1954–67 Autobook
1300 Beetle 1968–70		..	..		Bell	Volkswagen Beetle 1968–70 Autobook
1300 Karmann Ghia 1965–66	..	..			Ball	Volkswagen Beetle 1954–67 Autobook
1500 Beetle 1966–67	..	..	..		Ball	Volkswagen Beetle 1954–67 Autobook
1500 Beetle 1968–70	..	..	..		Ball	Volkswagen Beetle 1968–70 Autobook
1500 1961–65	..	..	..		Ball	Volkswagen 1500 1961–66 Autobook
1500N 1963–65	..	..	..		Ball	Volkswagen 1500 1961–66 Autobook
1500S 1963–65		..	..		Ball	Volkswagen 1500 1961–66 Autobook
1500A 1965–66	..	..	..		Ball	Volkswagen 1500 1961–66 Autobook
1500 Karmann Ghia 1966–67	..	..			Ball	Volkswagen Beetle 1954–67 Autobook
1500 Transporter 1963–67	..	..			Ball	Volkswagen Transporter 1954–67 Autobook
1500 Karmann Ghia 1968–70	..	..			Ball	Volkswagen Beetle 1968–70 Autobook

VOLVO

121, 131, 221 1962–68	..	..	..		Ball	Volvo P120 1961–68 Autobook
122, 132, 222 1961–68	..	..	..		Ball	Volvo P120 1961–68 Autobook
123 GT 1967–68	..	..	..		Ball	Volvo P120 1961–68 Autobook

WOLSELEY

1500 1959–65	..	..	..	..	Ball	BMC Autobook Three
15/50 1956–58	..	..	..	..	Ball	BMC Autobook Three
15/60 1958–61	..	..	..	..	Smith	BMA Autobook One
16/60 1961–69	..	..	..	..	Smith	BMC Autobook One
6/99 1959–61	..	..	..	..	Ball	BMC Autobook Four
6/110 1961–68	..	..	..	..	Ball	BMC Autobook Four
Hornet Mk 1, 2, 3 1961–70	..	..	..		Ball	Mini 1959–70 Autobook
1100 Mk 1 1965–67	..	..	..		Ball	1100 Mk 1 1962–67 Autobook
1100 Mk 2 1968	..	..	..		Ball	1100 Mk 2, 1300 Mk 1, 2, America 1968–70 Autobook
1300 Mk 1, 2 1968–70	..	..	..		Ball	1100 Mk 2, 1300 Mk 1, 2, America 1968–70 Autobook
18/85 Mk 1, 2 1967–70	..	..	..		Ball	1800 1964–70 Autobook
18/85S 1969–70	..	..	..		Ball	1800 1964–70 Autobook